MARTYRS

Contemporary Writers on
Modern Lives of Faith

'MARTYRS,

Edited by
SUSAN BERGMAN

HarperSanFrancisco
An Imprint of HarperCollins*Publishers*

A TREE CLAUSE BOOK

HarperSanFrancisco and the editor, in association with The Basic Foundation, a not-for-profit organization whose primary mission is reforestation, will facilitate the planting of two trees for every one tree used in the manufacture of this book.

FIRST EDITION
Book design by Ralph Fowler
Set in Bembo

Library of Congress Cataloging-in-Publication Data
Martyrs : contemporary writers on modern lives of faith / edited by Susan Bergman.
    p.   cm.
  Includes bibliographical references.
  ISBN 0–06–061120–0 (cloth)
  ISBN 0–06–061121–9 (pbk.)
    1. Christian martyrs—Biography. 2. Persecution—History—20th century.
3. Martyrdom (Christianity) I. Bergman, Susan.
BR1608.5.M38   1996
272'.9'0922—dc20
  [B]   96–14863

96 97 98 99 00 ❖HAD 10 9 8 7 6 5 4 3 2 1

For those true martyrs of our century who knew
what it was to cherish the cross:

This is your share of the eternal burden,
The perpetual glory. This is one moment,
But know that another
Shall pierce you with a sudden painful joy
When the figure of God's purpose is made complete.

Thomas Becket, in T. S. Eliot's
Murder in the Cathedral

Contents

ACKNOWLEDGMENTS

S itting on my desk were two books—*A Testament to Freedom: The Essential Writing of Dietrich Bonhoeffer* and *A Testament of Hope: The Essential Writing and Speeches of Martin Luther King, Jr.*—reminders to me that two of the wisest and most outspoken figures of our century had a shared faith in the dignity of people and the call of God to serve as they could, beliefs that demanded a fervent commitment, beliefs that cost them their lives. These two martyrs I hadn't ever considered in the same breath. There were others who came to mind: Edith Stein, Archbishop Oscar Romero, the Rwandan bishops who had been butchered that very week, the little-known martyrs whose letters or journals were hidden away in carefully catalogued archival boxes. With some writers I knew I began to talk about the figures of our age who through their lives and deaths had influenced the way we thought about faith in God, social engagement, what it means to follow Christ. For inspiration and conversation in the early stages of thinking about marrying these powerful stories with strong writers I want to thank Carolyn Forché (for breaking ground with her anthology *Against Forgetting*), Paul Elie (whose collection *A Tremor of Bliss: Contemporary Writers on the Saints* is my model), Ron Hansen, Anthony Walton, and Philip Yancey.

Once the idea had come clear and a careful search been conducted for the best-versed editor on the subject, John Loudon generously agreed to shepherd the project. His training and his even temperament have perfectly suited him to the project. Karen Levine has tended *Martyrs* like a garden. We couldn't have been nurtured by a better pair. Rhoda Weyr was instrumental in arranging the details of our agreements. I'm grateful for her experienced representation.

Tom Giles, my partner in research, brought his invaluable eye for detail, the needed skills of inquiry and documentation for a project of this scope, and his wonderful humor to bear as early on we sorted through the century's dead. Among the living to whom we owe sincere thanks, not only for difficult-to-find facts but also for the gift of their time and direction, are: Samuel Hugh Moffett (author of *The History of Christianity in Asia*); John Witte, Jr. (director of the Law and Religion program at Emory University); Steven Snyder (director of Christian Solidarity International); David Neff, Mickey Maudlin, and the news staff at *Christianity Today;* John Major (for his Asian expertise); Reginald Gibbons (editor at *TriQuarterly*); David Barrett (World Christian Encyclopedia); Mark Elliott (Institute for East-West Christian Studies); Aleksei Gregoriev (for alerting us to Aleksandr Men); Diane Knippers (Institute on Religion and Democracy); Jubilee Campaign (London-based human rights watch); Kim Lawton (News Network International); Nina Shea (Puebla Institute); the staff of Voice of the Martyrs; and the librarians at the Billy Graham Center Archives.

Meanwhile, writers with a heart for the subject and almost inordinately busy lives one by one took up their martyrs with a depth of commitment I had not envisioned possible. To write these stories cost them an examination of their own spirituality, in the light of manifest faith, in a way that often made the most proficient and authentic feel inadequate for the job. Their perseverance—sometimes their struggle to identify with a person whose faith bore few of the signs of common doubt or lapse—shows in certain essays. In others, the very human moments of agony or misgiving in a martyr's life let the writer approach his or her subject with just the lack of reverence needed to draw close. Some traveled to the place on the globe where the martyr whose story they were telling had died. Some made interior journeys into uncharted territories of the soul. Readers will go with them, gratefully, as I have. I can't begin to thank them enough for their contributions.

Finally, there are those whose support, in various and compound ways, resists all categorization and feels like grace: Beth Bergman, John Wilson, Jeff Thompson, Rose Johnson, my mother, Nancy Heche, my children, and in the simplest and most consequential of ways, as ever, Judson. To these my humblest thanks.

MARTYRS

INTRODUCTION

Twentieth-Century Martyrs: A Meditation

by SUSAN BERGMAN

And death is the reason
to begin again, without letting go.
And who can lament
such historical necessity?
If they are all dying,
the living ones,
they charge us with the improbable.

    Jay Wright, from "Death as History"

One sweltering August night of my early girlhood, while a slow electric fan hummed near the pulpit, the missionaries to China who visited our New Testament Baptist church unwrapped a pair of celadon porcelain dragons pried from the rafters of their house. No more evil spirits to ward off. No lingering demons to let slither through the open shutters once they'd prayed for God's protection. I was not yet ten years old, captivated as they unveiled their treasure trove of object lessons, and when the red lacquered *to pao ko* was passed to me, I balanced it on my lap, sure I could find all forty compartments in the box of hidden drawers, each concealed trigger that would spring the next choice riddle, and the next, as the missionaries told the story of a small village girl, just my age, who refused to "trample the cross and live." For this offense Communist soldiers opened fire as she raised her hands to the sky and sang in her own language "Jesus Loves Me."

I looked up from the magical box. She made it look so easy: *the pretzel bones of a small girl snapped in the desecration of her soul's house.* She let the body go, when I would have snatched it back, I thought. The girl's face shone with tears while *I* would move to the back of the line, watching what was happening to the others, waiting for the soldiers to grow tired of their game, or hungry, so they would order me to run and get the rice they could smell scorching on the bottom of the old enameled cooking pot.

I come from a country that holds the superpower of its youth in memory while in the mirror a swooning, feeble culture blinks back, unbelieving. This is an age of atrocity, a "tyrant century," as the Russian poet Osip Mandelstam calls it: "My animal, my age, who will ever be able / to look into your eyes?" One hundred years pregnant with corpses. Though there are ways to resist resignation, despair—bone sifting, grave trolling, call it what you will—I read the stories of the Christian martyrs of the twentieth century not so much to restore my hope in progress as to glimpse what it might mean to cherish God in such a time, to understand how they were able to profess belief in the Divine over all and through all and in all when what I have to go on is a seed of faith, an evidence I hope to uncover, a toehold. How did they live in the darkness? How did they die in the light? I sink roots into the tenacity of their affirmation to the end: Jesus is Lord.

The word *martyr* conjures scenes of ancient Roman arenas where early Christians were pitted against wild animals, or may bring to mind the gruesome sixteenth-century accounts in the best-selling *Foxe's Book of Martyrs*—that favorite text of Protestant children, featuring the etchings that were the Reformation's visual codex of torture and nakedness. A friend of another tradition recites the names of Jesuit priests and friars killed by Protestant heretics. "Did you have my mother in mind?" asks a woman in jest. Some will think of the recent story in a pamphlet, in a hand-circulated publication, in yesterday's newspaper, or never reported except in a letter home from a widow of the man whose body was discovered only yesterday.

Drawing my finger across a globe of the world, I find the places where the Chinese girl and others like her have died. She was the first of the dead to charge me with the improbability of faith, whatever the terms. To be a martyr you have to believe that something matters more than life. With the death toll of Christians rising throughout the world in recent years, my thoughts are drawn to the point of intersection between faith and death. In obscure archives and mission-agency offices I have been sorting through correspondences cut short, journals from the fields of missionaries' quiet labor and mostly unnoticed losses. I am responding to an almost overwhelming shadow narrative of this century's news—the world wars, the struggle for civil rights in the United States, the legacy of colonialism in Africa, the violently changing social landscape in Latin America—told through the stories of committed Christians whose faith in God not only did not spare them the peril of history, but often demanded their lives. How to account for such surety in a century of indifference and drift, such single-mindedness in a century whose plethora of deities, whose cultural and moral pluralism, disavows the singular?

Martyr, whose root meaning is "witness," was first used in reference to early Christians who were put to death for their confession of faith in one true God. These witnesses expressed not what they had seen with their eyes but what they envisioned in their hearts. They endured their present suffering because of their confidence in God's ultimate reign on earth and the hope they placed in a heavenly life to come. The term has broadened in current usage, but in the simplest understanding of martyrdom an individual is required to deny Christ and live, or confess him and die. Under such duress the martyr freely chooses death over life—death seals a life's belief—in order to act as a witness to the truth of Christ's claims and to his or her own faith.

These were the bald alternatives presented in the second century to Polycarp, bishop of the church at Smyrna. Unwilling to call Caesar God, he let his captors tie him to a stake and set him alight. "Come now," urged his captors, "where is the harm in just saying Caesar is Lord, and offering the incense, and so forth, when it will save your life?" Polycarp replied, "Eighty and six years have I served Him, and He has done me no wrong. How then can I blaspheme my King and my Savior?"

In our century, there are clear records of Christians being put to the choice between faith and life in Pakistan, the former Soviet Union, Armenia, Sudan, China, Chile, Iran—the list goes on. More often, though, a martyr's determination has been complicated by political or racial difference layered over the issue of direct spiritual opposition, making a martyr's choice whether to continue to follow a spiritual call and remain in known danger or to cease, whether to stay in the path of jeopardy or to find another place to serve. Archbishop Oscar Romero, who could have chosen to escape El Salvador, refused, while others working in the area felt their usefulness to be greater if they removed themselves from the situation of conflict. This does not represent a choice between suicide and survival (the martyr does not yield to the despair that suicide implies), but a willingness to accept the consequences of faith even when this means a threat to one's own safety. "The essential element in martyrdom," the contemporary Orthodox theologian Gerald Bonner writes, "is not the physical act of dying but rather a disposition of the will to live for Christ, with the necessary corollary that, by a strange but wholly Christian paradox, living for Christ may involve the necessity to lay down one's life for him."[1]

Martyrs have demonstrated this commitment within a spectrum of initiatives. Some through mission work directly proclaimed the gospel story of Christ's love; others, including relief-agency and medical workers, teachers, and translators, chose social or cultural service undertaken in the name of God as their means of witness. Still others (I think of Raoul Wallenberg and Steven Biko), perhaps not explicitly working to manifest God's grace, nevertheless worked within its breadth and so demonstrated God's love by spending their lives for others' benefit. "What does the Lord require of you," wrote the prophet Micah, "but to live justly, to love mercy, and to walk humbly with your God?"

The choice to live a moral and compassionate life, characterized by humility toward God, begins long before any ultimate decision must be faced to affirm faith at the cost of death. A martyr's first faith grows with continued affirmations of God's direction over her own disposition. "The true martyr," says Archbishop Thomas Becket, as T. S. Eliot imagines his final Christmas sermon in *Murder in the Cathedral*, "is he who has become the instrument of God, who has lost his will in the will of God, not lost it but found it, for he has found freedom in submission to God. The martyr no longer desires anything for himself, not even the glory of martyrdom." If we are not all called to this extremity of submission, we can at least recognize—in our own choices to persevere despite personal cost, to honor our beliefs in the contest with doubt—the significance of the daily, incremental decisions that influence who we become, and how we behave.

    —∞—

"When one member suffers, all the members suffer," the apostle Paul writes to the Corinthians. He refers to the members of the metaphoric Body of Christ as interdependent, each member's well-being crucial to the vitality of the whole. More recently, in a similar vein, Martin Luther King refers to "an inescapable network of mutuality." How untrue these statements about the metaphysical unity of those who suffer can seem from where I stand. *When one suffers, all suffer.* I read this as a challenge to awareness of conditions outside my own secured boundaries. To identify with those who suffer for their faith—a path that more have taken in this century than in any other—is not to pretend to possess extraordinary belief, but to remind ourselves of the plea that must have crossed the lips of so many martyrs faced with their own last breath, "Lord, help my unbelief."

Intent on understanding the relevance of my own faith to the world I live in, I find myself searching for an adequate response to the news of the crucifixions of Christians in the Nuba Mountains of Sudan and to the discovery of a slave trade in Christian villagers in that country; to young Salamat Masih charged with blasphemy—for his belief in Jesus—under Pakistan's penal code, which decrees death for anyone who "by any imputation, innuendo or insinuation, directly or indirectly, defiles the sacred name of the Holy Prophet Muhammad"; to the seven missionary children in Colombia who watched Marxist guerrillas throw their fathers into a truck and drive off, only to hear on June 19, 1994, over a year later, that they had been found dead after a gun battle between the government and rebel forces; to accounts of persecution of Christians in Sri Lanka, the Philippines, Uzbekistan, China. How to draw close to them? I find in the lives of a few martyrs, in the drawers and documents I am given to open, the seeds of affinity: it is their God I share, their willingness to live as if this God gives rise and meaning to our lives.

    —∞—

Our century begins in the fever of China's Boxer uprising, where Lizzie Atwater, a young American woman waiting to be executed, scratches a note to her sister: "They beheaded thirty-three of us last week in Taiwan. I was restless and excited while I thought there was a chance for life." The Boxers' puppet empress Tz'u-hsi issued a decree calling for the execution of all foreigners ("Death to the foreign Devils . . . exterminate the foreign religion"), and in June and July of that year, 1900, in the northern Shansi province alone, Governor Yu-hsien had slaughtered 159 Christian missionaries and their children.

Another drawer. Inside, a folded paper: Flossenburg, April 9, 1945, a few days before the Allies are to liberate the camp. Dietrich Bonhoeffer, the German pastor of the "Confessing Church," leads the morning prayers for his fellow prisoners and soon after is led to a Nazi gallows with five other "conspirators" against Hitler. A British fellow-captive recorded Bonhoeffer's parting words, spoken in English before he was hanged, "This is the end—for me, the beginning of life."

In the Huaorani territory of Ecuador, early 1956, the pilot of a low-flying search plane making its way along the Curaray River spots one of the five missing missionaries' bodies lying facedown in the water.

The Congo massacres erupt as Chinese-trained Simba rebels of the People's Republic of the Congo strike government posts and conduct recruiting raids on villages. At the Catholic mission station in Buta in the northeast, January 1964, thirty-one priests are stripped naked and bound together before they are marched to the riverbank. There Simbas hack them to pieces and throw their corpses into the current, or force the captive children of Protestants living there to parade the body parts on sticks through the mission grounds.

In San Salvador, on the afternoon of March 24, 1980, a soldier appears at the door of the chapel where Archbishop Oscar Romero, blessing the offering, is saying mass at a convent hospital for the terminally ill. That morning he had refused breakfast, walking alone instead of eating; his demeanor struck the sisters who cared for him as profoundly sad. The soldier opens fire, then is driven off in a red car.

What these Christian martyrs and others have contributed to the twentieth century is not their agonizing deaths but the legacy of their faith. *Martyrem non facit poena, sed causa* ("The cause, not the suffering, makes genuine martyrs," *Epist.* 89:2), wrote Augustine. Their stories document a struggle that has taken place in recent history across boundaries of nations and peoples and also between the realm of culture and the province of the sacred. They attest to the conviction of tens of thousands that to live is Christ and to die is gain.

⸺⸻⸺

"If anyone wishes to come after Me," says the red print of my old King James Bible, "let him deny himself and take up his cross and follow Me. For whoever wishes to save his life shall lose it; but whoever loses his life for my sake shall find it" (Matthew 16:24–25). Of all spiritual concepts expressed in language, redemption through death seems to me the most central to Christian faith and the most consistent to appear in the writings of twentieth-century Christian martyrs. It is in answer to this call to follow Christ that we begin to walk in the steps of a martyr's path. Bonhoeffer writes in *The Cost of Discipleship:*

> If we refuse to take up our cross and submit to suffering and rejection at the hands of men, we forfeit our fellowship with Christ and have ceased to follow him. But if we lose our lives in his service and carry our cross, we shall find our lives again in the fellowship of the cross with Christ . . . To bear the cross proves to be the only way of triumphing over suffering. This is true for all who follow Christ, because it was true for him.[2]

In an Edith Stein daybook I read: "*He who wants to keep his soul will lose it.* Thus the soul can only find itself when it is not concerned with the self . . . I believe that the more deeply someone is drawn into God, the more one must also come out of oneself; that is, come out into the world, in order to carry the divine life into it." Etty Hillesum, like Stein, born of Jewish parents and thought to be a convert to Christianity, did not return from Auschwitz, yet her diaries are free of despair: "By excluding death from our life we cannot live a full life, and by admitting death into our life we enlarge and enrich it."[3]

This pairing of life and death, this incongruous welcoming of their interrelation, the words opening into significance through their own opposites, has its prototype in the central story of Christianity. Through the willing sacrifice of Jesus on a cross the world witnessed the love of God. Only, paradoxically, through the shedding of blood could lives ruined by sin and death be reanimated: through death entered life. Martyrdom's often gruesome triumph reenacts this meaning-full suffering in each of its amplifications. But the Christian willingly identifies with the suffering and death of Christ in the full hope of also partaking in Christ's resurrection. *If we have died with Christ, we shall also live with him.* It is Christ's resurrection and the believer's reliance on the force of its ultimate effects that renders death and the fear of death powerless.

Where such faith is involved, those who suffer are not *victims.* Victims suffer loss, are injured, are massacred (passive voice) against their will. We speak of victims of war, victims of the Holocaust, victims of rape and incest, victims of nuclear and chemical warfare, which are vile and purposeless acts in and of themselves, conceived and carried out by human beings against human beings and so against God. Any commemoration of those who have died intentionally, securing meaning in their loss, must honor the memory of those crushed without choice. Implicit in the remembering of martyrs is the voice of resolve rising, however reluctantly, above the din, against the oppressor. Because of the clarity required of resistance, however many are slain, the martyr registers in history not en masse but as an individual, one perhaps too often expected to have lived a uniformly heroic life, but nevertheless in his or her conviction exemplary. But it is this privilege of ascent (of a life's declarative heft) that is silenced in the victim, "not because of the magnitude of the crime," the poet Czeslaw Milosz observes, "but because of its impersonal nature."

The atrocities enacted in our century strain our credulity at the possible meaningfulness of human existence. "Despair registers more authentically on our pulses than the rhetoric of hope," the Holocaust scholar Lawrence Langer writes in his provocative and intensely bleak work *Admitting the Holocaust.* Unwilling to find redemptive value in such extremity, Langer seeks to go beyond the pre–Holocaust linguistic salve of words like *martyrdom, choice, heroism,* and *resistance,* believing these "naive notions" to have been stripped from those subjected to the utter devaluation of their lives by the Nazis. He is right, of course, in saying that language is a tool we use to construct memory and to make sense of otherwise senseless loss:

> When we speak of the survivor instead of the victim and of martyrdom instead of murder, regard being gassed as a pattern for dying with dignity, or evoke the redemptive rather than the grievous power of memory, we draw on an arsenal of words that urges us to build verbal fences between the atrocities of the camps and ghettos and what we are mentally willing—or able— to face.[4]

He is not right to undermine the potential of individuals' volition and language to oppose the devaluation of life, on behalf of themselves and others—even those conscripted by a pernicious and devouring system because of an accident of ancestry. What tools have we but language and faith in our pursuit of meaning? I find myself drawn into mental dialogue with Langer on the subject of meaningful death as a result of my own exposure to the literature of witness written by Jewish martyrs. Nazis never possessed power over human souls any more than the Turks owned the spirits of the Armenians, or Idi Amin controlled the hearts of Ugandans, or Stalin triumphed over his millions of dead. The advantage of spiritual force over the powers that oppose freedom of any kind is not necessarily its power to change circumstance but its ability to respond to devastation by drawing on transcendent strength and perspective, which imbue circumstance with meaning, removing from circumstance its status as final and determined.

To banish the notion of martyrdom from any faith, Langer knows, deprives affliction of its message. Yet suffering becomes exemplary when it engages the will of the sufferer. I see this engagement in Langer's own proliferation of books and memory (is he not evidently persuaded of the value of the word to interrogate despair, to build the ruins against oblivion?), though he claims he would have preferred from Etty Hillesum and Victor Frankl (whom he calls desperate and misguided), and others who in their writing attribute value to their suffering, what he calls "the more modest role of recorder of human wretchedness." Record for the sake of clarity: better this, he attests (falsely comparing hope with obfuscation or squeamishness), than a chronicle of the human spirit's capacity for love and resolve that has matched and sometimes even mastered human abomination.

The impulse to transform terror, to resist its tide with language or music or love, flows from a perception that all history is caught up in meaning greater than a single event can reveal, meaning that has been showing itself through the ages, an act of faith Langer cannot allow himself in the dark aftermath of the death camps. In my experience his views are not particularly Jewish, nor mine peculiarly Christian. (French poet Edmond Jabes in *The Book of Questions:* "[G-d] is image in the absence of images, language in the absence of languages, point in the absence of points.") We have made different choices of belief, each available within the other's orthodoxy—the one to see certain events as beyond the scope of divine intention and therefore solely of human doing (secularism), the other to see all history as informed by the freedom of human choice but ultimately subject to God (theodicy), a difference Langer is first to identify, which lifts the death of a martyr from the sheer helplessness of victimhood to a purposed gain.

"Precious in the sight of the Lord is the death of his saints," writes the psalmist (Psalm 116:15). "Blessed are the dead which die in the Lord" (Revelation 14:13). Though tortured or persecuted or stricken, the lives of his children are never wasted in God's sight. In Aleksandr Solzhenitsyn's 1983 Templeton Address entitled "Men Have Forgotten God," we hear from the man who exposed the 60 million dead under Stalin to an incredulous world in language devoid of empty solace or evasion. He said, "The failings of human consciousness, deprived of its divine dimension, have been a determining factor in all the major crimes of this century."[5] The flaw of sensibility that lacks divine dimension is to see only oppressors and victims. Such a view refuses to acknowledge the moral force of the individual. To see clearly is to look intently, without flinching, at all that is human, the degradation and the rarer glory, and also to witness, in what is visible, all that we are given to see of God.

— ∞ —

I overhear in the record of fragments a quiet mingling of purpose and sorrow that speaks sometimes in letters home from the field or in journal entries or phrases of static-congested radio transmission. It is here that the unseen imprint of God seems almost perceptible in the martyrs' astonishment at God's presence in the dire straits of their circumstances, in their repeated insistence on an unfathomable peace that suffuses the elements surrounding them, or in some cases in the mere acquiescence to living, though near the end many begin to sense the circumvention of their days through premonitions of death. Here we glimpse what they themselves identify as the grace of God, perhaps somewhat nebulously for those of us looking on, reaching to catch the hem of his robe—where *is* God? With what can you compare God? They depend for strength on a power that reveals itself at the final gasp of their own frailty. In these fragments there is none of the requisite hyperbole of early martyrologies, but the resolution of those whose hearts have turned toward heaven. I mark the simple words: *peace, rest, quiet.*

From the Boxer uprising, more of Lizzie Atwater's letter to her sister, written August 3, 1900:

Dear ones, I long for a sight of your dear faces, but I fear we shall not meet on earth . . . I am preparing for the end very quietly and calmly. The Lord is wonderfully near, and He will not fail me. I was very restless and excited while there seemed a chance of life, but God has taken away that feeling, and now I just pray for grace to meet the terrible end bravely. The pain will soon be over, and oh the sweetness of the welcome above!

My little baby will go with me. I think God will give it to me in Heaven, and my dear mother will be so glad to see us. I cannot imagine the Savior's welcome. Oh, that will compensate for all these days of suspense. Dear ones, live near to God and cling less closely to earth. *There is no other way by which we can receive that peace from God which passeth understanding* . . . I must keep calm and still these hours. I do not regret coming to China, but am sorry I have done so little. My married life, two precious years, has been so very full of happiness. We will die together, my dear husband and I.

I used to dread separation. If we escape now it will be a miracle. I send my love to you all, and the dear friends who remember me.

Days after her husband's body was found in Ecuador, on January 12, 1956, Barbara Youderian writes in her journal:

God gave me this verse two days ago, Psalm 48:14, "For this God is our God for ever and ever: he shall be our guide even unto death." As I came face to face with the news of Roj's death, my heart was filled with praise. He was worthy of his homegoing. Help me, Lord, to be both mother and father, to know wisdom and instruction . . . I wrote a letter to the mission family, trying to explain *the peace I have.*[6]

All Lois Carlson hears is a screen of static from the shortwave radio, then these words pressing through the distance between them in her husband's weakened voice: "Where I go from here I know not, only that it will be with Him. If by God's grace I live, which I doubt, it will be to His glory." September 24, 1956, Dr. Paul Carlson radios again, this time from Wasolo, on the other side of the Ubangi River, to where she is waiting for him in the Central African Republic. He has stayed with his patients though the hospital he runs in the Congo has been overtaken by Simba nationalists. Lois waits near the static for days without a sound from him and then his last brief message, a bit of paper dated October 21, is thrust into her hand. She reads, "I know I'm ready to meet my Lord, but my thought for you makes this more difficult. I trust that I might be a witness for Christ." In the New Testament found in his jacket pocket, Carlson had written the date and a single word the day before the Simbas shot him. *Peace.*[7]

The martyrs' understatement of lack, dread, duration, their forward gaze, balances our own grief; their humility plays the counterpoint to overambitious eulogy. In our consent to suffering, the body weakens its claims.

All these persons died in faith. They were not yet in possession of the things promised, but had seen them far ahead and hailed them, and confessed themselves no more than strangers or passing travellers on earth. Those who use such language show plainly that they are looking for a country of their own. If their hearts had been in the country they had left, they could have found opportunity to return. Instead, we find them longing for a better country—I mean, the heavenly one. That is why God is not ashamed to be called their God; he has a city ready for them. (Hebrews 11:13–16)

Those who have wished to make of commemoration a warning or an idol have through history inflated the memory of the Christian dead. Though the spiritual purpose of the stories of martyrdom was clearly conceived from the beginning, over the years the telling began to accrue miracles and apocryphal codicils to supplement the facts. In the manner of Saint Stephen, who saw the heavens open to reveal the glory of God at his death, the fragrance of bread rose from Polycarp's burning flesh. His soul, it is said, lifted from his body in the symbolic form of a dove. This spiritualization makes Polycarp an allegorical Christ, the bread of life. The dove of his soul flying upward alerts readers to the presence of the Holy Spirit, which appeared first in the dove's form in records of the baptism of Jesus by John the Baptist.

The rare early *passione,* that is verifiable through court records or corroborative eyewitness accounts is far outnumbered by wholly fabricated incidents and by the extravagant inflation of the numbers of dead. In this trumped-up testimony of exotic deaths we glimpse the earliest impulses of an emergent genre consistent in style through the most recent of martyrologies. Tell me the story of her inspired expiration, and I will supply, along with allegorical miracles and rapturous apparitions, the demonized oppressors on stages hung with patterned psychic and political drapery. Lace collars, worn velvet shoes, a shriek on the tongue of a wild heifer.

The din of spiritual bliss equates with wretched death. *Under gilded domes and iced bridges, winter bent double. Blood like the tears of Jesus trickled from the old man's palm.*

This literature, written in a rush of scant facts, reports its news in a style foreign to those raised on contemporary journalism, not only because of its coverage of Christians and their activities (a subject usually presented in the media with mild derision), but also because the purpose has less to do with conveying historical detail than with imparting spiritual truths. What country are we considering now? What is the last name of the man who died hanging upside down in an airless cell? The anonymous authors embed their accounts with hope, resolve, and the spare, requisite goriness also indigenous to the genre. They are riven with inspiration and slim on information. (Though maybe we will find an address where we are asked to send words of comfort to a Pakistani widow and her ten orphaned children, maybe a request for correspondence appealing for a prisoner's release.)

I am both drawn to and repulsed by these excesses in the stories of martyrs. But I suspect another influence at work in the stories' break from everyday language into heightened style. Paired with the difficulty of finding words for spiritual experience is the problem of matching language to what we have been forced to see and hear and feel. Poets and scholars, particularly since the First World War, have noted the shattering of common language as it approaches its own inadequacy to describe reality: war and its aftermath, human slaughter and debasement. For our present consideration I would add the violent deaths of the martyrs; these tragedies are not new to our century, though they become central to any consideration of our age. In conditions of extremity, language either tends to revert to conventional usage as a means of retreating from the particulars to the protective distance of the familiar, the cliché, or we find it reaching *into* reality, experimentally, toward a diction that is sufficient for both incommunicable sorrow and the possibility of renewal. Czeslaw Milosz, speaking of the poet's role as witness, writes:

> I assume that in our century something has been born which we try in vain to name, and to which I give the provisional name of a new dimension of man and of society. I assume also that poetry, unless it is conscious of this and stays in that frontier area where it should strive to grasp the new dimension, by necessity lacks that vigor of being *which is necessary to redeem* the abnormality and moral ambiguity attending its birth. [Emphasis mine.][8]

Milosz urges on language the vigor necessary to attend the birth of horror, not simply to observe but, in his word, to redeem through witness. I imagine this redemptive vigor to have been an informing impulse in the writing of the martyrs' lives. First witness, then excess—it is the manner of all movements in writing and the arts—the real, then the imitation, the making use of.

Overcast memorials far outnumber any clear-sighted considerations of martyrdom—in our century there is none that stands more lucidly than T. S. Eliot's rendering of the life of Thomas Becket in *Murder in the Cathedral*. Modern martyrologies' most frequently used words: *genocide, brutality, atrocity, bloody, horror, unprecedented, anguish, calamity,* and *pogrom*. Whereas a cautious encyclopedia puts forth 600,000 Armenian Christians dead at the hands of the Turks in the first quarter of our century, poets and relief agencies estimate 1.5 million lost in all. The numbers vary depending on historical perspective and denomination, and must be considered with a grain of caution.

During a five-hour ceremony in Park Avenue's Russian Orthodox Cathedral of Our Lady of the Sign, November 1981, Tsar Nicholas, Alexandra, their entire family, and 30,000 other Russians killed in 1918 by the Bolsheviks were canonized and glorified as martyrs. The Orthodox communion of saints, determined by a less technical process than that carried out by the Roman Catholic church, includes hundreds of thousands of such martyrs and estimates as many as 12 million Christians to have perished under the most recent atheistic regime.

Since the papacy of John XXIII began in 1958, according to the *New York Times,* the official Roman Catholic Congregation for the Causes of Saints has added 1,100 names to the list of those beatified and canonized; most of these additions were made during the papacy of John Paul II, sometimes in groups of a hundred or more, bringing the total number of saints and martyrs to roughly 10,000. The politicized process involves lengthy appeals that require the demonstration of an exemplary moral life and, for sainthood, the proof of posthumous miracles.

"Chances that a Catholic saint canonized since 1978 is Vietnamese: 2 in 5" (*Harper's,* August 1995).

On the Protestant front, David Barrett and Todd M. Johnson have made it their job to maintain the database that counts Christian martyrs, defined without denominational distinction as "believers in Christ who lose their lives prematurely, in situations of witness, as a result of human hostility." In their book *Our World and How to Reach It,* they count 40 million Christian martyrs in 220 countries across twenty centuries, and estimate 26,625,000 Christians to have been martyred in this century alone—more than in all other centuries combined. A fan-shaped graph (reprinted in *The Almanac of the Christian World*) identifies history's fifty-six worst situations of mass martyrdom (over 100,000 each), the most recent being Idi Amin's Uganda massacres in 1971, where much of the population had been "Christianized" in the early years of this century.

The current annual count of Christian martyrs' deaths by Barrett and Johnson's estimate runs to 290,000, as of 1990. If one is a bishop, evangelist, catechist, or missionary the likelihood of being martyred this year is as high as 5 percent. Many would choose not to rely on these numbers as anything but rough approximations. "With such figures you need to exercise humility," says one director of a human rights watch organization. Pressed on their sources and methods of calculating, David Barrett acknowledges the difficulty of distinguishing between deaths owing directly to Christian belief and those owing to political causes, confirming that few martyrs of this century could be lifted cleanly from the political and cultural conditions in which they find themselves and identified as targets of a purely spiritual vengeance.

If the numbers tend, by overwhelming the particulars, to blur our view, to safely numb, then one young man's thick brown hair, the broken wheel of his bicycle, a gash over his right eye or one woman's dusty patch of garden and leaking water pipes, her taste for berries and cream, which she remembers from her prison cell, draws us to them until we can begin to feel their hurt. One member suffers and we suffer too. The menace to another's religious freedom matters because it breathes its threats near every truth.

―∞―

In Osip Mandelstam's influential "Journey to Armenia," he describes a country of ancient Christian churches and graveyards, a place he calls "a Sabbath Land," with its outlying islands of Malta, Saint Helena, and Madeira, its melancholy peninsula of Sevan where he finds "a porous calcified little crust of someone's cranium" and respectfully wraps it up in his handkerchief. In 1933, the year of his visit, the remnant Armenians who had survived the Turks were growing comfortable with their new Russian identity; a million and a half or so Armenians had been slaughtered in his lifetime in an attempted annihilation of the earliest of Christian peoples—driven into the desert, into the sea, into ditches, into massive burning pyres of corpses, into silence. *We will not be silent,* those who escaped whispered to their children and grandchildren, who now face their torturers in Azerbaijan. It was the year before his own sentencing to five years of hard labor under Stalin, and perhaps he sensed among these skulls of a distant land a fraternity of exile.

Now again Armenians are crying out under oppression. The director of a relief mission to Nagorno Karabakh describes to me their voices, what they need. In October 1994 a team from Christian Solidarity International (CSI) flew in food and medicine and offered the Armenians an assurance that the world was not unconscious of their plight. Since 1993, in the area of Nagorno Karabakh, the Muslim Azerbaijanis have murdered an estimated 3,200 Armenians, and continue to blockade food supplies and medical aid to this small nation, which suffered an earthquake in 1993 that also killed thousands. He regrets that CSI's small helicopter, in danger of being shot out of the sky, could carry only an hour's moral salve, half a week's food and bandages.

Human rights agencies' reports and missionary bulletins can only point in the direction of current crises. They stack bodies as names on a list. They publish the random, smuggled photograph. Do not think these pictures to be the most brutally telling, to be isolated instances. They appear beside appeals to readers to join in letter-writing campaigns to free others whose lives are threatened. They document the results, the releases from prison, as well. Here is the naked body of Sylvio Claude, a Protestant pastor and human rights campaigner active since the Duvalier regime in Haiti. He is surrounded by the mob who lynched him for protesting injustice under President Jean-Bertrand Aristide. Method of torture: "the necklace," a tire doused with gasoline hung around the victim's neck and set on fire. One man with his hands on his hips steps on the dead man's face. Another agency must certainly document the atrocities committed against the supporters of Aristide. Here is sixty-seven-year-old Asrat Waldeyes, a prominent Ethiopian physician imprisoned on June 28, 1994, for "inciting rebellion." He has formed the All Amhara People's Organization (AAPO) to help protect the human rights of all Ethiopians and the religious freedom of Amharas, an ethnic group of Orthodox Christians subject to violence and religious repression by the current government.

Here is a black-and-white image of Lai Manping, age twenty-two, who lies dead from beatings inflicted by the Public Security Bureau (PSB) following a raid in 1994 on a house church meeting in Taoyuan, Shaanxi province. In the photograph the bloodied offering bag thrown on top of him rests across his chin. The PSB has arrested more than ninety Christians in an attempt to cover up this murder.

Paul Uchibori's children were martyred before his very eyes. He fell in a faint. When he revived, he said that he had seen his children in heaven and that they gave him great consolation. He died by being plunged into boiling water.

Leonard Massadeodezu was beheaded. He was encouraged to face death by seeing an apparition of his wife, Magdalene, who was martyred before him . . . Others had their ears and noses cut off. Apples don't fear the knives that peel them, because the cutting yields an aroma and a sweet taste that produces joy in children.

Brother Saw Ting Jing, a helper and co-worker of our mission, smuggled 20,000 copies of Bibles and *Tortured for Christ* into China. He was arrested by the Communists in China and we do not know if he is alive. Let us pray for him.

In Salair (Russia), during the Communist revolution of 1917, a Christian named Raphael and deacon Terenty were serving in church when the God-hating Reds broke in. While the deacon fled, Raphael continued his prayers. The Communists took hold of him, tied his legs to the tail of a horse, and rode off dragging him over streets, stumps, and bushes to the edge of a pit, where they dumped him. One would think that he would have entered into his rest. But saints don't rest when their friends endanger their souls by not enduring to the end.

In a dream the next night, Raphael appeared to the deacon with a golden crown on his head and said, "Brother, were you afraid to get a crown? It waits for you. Get it!" The next day the deacon went to the Communists and confessed his faith. They killed him and threw him, as well as nine laymen, into the same pit. Later, on the same spot, a spring of water appeared that never freezes. Such men endured unto the end and were saved! (*The Voice of the Martyrs,* March 1995)

The voice telling these stories is that of Pastor Richard Wurmbrand, a Romanian Jewish Christian who spent fourteen years in prison, three of those in solitary confinement, because he claimed aloud what he believes is true—*Huh echad veein sheni* (He is one and there is no second). His work continues around the world in areas where Christianity is forbidden by law and by physical force. He calls his mission organization "The Voice of the Martyrs." His monthly newsletter raises the impassioned plea that we love—with the love that Christ offers—those who persecute Christians, that we assist (with supplies and letters and books) those Christians who are being imprisoned and killed by those opposed to the free exercise of religion, that when faced with opposition to the truth of the gospel we endure to the end. He is now eighty-six years old, the age of Polycarp when his soul flew dovelike toward the sky.

Part of Pastor Wurmbrand's service has been to document with photographs and letters the history of Christian martyrdom in the latter half of the twentieth century. His offices, I imagine, house a paper mausoleum unlike any the world has ever witnessed, save perhaps in the chronicles of John Foxe, whose multivolumed account of martyrs through the sixteenth century might compare, though it lacks something of the color and immediacy engendered by one who has suffered torture himself.

Wurmbrand issues his newsletters as an exhortation to prepare ourselves. *Christians, don't be caught off guard. When you are captured and imprisoned it will be too late to equip yourselves to face the enemy with love. Practice today. Practice breathing so that you are calm when questioned. Practice physical pain so that you don't betray your brothers and sisters when put to the test.* A third of the Christian church today must operate in secrecy, under the threat of extermination, he reminds his readers. His message exhorts to prayer rather than fear, to discipline instead of complacency. Almost at a wailing pitch, he warns against distinguishing ourselves from those suffering, a stance that in our century has allowed the perpetration of atrocity.

———⚬⊗⚬———

I think what it would mean for me, today, to prepare not to have my faith taken from me—pilfered by my own inward doubts or seized by some external tyranny. No one is demanding that I deny what I believe; but have I denied myself—living within conditions of privilege and safety that much of the world has never known—and taken up my cross, daily, in order to follow Christ? *Were you there when they crucified my Lord?* The spiritual invites us into the discomfort of his presence. I wonder, trembling, if I had been there, if I would have done what Peter did (after Jesus had washed Peter's feet and served him a meal), insisting that he'd never known Christ, or what the Chinese girl did, freely testifying, centuries later, to the love of Jesus.

I am reminded by the vigilance of another witness, by his intimate identification with those who suffer, of one who carried a message of compassion and restraint despite the tortuous climb of the path ahead of him. Perhaps readying himself, along with all who sorrow for our century's devastation, for what was to come, Martin Luther King, Jr., addressed those gathered at the funeral of the children killed by a bomb as they attended Sunday school at the Sixteenth Street Baptist Church in Birmingham on September 15, 1963:

> I hope you can find some consolation from Christianity's affirmation that death is not the end. Death is not a period that ends the great sentence of life, but a comma that punctuates it to more lofty significance. Death is not a blind alley that leads the human race into a state of nothingness, but an open door which leads man into life eternal. Let this daring faith, *this great invincible surmise,* be your sustaining power during these trying days.

Notes

1. Gerald Bonner, "Martyrdom: Its Place in the Church," *Sobernost* 2(5):15.

2. Dietrich Bonhoeffer, *The Cost of Discipleship,* in *A Testament to Freedom,* ed. Geffrey B. Kelly and F. Burton Nelson (San Francisco: HarperCollins, 1990), 332.

3. Edith Stein, *An Edith Stein Daybook: To Live at the Hand of the Lord,* trans. Susanne Batzdorff (Springfield, IL: Templegate, 1994), 87, 99; Etty Hillesum, *An Interrupted Life: The Diaries of Etty Hillesum, 1941–1943,* trans. Arno Pomerans (New York: Pantheon, 1983).

4. Lawrence L. Langer, *Admitting the Holocaust* (New York: Oxford University Press, 1995), 6.

5. Aleksandr Solzhenitsyn, Templeton Address, London, 1983. For complete text of the speech, see *National Review,* July 22, 1983.

6. Diana Dewar, *All for Christ: Some Twentieth Century Martyrs* (New York: Oxford University Press, 1980), 120.

7. James Hefley and Marti Hefley, *By Their Blood: Christian Martyrs of the Twentieth Century* Grand Rapids, MI: Baker Book House, 2nd ed., 1996), 477ff. For renditions of these and other stories (though documentation and often crucial details are absent from their accounts), I highly recommend the Hefleys' book, which we came to call the "Protestant Martyrs Bible" as we conducted research for this project. Other details of this event appeared in *Stanford Magazine* (1993 Centennial Issue).

8. Czeslaw Milosz, "On Literature and Writers," in *Beginning with My Streets* (New York: Farrar, Straus & Giroux, 1991), 159.

For Further Reading

Diana Dewar, *All for Christ: Some Twentieth Century Martyrs.* New York: Oxford University Press, 1980.

Georges Duhamel, *The Life of Martyrs.* New York: Gordon Press, 1990.

Paul Elie, ed., *A Tremor of Bliss: Contemporary Writers on the Saints.* New York: Harcourt Brace, 1994.

John Foxe, *Foxe's Book of Martyrs.* Old Tappan, NJ: Fleming H. Revell, 1980. First published in the late sixteenth century, this account of early Christian and Protestant martyrs was a best-selling book through the nineteenth century.

James Hefley and Marti Hefley, *By Their Blood: Christian Martyrs of the Twentieth Century.* Grand Rapids, MI: Baker Book House, 2nd ed., 1996.

Herbert Musurillo, *The Acts of the Christian Martyrs: Text and Translations.* New York: Oxford University Press, 1972.

Diana Wood, *Martyrs and Martyrology.* Cambridge, MA: Blackwell, 1993.

ALEKSANDR MENN

Russia, 1990

A Martyr Who Lives

by LARRY WOIWODE

Two months before Aleksandr Menn was felled by an ax, he was asked in a radio interview broadcast across Russia, "Does one need to be a Christian, and if one does, then why?"

"I think there is only one answer and it is as follows," he said. "Man always seeks God. The normal state of man is, to some extent, to be connected with a higher power, even when the higher power in the human mind is distorted, and turned into something secular. Still, eras of Stalinism, Moldesuism, and all other isms seek some false god even if God is taken away. This turns to idol worship, but still the inner instinct of seeking God is there."

One can imagine Menn, in the austerity of the Moscow studio, drawing closer to the microphone as he continued, on the spot, his careful answer:

"The question is totally different when it is put this way: Why Christianity? Is it because of the sacred scriptures? No, every religion has sacred scriptures, and sometimes with a very high quality of spiritual content . . .

"Then why Christianity? Morality? Certainly. I am happy that in our society high moral values of Christianity are accepted, but it would be totally erroneous to maintain that there are no moral values outside Christianity . . .

"Then why Christianity? Should we embrace pluralism of religion; or should we embrace a position that God is revealed and therefore can be found in any kind of religion? No, because then the uniqueness and absolute character of Christianity will disappear.

"I think that nothing will prove the uniqueness of Christianity except one thing—Jesus Christ Himself."

In the reflex of an Orthodox priest to the name of Jesus, Menn placed his right hand—his tapered fingers like a concert pianist's—across the crucifix suspended over his chest, below his gray-streaked beard. "Many religious teachers, I'm sure, have a degree of truth in what they preach, but let's listen to them: Buddha said that he could reach the state of absolute nothingness only after long and hard exercise. Can we believe him? We can. He is a good man. He reached what he worked hard for. Greek philosophers tell us how difficult it is for the mind to reach the idea of God and the truth. Mohammed says he felt miserable before God. He felt like nobody, but God simply revealed Himself to him. Mohammed was like a little fly before God. Can we believe him? Yes.

"Among these religious teachers there is only one who says, 'And I say to you,' as if he is speaking on behalf of God." Menn's fingers curl around his crucifix in a gesture that sets his Semitic features into pure relief. "As the Gospel of John would say, 'I and the Father are one.' Among the great teachers of world religions, nobody ever said anything like that. This is the only instance in history when God so fully revealed himself through a man—Jesus Christ, the God-man.

"It is a historical myth that Jesus simply preached morals. He could not be crucified for just doing that.

"Someone might say, 'He called himself Messiah.' Yes, but Berkeley also called himself messiah, and he was not crucified for that. There were many false messiahs. Why was he so loved and hated? He said, 'I am the door'— the door into eternity.

"I believe that everything that is of value in Christianity is valuable only because it belongs to Christ. If it doesn't belong to Christ, it belongs to the same degree to Islam or Buddhism. So every religion is an *attempt* to reach God. But Jesus Christ is the only answer."

The Moscow State Radio interviewer must have nearly tipped over in his chair. But Menn went on, quietly carrying his point home: "On one hand He is the framework of history. On the other He is totally unique. Christianity is unique because Christ is unique."

That was his answer, pared down, given under the constraints of an interview to which the KGB was listening, as Menn was aware. And he wasn't finished; that was only the opening. He spoke with the same alert eloquence for another half-hour. It was July 19, 1990, and the disassembly of the Soviet system was nearly complete, or so consumers of television and newsweeklies in the United States would have liked to believe.

But before glasnost and perestroika were bywords on the nightly news, Menn was known across the Soviet Union as a beacon of spiritual reform. In his humble church in a Moscow suburb, where intelligentsia flocked, even unlettered workers could understand Menn's plain sermons and lecture presentations of the gospel. That gospel teaches how particular talents are given to believers, but the honed clarity that Menn exemplified does not drop from the stars.

———◦◦◦———

Menn was born in Moscow in 1935. Both parents were Jews. His father, an engineer, was an official atheist and nonpracticing Jew, but sympathetic to the Jewish community. In the early 1930s, during a period of bloody anti-Christian purges, Menn's mother, Elena, met Father Serafim Batukov, a priest in the catacomb (or underground) church. As a child, Elena had been a seeker after truth, and as a young woman she became active in the Russian Zionist movement. Now she happily received Father Serafim's teachings.

Seven months after her first son, Alik, was born, Elena took him secretly to Father Serafim's house in Zagorsk. There she and her infant were baptized together. She joined Father Serafim's community and moved to Zagorsk. Seven years later, as the elderly priest lay dying, he said to Elena, · "Thanks to what you are enduring and to the serious way you are raising him, your Alik will someday be a great man."

Young Menn received the nurture of Father Serafim until the priest's death and then turned to Boris Vasilev, a scientist and theologian who was also a member of Serafim's church. At the age of thirteen, Menn knocked on the door of the Moscow Theological Seminary, located in Zagorsk, and asked to be admitted. He was turned down, but the dean of students was so impressed by his abilities—Menn had begun to master Latin, Greek, and Hebrew as well as several modern European languages—that he became Menn's lifelong confidant.

Menn's younger brother, Pavel, an Orthodox believer who later taught Hebrew in Moscow, says Menn felt called to the ministry when he was twelve. "He sought out religious literature wherever he could find it. I can still see him in a Moscow market, poring over books by great religious philosophers. 'They inoculated me against the pestilence of Stalin,' he once told me. 'I trembled as I read.' "

At the age of fourteen, Menn began writing a life of Christ. Within the year, he finished a first draft—a book that eventually became volume one in a series on the history of world religions. Menn loved the natural world and hoped to know it better, so he studied biology—first in Moscow, then at Irkutsk, in Siberia. He later said that because of his training under Vasilev he never sensed any contradiction between faith and science.

His roommate at Irkutsk was Gleb Yakunin, a biology student and an atheist. Menn persuaded Yakunin to rejoin the Russian Orthodox church, where he had been baptized. (Yakunin was later ordained a priest: he became an outspoken defender of human rights in the Soviet Union and, after the overthrow of communism, served as a deputy in the Duma, the lower house of Russia's parliament.) The year Menn was to receive his degree in biology, he was expelled from the institute as "a practicing church member."

Since he had sensed his call earlier, he entered the seminary at Zagorsk. The call was confirmed, he felt, in 1948, when Israel became a nation. He believed that if Jesus was the Messiah of Israel, the people of Israel would someday acknowledge that. Once they did, and were gathered from diaspora into a national identity, he believed they would begin to study what he called their "Jewish legacy—the New Testament." The need for Jewish preachers of the gospel at that time, he felt, would be momentous.

In 1958 he married, and that summer, on the feast of Pentecost, he was ordained a deacon. Two years later he was ordained a priest. He served parishes near Moscow, but only as an assistant, because of the popularity of his ministry. Worship services, once attended only by elderly women, began to overflow with crowds attracted by his preaching. Menn baptized the songwriter Aleksandr Galich, the memorialist and cultural commentator Nadezhda Mandelstam (widow of the great Russian poet Osip Mandelstam, who died in 1938 in a Soviet labor camp), and the writer Andrei Sinyavsky, whose pen name was Avram Tertz, and who later spent nearly seven years in the Gulag. Menn was a spiritual adviser to Aleksandr Solzhenitsyn and the Nobel Prize–winning physicist Andre Sakharov.

Parishioners and friends, saved souls, described him as a man of joy with unusual gifts of discernment; he seemed to sense spiritual needs intuitively and conveyed to others the love of Christ—a lighthearted spiritual healer. In nearly every photograph he is smiling the broad clear smile of one whose joy springs straight from the heart.

Menn read all he could, and his memory was encyclopedic. He wrote a six-volume history of religious and philosophical thought in Eastern and Western cultures before Christ—beginning with the volume he drafted when he was fourteen, *Syn chelovecheskii* (*Son of Man*), his life of Christ. The series ended with the New Testament teachings of Christ being spread throughout the world. That work, according to his biographer, Yves Hamant, exceeds 4,000 pages. In addition to another encyclopedic work, a seven-volume dictionary of biblical studies, Menn wrote many other books and essays, including books on Orthodox worship and on how to read the Bible—a necessity in tradition-fogged, officially atheist Russia.

The vibrancy of Jesus as revealed in the Gospels, Menn felt, had to re-animate the thousand-year-old Orthodox church. And he was aware that its Russian branch had undergone compromises with the Soviet regime merely to exist. His books, circulated in samizdat (the underground press) undid the Soviet claim that atheism was a science; they advanced Christianity as the true intellectual Way. These writings, Michael Meerson says, breathe out the appealing person of Christ. They brought about revival in the Orthodox church; thousands of young people were converted through them. Menn's popularity aroused the ire not only of government officials but also of clerics in the established church. They moved him from Moscow to the small parish of Novaya Derevnya.

Michael Meerson once visited Menn there, at the house where he lived for more than twenty years: "I found him working in his garden, watering plants. He was reading a book held in his left hand, reciting something to himself, while watering with his right hand. 'What are you reciting, Father?' I asked him. 'Dante's *Divine Comedy,*' he replied. 'I cannot live without it, I know it almost by heart, and reread it several times a year to keep it in my memory.' . . . Conversation with him was an intellectual feast: his language was picturesque, full of puns, literary allusions, and quotations from memory of poetry, of the mystical literature of East and West, and of Scriptures, which he knew brilliantly."[1]

Certain members of the hierarchy of the Orthodox church hoped to suppress Men—denouncing him within the church and even publicly to the press and Soviet authorities. Those authorities, who had shadowed Menn for years, finally moved in. For six years the KGB kept him under surveillance, and in 1985 and 1986 subjected him to searches and seizures and harassment. During this time Menn often had to meet with the KGB several times a week. They threatened him with deportation and prison, trying to force him to sign a public denunciation of his ministry.

He refused. He was somehow able to negotiate his own terms, finally stating only this: that in the past he hadn't always behaved with proper caution and had made mistakes—a rudimentary confession for any sinner redeemed by Christ. Menn was asked how he felt about being called in by the KGB so often, facing questions and threats. He said, "I'm a priest, I can talk to anybody. For me it's not difficult."

When the recent change began in Russia, he said to a group of young professionals, "People see perestroika as a kind of panacea. 'Ah! Here's the solution for everything!' But that's not the way it works. We are living with the consequences of a colossal historical pathology [communism]. Our Church, our Russia, have been virtually destroyed, and the damage lives on, in people's souls, in the work ethic, in the family, and in the conscience."

But as the restrictions on religion lifted, Menn moved more freely and broadened his ministry. He visited schools and spoke to students, he gave public lectures—often taking on twenty speaking engagements a month, besides Bible studies and prayer meetings and daily pastoral duties at his church. He put in regular appearances on radio and TV. He was instrumental in organizing an ecumenical institute in Moscow. Asked how he kept up, he said, "I volunteer; God provides the time."

In the eyes of the Russian public he began to assume the dimensions of a Solzhenitsyn or a Sakharov. And when Solzhenitsyn, then in exile in the United States, said that the single greatest hope for Russia was its underground church, he probably had Menn in mind. To American journalists Solzhenitsyn's statement simply confirmed the "reactionary" attitude revealed in his Harvard address. Clearly the rumbling dinosaur was out of touch. Yet as it turned out, Solzhenitsyn's statement was one of the most prophetic ever spoken about modern Russia.

To his brother, Menn confessed that after all the years of restrictions and imposed silence he felt like "an arrow finally sprung from the bow." But a darker shadow was dogging him now. Death threats arrived in the mail. They may have originated with the KGB, or a worse tyranny—one of the heart. Menn had been emphasizing an ecumenicity not compartmentalized by denominations—a faith of universal victory in Jesus Christ—and zealots in the Orthodox church began to vilify him as a secret Catholic and crypto-Jew.

Those close to him believe that an ultraconservative element of the KGB, or the church, or the two in concert, stirred members of the nationalistic group Pamyat to action against Menn. This Russian cult believes that being a Jew is a curse and blames all of Russia's troubles on the Jews. In some of the later lectures Menn was giving, there were disruptions, and one night a group started shouting, "Get out, you Yid! Don't tell us about our Christian religion!"

In September 1990, Menn was invited to host a regular television show, broadcast from Moscow, on religion and culture. He was also asked to assume the position of rector at the Moscow Christian Sunday University. Threatening mail arrived, and it was blunt: accept either position and you're dead. Menn set these threats aside, or read them in public, trying to pass them off. But parishioners and friends started accompanying him home from public appearances, and somebody close to him suggested he should emigrate to the West.

"Why?" Menn asked. "If God hasn't turned away from me, I have to stay and serve Him. And if He *has* turned away, where could I hide?"

It took nearly three years for journalists in the West to piece together the events of Menn's last hours. The following account appears with Michael Meerson's chapter (1993) on Men's life.

> In the morning twilight, the village priest opened the door and headed for the train platform less than a half-mile away. It was Sunday, and Father Alexsander Men' always caught the 6:50 A.M. *elektrichka* from his village near Zagorsk to his parish church in Novaia Derevnia, a small town outside Moscow. The priest kept walking along the asphalt path through the Semkhos Woods. Suddenly, from behind an oak, someone leapt out and swung an axe at Aleksandr Men'. An ax—the traditional Russian symbol of revolt, one of the symbols of the neo-fascist group Pamiat'. The blow hit Men' on the back of the skull. The wound was not very deep but it severed major arteries. The killer, police sources said, grabbed the priest's briefcase and disappeared into the woods. Father Aleksandr, bleeding, stumbled toward his home, walking a full three-hundred yards to his front gate at 3-A Parkovaia Street. Along the way, two women asked if he needed help. He

said no, and they left. From her window, Natasha Men' saw a figure slumped near the gate and pressing the buzzer. She could not quite make out who it was in the half-light. She called an ambulance. In minutes, her husband was dead.[2]

—⊶⊷—

On the evening of September 8, the night before he was struck from behind by an ax, Menn gave a lecture in Moscow, with this at its very heart:

> Some ants build; some ants sow and later reap the crop; and some apes fight and have wars although they are not as cruel as people are. But nothing in nature, except for man, ever tries to think of the meaning of life. Nothing climbs above its natural physical needs. No living creature, except for a man, is able to take a risk, and even the risk of death, for the sake of truth. Thousands of martyrs who have lived are a unique phenomenon in the history of all our solar system.

One pauses at that final sentence—so filled with implications. The conventional way to put it would be "martyrs who have died," and perhaps that was Menn's first choice. But he had just used "death" and, as a biologist, was speaking in a larger sense of life on the earth; so, "martyrs who have lived." But he understood the endlessness of every martyr's death; they live on in the memories of others and in their present-day effects on others' lives. More clearly than most, they live eternally in Christ.

As Menn had said about Jesus only two months before, responding to that Moscow radio interviewer, *"Why was he so loved and hated?"*

After Menn's death, the highest officials in Russia, Gorbachev and Yeltsin, decried the brutality of his murder and demanded justice. But to this day, more than five years later, no one has been accused, and not even one person has been arrested. All official reports of the police claim that the motive for his murder was robbery.

How? What self-respecting thief, much less one willing to murder, would imagine a priest carrying a briefcase to a 6:00 A.M. train on Sunday a likely mark? No, what took place perhaps originated in the government itself; the hidden factions conferred and decided they had had enough. They were aware of the symbology for Russians of the icon and the ax: the one a symbol of enduring religion, the other of brute force— and thus designated by Stalin to be used on Trotsky. They would smash Menn the icon with an ax.

It was probably actually a camper's hatchet, chosen for its suitability to their plan of stealth. They had shadowed Menn enough to know he walked alone on Sunday to the train to make his morning service. A central patch of the woods he passed through was deserted then. One of them—no, cowards must have company—*two* would loiter on the asphalt path, acting as lookouts and bait, one for each arm if Menn should resist. They would look confused, act lost, perhaps hold a scrap of paper with a map scrawled on it.

Better, they would have a transcript of Menn's talk, distributed the night before, audaciously entitled merely "Christianity." They would approach him with concern, saying, "Father, is it true you really said this?"— pointing to the central statement. "Martyrs who have *lived?*"

That was the cue to strike for the man behind the oak, hidden in the spot where police found underbrush trampled—trampled first to silence his rush, then from the fellow's restless fear primed for action by liquid courage, vodka, sweating as he writhed to bring himself under control yet remain hidden.

But quiet, here he comes.

No one who leads a straightforward life imagines he'll be attacked from behind. Menn saw the pair ahead and braced himself, then noticed their bedraggled state, their worn clothes and scuffed shoes and slack-lipped look of apprehensive shame—more of the pitiable alcoholics who'd been bedding in Semkhos park.

"Father?" one said, and seemed so sorrowful he had trouble swallowing. Since Menn had been appearing in newspaper stories and on television, strangers everywhere spoke to him. "Father, is it true?" the other asked, and seemed unable to get his breath, his mouth hanging open. "Did you say this?" He held the printed pages up.

Menn set his briefcase on the walk, drew his reading glasses from a pocket of his windbreaker, and slipped them on. "Now, my friends, what?"

At his voice, the one hidden sprang and struck. Menn fell to the ground, silent. In the silence one grabbed his briefcase, snapping it open, and the assassin dropped the hatchet inside. The other snapped it closed— a sound like a pair of dull pistol shots in the morning woods—and walked off one way while the other two set off in separate directions of their own, as prearranged.

In Menn consciousness trembled to life. Like most who suffer a blow to the head, he had no memory of the moment leading to it. He was on his way to the train for morning services and somehow had fallen. He got to his feet, off balance, feeling faint, and understood he should have—he couldn't draw the thought to completion. In the distance he heard the gathering sound of his approaching train.

He started for it, his legs like shattered tree trunks shedding their substance, and felt he was pouring sweat. He put a hand to his neck and in the dim morning light it came away black. Perceptions reversed. Or he cut himself when he fell. In a swirl of darkness he felt suspended across the distances of time and space he imagined Jesus occupying, and then he remembered his briefcase.

He swung around and when he came to the place where he'd started from, he wanted to lie down. Two women were approaching. Natasha? No. But now that was his purpose: to see her. He shoved his hand in his pocket and steadied his walk. "Are you hurt, Father? Do you need help?"

"No, fine."

He jolted above them like a striding colossus, the riddled trunks of his legs spanning nebulae, and then his consciousness started fraying at its edges like window screen being ripped to shreds. His heart hit his ribs so hard he had to admit he was dying. He squinted out one dim chink of consciousness left. *In the Garden of Gethsemane, Jesus*—the words matched his gait, drawing him along a line he couldn't otherwise manage, and he repeated them until he could see his house ahead, a light in it, the gate.

He was there when he knew he wouldn't make it. He forced himself to take a last step and dove, striking the palings of his garden fence—like bars holding him from the garden where his Savior suffered. He was jolted awake by that last vestige of pride, what he said to the women along his route who offered him help: *No, fine.* His body would not respond when he tried to move, but finally he forced a hand as far as the bell. Then the subatomic insubstantiality of the world gave way, its veil parting, and he passed through the palings and everything he had known to exist into the solidity of everlasting light.

⸺⸙⸺

Natasha Menn saw a man slumped against the garden gate and phoned for an ambulance, assuming she was ministering to a drunk. When the man didn't move, she felt drawn to him and cautiously opened the door. "Don't tell me," she said to the crowd already gathering, meaning she now knew.

At Menn's burial, in the churchyard of the parish he served for twenty-two years, a peasantlike crowd gathered with the intellectuals, and Gleb Yakunin, putting himself at considerable risk, delivered Menn's eulogy.

After the burial, a reporter for the *New York Times* found a woman praying at Menn's grave. She was in her eighties, a member of Father Serafim's catacomb church, as it turned out. She had known Menn since he was baptized. "The final path of this holy man was marked with his own blood!" she cried. And then, "I remember when he was a boy his mother showed me that he had written 'Defeat evil with good.' That is exactly how he turned out."

--- ⚭ ---

Four of Menn's television shows had been taped, but an unknown hand erased the tapes. In 1994 the Radio–1 division of Russian State Radio began to air audiotapes of his lectures, and 70,000 letters from listeners arrived at the studios. The director of Radio–1, in a weekly report his duties demanded, wrote that owing to the response the program was being moved from midnight to 10:30 P.M., and added, "The strength of the program consists in Aleksandr Menn's amazing understanding of the Russian soul and his remarkable intellect of truly global range."

When a parishioner of Menn's heard about this, he remembered that one of Menn's last sermons was taken from the first chapter of the Revelation of Saint John—when John beholds the glorified Christ. And the parishioner heard Menn's voice again as he placed an electrifying emphasis on this statement of Jesus, "I am he who lives and was dead; and behold, I am alive forevermore."

Notes

1. Michael Meerson, "The Life and Work of Aleksander Men," in *Seeking God: The Recovery of Religious Identity in Orthodox Russia, Ukraine, and Georgia,* ed. Stephen K. Batalden (De Kalb: Northern Illinois University Press, 1993). I have also drawn heavily on Meerson's chapter for the facts of Menn's life. From all I've sorted through, Meerson seems (given my admittedly imperfect perspective) to be the most consistently accurate. Other aids have been the article from *Frontier* quoted; Mark Elliot's reports from the Institute for the Study of Christianity and Marxism at

Wheaton College in Wheaton, Illinois; News Network International reports; and the Keston News Service of Keston College in Kent, England.

2. The issue of *Frontier* magazine for January–March, 1993, contains a similar reconstruction, with varying details, of Menn's slaying.

For Further Reading

Yevgenia Albats and James Yuenger, "A Murder Most Unholy in USSR." *Chicago Tribune,* September 16, 1990, 1, 18.

James H. Billington, *The Icon and the Axe: An Interpretative History of Russian Culture.* New York: Knopf, 1966.

Francis X. Clines, "Killing of Soviet Priest: Robbery or an Assassination?" *New York Times,* September 15, 1990, A1.

Lawrence Elliot, "Murder of a Russian Priest." *Reader's Digest,* September 1994. Remarkably accurate, collating the other sources, and not the usual *Reader's Digest* piece.

Yves Hamant, *Alexandre Men: Un témoin pour la Russie de ce temps.* Paris: Editions Mame, 1993. Translated into English by Father Stephen Bingham as *Alexander Men: A Witness for Contemporary Russia, a Man for Our Times* (Torrance, CA: Oakwood, 1995)—the only biography of Menn presently available.

Dmitry Sidorov, "Priest Is Murdered in Zagorsk." *Moscow News,* September 1990, no. 37, p. 5.

JESUIT PRIESTS

El Salvador, 1989

Hearing the Cry of the Poor

by RON HANSEN

Theologian Jon Sobrino was offering a brief course in Christology in Thailand when, on the night of November 16, 1989, a fellow priest awakened him with the news that a Jesuit had been killed in El Salvador. The Irish priest said he'd only half-heard it on the BBC's World Service radio broadcast so for further information he'd phoned London and Julian Filochowski, the director of an international aid agency and a great friend of the Central American Jesuits. Filochowski, hearing that Sobrino was presently there in Hua Hin, asked to speak to him directly.

Walking to the phone, Sobrino feared the news concerned his friend Ignacio Ellacuría, the well-known and frequently threatened rector of the Central American University in San Salvador. And so when Filochowski told him, "Something terrible has happened," Sobrino at once said, "I know. Ellacuría." But he did not know. His friend told him that Ellacuría indeed had been killed, and then he went on. Also killed were Ignacio Martín-Baró, Segundo Montes, Juan Ramón Moreno, Amando López, and Joaquín López y López. Even a cook, Elba Ramos, and her sixteen-year-old daughter, Celina. "My friend read the names slowly," Sobrino remembered, "and each of them reverberated like a hammer blow that I received in total helplessness. I was writing them down, hoping that the list would end after each name. But after each name came another, on to the end. The whole community, my whole community, had been murdered."[1]

––––∞∞∞––––

Ignacio Ellacuría had celebrated his fifty-ninth birthday just a week before his murder. He was born in the Basque region of Spain—as was Saint Ignatius, the founder of the Society of Jesus—and was the fourth of five boys in his family to go into religious life, entering the Jesuit novitiate in Loyola in 1947. Encouraged to be a missionary by Miguel Elizondo, the novice master who would form five of the six martyred Jesuits, young Ellacuría went to El Salvador with six others in 1949 in order to found a new novitiate in the vice-province of Central America—comprising Costa Rica, El Salvador, Guatemala, Nicaragua, and Panamá. (Forty years later, a columnist for *Diario de Hoy* wrote of Ellacuría that shortly "after World War II, a sinister person arrived in the country, and it wouldn't be much of a surprise if he turned out to be a KGB agent."[2]

After five years of humanities, classical languages, and philosophy at the Catholic University in Quito, Ecuador, Ellacuría returned to San Salvador for his three-year regency, teaching in a high-school seminary. Then he was sent to Innsbruck, Austria, for four years of theology, having as one of his Jesuit professors there the formidable and influential Karl Rahner, one of the principal architects of the *aggiornamento*, or updating, of the Catholic church in the Second Vatican Council.

Ellacu, as he was called by his friends, was unhappy in Austria. While he was the acknowledged leader of his Hispanic peers, he was perceived by his father superiors less favorably, as an intense, imperative, lofty man with fierce magnetism and often forbidding intellect. A Jesuit examiner wrote of him: "While he is highly talented, his character is one that is potentially difficult; his own spirit of critical judgment is persistent and not open to others; he separates himself from the community in small groups amongst whom he exercises a strong influence."[3]

Ellacuría was ordained in 1961 and, following a fourth year of theology in Austria, commenced work on his doctorate in philosophy at Complutense University in Madrid, writing his dissertation on the Spanish philosopher Xavier Zubiri, a theoretician of popular political movements whose work investigated, as Ellacuría later put it, "the truth of what seemed to him to be the fundamentals in human life."[4] In 1967, nine years after he left for theological studies, Ellacuría returned to San Salvador to teach philosophy at the Universidad Centroamericana José Simeón Cañas—named after a nineteenth-century Salvadoran priest who fought for the abolition of slavery—which was then little more than a handful of courses and a fifth year of high school.

The Central American University had been founded in 1964 by wealthy parents, politicians, and a Catholic church hierarchy that wanted an antidote to the toxic Marxism that was poisoning education at the federally run National University. Without a site or financial foundation, with only a few fervent Jesuits, secretaries, and faculty members who taught for free as a favor to the fathers, the Central American University at first relied solely on the high repute of the Society of Jesus for its prestige and seriousness. But that was enough. Within a few years a sloping, coffee-growing plantation in the hills south of the city had given rise to a palmy campus that housed highly regarded faculties in industrial engineering and economics, finally enrolling 7,000 students who were generally from Salvadoran high society, young men and women who, "privileged for having received a greater culture, would then be the natural leaders of others."[5]

Ellacuría, who was put on the university's five-man board of directors, found that premise troubling. While the institution's orientation was formally that of providing technicians for the economic and social development of El Salvador, he thought it was essentially affirming European values and structures, and fostering prosperity for the prosperous. Ellacuría felt the institution ought to fully engage the harsh realities of the third world and, through teaching, research, and persuasion, to be a voice for those who have no voice, to change or annihilate the world's inhuman and unjust structures, and to help assuage the agony of the poor. With his forceful guidance and his editing of the monthly magazine *Estudios Centroamericanos,* the Central American University would undergo an epistemological shift, having its ethos in the fundamental option for the poor and in the liberation theology formulated by Gustavo Gutiérrez, a theology with origins in "the contrast between the urgent task of proclaiming the life of the risen Jesus and the conditions of death in which the poor of Latin America were living."[6]

There was much to do. El Salvador was a tiny country of just over 8,000 square miles—about the size of Israel, or New Jersey—but with the greatest population density in the Western Hemisphere. Coffee had created

El Salvador's foreign exchange, financed its public works, furnished jobs to its wage earners, and bestowed huge fortunes on fourteen families that had formed an oligarchy in what was still a feudal society. El Salvador did not fit well into the first- and second-world models of a free-market, trickle-down, privatized economy, but the wealthy had persisted in holding onto a fierce capitalism that went far beyond avarice. Eight percent of the population owned 50 percent of the gross national product, while 92 percent fought to find a fragile subsistence on what was left over, getting by, or not, on an average income of $141 per year. Half the children did not finish primary school. Two percent of the population owned cars. Life for the landless majority was one of rootlessness, wattle huts, filth and illness, and half-mile walks to fetch contaminated water in a bucket, hunger forever there with them like a dog at heel. *Wish for* and *want* may have been the only necessary verbs.

And he came to Nazareth, where he had been brought up; and he went to the synagogue, as his custom was, on the sabbath day. And he stood up to read; and there was given to him the book of the prophet Isaiah. He opened the book and found the place where it was written,

"The Spirit of the Lord is upon me,
because he has anointed me to preach good news to the poor.
He has sent me to proclaim release to the captives
and recovering of sight to the blind,
to set at liberty those who are oppressed,
to proclaim the acceptable year of the Lord." (Luke 4:16–19)

Ellacuría once argued that priesthood and religious life found their meaning in the third world, for there the professed vows of poverty, chastity, and obedience offered a liberating freedom from first-world values of wealth, hedonism, and power. At a disputatious retreat for Central American Jesuits, Ellacuría spoke compellingly of "the sin of the vice-province," of possible collaboration of the Society of Jesus in shoring up unjust structures and oppression in the third world by favoring the rich with their schools and ministries in the past, and of the future need for effective action in liberating the poor from sin, hunger, ignorance, misery, and persecution.

Older Jesuits felt their former efforts were being nullified, but Jesuits still in formation felt inspired to take a far more activist role in countering injustice, some of them joining Salvadoran Jesuit Rutilio Grande and his pastoral "accompaniment" of the campesinos in the parish of Aguilares. These seminarians were firebrands in their late twenties and thirties from well-to-do families, for whom third-world poverty became a hard reality for the first time. They'd study books such as Jon Sobrino's *The Historical Jesus* at the Center for Theological Reflection founded by Ellacuría and Sobrino, and then go out to the parish, where they'd see at firsthand a crucified people. A few scholastics began to feel more strongly called to organize a popular revolutionary movement than to pursue their studies for the priesthood.

> [Ellacuría] took them to task for the neglect of academic studies he believed a fundamental base from which analysis, free from any one ideology, could be constructed. Then he argued that by actively assuming a role within the political process they would be absorbed by it, becoming just a few more individuals in a mass of actors. His position was that the university and the Society of Jesus were entities capable of playing an important and original role in the process of change, but that that capability was dependent on their autonomy.

Unfortunately, three Jesuit seminarians left the order to take up arms against the so-called national security forces that were wreaking vengeance on those nuns and priests and Protestant missionaries who had allied themselves with the poor. Often the presence of a New Testament in a house was enough to have that house destroyed by the police. Whole villages were wiped out. Writer and television producer Teresa Whitfield wrote that after the 1979 Young Officers' coup, which brought in a civilian-military junta, "El Salvador had hit and held the international headlines as a Central American hellhole where death squads ran riot, unarmed *campesinos* were slaughtered by the score, and unidentified bodies, or parts of them, turned up on the roadside each morning."

Rutilio Grande was also one of those that *los escuadrones de la muerte* (death squads) sought out. In the parish of Aguilares, Father Grande and his team of three priests officiated at formal religious functions and furnished pastoral care as before, but they also worked to form a tightly knit community of brothers and sisters in Christ that could fashion a new world. Within a short time 300 people there were committed to the ministry of the Word, coordinating liturgies and catechism classes and stressing the gospel message that God's will was the building of a kingdom of heaven on earth.

Then the wealthy owner of a sugar plantation in Aguilares was killed outside his home while, coincidentally, the ordination of three Jesuit priests was being celebrated by the archbishop, 40 Jesuits, and 2,000 campesinos—who were soon being called "hordes of assassins." Again the Latin American Society of Jesus was accused of favoring the rebels and fostering subversion.

A presidential candidate promised to rid El Salvador of the Jesuits within three months of his election. The Committee for the Defense of the Fatherland, the Catholic Association of Mothers, and other government front organizations found their greatest enemies were not hunger and misery but liberation theology and its Jesuit teachers. Ellacuría was among those priests exiled from El Salvador for a time; other foreigners were interrogated with torture or expelled, including a Colombian priest from the parish next to Aguilares for whom Rutilio Grande filled in at a mass. In his homily, Grande said:

> I greatly fear, my brothers, that very soon the Bible and the Gospel will not be allowed within our country. We'll get the covers and nothing more, because all its pages are subversive. . . . And I fear, my brothers, that if Jesus of Nazareth returned . . . they would arrest him. They would take him to the courts and accuse him of being unconstitutional and subversive.

On the afternoon of March 12, 1977, Rutilio Grande got into his white Jeep with an old man, Manuel Solórzano, a fifteen-year-old boy named Nelson Rutilio, and three children, and headed for a mass in the village of El Paisnal, where he'd been born forty-nine years earlier. Waylaid by heavily armed soldiers on his right and left in the sugarcane fields, Father Grande was heard to say quietly, "We must do as God wills," and then he and the old man and boy were cold-bloodedly killed. The children in the back of the Jeep got away.

Late that night Archbishop Oscar Romero concelebrated a mass for the dead in Aguilares, and afterwards humbly begged the gathered priests and nuns to tell him what the church ought to do next. The Jesuits there were surprised. Although he'd been educated by them in San Salvador and at the Gregorian University in Rome, Monsignor Romero was hardly friendly to the Society of Jesus in El Salvador, having gotten its men removed from the faculty of the National Seminary, having warned a pontifical commission about their politicization of the clergy, and having been a longtime follower of the highly conservative Opus Dei movement. And he was hampered, too, by the fact that when the papal nuncio consulted wealthy businessmen and government officials about their choice for the archdiocese, he was the one preferred.

Either they'd got him wrong or he was changed by the office or by grace, for from the time of Rutilio Grande's murder, Oscar Romero was a different man, offending the right-wing press, the papal nuncio, his fellow bishops, and those in high society who'd thought he was one of them. And now his friends and allies were the hated Jesuits. His press secretary, the president of the governing board of the archdiocese, the general manager of its radio station, his consultors and writers, even his confessor—all were Jesuits. And Romero inspired them with his evangelization of the culture and his serenity, prayerfulness, and fortitude in the face of evil, giving the university a greater consciousness of its own Christian mission in the third world. Ellacuría would say of him, "With Monsignor Romero, God passed through El Salvador."

Leaflets had been floating around San Salvador that read: "*Haga patria, mate un Cura!*" "Be a patriot, kill a priest!" Eleven would be killed between 1977 and 1980, but also killed were four North American churchwomen, and Lutheran, Episcopalian, Mennonite, and Baptist missionaries— any of those who imitated Christ in opting for the poor. And yet they stayed. "We have not remained because we are obstinate," the Jesuit provincial wrote, "but because we are thinking of our brothers, especially the dispossessed, who have suffered more than we . . . We have remained to make a small testimony to the loyalty of the church."[7]

Archbishop Romero said in a homily, "I am glad, brothers and sisters, that they have murdered priests in this country, because it would be very sad if in a country where they are murdering the people so horrifically, there were no priests among the victims. It is a sign that the church has become truly incarnate in the problems of the people."[8]

Ellacuría was with him when he planned his homily for March 23, 1980. Romero would talk about the fifth commandment and the thousands who were being slaughtered, and he would implore the soldiers and police to heed God's law, not the godless commands of their superiors. "In the name of God," Romero said, "and in the name of this suffering people whose cries rise up to the heavens every day more tumultuously, I beg you, I beseech you, I order you in the name of God: Stop the repression!" Early in the evening of the following day, while he was celebrating mass in a hospital chapel, preparing the gifts for the offertory, a national policeman walked in, shot Archbishop Romero through the heart, and hurried out.

Of course the government offered its condolences and there was an official investigation of the murder, but over fifteen years have passed and no one has been charged with the crime.

> What does it profit, my brethren, if a man says he has faith but has not works? Can his faith save him? If a brother or sister is ill-clad and in lack of daily food, and one of you says to them, "Go in peace, be warmed and filled," without giving them the things needed for the body, what does it profit? So faith by itself, if it has no works, is dead. (James 2:14–17)

Archbishop Romero had walked through a door that he'd left open for his Jesuit friends. In 1979 Ignacio Ellacuría had been named rector, or president, of the Central American University, and he became a far more public man. Two years later Ignacio Martín-Baró was named academic vice-rector, Ellacuría's right-hand man.

Twelve years younger than his friend Ellacu, Ignacio Martín-Baró, or Nacho as he was called, was born in Valladolid, Spain, in 1942. In formation he was thought to be hugely talented but too serious and intense, an uptight perfectionist whom his Jesuit classmates finally humanized to such an extent that friends later characterized Nacho as a "boon companion."[9] While studying humanities and philosophy in Bogotá, Colombia, Martín-Baró became engrossed by psychology and filled his nights reading whatever books on it he could find. Right after his ordination to the priesthood, he was assigned to the Central American University, where he taught psychology and was a popular dean of students until he left for the University of Chicago, where he was awarded a Ph.D. in social psychology in 1979—his dissertation considered population density in El Salvador—before returning to UCA.

With his *norteamericano* colleagues, Martín-Baró often wisecracked, "In your country, it's publish or perish. In ours, it's publish *and* perish."[10] And publish he did, writing frequently for Ellacuría's *Estudios Centroamericanos* on a wide variety of subjects, "from the latest Nobel Prize for literature to James Bond, from *machismo* to marijuana." Chair of the psychology department at UCA, vice-rector, a member of the five-man board of directors, and founder of the Institute of Public Opinion—which did polling and canvassing of the people to counteract the government-controlled media's "public disinformation"—Martín-Baró was of necessity a workaholic, getting to his office before 6:00 A.M. and generally staying until 8:00 P.M., and often following formal meetings with late-night chat sessions at which he'd sing and play guitar. Weekends he spent in a parish in Jayaque, where he left behind his harried, intellectual life to become "Padre Nacho," his trouser pockets full of candies for the children, his face lighting up with love and joy as he ministered and preached to his congregation. "A Cervantes with his pen or at the computer," as a friend described him, "as an orator he could have captivated an auditorium of the deaf."

Martín-Baró was internationally famous for a psychology of liberation that eschewed Western scientism, ahistoricism, and self-centered individualism in order to orient psychology toward service to communities and to the rights of workers, campesinos, union organizers, and mothers of the "disappeared."

Writing in the *International Journal of Mental Health,* Martín-Baró pointed out that the Reagan-Bush White House pretended that El Salvador was premier among the Latin American democracies, having, as it seemed, a government chosen in free elections, an ever-increasing respect for human rights, and a highly professional army under civilian control. What few problems there were in the functioning of the judicial system, the White House proposed, were in fact fomented by Marxist-Leninist terrorists.

The hard realities were far different. Civil war had brought not only violence, polarization, and the "institutionalized lie" to El Salvador, but also psychological trauma that would have far-reaching effects on a whole generation. Looking at a tiny village used as a hiding place by the insurgents of the Farabundo Martí National Liberation Front (FMLN) and periodically wiped out by the Salvadoran armed forces solely for that reason, he found that whenever even a far-off military operation was begun, "the people take shelter in their houses gripped by a series of psychosomatic symptoms: generalized trembling of the body, muscular weakness, diarrhea."[11] His fieldworkers collected "clear evidence that government soldiers practice systematic sexual abuse of the *campesina* women," and found that campesinos were afraid even to talk about the civil war. Of those interviewed, who had expressed themselves freely up to that moment, 59.1 percent appeared frightened and answered that they did not know anything about it. Even when they were shown obvious results of the war—burnt crops, the marks of bullets or bombs on their own houses—they insisted on their ignorance, saying that these things had happened when they were not at home.

And when children from the higher economic sectors were asked what would have to happen for there to be no more poor people, a few answered, "Kill them all."[12]

Working in much the same areas as Martín-Baró was Segundo Montes, who was famous in both El Salvador and the United States for his analysis of exiles, refugees, and the displaced. Like Ellacuría and Martín-Baró, he was punishingly overworked: he was the religious superior of the Jesuit community—often a full-time job at other universities—as well as the chair of sociology and political science, one of the five on the board of directors, the head of the Human Rights Institute, and a weekend pastor at a parish in Santa Tecla.

A tall, hot-tempered, passionate Spaniard with a fierce scowl and beard, Segundo Montes was called Zeus by his students, for whom he had a fatherly affection. Educated initially in the hard sciences, he taught physics at the Jesuit high school in San Salvador—the Externado San José—during his regency, and after his Austrian theology studies and ordination he went back to be prefect of discipline and headmaster there. But he saw he could do far more good as a social analyst than as a physicist, so he went on to get a doctorate in anthropology at the University of Madrid and fulfilled his former penchant for numbers with statistics.

Researching subjects as varied as land holdings, social stratification, patronage, and the pervasive theft of dollars mailed from workers in the United States to their Salvadoran families, Montes stirred up as many enemies as Ellacuría had. In 1980 a high-powered bomb exploded at the foot of his bed in the old Jesuit house on Calle Mediterráneo, blowing out a hole in the floor the size of a trash-can lid. On another night he and Ellacuría left a dinner and found their little white car painted with blood-red swastikas and slogans, including "Death to the Communists of the UCA!" And in the early 1980s he heard from army officers who'd formerly been his high-school students that there was a plan to murder Ellacuría first and then himself and the three other men who directed the university. Segundo Montes shrugged and told a worried staff member, "What am I going to do?—if they kill me, they kill me."[13] When a journalist asked in 1988 if he'd thought about seeking freedom elsewhere, Montes told him, "We here are not just teachers and social scientists. We are also parish priests, and the people need to have the church stay with them in these terrible times—the rich as well as the poor. The rich need to hear from us, just as do the poor. God's grace does not leave, so neither can we."[14]

The fourth member of the board at the Central American University was the Spaniard Juan Ramón Moreno, who was born in 1933 and was known to his friends as Pardito. He was a highly intelligent, haltingly shy and sensitive man whose first assignment as a regent was biology classes in the high school of the San Salvador seminary where Ellacuría taught. But other than some work in bioethics, that was as far as he went with his great love of science, and he failed to get a doctorate or even a master's degree in any field, a humiliating oddity among Jesuit priests. Moreno held a host of jobs in vice-province service and formation, having been a novice master, a teacher in the juniorate, a province consultor, a secretary to the provincial, an editor of the province newsletter, and a spiritual director for a great number of sisters and priests in religious orders throughout Latin America.

Ever tactful and self-effacing, Moreno was named interim rector of San Salvador's Externado San José in 1972 in order to investigate charges by high-society parents that their sons and daughters were having their heads filled with talk of the class struggle and then going on field trips among El Salvador's poor, after which they were angrily denouncing their families for being bourgeois, "as if the effort to maintain an economic well-being was a crime." Looking carefully into the matter, Moreno found out that the high-school students were not reading Marxist tracts but papal encyclicals and that they were shocked because the injustice and poverty were shocking. Quiet rationality was not what was wanted, however, and the pro-government newspaper *Prensa Gráfica* hounded Moreno out of office with fulminations about him wrapping Christ and the Gospels in communism.

The founder in Panamá of a magazine for religious called *Diakonia*, which in Greek means "service," Moreno brought the publication and its library with him to the Central American University in the 1980s, where he was librarian for the Center for Theological Reflection and assistant director of the new Oscar Romero Center. There, on the night of his martyrdom, in wanton retribution for his crimes of thoughtfulness and conscientious administration, soldiers would firebomb his filing cabinets and wipe out the hard disks on the computers he'd installed.

In the 1970s, when Juan Ramón Moreno was assisting in a nationwide literacy campaign in Nicaragua, Amando López was one of his superiors.

López was then head of the Central American University in Managua, having moved there from the post of rector at the Colegio Centro América. Amando López was born in Spain in 1936, studied in Rome, got his doctorate in theology at Strasbourg in 1970, and, at age thirty-four, was put in charge of San Salvador's diocesan seminary. Within no time the bishops who'd been impressed by his credentials were woefully disappointed. Expecting López to form the seminarians as they themselves had been formed, the prelates were offended at finding out that López was instituting changes that were prompted by Vatican II: the faculty were far less aloof, regulations were far less intrusive, soccer was now being played inside the walls, old-fashioned cassocks were being discarded, and the seminarians were going over to the UCA to get their philosophy classes from that wild man Ellacuría. In 1972, after heated deliberations, López and the full faculty of Jesuits were fired from their jobs.

López had taught at the high school in Managua as a scholastic, so it was a good fit for him to be assigned as rector there, and then at the Central American University of Nicaragua after the Sandinista revolution. The United States Congress was up to then following the urgings of the White House in financing the governments of infamous autocrats like Anastasio Somoza and the Shah of Iran if that meant fending off for a few more years a regime of communism, and Reagan foreign policy advisers like United Nations Ambassador Jeane Kirkpatrick and Secretary of State Alexander Haig so frowned at "the affinity of liberalism, Christianity, and Marxist socialism"[15] that they found themselves telling journalists that four American churchwomen[16] raped and slaughtered by the Salvadoran National Guard on the highway to La Libertad were political activists who'd probably brought it on themselves—Haig even offered the ludicrous suggestion that the four churchwomen first engaged the soldiers in gunfire.

López found no difficulty in choosing sides, aligning himself against the tyranny and terrorism of the former Nicaraguan regime and with the progressive, if imperfect, government of the Sandinistas. Word of his friendly relations with them got back to the Vatican Curia, however, and López was sent an official "visitor" from Rome who filed a confidential report, the upshot of which was that López was forced to give up his post as rector and went back to Spain for a sabbatical before heading to the Central American University in San Salvador.

López's spirit seems to have been broken for a time by his conflicts with the Catholic church hierarchy, for though he was a forthright and sympathetic counselor to those who sought him out, he seemed hidden in the Jesuit residence, and his theology classes, though well prepared, were frankly thought to be dull. Yet in 1989 López found fresh vigor and happiness in his Sunday pastoral work in the farming region of Tierra Virgen, where his parishioners had such affection for him that twenty-five walked through San Salvador's killing zones in order to go to his funeral.

The oldest and most taciturn man in the Jesuit community was also the only native Salvadoran. José Joaquín López y López, who was called Lolo, was born in 1918 to a wealthy family that owned coffee plantations and a famous dairy in Santa Ana. Lolo felt called to the Catholic priesthood from his youth, finishing high school in a minor seminary before he was accepted into the Society of Jesus. While teaching upper-class boys at the Externado San José, he got the idea to hold weekend catechism classes for the poor, a ministry that finally became part of the Latin American organization Fe y Alegría, "Faith and Joy," and furnished El Salvador with thirteen schools and twelve workshops, as well as two health clinics with 50,000 patients. Lolo financed it all in the old-fashioned way, with fund drives, government aid, and highly successful raffles.

Early in the 1960s López y López began campaigning for a Catholic university in San Salvador by going to right-wing politicians and the wealthiest families he knew with the hope of constructing a private alternative to the radicalized National University, so his humility and loyalty were put to the test when the focus on liberation theology offended the very groups he'd depended upon to found the UCA. Yet for many years he was general secretary to the faculty there, and, at Ellacuría's behest, he joined the Jesuit community in 1988, knowing the threat of violence to them was persistent and gathering force, and knowing too that he had prostate cancer and had few years or months more to live.

When the Son of man comes in his glory, and all the angels with him, then he will sit on his glorious throne. Before him will be gathered all the nations, and he will separate them one from another as a shepherd separates the sheep from the goats, and he will place the sheep at his right hand, but the goats at the left. Then the King will say to those at his right hand, "Come, O blessed of my Father, inherit the kingdom prepared for you from the foundation of the world; for I was hungry and you gave me food, I was thirsty and you gave me drink, I was a stranger and you welcomed me, I was naked and you clothed me, I was sick and you visited me, I was in prison and you came to me." Then the righteous will answer him, "Lord, when did we see thee hungry and feed thee, or thirsty and give thee drink? And when did we see thee a stranger and welcome thee, or naked and clothe thee? And when did we see thee sick or in prison and visit thee?" And the King will answer them, "Truly, I say to you, as you did it to one of the least of my brethren, you did it to me." (Matthew 25:31–40)

By 1989, El Salvador's ten-year civil war had killed more than 70,000 people and caused homelessness and misery for far more. Ellacuría had for a long time been urging dialogue between the factions and a negotiated settlement to end the war, and progress seemed slightly more possible when Alfredo Cristiani, the Nationalist Republican Alliance (ARENA) candidate, was elected president on March 19 and publicly committed his government to good-faith negotiations toward peace with the rebel forces of the Frente Farabundo Martí de Liberación Nacional (FMLN). But the Salvadoran government was arrogant, even belligerent, in its talks while—seemingly without Cristiani's awareness—the High Command heightened the violence against human rights organizations such as the National Trade Union Federation of Salvadoran Workers, the Committee of Mothers of the Detained, Disappeared, and Assassinated, and even a primary school operated by the Lutheran church. The FMLN halted negotiations and on November 11 initiated the largest offensive of the war, firing missiles at Cristiani's private home, the presidential residence, and the homes of the president and vice president of the Salvadoran Constituent Assembly.

Cristiani's response was to suspend all constitutional guarantees and announce a state of siege and a curfew between six at night and six in the morning. A huge counteroffensive of artillery and aerial bombardments of presumed guerrilla hiding places in the poorest and most heavily populated areas of the city trapped families in their homes without food or water, or forced them to flee their neighborhoods and face the gunfire in the streets. The government and armed forces seized the radio and television stations in order to have a national channel on which citizens could report guerrilla activities and find lost members of their families, but the phone-in shows also became forums on which to broadcast attacks against what was thought to be the intellectual leadership behind the FMLN: Archbishop Rivera y Damas, the "Communists" infiltrating the Catholic church, and, of course, the Jesuits. "Bring them to the public places and lynch them," said one of the radio announcers. Ellacuría, it was said, ought to be "spit to death."[17]

President Cristiani was a graduate of Washington's Jesuit-run George-town University and was friendly with Ellacuría, but he was also thought to be in the thrall of the ultrarightist Roberto D'Aubuisson, president of the assembly and founder of Cristiani's ARENA party, composed of para-military groups and wealthy industrial and farming interests. A "homici-dal killer," as a former U.S. ambassador said of him, D'Aubuisson was fond of the Nazis and their holocaust of the Jews, had ordered the murder of Archbishop Oscar Romero, was the chief architect of the political assassi-nations, kidnappings, and terrorism of the underground death squads, and was officially ostracized by the United States in 1984 when it was found he'd tried to have Ambassador Thomas Pickering killed. Closely allied with D'Aubuisson was Colonel René Emilio Ponce, a shrewd tactician and former death-squad member who was now chief of the Joint General Staff and of a powerful corporate network of brutality and corruption that was financed by the United States.

On the afternoon of Monday, November 13, government officials es-tablished a zone of security around its Joint Command headquarters, the military academy, and the Arce neighborhood, which were in front of the main gate to the UCA. Three hundred soldiers were stationed around the campus, so presumably it was safe.

On Wednesday, November 15, 1989, an evening meeting of the High Command was held at the general staff headquarters, the *estado mayor*. Among the twenty-five present at the meeting were Colonel Ponce as well as Colonel Juan Orlando Zepeda, vice-minister of defense, and Colonel Guillermo Benavides, director of the military academy. Worried about the offensive, the officers held hands and prayed for divine inter-vention, after which Chief of Staff Ponce ordered the "elimination of ringleaders, unionists, and known members of the FMLN leadership," and Minister of Defense Bustillo further authorized Colonel Benavides, com-manding officer of the security zone between the general staff headquar-ters and the UCA, to organize a commando unit within the Atlacatl Battalion for the purpose of assassinating Ellacuría and the other Jesuits. They were to leave no witnesses.

Ellacuría was in Spain at the beginning of the offensive, visiting old friends and his ninety-three-year-old father, giving thanks for the $5,000 Alfonso Comín Prize awarded to the UCA for its commitment to justice for the oppressed, celebrating his fifty-ninth birthday, and being unanimously elected president of the coordinating council of postgraduate institutions in Spain, Portugal, and Latin America, at which meeting he offered to host the council in his country in two years, "if I am still alive."

Ellacuría flew back to El Salvador on Monday, November 13. With a curfew in effect and a state of siege having been declared, the twenty-three buildings on the shut-down university campus were bleakly empty but for the new Archbishop Romero Theological Reflection Center, a functional construction of concrete block that housed offices on the first floor and, on the second, the kitchen, dining room, guest room, and corridor of bedrooms of the Jesuit residence. Jon Sobrino had moved in before flying off to Thailand, but the six other priests were still shifting their hundreds of books and few other possessions from the old residence when Ellacuría got there.

A half-hour later, as he was talking to his friends about Europe, they heard the doors to the Romero Center below them being kicked in. Hurrying downstairs the Jesuits found twenty soldiers from the elite Atlacatl Battalion working through the offices. An officer who knew the Jesuits by their first names but who refused to identify himself told Ellacuría they were looking for hidden weapons and, given the state of siege, needed no permission to do so. After a thorough and orderly inspection of the upstairs rooms, the two patrols left, searching no other buildings.

Ellacuría was fuming about it Tuesday morning when his Jesuit assistant, Rolando Alvarado, recalling his teens in Somoza's Nicaragua, told the rector it was in fact a reconnaissance. Wouldn't it be wise for the Jesuits to go somewhere else?

Ellacuría replied that Alvarado was being paranoid, that the soldiers found nothing incriminating, and there were no other housing options anyway. "We have fought them from here and here we will stay."

His friend Rubén Zamora would later say, "Ignacio was a Cartesian, with absolute faith in logic. This time his analysis failed him."[18]

Elba Ramos was the forty-two-year-old housekeeper at the Jesuit school of theology, a fifteen-minute walk away, and her husband, Obdulio, was a night watchman at the university when Father Amando López, who was in charge of buildings and grounds, gave the family of four the chance to live in a little guardhouse not far from the Jesuit residence. But the guardhouse was on Avenida Albert Einstein, where the hammering noise of bombing was so frightening that Elba phoned the Jesuits to find out if there was a quieter place where she and her daughter Celina could stay for a while. Celina was sixteen and in the first year of a high-school commercial course that was rigorous enough that she'd been forced to give up basketball and the band. She was having a hard time doing homework. On Sunday López offered Elba and Celina the guest room in the Archbishop Romero Theological Reflection Center, where it was thought they'd have more peace and quiet.

Segundo Montes was installing telephones in the residence on Wednesday night, and Ignacio Martín-Baró took advantage of one to call his sister Alicia in Valladolid, Spain. He told her he was all right but that San Salvador was being besieged. " 'Listen, listen—wait—can you hear the bombs?' he asked as, at his end of the telephone, her voice was drowned out. 'Oh, Nacho and when is this going to end?' she asked. 'A lot more people will have to die yet,' he answered. 'A lot more people will have to die.' "[19]

Lieutenant José Ricardo Espinoza was the twenty-eight-year-old commander of the commando unit within the feared Atlacatl Battalion and a graduate of the Special Warfare Center at Fort Bragg, North Carolina. In fact, only the week before, thirteen U.S. Green Berets from there had flown in to oversee his company's training exercises. With the exercises called off because of the offensive, Espinoza's first assignment—an order hand-delivered by Colonel Ponce and signed by President Cristiani—had been the Monday-night search of the Archbishop Romero Theological Reflection Center. A few of the Jesuits there he knew well, having been a high-school student at the Externado San José. And so he was thought a natural for Wednesday night's assignment. Colonel Benavides had told him, "This is a situation where it's them or us; we are going to begin with the ringleaders. Within our sector we have the university and Ellacuría is there."[20] Espinoza was told to use the tactic of Monday's search, but this time he was to eliminate Ellacuría. "And I want no witnesses," he said.

Espinoza objected that this was serious, but Colonel Benavides told him not to worry, that Espinoza had his support, meaning that of the High Command. On leaving, Espinoza asked the colonel's assistant, Lieutenant Yusshy Mendoza, for a bar of camouflage grease so that he could paint his face.

Espinoza's four patrols of thirty-six commandos assembled at the Captain General Gerardo Barrios Military Academy after midnight on

Thursday, the sixteenth. With only two beige Ford 250 pickup trucks to get them to the university, five minutes away, there would have to be a return trip. The trucks took the Southern Highway, then went uphill to the Mortgage Bank behind the UCA where the patrols finally were told who they'd be killing: priests who were in on the FMLN's offensive up to the hilt, furnishing logistical assistance to the guerrillas and even overseeing their campaign against the armed forces and the people of El Salvador. Lieutenant Yusshy Mendoza, who was in charge of the operation, told Private Oscar Mariano Amaya, nicknamed Pilijay, or "Hangman" in the Nahuatl language, that it was he who would have prime responsibility for the assassinations because of his familiarity with the AK–47 rifle, a Soviet-made assault weapon wholly associated with the FMLN. When Pilijay was finished there would be a flare, at which time the four patrols would fire their rifles as if they were fighting off the fleeing terrorists.

Espinoza ordered them to form a column and head toward the university at about 1:00 A.M. on November 16, 1989. Electrical power was gone from the area but there was good light from the moon. The pedestrian gate was forced open and the commandos hustled past the Chapel of Christ the Liberator to a parking lot where they feigned a first attack by the FMLN by riddling cars with bullets and throwing a grenade. A few soldiers must have then strayed off in the wrong direction, because a night watchman heard a voice say, "Don't go over there, there are only offices over there."

While some soldiers got on roofs of neighboring houses to watch, another group encircled the Archbishop Romero Theological Reflection Center and began banging on the doors and windows, and a high fence of wire mesh was climbed so a first-floor door could be unlocked from the inside.

Sub-sergeant Tomás Zarpate went a few steps down a passageway when he heard a sound in a guest room and found Elba Ramos worriedly sitting on a divan bed beside a pretty teenaged girl who was lying under covers. Lieutenant Yusshy Mendoza held a lamp up to see them and then told Zarpate to stay there and not let anyone leave. Ignacio Martín-Baró was being hauled down the passageway by a soldier when he saw Zarpate holding his rifle on the women. Eyewitness Lucía Barrera de Cerna heard Nacho say, "This is an injustice. You are carrion."

Pilijay saw a soldier forcing a piece of wood between a frame and a door when a priest in a coffee-colored robe frowned at them from his hammock on the balcony. Ellacuría said, "Wait. I am coming to open the door, but don't keep making so much noise." And then Pilijay heard his name being called and was told the priests were in front of the building.

Pilijay hurried out and found Sub-sergeant Antonio Ramiro Ávalos, whose nickname was Satan, holding a rifle on five grim priests in pajamas or trousers and shirts, priests whom other Jesuits called *los viejos,* the old men, because their fifteen-hour days of hard work and anxiety had hurt their health and prematurely aged them. Ellacu, Nacho, Zeus, Pardito, Amando. Worried that it was five against two, Sub-sergeant Ávalos ordered them to lie facedown on the grass and then was called over by Lieutenant Espinoza, whose eyes were filling with tears because he saw that Segundo Montes, his headmaster at the Externado, was among those on the ground. Espinoza impatiently asked, "When are you going to proceed?" Sergeant Ávalos walked back to Pilijay and told him, "Let's proceed."

The five priests were prostrate just as they were in their rites of ordination when the litany of the saints is chanted. And they seemed to be whispering a psalmody when Sub-sergeant Ávalos yelled, "Quick, quick, give it to them quickly!" and Pilijay fired the AK–47 at the heads of the three men in front of him, thinking their brains were the problem, killing Ignacio Ellacuría, Segundo Montes, and Ignacio Martín-Baró. Ávalos fired his M16 at the heads and bodies of the two priests closest to him, Amando López and Juan Ramón Moreno, and then Pilijay finished off all five with a long burst from his fully automatic rifle. Only with difficulty would friends later be able to find features in the hacked-apart face of Amando López.

Sub-sergeant Zarpate heard the gunfire and then someone shouting, "Now!" Obediently he turned to Elba and Celina Ramos and, though they were far from being Communist agitators, Zarpate fired at them until "they no longer groaned," hitting Elba in the vagina in the signature style of the death squads. And then he glumly walked off.

In the first-floor Theological Reflection Center, offices were being trashed and commandos were firebombing the file cabinets, wiping out computers, burning books and tapes. When he heard the gun noise outside, one inflamed soldier looked up at a framed picture on the wall of a genial Archbishop Romero and fired a bullet at his heart.

A frail old man in a white undershirt walked out into the corridor and then to the front of the building. López y López was in hiding until he heard the gunfire, and then must have felt he had to go out. But when he saw his friends massacred on the grass, fear overtook him and he said, "Don't kill me, because I don't belong to any organization." And then he turned to go back inside the house.

"*Compa,* come here," a soldier called. FMLN members are affectionately called *Compa* by their supporters. Lolo walked on. But as he was entering a bedroom, he was hit with a shot and fell. Corporal Ángel Pérez walked into the room to find what was in there. Like Sub-sergeant Ávalos, he was a graduate of a Small Unit Training Management Course in the United States. Lolo's hand took hold of his foot and in his astonishment Corporal Pérez fired twice at Joaquín López y López. And then, flushed with embarrassment at his surprise, he fired at the old man twice more.

Walking a passageway toward the garden gate, Sub-sergeant Ávalos heard groaning and lit a match to look into the guest room where Elba and Celina Ramos were still painfully alive and hugging each other in a widening pool of blood. The sergeant told Private Jorge Alberto Sierra to finish them off, and Sierra fired the full magazine of his M16 into them and trudged off, leaving bootprints of blood on the floor.

And then they were through. The whole operation had taken no more than an hour. Pilijay headed back inside the Jesuit residence, wrecked the kitchen, and helped himself to a Pilsner beer. Hoping to hide the fact that this was a formal execution, other commandos hauled the bodies back inside, but there was only time for Corporal Cotta Hernández to drag Juan Ramón Moreno along the tile floor to Jon Sobrino's bedroom, the red bundle of his brains hanging from his head. A book fell from its bookshelf there and into his flowing blood. The book's title was *The Crucified God.*

Behold, my servant shall prosper,
he shall be exalted and lifted up, and shall be very high.
As many were astonished at him . . .
so shall he startle many nations;
kings shall shut their mouths because of him;
for that which has not been told them they shall see,
and that which they have not heard they shall understand.
(Isaiah 52:13–15)

The official story was that the murders were committed by the FMLN, and at first even Secretary of Defense Richard Cheney was firm in saying,

"There's no indication at all that the government of El Salvador had any involvement."[21] Witnesses to the slayings were harassed and intimidated by the FBI; Colonel René Emilio Ponce, of all people, was put in charge of the official investigation of the murders; and the United States embassy all but stonewalled on the crimes. Word of the truth was getting out, however, and Massachusetts Representative Joe Moakley's congressional task force finally embarrassed the Cristiani government into action, reflecting an old pattern in our relations with El Salvador over human rights issues in which, as Martha Doggett of the Lawyers Committee for Human Rights put it, "Washington plays the parent to the unruly Salvadoran child. When threats fail to curb behavior, punishment sometimes follows, though not as a rule."[22] Eventually the Salvadoran Supreme Court charged four officers and five enlisted men with the crimes—a half-measure certainly—and even though there were confessions from those who committed the atrocities, a jury that was possibly tampered with found only Colonel Guillermo Benavides and Lieutenant Yusshy Mendoza guilty of murder, the first officers ever convicted of a human rights violation. They would finally serve a little over a year of their thirty-year sentences. Each and every other member of the Atlacatl Battalion went free.

But the two-year investigation of the Jesuit murders shone a light on villains in the High Command, put an end to the hated security forces and the Atlacatl, focused attention on other crimes and inequities in El Salvador, and changed U.S. policy to one of full endorsement of negotiations, resulting in a peace agreement being signed in Chapultepec.

At the funeral of the six Jesuits, José María Tojeira, their provincial superior, offered a homily in which he ringingly said, "They have not killed the Central American University and they have not killed the Society of Jesus in El Salvador."[23] And the filled auditorium affirmed that with a two-minute standing ovation.

Two Salvadorans, two Americans, a Mexican, and a Canadian joined Jon Sobrino in the university's Jesuit community, and off the balcony where Ignacio Ellacuría frowned at the soldiers, a building extension was constructed to accommodate the growing numbers of theology students.

The blood of martyrs is the seed of the church, wrote Tertullian. All the faithful do not perish, nor suffer infamy or risk, but we as a church are expected to be witnesses to those who did, and do. And then we will find that like the martyrs before them, the two women and six Jesuits murdered in El Salvador are, as José María Tojeira has written, dead "who continue to be profoundly active and alive . . . generating human spirit, generating human dignity, generating the capacity for dialogue and humane rationality, generating a critical capacity, a constructive capacity, and generating imagination."

Notes

1. Jon Sobrino and others, *Companions of Jesus: The Jesuit Martyrs of El Salvador* (Maryknoll, NY: Orbis Books, 1990), 5.

2. *Diario de Hoy,* June 13, 1988; quoted in Martha Doggett, *Death Foretold: The Jesuit Murders in El Salvador,* Lawyers Committee for Human Rights (Washington, DC: Georgetown University Press, 1993), 17.

3. Quoted in Teresa Whitfield, *Paying the Price: Ignacio Ellacuría and the Murdered Jesuits of El Salvador* (Philadelphia: Temple University Press, 1994), 28.

4. Ignacio Ellacuría, "Zubiri sigue vivo," *Estudios Centroamericanos,* no. 420 (October 1983); quoted in Whitfield, *Paying the Price,* 32.

5. Whitfield, *Paying the Price,* 35. Unless otherwise noted, the quotations throughout this article are from Whitfield's book.

6. Gustavo Gutiérrez, *A Theology of Liberation* (Maryknoll, NY: Orbis Books, 1988), xxxiv.

7. Cézar Jerez, S.J.; quoted in Doggett, *Death Foretold,* 25.

8. Sobrino, *Companions of Jesus,* 54.

9. Sobrino, *Companions of Jesus,* 76.

10. Review of *Writings for a Liberation Psychology,* by Ignacio Martín-Baró, *Catholic Book Club,* February 1995, 2.

11. Ignacio Martín-Baró, "Political Violence and War as Causes of Psychosocial Trauma in El Salvador," *International Journal of Mental Health* 18:1 (1988); quoted in Sobrino, *Companions of Jesus,* 80.

12. Sobrino, *Companions of Jesus,* 81, 82.

13. Whitfield, *Paying the Price,* 333, 338.

14. Interview with Rev. Stan Granot Duncan, Disciples of Christ, April 1988; cited in Sobrino, *Companions of Jesus,* 137.

15. Jeane Kirkpatrick, "Dictatorships and Double Standards," *Commentary,* November 1979, 40.

16. Sisters Ita Ford, Maura Clarke, Dorothy Kazel; and Jean Donovan, a laywoman; on December 2, 1980.

17. Sobrino, *Companions of Jesus,* xiv; Whitfield, *Paying the Price,* 347.

18. Philip Bennett, "Letter from El Salvador," *Vanity Fair,* November 1990, 115.

19. Bennett, "Letter from El Salvador," 352.

20. Doggett, *Death Foretold,* 65. All further quotations in the narrative of the crime are from Doggett's edited and abridged version of "Narracíon de los Hechos," which was prepared by the Jesuits in early 1990, and from extrajudicial statements of those charged with the murders.

21. Sobrino, *Companions of Jesus,* xix.

22. Martha Doggett, "A Study in U.S. Human Rights Policy Toward El Salvador: The Jesuit Case," *America,* October 12, 1991, 246.

23. Joseph E. Mulligan, "The Blood of Martyrs: The Seed of Hope and Commitment," *America,* February 17, 1990, 146.

For Further Reading

Martha Doggett, *Death Foretold: The Jesuit Murders in El Salvador.* Washington, DC: Georgetown University Press, 1993.

————, "A Study in U.S. Human Rights Policy Toward El Salvador: The Jesuit Case." *America,* October 12, 1991, 246.

Joseph E. Mulligan, "The Blood of Martyrs: The Seed of Hope and Commitment." *America,* February 17, 1990, 146.

Jon Sobrino and others, *Companions of Jesus: The Jesuit Martyrs of El Salvador.* Maryknoll, NY: Orbis Books, 1990.

Teresa Whitfield, *Paying the Price: Ignacio Ellacuría and the Murdered Jesuits of El Salvador.* Philadelphia: Temple University Press, 1994.

OSCAR ROMERO

El Salvador, 1980

Seed of Liberty/Sign of Hope

by CAROLYN FORCHÉ

I awaken every two hours during the night, on my pallet in the mud hut, a rooster's eye fixed on mine in the pitch dark. He crows, alerting the dogs, whose barking ricochets among the coco-palms until the darkness is filled with the strains of "the symphony of Santa Marta": burros, sows, piglets, wild birds, in a village high in the mountains of Cabañas without lights or running water, five hours and forty-five minutes by plane from Washington, D.C., then another three or four by truck depending on the roads, the rains.

Santa Marta shares its poverty with every other village in El Salvador, along with the ghosts and shallow graves of the war, so that it's possible to walk through a field and fill a sack with bones. It has a cinder-block school built by the Swedes, and a clinic with no physician, where the armless, blind boy in the hammock was taken the day a land mine exploded. In the morning, the women beat their clothes on wet *pilas* (stone tables used for washing clothes), hang them in blue veils of cook-smoke, eat their palm-sized tortillas, their lump of beans. They bathe at the common spigot, deftly soaping and rinsing themselves beneath their clothes. The water is clear, tepid, contaminated.

There is tuberculosis here, and dysentery, illiteracy, malnutrition, paraplegia, and also patience, camaraderie, and uncommon courage. The people fled the war in a *guinda* (evacuation), babies on their backs single-file through the jungle, in silence and mortal fear, leaving behind them the first Santa Marta, gutted and burned. They lived together for several years in a refugee camp in Honduras, until as one they decided to return home without the permission of anyone but themselves. The second Santa Marta was built on this ground, with the houses clustered for security, and it was here, in this resurrected village, that the war actually began to end. So it is fitting that this village has what no other can claim, a holy thing, given to them by Catholic sisters in San Salvador, a frayed swatch from the vestment of Archbishop Oscar Romero, washed with the blood he gave for them, the blood he hoped would seed their liberation.

It has been seventeen years since I first traveled to El Salvador, before the war, while the country was still at peace: the silence of misery endured; fifteen years since I left the country at Monsignor Romero's urgent behest; fifteen years and six days since he was shot while saying mass in the chapel of Divine Providence Hospital for the terminally ill poor before a tiny cluster of the sick and their caretakers. Monsignor celebrated the mass alone, in his Lenten vestments. "This Eucharist . . . is just an act of faith," he said in his homily. "May this body immolated and this blood sacrificed for humans nourish us also, so that we may give our body and blood to suffering and to pain—like Christ, not for self, but to bring about justice and peace for our people. Let us join together, then, in faith and hope at this moment of prayer for Doña Sarita and ourselves."[1] He returned to the altar, facing the open doorway of the chapel, looked out at his tiny congregation, then down at the unconsecrated host and the cup of wine.

For three years Oscar Arnulfo Romero y Galdámez had served as archbishop of San Salvador. If we are to find his predecessor among martyred Christians, we must turn to another bishop, Ignatius Theophorus of the metropolitan see of Antioch in Syria, immolated in the Flavian amphitheater in A.D. 107. Little of Ignatius's life is known, and nothing of the charges resulting in his persecution, but like Monsignor Romero, he is revered for his strength of character, his pastoral letters, and his transformation of the Christian view of martyrdom. "I am God's wheat ground fine by the lions' teeth to become purest bread for Christ,"[2] Ignatius wrote, turning from the pain of death toward an inexorable, eucharistic destiny, the apotheosis of a holy life, unambiguous and spiritually complete.

"I have frequently been threatened with death," Monsignor Romero said near the end of his life. "I should mention to you that I do not believe in death, but in resurrection. If they kill me, I will live on in the Salvadoran people."[3] Nineteen centuries earlier, Ignatius pronounced that the martyr is "no more to be found in himself."

Oscar Romero was born in the remote village of Ciudad Barrios on August 15, 1917, to Santos Romero and his wife, Guadalupe de Jesús Galdámez. He spent his adolescence with the Claretians, then attended the major seminary in San Miguel, and finally studied with the Jesuits at the National Seminary in San Salvador. In 1937 he began six years of work at the Gregorian Seminary in Rome, where he was ordained and awarded a degree in theology. Italy was at war, and the young Romero lived in extreme poverty under Mussolini's dictatorship. It was there, perhaps, that he was first drawn to the conservative Opus Dei, a prelature of the Catholic church dedicated to personal sanctity.

When he returned to El Salvador, he served his own community as one of the few rural priests administering to the spiritual needs of the very poor. Devoutly dedicated, he is remembered for his openness, compassion, and strict discipline. The priesthood for him was not a business founded to extract a comfortable life from the needy; upon his elevation to the bishopric in 1967, he imposed the same discipline upon his working priests. After three years, he became auxiliary bishop of San Salvador and was then assigned to the impoverished diocese of Santiago de María, where, it is believed, his soul embarked on the path toward sanctity.

In the aftermath of a martyr's death, mythologizing begins in earnest, a narrative constructed of apocryphal stories and documentable facts conforming to the meta-narrative: whether the martyr's origins are humble or privileged, there must be a decisive turn, an awakening or conversion, temporally fixed and irrevocably decisive. For Monsignor Romero, this epiphanic moment was said to be the murder of his close friend, the Jesuit father Rutilio Grande, near the village of El Paisnal. The priest was riding in a jeep through the cane fields, along with an elderly man and a sixteen-year-old boy, when security forces machine-gunned them on March 12, 1977. The first among the country's clerics to be murdered, Father Grande had, a month earlier, denounced the expulsion of a missionary priest in these words:

It was a matter of being or not being faithful to the mission of Jesus here and now. And for being faithful there would be reprisals, calumnies, blows, torture, kidnappings, bombs, and if one was an outsider, expulsion. But there always remained the fundamental question: it is dangerous to be a Christian in our milieu! . . . precisely because the world which surrounds us is founded radically on an established disorder before which the mere proclamation of the Gospel is subversive . . . in Christianity one has to be ready to give one's life in the service of securing a just order, in saving the majority and in helping defend the values of the Gospel.[4]

Within the church, these values were in some dispute. The Second Vatican Council's restoration of popular biblical study, together with its approval of liturgical worship in local languages, authorized the often illiterate and impoverished laity to study Scripture without intercession, eroding the concept of religious and, ultimately, secular hierarchies. In Latin America, the historically conservative and defensive institutional church, long allied with oligarchic economic elites, addressed the precepts of Vatican II in a conference of bishops held at Medellín, Colombia, in 1968. While these convocations marked apparent doctrinal shifts, it would be a mistake to view them as causal; they were, rather, responsive to the growing demand among ordinary Catholics for a living faith, founded on praxis in the modern world. This spiritual renewal coalesced in "liberation theology," in which "the very enterprise of doing theology moves from a deductive and axiomatic logic to become an interpretive discipline, shaped and limited by the context in which it evolves and by the interests and experiences of the Christian community itself. As a practical matter, these interests and experiences are the way they are because of historical realities of exploitation, injustice and oppression."[5]

In Latin America, the members of this renewed, "popular" church formed Christian "base communities," studying Scripture by candlelight, celebrating masses anywhere possible, often in the open on makeshift altars. For them, the kingdom of God and the world of humanity coexist, one emerging from the other. Poverty and misery are distinguished: the one a condition of simplicity and renunciation; the other, of humanly imposed suffering. Social injustice and the exploitation of labor are condemned. Nuns and priests commit themselves to "a preferential option for the poor," living in solidarity with them and sharing their fate. This church views historical change as the salutary and inevitable work of God in the world, advocating action to promote justice, critiquing society, and interpreting faith through the experience of the most oppressed. They activate Scripture: "For Thou has been a defense for the helpless, A defense for the needy in distress" (Isaiah 25:4) and "The Spirit of the Lord is upon me, because he has anointed me to preach good news to the poor. He has sent me to proclaim the release of the captives and recovering of sight to the blind, to set at liberty those who are oppressed, to proclaim the acceptable year of the Lord" (Luke 4:18–19). In this church, the poor have compassion for the poor.

Monsignor Romero hurried to the Jesuit house in Aguilares on the news of Father Grande's death. Only weeks before, he had been appointed archbishop of San Salvador, the most powerful office in the Salvadoran church hierarchy. The priests of the emergent church viewed his elevation with dismay: as a candidate acceptable to the country's wealthy elite, he had apparently been charged to suppress the young activists, discipline their ranks, and restore their mission to feudal pastoral ministry. The bishop who arrived that night, however, was deeply troubled and determined to respond to the murder. After concelebrating the memorial mass with more than a dozen others, he asked the priests and nuns to remain with him, and together they talked into the morning, the new bishop soliciting the counsel of those who had worked closely with the dead priest and his parish of laborers, and who were vulnerable themselves. The three corpses had been laid on simple wooden tables in the church, covered with white sheets. It was said that Monsignor kept vigil over the remains of Father Grande for several hours.

By this time, more than three hundred campesinos had been killed in El Salvador, among them catechists and labor organizers who were dragged from their makeshift cardboard *champas* (shacks) in the night, from the fields, the roads, from Bible studies and mud-brick chapels, tortured with machetes and coals, their eyes gouged, their limbs hacked away, their entrails pulled from them, and then left in the field or at the doorstep of one who might be next. Others were "disappeared," made to vanish, and a new word entered the language: *desaparecido,* one who *might* be dead but could be suffering in secret detention.

The smallest and most populous country in Central America, El Salvador had been under military dictatorship for almost fifty years. Two hundred families owned 60 percent of the arable land and controlled 75 percent of export earnings; they lived aristocratically, protected behind high walls and on massive estates, with houses in Miami, Houston, and Switzerland. Among the poor, half were unemployed, and more than 90 percent earned less than $100 a year. Agricultural unions were forbidden by law. Eighty percent of the people had no running water, electricity, or sanitary services. The chief cause of death was amebic dysentery. One out of four children died before the age of five; the average life expectancy was forty-six years.

The murder of Father Grande was viewed as Monsignor Romero's moment of truth, his "Saul to Damascus" conversion; in the myth, he arises from his mournful vigil transformed. The activist priests who feared his archiepiscopal discipline interpreted his resolve in the succeeding months as evidence of conversion, "that passage that never ends . . . which is the unceasing demand to kill in oneself all that is sin and make live, with ever growing power, all that is life, renewal, holiness and justice . . . It is a great joy to me to emphasize this sense of service in a letter whose purpose is to introduce to you a pastor who wants to live out, and as closely as possible, to share in, the feelings of the Good Shepherd, who 'came not to be served, but to serve, and to give his life' (Matthew 20:28)."[6] A year earlier, as bishop of Santiago de María, Romero had criticized "rationalistic, revolutionary, hate-filled christologies."[7] Was this the reversal it seemed? The activist priests thought so and embraced him as their spiritual guide; the ruling class also thought so and would soon condemn him to death.

We drive through the stench of rotting coffee husks, past pit fires and roadwork, toward the church of San Antonio del Monte, one of the oldest in the country, starkly white against the pewter-clouded afternoon. The verandas give onto a courtyard dripping with wisteria, where chickens forage and the new cistern sits full but inaccessible because of a power outage. I have not seen Father Guerra in seventeen years. There is a high, pulsing hum in the trees, which has been there since my arrival, mysterious and pervasive, linking me to the past, years of horror and immeasurable love. It is the song of cicadas.

In the high-ceilinged rectory kitchen, we share a meal of lemonade, white cheese, and beans in the near dark. Father Guerra comes in, silvered from his years, but essentially the same: quiet, intense, wearing a white *guayabera,* his hands clasped in sincere joy that we've come, but asking us to make ourselves at home while he frees a few moments from his busy ministry.

"They captured him," my friend whispers, "and beat him almost to death."

It is *semana santa*. In an hour, the people will carry Christ shouldering the cross on a litter through the streets, lighted by fluorescent tubes powered by a portable generator, followed by an unlit Madonna, borne by women. Seventeen years ago, the litters were candlelit and accompanied by plainsong. Now the music issues from a cassette player. Still, the townspeople are dressed in Lenten violet robes and positioned in medieval tableaux. A man is squatting before the Christ, gesticulating and asking the statue to acknowledge the beautiful flowers, the elaborate preparations he made for this moment; it is a conversation, but we hear only his side.

"Well," Father Guerra asks, when we meet him later on the blacked-out terrace, "did you see the procession?"

"You were captured . . . "

He smiles and offers us Coca-Colas and a flashlight, then enthuses over what has been accomplished in his poor parish: the orphanage; the school; the soybeans sandbagged against the walls of the vestibule, enough to feed the children for a year; and the church itself, rebuilt after the earthquake, of cement blocks this time, but in the old colonial style.

A candle gutters in the mild breeze and goes out. I ask about Monsignor Romero.

"He was always with us."

"Always?"

"Monsignor Romero's process began in Santiago de María, before Father Grande was killed, with the people of that parish, or before, but I think he was greatly affected by Santiago, where he openly defended the poor."

His "conversion" to liberation theology was a gradual process of interrogating the new thought, measuring it against traditional teachings, testing its theological soundness, and warning his priests that the apprehension of God in history must be commended in a language of compassion rather than combative fervor. "There is a Spanish saying, *love must be paid with love*. And that is the purpose of my pastoral message: to repay a debt of love. I have no other reason to be here."[8] For him, the realization of the kingdom of God on earth was something more than the spiritual template of a secular ideology. "The church does not exist for itself,"

Monsignor wrote in his first pastoral letter. "Its raison d'être is the same as that of Jesus: service to God to save the world."[9]

He called for the schools to recess for three days of reflection and announced a single memorial mass for Father Grande to be celebrated in the cathedral on Sunday; the wealthy protested that this mass would deprive them of the opportunity to fulfill their Sunday obligation, as they seemed unwilling to drive to the cathedral and join the congregation of the poor. The papal nuncio questioned the "canonical" correctness of the decision, and others in the institutional hierarchy warned that such a gathering would be dangerously provocative. Cardinal Casariego of Guatemala intimated that Father Grande's death was his own fault.

One hundred thousand people attended the mass, the largest in Salvadoran history, filling the dark interior of the still unfinished edifice and spilling onto the plaza and side streets to stand in the sun, singing, praying, and listening to Monsignor's voice over loudspeakers; others in the countryside heard him by radio. From then on, he would celebrate mass before a spray of microphones, transmitting his voice to the streets and to radios in the *campo* and around the world.

On May 1, 1977, Jesuit father Jorge Sarsanedas, a Panamanian, was captured. Before his deportation, Monsignor visited him and was asked by the commander of the Guardia Nacional to sign a statement affirming that Father Sarsanedas had not been harmed. The priest had been blindfolded, beaten, and fed almost nothing; Monsignor refused to sign, then followed the Guardia car to the airport to see the priest safely out of the country. Repeatedly, bombs went off in the archdiocese print shop. A second priest, Father Alfonso Navarro, was murdered in the capital on May 11, along with a fourteen-year-old parishioner. Navarro died in the hospital, pardoning his killers. Meanwhile forty nuns were deported, and campesinos continued to die.

Government troops attacked Aguilares on May 17 in a violent attempt at mass eviction. At least fifty townspeople were murdered, among them one attempting to ring the church bell, and hundreds disappeared. Houses were torn apart, and the three remaining Jesuits were deported. A visiting priest was arrested and beaten. Monsignor Romero went himself to Aguilares but, barred from entry, asked the chaplain of the Guardia to go in his place. Security forces arrested and held the chaplain prisoner while they shot open the tabernacle and ground the host into the floor.

The church is persecuted, Monsignor Romero said later that year, because "it denounces sin. It says to the rich: do not sin by misusing your money. It says to the powerful: do not misuse your political influence. Do not misuse your weaponry. Do not misuse your power. It says to the sinful torturers: do not torture.You are sinning.You are doing wrong.You are establishing the reign of hell on earth."[10]

The security forces, comprising the National Guard, the National Police, the Treasury Police, the Air Force, the Army, and a small Navy, were all under brutal commands, but the Army controlled the government and its highest offices. The institutional culture of the military fostered participation in graft and corruption so extensive and lucrative that the highest-ranking officers from the most powerful military cliques (called *tandas*) amassed millions and fiercely protected the hegemony they began to share with the landed rich.

Paramilitary groups, although officially disbanded, terrorized the countryside. "Death squads" composed of the military and civilians closely linked to them, and financed by wealthy families, began clandestine operations, targeting union organizers, teachers, human rights activists, and members of the growing "popular organizations," as well as nuns and priests. The *desaparecidos* grew by the thousands; corpses of the unidentified dead filled the morgues and were recovered from ditches, fields, and the long, pristinely beautiful coastal beaches. Campesinos stopped fishing the lakes, not wishing to eat fish that had fed so abundantly on human remains.

Between 1978 and 1980 I made several long trips to the country, initially to translate Salvadoran poets, whose work bore poignant witness to repression, at times so explicitly that it was difficult to distinguish literal from figurative truth. The brutality of the security forces, uniformed and clandestine, intensified during my initial visit, which corresponded to the first human rights investigation in El Salvador.[11] A young, lapsed Catholic poet, I observed the proceedings at the remove of one who finds herself assimilating unprecedented horror while encountering living faith for the first time. When the investigators left, I remained and asked my Salvadoran friends what would happen to the campesinos who had commended their dignified, tearful testimonies to the tape recorders, the priests and nuns who had so courageously provided meticulous documentation of repression.

"Most of them will die," my friend said.

"But they must be protected!"

"Yes, they *should* receive protection—but from whom?"

Over the next months, I traveled throughout the country, compiling a report on the growing repression, replete with pseudonyms and detailed atrocities, which I sent to Amnesty International's secretariat. A few weeks later, I received a reply,[12] couriered from the United States, asking me to continue providing information, particularly regarding the possible fates of the disappeared.

For this work, it became necessary to learn to compare a child's school photograph with the face of a mutilated corpse, control my emetic reflex, search without prospect of recovery, impart hope without hoping. In this I was continually accompanied by Salvadorans, who guided me with patience through the labyrinthian military security state, permitting me to discover for myself my own embassy's complicities. They were with me when I feared more for myself than for others, when I wanted respite or the comforts of home. Within months, I could no longer regard my fate as other than inextricably linked with their own.

During the next two years, every peaceful demonstration and protest march was fired upon, even when the marchers numbered 200,000, as on January 22, 1980, when it seemed that all of El Salvador converged on the capital in jubilant defiance, unfurling the bright red and yellow banners of the growing popular organizations. They sang, chanted, linked arms, and marched inexorably toward an attack that left twenty dead. A coup d'état by younger officers on October 15, 1979, had replaced the old military guard with a succession of three military-civilian juntas, each more repressive than the last.

In the countryside the mass killings of Salvadoran campesinos continued. We encountered villages so newly abandoned that the little corncribs near the mud huts still smoldered, and their *champas* had become smoking mounds of ash, burnt enamel cookware, melted plastic washbasins. The fields around these villages had been torched, and where hours ago there had been children, women bearing water jugs, and men bent over their work, there was no one. Flies clouded the carcasses of horses and goats. Only a few hours from the pillage, in the makeshift refugee camps, I knelt beside women whose breasts had been slit open with machetes, and with children newly orphaned. There were very few men.

In the city, the death squads pulled victims into panel trucks and Jeep Cherokees and slit their throats. Years later, a young soldier active in the death squads told me about the people he had taken into dark-windowed vehicles "with no hope. The person is tied up, their hands tied . . . to see their expressions as their face is covered with a mask . . . to see their chests and arms and hands and feet tremble! The memory comes back to me." He had been intrigued, he said, at the way the blood from a slit throat makes a soft bubbling sound. Sometimes the victims were shot and left on the sidewalk for buzzards and schoolchildren to find in the morning. A throng of children was often the sign of a corpse. For the targeted union leaders, priests, nuns, human rights workers, teachers, and organizers, the nights were often long and sleepless, as the hypervigilant listened for cars or footsteps, any unusual sound, and dreaded the telephone, which, in the early hours of the morning, could only bring death threats or terrible news. We tried to maintain our spirits and humor, and there were moments of levity, as when the screaming woman beyond my window turned out to be a parrot in the light of day.

Having suspended construction work on the cathedral in order to give money to the poor, Monsignor said mass there on Sundays, or else in the Sacred Heart basilica, but always for crowds standing shoulder to shoulder in the vaulted concrete carapace, spilling onto the steps and into Cathedral Square. Long columns of sunlight passed from the louvered towers to the cement floor, where children gathered at the communion rail with the coffins, windows cut into the lids to reveal the faces of the dead. Monsignor called the roll of those murdered by security forces during the previous week, to which the congregation responded *"Presente!"* as schoolchildren would answer a teacher, *"Here!"* The dead were present among us. Journalists crowded the sanctuary in the final months, holding aloft their cameras and microphones, which had also been arrayed in metal bouquets on the altar, at times nearly hiding the face of the mild, bespectacled bishop, who with each passing week seemed at once more tranquil and more resolute.

In his homily on the Sunday before he was killed, Monsignor Romero addressed the Salvadoran military:

> Brothers, you are from our same pueblo, you kill our brother campesinos;
> and before an order to kill given by a man you ought to reflect on the law
> of God which says: do not kill. No soldier is obliged to obey an order that is
> contrary to the will of God. Nobody has to fulfill an immoral law. Now it
> is time that you recover your consciences and that you first obey your con-
> science rather than an order to sin. The Church, defender of the rights of

God, of the law of God, of the human dignity of the person, cannot remain shut up before such an abomination. We want the government to take seriously that reforms achieved with so much blood serve no one. In the name of God, then, and in the name of this suffering pueblo, whose cries rise to the heavens, every day more clamouringly, I beg, I ask, I order you in the name of God: stop the repression.[13]

The last time I saw him alive, we talked in the hospital of Divine Providence, where he lived in a tiny casita (having from the beginning refused the grand house offered him in the wealthy suburb of Colonia Escalón). He arrived alone, walking under the fire trees and bougainvillea in his white cassock. It was 5:00 P.M. on March 14, the hour when the little parrots flock over the city so punctually that people set their watches by the passing. We sat at a table at one end of a community room, drinking water, with a fan turning back and forth and Monsignor tapping lightly on the Bible he always carried. A Venezuelan journalist was there, and when he began asking questions, I turned on my little cassette recorder and preserved what may have been Monsignor's last words for the foreign press.

When asked whether peaceful means for finding a solution to the conflict had been exhausted, Monsignor replied, "No. For if that were true, we would already be in the midst of a full civil war."

The sisters of Divine Providence hurried in and out, carrying brief messages, bringing fresh water, and remaining at hand should Monsignor need anything. The journalist wanted a *story* from the archbishop, something new, controversial, and "newsworthy," and so he pressed Monsignor about his relationship with the popular organizations, which now had military wings.

"My relation with the organizations is one of a shepherd, a pastor with his people, knowing that a people has the right to organize itself and to defend its right of organization. And I also feel perfectly free to denounce those organizations when they abuse the power, and turn in the direction of unnecessary violence. This is my role as pastor: to animate the just and the good, and to denounce that which is not good."

But what about the government? the journalist wanted to know, which claimed that it was seeking a road neither left nor right, but a center road, and which recently had announced banking and land reforms?

"I have always said that any reform truly beneficial to the people can never be imposed and should always depend on the popular bases. The people will not see its liberation as something given to them, but rather that the government is assisting in a process which the people have *already* developed." He patted the Bible for emphasis. "Social programs must be supported by the will of the people. Therefore I have always said that it's not enough to follow a neutral path, neither left nor right, nor is it correct to conflate the two. In this case, the right definitively signifies social injustice . . . One must be aware that what sometimes passes as 'violence' on the left may be the fruit of anger at this social injustice. And therefore one cannot judge the violence of the left in the same way. One must see whether one cannot, in dialogue with the government and the people, begin advancing changes in the social structure."

The journalist seemed frustrated and wanted to know if there really were forces on the left and in the government capable of dialogue.

"I don't use the expression 'forces of the left,' but rather 'forces of the people.' What are frequently called 'organizations of the left' are organizations of the people, and this we must bear in mind. I believe that a government that does not have a popular base is not a government of the people."

But weren't the popular organizations socialist? the journalist wanted to know, and I remember that Monsignor smiled with the patience of a teacher helping a child solve a particularly intransigent problem.

"Look," he said, "the processes of peoples are very original. Our process is a Salvadoran one. Our people are an autonomous force and therefore our process is Salvadoran and has to be interpreted as Salvadoran. If you want to call that 'socialism,' well, that's only a cliché, a name. That makes it a question of a cliché or a name. However, if we want to speak in terms of justice, what we are seeking is social justice, a more fraternal society, a redistribution of wealth—all the rights of the common good. That is what is being sought. It is *more* that the cliché of what is called 'socialism' . . . Anything imposed doctrinally, whether from the left or the right, cannot possibly be successful. There has to be an opening to critical dialogue in which *the people* are really informing *the government* as to their wishes . . . The people forge the government they desire."

Did Monsignor feel optimistic?

"Lamentably, there's not much optimism at this particular juncture in Salvadoran history. But I think we aren't fatalist. As free beings, we must use our liberty. Historical moments are original and new. It is a question of definitively escaping from the structures of injustice. And if there is hope, it is because of the human capacity to discover new things."

A wind rose in the palms, and the fan was unobtrusively silenced by one of the sisters. It was almost dark, but the lights in the room were not turned on. The sisters didn't want Monsignor to become tired; they wanted him to join them in the little convent kitchen for supper; they wished to allow him a few hours of peace. The journalist, however, wanted Monsignor to clarify precisely his position with regard to the popular organizations, now that the people were beginning to take up arms.

"The true political process must always proceed from the people, and the organizations are the *voices* of the people. They're not the only voices. When I use the word 'organization,' I mean the critical sense of the people . . . The church is the halo of God at the service of the people, and therefore its role is not political . . . Our task is not to say to the popular organizations 'this is good' or 'this is bad,' but rather to support the *right* of popular organization. That's what I am responsible for . . . I have to maintain a position of autonomy and freedom and if that is what some would call vacillation, that is the law of my ministry . . . My reason for being is the word of God, the illumination of God, and to be a pastor who tries to provide direction. I believe that this is the greatest service that I can provide to my people. I know already that many times that hasn't sat well with the Bloque[14] or with the government, neither with the rich, nor with the others. That really isn't of great importance to me because I'm not seeking popularity. The reason for being is to find oneself in the light and the word of revelation."

It was late, but as always during the past three years, Monsignor didn't seem tired—pensive, yes, and perhaps a bit wary of this ambitious young man, but not tired. His interlocutor continued to press him about his political views.

"As I have told you, I do not have a political role in El Salvador, but rather a pastoral one. As a pastor, it is my duty to construct this Church, my community, the Church. That is what I am responsible for. And this Church, as a people, illuminated by God, has a mission, too, among the people in general."

Don't the wealthy also consider themselves part of this Church?

"The documents of Puebla[15] are very clear and determinant in saying that a society which calls itself Christian but does not practice a 'preferential option for the poor' is in a certain way a traitor to the gospel. A true Christian cannot be a protagonist in social injustice . . . There is much talk about the dangers of communism as a possibility, but they do not notice the reality in which they are living, the reality of capitalism, which has also done great evil."

The journalist then asked about the Christian Democratic party, which had decided to remain in government, as part of the military-civilian junta.

"The qualifying word 'Christian' in a political party doesn't mean that the party is Christian. It's a name. What interests us is the reality and not the name. Concrete actions will determine whether a party is Christian or not . . . It is a very serious risk for a party to be in government where there are certainly good intentions for structural reforms but at the same time enormous repression. The party can serve as a protection, a mask, an umbrella, something which is of no benefit to the people. In that case, it is not meeting its duty as a true government. Rather, it is making itself complicit in the crushing of the people. And this—for journalists from other countries—I would really recommend that they be extremely clear and objective in what they say about what is happening in El Salvador . . . because if the Christian Democrats are there, and are beginning reforms, one might say 'what more do they want?' But this is to ignore the other aspect. Yes, there is a democracy, and yes, there are reforms, but what the people are feeling is a terrible repression. The repression we are seeing is horrific, and that is a fact . . . Union leaders are being killed, members of organizations, all of which demonstrates that the organizing force of the people is being made the object of a *systematic* repression."

The young man then asked Monsignor about the United States.

"A delegation came from the U.S. embassy," he said softly, "saying that the aid was for development of the people, and that the $5 million in military aid was not *directly* for the security forces, but rather for supplies the army lacked. In one operation, for instance, they didn't have walkie-talkies or proper transport, and other things of that nature. I said to them that this may be *their* wish, but the very same Minister of Defense is the one in charge of the security forces—and who is going to tell *him* that this aid should not go to strengthen the repression?"

The previous month, Monsignor had sent a personal letter to President Carter that read in part:

Because you are a Christian and because you have shown that you want to defend human rights, I venture to set forth for you my pastoral point of view in regard to the news [of pending economic and military aid] and to make a specific request of you . . . to forbid that military aid be given to the Salvadoran government; to guarantee that your government will not intervene directly or indirectly, with military, economic, diplomatic, or other pressures, in determining the destiny of the Salvadoran people.

He did not receive a reply to his letter until the day after his death. It came in the form of U.S. congressional approval of $5 million in military aid and the sending of twelve "trainers" to assist the Salvadoran military.

As delicately as he could, the journalist raised the issue of Monsignor's own safety.

"I have a great confidence in the protection of God," he said to us. "One does not need to feel fearful. We hear from Jesus Christ that one should not tempt God, but my pastoral duty obliges me to go out and be with the people, and I would not be a good pastor if I were hiding myself and giving testimonies of fear. I believe that if death encounters us in the path of our duty, that then is the moment in which we die in the way that God wills."

Monsignor Romero had received numerous death threats. According to the sisters of Divine Providence, two plots had been discovered and blocked: one to involve him in a fatal car accident, another to poison him at a formal dinner. Just a few days before, a bomb containing seventy sticks of dynamite failed to detonate in the basilica where he was saying mass. Yet he eschewed protection, preferring to drive himself around the capital unaccompanied, and once offered himself in exchange for the disappeared.

After the journalist left, we went to the convent kitchen, and as the sisters hurried the food to the table, they joked with him, this mild-mannered bishop whom they had attended for three years. Over platters of *frijoles, plátanos,* cheese, and fruit, Monsignor asked me about something that had happened to me the previous week. I'd been talking to a young Christian Democrat who had decided to defect from the party, no longer believing it moral to remain providing a "mask" for the military government. As it happened, we lost track of time, and at midnight I asked him to drive me home.

"But it's past curfew . . . "

The government had declared a state of siege, and only the security forces were permitted on the streets.

"I could call."

"There's no telephone."

"Then I have to try to go back. If I don't come home, they'll think I've disappeared and they'll look for me. That would be dangerous."

So we got into the car and had driven out of the compound almost past the gate when we saw a taxi parked so as to block the street, and over its roof, three hooded men crouched with machine guns aimed at our windshield. My friend threw the car into reverse, then floored the accelerator before slamming to a stop behind the wall. He told me to get out and run back to the house, where he arrived moments later, pale and out of breath.

"Death squad . . . "

"Why didn't they come after us?"

"They think we have security guards."

"Do we?"

He shook his head. "They think we have weapons. They never want to risk being killed themselves."

"Do we? Have weapons?"

"No."

He went into the bathroom and flushed the toilet, then cursed as the toilet began to overflow. "Help me—get some towels."

So we spent the next minutes sopping up the toilet water and wringing it into the sink, until he found the shut-off value, and I thought to myself: this is how I am going to spend the last moments of my life—cleaning up after a toilet.

The nuns saw the humor in this.

"We can't go out tonight. We'll have to wait here and go in the morning. Maybe they'll come, but maybe they won't."

I tried to sleep, but every hour or so a cashew nut dropped from its tree to the roof, skipping down the corrugated lamina like machine-gun fire.

Romero listened, and said: "You must return to the United States and speak about conditions in El Salvador. You must help the North Americans to understand . . . "

"I plan to go home soon."

"You must go now."

"And you, Monsignor? Your name is first on the death list. Why don't you leave? *Please*," I said.

"My place is with my people. And your place, now, is with yours."

I had never contemplated the idea of having "a people," and it's with some regret that I recall having spent my last hour with him pleading my case to remain in the country a little while longer, and that I so misjudged the depth of his commitment that I would suggest exile, but that is what happened, and time will not alter this. During his hours with the journalist, and later at supper, I noticed a luminosity about him that I had not seen issue from anyone else. *He is holy,* I thought, *he is already a saint.*

A week and a half later, on the morning of his death, he refused breakfast and seemed to the sisters inconsolably sad. One of the younger nuns looked him in the eyes and said: "Don't worry, Monsignor. Nothing is going to happen to you before your time. Nothing!"

"You're right, nothing will happen before my time." Then he asked to see his confessor, and later a friend took him to the sea for a walk along the beach. They wanted to raise his spirits, they said, and he always loved the sea.

"In the newspaper that day, there had been an announcement that Monsignor would say mass at 6:00 P.M. in the chapel of Divine Providence, to mark the anniversary of a death," Sister Ana María told me, "and we found this a bit strange, that an announcement would appear publicly providing details of Monsignor's whereabouts, and having seen this, someone called to ask Monsignor not to go ahead with it. Of course, he never took this kind of advice."

After fifteen years, I found myself sitting again on the little terrace of the hospital, beside the well-tended roses, as the hymns of the late-afternoon mass filled the courtyard.

"He wanted to live here with the poor who are sick," the nun said quietly. "This was the oasis where he rested. He trusted our work here. We knew him before he was archbishop. He used to come from Santiago de María to celebrate mass on the first day of every month, as today, the mass and the Holy Hours. That's how we met him, and that's how he began to build trust in us, and that's why he came to live here."

"Was he ever afraid?"

"If he was, he didn't show it. But he said that sometimes his legs trembled, in certain situations. When the guerrillas took the Rosario church, which outraged the National Guard, they called Monsignor Romero at midnight and said that they had killed them, but it wasn't true. The guerrillas had lighted candles in the church for their friends who had died. Monsignor went to the church alone, because the National Guard refused to allow anyone else to accompany him. Two or three trucks filled with National Guard were at the church. Imagine what he felt. They took him inside and told him to tell the guerrillas to give up. They were moving their weapons, as if they were going to attack him. His legs were trembling. It was human and logical that he would feel fear. But he said, 'Even though I was afraid I could keep my serenity.' He went from body to body and realized that while they had been detained, they were not dead."

"Sister, were you there at his last mass?" She nodded and removed her eyeglasses, rubbing them against her habit.

"There was a little cloth on the altar, and he looked down on the little cloth. They took advantage of this moment. That is when they shot him."

"Did you hear the shot?"

"It seemed to me like a bomb had gone off. I don't know if it was the kind of ammunition, or it was near to the microphone, but it seemed like a bomb. In this moment, Monsignor clutched the altar cloth and pulled it toward him. The cup of hosts fell down. They weren't consecrated. They were dispersed on the altar. In this moment, he fell. Backwards. My reaction was very aggressive. I felt no fear. Everyone went to the other side and threw themselves to the ground because they were afraid. I didn't feel fear. I went because I wanted to help him. I saw the hemorrhaging, the blood from the nose, the ears, and the mouth, and there was nothing I could do. I looked outside to see if I could see the assassin, but he had time to leave, because everyone was so panicked about what had happened."

"Was Monsignor still alive?"

"He was alive for a few minutes. We all knew, and we were all waiting—but we never thought it would be during a mass. This was the most sublime moment. He was with God. He was celebrating the mass. He was performing a sublime act, doing his work until the last moment, finishing his life, as he had lived it: authentically, wholly, a saint bishop."

<hr />

By now the afternoon mass had ended, and the sisters rose, cicadas still humming in the trees, the sky roiling with clouds so close to the rainy season. I went into the empty chapel, whose front doors were flung open as they had been when the red Volkswagen had pulled to the curb and the shooter had either leaned from the driver's window, as some suspect, or left the car to stand in the panel of light and fire the exploding round into Monsignor Romero's sternum, shattering the bone and flooding his chest cavity with blood, after the Word and before the Offertory. I paced the polished aisle and stood where the killer had stood, facing the altar, not twenty feet away. Monsignor had looked out at his congregation and then down at the hosts waiting to be transubstantiated to the body of Christ. It is possible, then, that he saw the man who had come to take his life. Standing where he stood, I was overcome by a desire to know his identity.

The nun turned the key in the lock of the little casita and left me alone there, in his room among his things. His bloodied surplice hangs in his narrow closet, now behind glass, along with the blue oxford-cloth shirt with its small bullet hole. In the cabinets are his worldly goods: a wristwatch, cuff links, a briefcase, his driver's license, his chalice, bishop's staff, miter, the vestments he wore, the books he studied, his breviary and the complete papal encyclicals. The desk where he often worked into the night has been left as it was, with its IBM electric typewriter, cassette recorder, and bronze pietà. A crucifix was on his pillow, and a visitor had left a tiny origami crane on his bedside table. There is a book for such visitors to sign, and it is filled with names from all over the world. The room has become at once a shrine and a museum, and the nuns maintain a small bouquet of fresh flowers beside his bed. It is a peaceful place, but the spirit of Monsignor has not remained in it.

On Sunday I drove to the cathedral, not realizing that it had been boarded up for two years, behind fencing and concertina wire, undergoing what some believe will be an interminable renovation. The building is so obscured now that I had difficulty finding it in the maze of the old city, but when I asked people for directions, saying that I wished to attend mass, they patiently told me which turns to take, and not one divulged that there had been no masses for a long time. Monsignor is interred here, and visited now only by rock doves. Cathedral Square is nearly empty, as is its fountain, but some of the vendors are still there selling paschal candles and holy cards.

For the funeral mass on Sunday, March 30, an altar was set up before the cathedral's front doors, and thousands of mourners crowded the steps and the plaza. My husband remembers that he was standing on the walk when the bomb went off and the shooting began, and as the crowd rushed toward the cathedral for shelter, he began to lift people over the locked gate, as many as he could until it was no longer possible. The sea of mourners spilled into the side streets, surging toward, then away from the cathedral walls. Nearly forty people were trampled to death. "When it was over," he said, "the steps and the square were deserted, but covered with abandoned shoes."

I have spent many hours sorting through reports of the decade-long "investigation" of the murder and have talked to former death-squad members, both in prison and out, hoping for information that would clarify, finally, what happened. What many believe is that a former National Police detective, Edgar Pérez Linares, probably pulled the trigger. He was himself later assassinated. Hector Antonio Regalado, a dentist known as "Dr. Death," who still lives freely in El Salvador and once organized a Boy Scout troop of Santiago de María into a death squad, was also allegedly involved, and many people believe *him* to have been the gunman. Captain Alvaro Saravía, an associate of the notorious former major Roberto D'Aubuisson, was said to have given the order. The driver of the vehicle, by his own admission, was Antonio Amado Garay, now living in Miami "surrounded by lawyers."

"The man who pulled the trigger is in the States," I was told in March by a Salvadoran who has spent fifteen years investigating the murder through contacts in the military and on the right. "The official story says the driver didn't shoot Monsignor Romero," he alleged. "The truth is that the driver *was* the shooter. There was just somebody else in the car."

For years, D'Aubuisson was said to have been responsible.

"D'Aubuisson was very useful," he continued. "*What was the role of the high command of the army?* D'Aubuisson did it. *What was the role of the American embassy?* D'Aubuisson did it. This man has been in the States for years, but that's not important because *D'Aubuisson did it.*"

He dismisses as meaningless the myths surrounding the murder: the legendary secret meeting at which straws were drawn, the months of elaborate planning, even the necessity of procuring a large sum of money—the net of complicity was cast wide, the money a guarantor not of a successful operation but of widely dispersed culpability that now is said to taint President Calderón Sol himself.

Monsignor Romero was assassinated not because he defended the church but because he defended the poor, and as the only institutional voice denouncing the repression in morally unimpeachable terms, he was in a position possibly one day to succeed in his appeal to the United States. That the landowners feared this, and wanted him dead, is not in dispute; that the military-civilian death squads would oblige was never in question; but that nothing of such magnitude could occur in El Salvador in those days without the tacit approval of the highest military command and at least without the *opposition* of the United States has never had to be openly acknowledged because *D'Aubuisson did it.*

This country named for the Savior of the world, its cities and villages for the saints, endured twelve years of civil war following Monsignor Romero's death. More than 75,000 people died, most of them civilians. Excluding funding for Central Intelligence operations, the United States provided $4.5 billion in combined military and economic aid to the Salvadoran government. On January 16, 1992, a peace accord was signed between the government and the combined oppositional forces of the FMLN.[16]

Monsignor Romero was called "the voice of the voiceless," but it seems a misapellation; the four million poor that he defended weren't lacking in ability to articulate their condition; their bishop was rather the spokesman for those to whom no one would listen. As a martyr, he partook of the eighth sacrament, accepting the ultimate sacrifice. But *martyr* does not connote in the original Greek the acceptance of death—*matur* means "witness," one who testifies with his very being, body and soul, and this he accomplished as an ordinary man, intractable and patient in his defense of truth.

In one of his homilies he said, "If they manage to carry out their threats, I shall be offering my blood for the redemption and resurrection of El Salvador . . . May my blood be the seed of liberty, and a sign of the hope that will soon become a reality . . . May my death, if it is accepted by God, be for the liberation of my people, and as a witness of hope in what is to come."[17]

The people of Santa Marta suffered the war, in flight and in exile, and now live in a village raised from the dead, whose greatest treasure is a tiny piece of cloth worn by their murdered brother in God. But if you ask them about Monsignor Romero now, they will tell you that he isn't dead but is living among them, and they will sit you down and give you the last of their tortillas and beans and a place to sleep, where you will be able to listen all night to their symphony.

Notes

1. Oscar Arnulfo Romero, Homily of March 24, 1980.
2. Ignatius of Antioch, as quoted in *Early Christian Writings: The Apostolic Fathers,* trans. Maxwell Staniforth (New York: Dorset Press, 1968).
3. From one of Romero's last interviews, given to *Excelsior* (Mexico City) two weeks before his death.
4. Rutilio Grande, as quoted by Dermot Keogh, *Romero: El Salvador's Martyr* (Dublin: Dominican Publications, 1981), 59.
5. Daniel H. Levine, *Popular Voices in Catholicism* (Princeton: Princeton University Press, 1992), 42.
6. Oscar Arnulfo Romero, First Pastoral Letter, Easter Day, April 10, 1977.
7. Jon Sobrino, *Archbishop Romero: Memories and Reflections,* trans. Robert R. Barr (Maryknoll, NY: Orbis Books, 1990).
8. Oscar Arnulfo Romero, Pastoral message to the National Council of Churches, delivered at the meeting of the governing board, New York City, November 8–10, 1979.
9. Romero, First Pastoral Letter, April 10, 1977.
10. Romero, December 8, 1977.
11. Conducted by Father John Drinan, S.J., Democratic congressman from Massachusetts.
12. Sent from Michael McClintock of the Latin America Research section, London.
13. Romero, Homily, March 24, 1980.
14. Bloque Popular Revolucionario, one of the popular organizations.
15. A conference of bishops held at Puebla in 1979.
16. Farabundo Martí National Liberation Front.
17. Romero, March 1980; quoted by Sobrino, *Archbishop Romero,* 165.

For Further Reading

Dermot Keogh, *Romero, El Salvador's Martyr.* Dublin: Dominican Publications, 1981.

Oscar Romero, *A Martyr's Message of Hope: Six Homilies by Archbishop Oscar Romero.* Kansas City, MO: Celebration Books, 1981.

Jon Sobrino, S.J., *Archbishop Romero: Memories and Reflections.* Translated from the Spanish by Robert R. Barr. Maryknoll, NY: Orbis Books, 1990.

Janani Luwum

Uganda, 1977

Janani Leads Me to the Cross

by Nancy Mairs

Lent. Once again, I am trying to penetrate the folds that shroud "crucifixion" in my head even more densely than purple fabric drapes the cross during this penitential season: agony, betrayal, humiliation, suffering, death. Who would choose these experiences? Not I, I feel sure. How then can I possibly fathom the ordeal of one who has done so? Hoping that the stations of the cross, which I have never formally traveled before, will illuminate this mystery, every Tuesday I join a small gathering at a nearby Episcopal church. Because Lent is late this year, and spring comes early to Tucson, fourteen crosses have been affixed at intervals around the weathered brick exterior, and we make our halting progress out from under a canopy of orange blossoms, past plantings of prickly pear and bright bird-of-paradise, over the slippery dark fruit dropped from olive trees, our voices small and uncertainly pitched in the late-afternoon stillness.

The others walk but I, of course, do not, and there seems to me to be something incongruous about tracing this particular route on four rubber tires, the wheelchair quiet except for the click of the locking and unlocking brakes as I stop and start. I could never have accompanied Jesus through rutted, dusty streets to the outskirts of the city, stood at the foot of the cross, anointed and wrapped his lifeless body, and laid it in a borrowed tomb. Some people have told me that multiple sclerosis constitutes my cross to bear, but I don't think so. It's just not hard enough. Whatever martyrdom may be, it's not this slow rolling through a life graced by affectionate friends, more than enough to eat, books to write with people to read them, a house and a car and a cappuccino maker, even two cats and a corgi for company.

This Lent, as I circle the perimeter of Grace Saint Paul's, my contemplation strays more often, and more anxiously, to modern Africa than to the *via dolorosa* 2,000 years in the past. Every day's dispatches prick my heart anew: when restless students are massacred in Lubumbashi; when Kinshasa's shops and factories are looted and destroyed by soldiers who have not been paid in months; when hundreds of thousands of Hutu and Tutsi lie butchered in the streets or flee to squalid camps to die of cholera, starvation, or despair; when filthy, understaffed, undersupplied hospitals fail to prevent, indeed contribute to, the spread of Ebola and AIDS. The whole continent reeks of greed and turmoil and death. But here and there redemption flickers, as in the case of Uganda's Janani Luwum, whose murder twenty years ago by military dictator Idi Amin haunts me. I sense that unless I can make some sense of Jesus' death, I can't possibly understand Janani Luwum's. Or perhaps it's the other way around. At any rate, I need to plumb an experience that's quite beyond me, and probably will remain so my whole life: the willingness to turn one's life over to people one knows to be wicked rather than repudiate what one believes to be good.

For a little over two years in the late 1980s, my heart lived in Africa. My daughter, a Peace Corps volunteer, was sent to Zaïre to teach farmers to build ponds, stock them with *Tilapia nilotica,* and harvest the fish for food. Anne's lengthy and detailed letters guided us from Kinshasa's smelly, teeming streets to the training center on the shores of Lake Kivu and even into Kahuzi-Biega National Park for a glimpse of gorillas, then back across the country to Chez Corps de la Paix in Mbanza-Ngungu, the capital of Bas-Zaïre, up to the hospital at Gombe-Matadi where Tata Nzulu's son died of sickle-cell anemia and the clinic where Ma Charlotte gave birth to her sixth child on a *pagne* on the ground, and on out into the forest to Anne's whitewashed bungalow in the village of Mfuatu, so that when we went to visit her, we had an odd sense of returning to a place we'd never been. Once your heart has lived somewhere, it never entirely abandons the place, no matter how remote in time or geography. This has become, in some sense, home.

Through these reminiscences and reflections, I tunnel my way toward Janani Luwum, whose death so eerily resembles that Passion I have been struggling to fathom. I first glimpse him as an Acholi boy herding his family's cattle, sheep, and goats over the grasslands of northern Uganda. Ah yes, goats. Infernal beasts, we quickly discovered in Mfuatu, who wake you with their shrill bleating at three in the morning and, at the first sign of rain, flock under the porch roof and beat their hooves on the door. When the doors are thrown open during the day to air out the stench of guano from the *tumfukunia*—much smaller than *ngembo,* the fruit bats relished as a delicacy here—massed under Anne's tin roof, the goats wander in at will. "*Katooka! Katooka!*" we learned to shout, flapping our hands and stamping our feet, but even in our impatience we could appreciate their investment value in an economy where paper money loses value almost by the minute. Cattle are even more precious: in fact, I was advised to accept nothing less, in exchange for my daughter in marriage, than a cow, 10,000 units of local currency, and a Coleman lantern (none of which I ultimately got). I can envision Janani herding his family's wealth.

At ten, he began primary school, followed by high school and a teacher training college: an excellent student who became a respected teacher and would eventually, his family expected, be a chief. But one day in 1948, when two members of the *Balokole* ("saved ones"), an East African revival movement, visited his village, he plunged into Christianity with these words: "Today I have become a leader in Christ's army. I am prepared to die in the army of Jesus. As Jesus shed his blood for the people, if it is God's will, I will do the same."[1] Any vigorous convert might make such a boast, I think. He would not expect—a young husband, the father of a baby girl—one day to be called on it.

Instead of becoming a chief, then, he enrolled in Buwalasi Theological College, preparing himself first as a lay reader, later a deacon, and finally, in 1956, a priest in the Anglican communion. He spent a year studying at Saint Augustine's College, followed by three years in an exceedingly difficult parish, then returned to England for two more years of study at the London Divinity College. There followed stints as principal of Buwalasi and as provincial secretary; in 1969 he was consecrated bishop of the newly formed diocese of Northern Uganda; and by 1974 he had been elected archbishop of Uganda, Rwanda, Burundi, and Boga-Zaïre, moving to the country's capital, Kampala. Although I have never been there, periodically I pack up a shipment of books for a women's club there,[2] among them my own work, and so my words have gone, without me, to the city where Janani Luwum spent his last years.

Kampala, like the rest of Uganda, was a perilous place in the 1970s. This was an inauspicious time for assuming a position of such prominence. Nine years after Uganda gained political independence from Britain in 1962, in a coup supported by Western intelligence agencies, General Idi Amin Dada deposed the elected president, Milton Obote, instituting a reign of terror that would destroy the economy and claim at least 300,000 lives before Obote recaptured power (and another 200,000 were killed).[3] Not quick, merciful deaths, either, but torments designed to terrify the populace, like the young thief tied to the ground in a stadium and crushed by soldiers' motorcycles in front of a captive crowd.[4] A Muslim in this predominantly Anglican and Roman Catholic country, Amin curried favor with (and arms from) Arab states by "Muslimizing" Uganda (although, oddly, he expelled Bangladeshis along with Pakistanis, Indians, and Israelis), confiscating Christians' property and replacing Christian government officials with Muslims. I recall all too well from Zaïre (where for decades another dictator has scourged his compatriots) the kind of economic and social devastation that rapacity and ruthlessness wreak in formerly prosperous, resource-rich countries: roads, once paved, now falling to rubble; schools and clinics abandoned; all the children under two years old in a village wiped out for want of measles vaccine; dense forests reduced to charcoal for cooking fires; wattle-and-daub huts, lighted by kerosene lanterns, clustered in the shadow of a giant pylon bearing electricity hundreds of kilometers away to the city, to the mines, anywhere where there's still money to be made.

Under Idi Amin, according to one eyewitness, "Life had become cheap. Bodies were regularly found floating on Lake Victoria or caught amongst the papyrus, or buried carelessly in shallow graves. Others were burned in petrol fires or simply thrown into the bush and left there to rot or be eaten by wild beasts. There was a smell of death from the marshes. The crocodiles which basked contentedly on the banks of the River Nile were fat."[5] Anyone who defied such a regime clearly courted death, yet how could people of conscience refuse to condemn these atrocities? In August 1976,

> Archbishop Luwum, the Roman Catholic Cardinal Nsubuga, and the Sheik Mufti of Uganda called together their bishops and sheiks and "passed resolutions deploring the killings, the harassment, the looting, and the excessive

power given to intelligence officers to execute people. They respectfully requested an interview with His Excellency. The permission was not granted. Instead, the president sent a very angry reprimand to Archbishop Luwum for holding this meeting without permission!"[6]

In chairing this meeting, Janani very likely marked himself for death, as he must have known, for in December he said, "I do not know how much longer I shall be occupying this chair. I live as though there will be no tomorrow."[7] And in truth, after that, there weren't very many tomorrows. He had already begun his *imitatio Christi*. There was even a Palm Sunday, January 30, 1977, when thousands of people, among them representatives of the government, gathered at Bushenyi for the consecration of Bishop Bamunoba of West Ankole and Bishop Festo Kivengere preached: "Many of you have misused your authority, taking things by force, using too much force . . . If you misuse the authority God gave you, God is going to judge you, because He is the One who gave it to you."[8] To Idi Amin, agitated by an attempted coup on January 25, this must not have sounded like Good News.

Under merciless torture, a man arrested for smuggling arms identified Janani as a "possible" subversive, and early on the morning of February 5 Janani's home—bedrooms, study, chapel, storerooms, toilets—was searched at rifle point. In response, the bishops, denied a meeting with Amin, drafted a protest against not only this outrage but a whole litany of wrongs that underlay it: "preferential treatment of Muslims; growing hatred of the security forces by the population; the war against the educated and the resulting brain drain out of the country; the confiscation of private property . . . by the military; the inordinate power granted to the state research officers to arrest and kill at will; the increasing communication gap between [the people] and the president . . . due to the influence of outsiders . . . who had become a menace to Ugandans."[9]

On February 11, meeting with his bishops for what would be the last time, Janani shared with them the Gospel passage in which Jesus calmed the Sea of Galilee for the frightened disciples, concluding: "The Lord has seen us in the past four days making headway painfully. But I see the way ahead very clearly. There are storms, waves, wind, and danger, but I see the road clearly!" It was—did he know this?—the road to his death, and I try to trace his passage along it in my heart as I move from cross to cross in the fading spring sunlight. On the morning of February 16, the army, government officials, diplomats, and religious leaders were summoned to the Conference Centre, where they spent hours without food or drink under the midday African sun while tortured prisoners read confessions implicating Archbishop Luwum and one of his bishops in a plot to overthrow the government.

"They are going to kill me. I am not afraid," Janani whispered to Bishop Festo Kivengere.[10] By this time, he can have had little doubt, especially when the vice president shouted, "What shall we do with these traitors?" and the soldiers responded, "Kill them! Kill them now!" But no, instead of an immediate public shooting, the vice president decreed that they'd be given a fair trial by military tribunal. After the crowd was dispersed, the dignitaries went into the Conference Centre, where the religious leaders were detained for an hour or so and then dismissed: all but Janani. When one of the bishops tried to accompany him, the soldiers pushed him back, saying, "We don't need you. His Excellency wants to talk with the archbishop."[11]

"I can see the hand of the Lord in this," Janani smiled.[12] Two of the bishops, who waited for him until they were turned away at gunpoint at 5:00, saw him being led from the Conference Centre to the nearby Nile Hotel at 4:10. By the time that Mary Luwum, frantic with worry, was driven to the Conference Centre and turned back by armed guards, her husband and the two cabinet ministers arrested with him were probably already dead. Having refused to sign a confession, he prayed for his captors as he was undressed and thrown to the floor, whipped, perhaps sodomized, and then, at about 6:00, shot twice in the chest.[13] Prison vehicles were driven over his body to suggest the automobile accident the government announced the next morning (showing one wrecked car in the newspaper and quite another on television), and then it was sent to his home village for hasty burial.

As a result, the grave dug for him outside the cathedral in Kampala remained empty on Sunday, February 20, when 4,500 people gathered for a funeral service. Beside the excavated earth, the retired archbishop Erica Sabiti read the angel's message to the women seeking Jesus' body on Easter morning—"He is not here. He is risen!"—and went on: "Our brother's body is not here, but we know that his spirit has gone to be with the Lord Jesus. He has risen. Praise God!"[14] Spontaneously, the people began to sing a *Balokole* hymn: "Glory, glory to the Lamb!"

Like others who have written about Janani, I am struck by the surface similarities between his final journey and Jesus'—the defiance of political authority, the jubilant celebration quickly followed by reprisal, the final meeting with his friends, the arrest, the rabble howling for his death, the stripping and scourging, the ignominious end—and so for a long while I miss their deeper significance. For, in retrospect, such correspondences can doubtless be traced in most martyrs' deaths, and this very banality constitutes their point: in the face of cruelty, greed, and injustice, the crucifixion must occur again and again and again. Jesus' death was not a finite event, either historically or spiritually, but a paradigm. Each one of us may be called upon to reenact it, with whatever grace we can muster, for the sake of God's simple but stringent law: that we love God and one another.

This is Janani's ambiguous gift to me: to recognize the presentness of martyrdom. This Way of the Cross I have been tracking is not merely, as I have conceived it, a commemoration of the agony and courage of a Nazarene carpenter who refused, 2,000 years ago, to hold his tongue to please the powerful, or even, in more mystical terms, an awed backward gaze at God's own suffering in human form. Also, and foremost, it provides discipline—the opportunity to perform imaginatively the acts that our obedience to God's law may in fact require of us—and thus commits us to the present and the future. People are dying for the sake of justice and peace today. Others will die tomorrow.

Oh, but I hope I don't have to be one! I haven't Janani's faith, Jesus' fortitude. As I leave the fourteenth station to sit for a moment in the quiet, darkened chapel, I feel sure that I'd never see such an ordeal through. This, though, is the final gift of the cross: consolation. Jesus wept, he sweated and stumbled and fell, he cried out. But he went the whole way nevertheless, to and through death, and his example reassures us that we can do what we have to do. Janani, like centuries of martyrs before him, did just that. No longer a stranger, Janani has become a traveling companion, and in recollecting his sacrifice, I have followed him home, here, to the cross. If I must mount it, he assures me, I will not do so alone.

Notes

1. Margaret Ford, *Even unto Death* (Elgin, IL: David C. Cook Publishing Co., 1978), 21.

2. One can post books overseas via surface mail quite cheaply, and I urge everyone to pack up discarded books in English and direct them to M. J. Collins, Executive Secretary, K Executive Club, P.O. Box 3092, Kampala, UGANDA, East Africa.

3. Robert A. Evans and Alice Frazer Evans, "Uganda: Church of the Martyrs," *Christian Century*, August 14–21, 1985, 726.

4. Ford, *Even unto Death,* 48.

5. Ford, *Even unto Death,* 67.

6. Festo Kivengere with Dorothy Smoker, *I Love Idi Amin* (Old Tappan, NJ: Fleming H. Revell, 1977), 42.

7. Ford, *Even unto Death,* 75.

8. Kivengere, *Idi Amin,* 44.

9. Kivengere, *Idi Amin,* 49.

10. Ford, *Even unto Death,* 86, says that Bishop Festo reported these words to her, although the bishop does not include them in his own account.

11. Kivengere, *Idi Amin,* 53.

12. Ford, *Even unto Death,* 87.

13. James and Marti Hefley, *By Their Blood: Christian Martyrs of the Twentieth Century* (Milford, MI: Mott Media, 1979), 436.

14. Kivengere, *Idi Amin,* 56.

For Further Reading

Robert A. Evans and Alice Frazer Evans, "Uganda: Church of the Martyrs." *Christian Century,* August 14–21, 1985.

Margaret Ford, *Even unto Death.* Elgin, IL: David C. Cook Publishing Co., 1978.

Festo Kivengere with Dorothy Smoker, *I Love Idi Amin.* Old Tappan, NJ: Fleming H. Revell, 1977.

STEVEN BIKO

South Africa, 1977

A Bump on the Head

by PAUL ELIE

O ne morning in June 1990 I left my apartment to get a Pepsi, and
walked into the new South Africa.

I was a graduate student at Columbia University, and I lived
in a neighborhood near the campus that might be called a religious
ghetto. Union Theological Seminary and Jewish Theological Seminary
face each other on Broadway, and Corpus Christi Church is shoehorned
between apartment houses on West 121st Street; behind Union are Riverside Church, its tower looming overhead like a displaced part of Chartres,
and the Inter-Church Center, a concrete-and-glass building known (this
is what passes for humor among divinity students) as the God Box.

It is a neighborhood where, perhaps more than anywhere else in Man-
hattan, religion is still seen and felt to be a going concern. That day it was
the setting for the greatest local religious event since the Rev. Dr. Martin
Luther King, Jr., preached at Riverside Church in 1962. After serving
twenty-seven years in a South African prison for his opposition to
apartheid, Nelson Mandela had come to New York, free at last. That
morning he would be meeting with American religious leaders at Riverside Church. The neighborhood had been transformed in anticipation.
Television crews had laid down their cables, the police their sawhorses.
Several thousand people, most of them African Americans, had gathered

outside the church, wearing dashikis and robes embroidered with *kinte* cloth, or T-shirts screened with images of Mandela and the African continent.

I wandered through the crowd, sipping my soda. I was used to seeing Africa celebrated in the neighborhood. On summer Wednesday evenings a festival of African crafts, food, music, and the like is held at Grant's Tomb, just north of the church. What struck me as odd was that this African feast had a Christian dimension as well as a civic and cultural one. I couldn't remember a time when I'd seen Christianity so closely linked with unfolding world events. It was powerful, and it was nervous-making. I found myself slipping into the role of devil's advocate. Mandela wasn't a Christian, was he? Not so far as I knew. And wasn't there something opportunistic in the welcome the church people were giving him? Sure, in recent years the mainline Protestant churches had publicly opposed apartheid, and as churches go, the nondenominational and racially diverse Riverside Church was an ideal place to honor Mandela. But I couldn't suppress the thought that the event and all its trappings were one more instance of progressive Christians trying to get on the right side of history—to romanticize prophetic movements abroad, where good and evil were sharply drawn and the very stones cried out for justice, rather than attending to the more mundane and ambiguous task of Christian witness at home.

Six years later, Nelson Mandela is the president of South Africa. No one would deny that he is the leader of the South African people and a man utterly fit for the calling, but under the circumstances of the last half-century he is an unlikely president. While he was in prison, and even after he was set free, few people expected the white South African minority government to surrender its power at all, much less as swiftly as it did. Well into the 1980s it was thought that Mandela would die in jail, a martyr to the cause of a free South Africa.

The man who would have been a likely president of his country did die in jail, a martyr to the cause of a free South Africa. Steven Biko was only twenty-six years old when the apartheid government placed him under a "banning order," which forbade him to speak in public, to write articles, or to leave his hometown. Three years later he was imprisoned, then released; the next year, 1977, he was imprisoned again, and he died while in custody, supposedly a suicide. He was thirty. A lengthy inquest suggested that prison guards had beaten him to death, but the apartheid government conceded nothing.

Steven Biko was banned and imprisoned for his role in the Black Consciousness movement, which he had led since his student days. "Black Consciousness," he wrote, "is in essence the realization by the black man of the need to rally together with his brothers around the cause of their operation—the blackness of their skin—and to operate as a group in order to rid themselves of the shackles that bind them to perpetual servitude."

Biko was by all accounts brilliant, charismatic, and patient with his adversaries, and he had a profound understanding of the condition of black South Africans under apartheid and a vision of their future in a free state. It is reasonable to suppose that had he lived to see a free South Africa take shape, he would have become its leader.

If he would have been a likely president, Biko was an unlikely martyr, in the conventional Christian sense of the term: a person who gave his life for his faith, who died so that Christ might live. Biko's namesake was the first martyr, Saint Stephen, but in its outlines his death is a stark contrast to the dramatic account of Stephen's death given in the Acts of the Apostles, where Luke tells of Stephen's long and faith-filled address before the council, his vision of the glory of God, his stoning at the hands of the crowd, his dying words ("Lord, do not hold this sin against them"), and the witness of his companions, who laid their garments at the feet of Saul, soon to be Paul.

Biko's death was less like a biblical apotheosis than like the pointless murders described in *The Executioner's Song* and *In Cold Blood*. Not much is known about his time in prison or what led the guards to beat him to death. There is no account of heroic refusal, no valedictory speech, no final act of faith. Biko died naked, bloody, and manacled in the back of a Land Rover (the accounts invariably give the make of the vehicle, as though to stress the modernity, and the banality, of the incident) while guards drove him to a distant prison hospital rather than having his injuries treated in a civilian one nearby. The authorities announced his death a few days later.

Only in an inclusive sense can Steven Biko's death be called a Christian martyrdom. Biko was raised an Anglican and was educated by Anglicans and Roman Catholics, and on several occasions he examined the relation of the Black Consciousness movement to liberation theology and church activism in South Africa. But he frankly dissented from historic Christianity. Through Black Consciousness he hoped to liberate black people from oppressive social forces, the Christian churches among them.

Yet upon his death church leaders eulogized Biko as though he had been a Christian. At his funeral the Reverend Desmond Tutu compared Biko to Christ, and in services at American divinity schools he was memorialized as a liberator and martyr.

The efforts to present Steven Biko as a Christian martyr have some of the complications that I felt the day Nelson Mandela came to Riverside Church. To claim Biko as a Christian is in some way to eviscerate him, to diminish his view of the scope of black liberation and accommodate it to the moderate, inclusive, liberal activism he opposed in South Africa.

The fact that Biko's Christianity was vexed and elusive, however, makes the matter of his martyrdom all the more profound. With this fact in mind, Christians are forced to see his life and death in the shifting light of uncertainty—now as an affirmation of Christian beliefs, now as a reproach to them. Steven Biko was a hero and a visionary, and it may seem petty and reductive to ask just what he died for: but we must do so if we are really to understand him, and understand just what it is we are living for.

<hr />

Biko is the subject of books, a movie, and at least one rock song, and by considering the best known of these we can piece together an account of his life and consider the nature of his death, the way the auditors of the Congregation of Causes—the Vatican agency that evaluates candidates for sainthood—review the accounts of a would-be saint's life, looking for signs of great holiness, defects of character, and evidence of miracles.

Steven Biko was born on December 18, 1946, in East London, a black district of King William's Town about 600 miles from Johannesburg. He was the third of four children; his father died when he was four, and he and his mother were very close. He was educated in Anglican schools, where as a teenager he wrote to Aelred Stubbs, a white Anglican priest who was a friend of the family, with agonized questions about his faith, which he had begun to abandon. Father Stubbs would later write a memoir of Biko as a postscript to *I Write What I Like,* a collection of Biko's writings.

Upon graduating from Mariannhill, a Catholic secondary school in Natal, Biko entered medical school in Durban (called the University of Natal Non-European because it was for blacks, mixed-race "coloureds," and Indians). There he joined the National Union of South African Students (NUSAS), a liberal, multiracial organization founded a half-century earlier, and became a leader of the local chapter. But in 1968, the year of student uprisings, there emerged a need for an all-black student group; at a University Christian Movement conference Biko and others (among them Barney Pityana, who would later become a priest) founded the South African Students Organization (SASO), and Biko became its first president.

In 1971 Biko married Ntsiki Mashalaba, a nurse in Durban, while continuing to study toward a medical degree. The next year, however, he was expelled from medical school—ostensibly for poor grades, but in all likelihood for his political activities as well. He went to work for Black Community Programmes (BCP), a black-run social-service agency in Durban, while continuing to lead the SASO. In 1973 the government summarily banned eight NUSAS leaders, and then, shortly afterward, eight SASO leaders, including Biko, who was forced to return to King William's Town.

Under the five-year banning order in "King," as it was called, Biko was prohibited from writing, publishing, giving quotes to reporters, receiving visitors, or attending any public gathering other than church services. (It isn't clear whether he did go to church services.) Biko and his wife now had two sons, whom she supported by working at an Anglican hospital some distance away while he pursued a law degree by correspondence. At the same time, deprived of a public role, he developed a King William's Town branch of the BCP; headquartered in a disused church, it became a vital agency for blacks of the district, and a focal point for political activity as well. Then and until the end of his life he led the Black Consciousness movement by working in stealth mode—holding clandestine meetings, using associates as go-betweens, and flouting the banning order as much as he dared.

In 1974 Biko laid plans for a medical clinic for blacks in King William's Town, called the Zemphilo Community Health Centre. Besides providing necessary services in the district, the hospital embodied one of the main tenets of Black Consciousness—Biko's belief that South African blacks could not depend on white liberals' sense of obligation to blacks but had to provide for themselves, and thereby increase black pride, by building up their own institutions.

After the BCP and SASO sponsored rallies in favor of the newly installed black nationalist government of Mozambique later that year, the South African government cracked down, arresting nearly thirty black leaders, and the trial of some of them early the next year became "the trial of Black Consciousness." In the meantime, a group called the Black People's Convention (BPC) had emerged as something like a political party for blacks, and Biko, still banned, served as main adviser to its leaders. One leader, Mapetla Mohapi, had been detained on Robben Island (where Nelson Mandela was jailed), and when he was released Biko founded the Zimele Trust Fund, an agency to ease newly released detainees' reentry into society.

Within the year Biko would be a detainee. In June 1976, after a number of black students were killed in the uprising in Soweto, black groups organized a protest march on Cape Town. In response, the government detained black leaders, and this time Mapetla Mohapi died while in detention. The authorities said that he had hanged himself. Biko demanded an inquest. Two days after Mohapi's funeral (which 4,000 mourners attended), Biko and a black woman reporter, Thenjiwe Mtintso, were themselves detained. *Detained*—it is a strange word, and one that suggests everything that was insidious about the apartheid regime of South Africa: the use of euphemism to disguise evil, the reliance on passive constructions (he "was detained") to hide the active forces of oppression, and above all, the way the word implies, negatively, movement, progress, growth. What was being detained was the development of justice in South Africa, the long march toward notions of universal human rights.

Biko spent 101 days in detention, where he was treated relatively civilly, and soon after his release he was made honorary president of the Black People's Convention. Early in 1977, working behind the scenes, he was a key figure at the inquest into Mohapi's death. It was established that Mohapi had "died by strangulation" but that no one was at fault—a blatant equivocation on the government's part, but nonetheless a rare acknowledgment that a detainee had died suspiciously.

Biko had by then established a friendship with the man who was to become his chief advocate in the English-speaking world. Donald Woods, the editor of the *Daily Dispatch,* a liberal newspaper, had written a column critical of Biko, contending that the separatist aims of Black Consciousness made the movement as racist in its way as the apartheid regime. Biko invited the editor to visit him, and soon afterward Woods ventured into King William's Town in his Mercedes-Benz. "I found Leopold Street easily enough," Woods recalls in his 1978 memoir of their friendship, "but where number 15 should have been was a little church whose main door was uncompromisingly closed . . . I knocked on the door to rouse the churchwarden in hopes that he might solve the mystery. The door opened almost immediately and I was beckoned in by several blacks who appeared to be expecting me." By the end of their clandestine meeting Woods had been won over by Biko's arguments and personality, and during the "trial of Black Consciousness" he, his wife, Wendy, and his newspaper vigorously supported Biko's positions.

In Woods's book, a transcript of the trial is immediately followed by the account of Biko's death seven months later, and by all accounts Biko's death came with great suddenness. On August 17, 1977, Biko and a friend were driving outside King William's Town when they were pulled over by the police and Biko was found to be in violation of his banning order. Both were jailed. A month later, Biko was dead. He was the forty-fifth South African prisoner to die while in custody.

Why did he die? Posed that way, the question includes two very different questions about Steven Biko's death: *How did he die?* and *What did he die for?* Biko's several expositors, so to speak, answer the question in different ways, and each comes to a different conclusion about the nature of his martyrdom.

Donald Woods was of necessity obsessed with how Biko died. Shortly after Biko's death Woods was banned because of articles he had written about the incident for the *Daily Dispatch,* in which he proclaimed that Biko was a martyr and his death an example of the injustice of apartheid. While under house arrest he wrote *Biko.* The book is passionate, full of the heat of the moment, and thickly detailed, with long sections of source material. It reached the West when Woods, dressed as a priest in order to evade the authorities, escaped from South Africa in 1978.

Owing to his banning order, Woods was not allowed to attend the inquest into Biko's death. Wendy Woods did attend, though, and from her notes and the transcript, Donald Woods assembled a hundred-page account of the official inquiry into how Steven Biko died. From page to page it is often dull reading, but in aggregate it is a fascinating, and appalling, document. The questions in three weeks of legal jousting between the advocate for Biko and the prison officials and doctors of the apartheid regime are focused on the particulars of Biko's last hours.

Forensics comes to seem a modern counterpart of the medieval obsession with relics—splinters of bone, strands of hair—as the gnosis of mortality (now made part of our common knowledge by the beating of Rodney King and the trial of O. J. Simpson), and the examination of evidence that is often invisible to the naked eye seems to define the way we live, and die, now. The twentieth-century martyr does not die in public, on crucifix or rack or gallows; he dies out of the world's sight, his death caused by factors only a coroner can determine beyond a reasonable doubt.

Early in the inquest the government was forced to abandon its contention that Biko had committed suicide through a hunger strike, for Woods and others had viewed Biko's corpse, and there was no mistaking the features disfigured as though from a beating, the large bump on the forehead, but the body otherwise reasonably healthy—not the body of a man who had starved to death. So the government witnesses contended that Biko had banged his head against a wall during a scuffle with guards, which he had provoked by throwing a chair at them.

The details of the ensuing days suggest just how degraded the conditions of political imprisonment were in the South Africa of the period. Had Biko used the toilet? Had he wet his blanket? Was there evidence of a bump on his forehead? Was there foam around his mouth? The government witnesses suggested that Biko had been "shamming"—feigning injury after the scuffle—or that he had practiced hyperventilation, a controlled breathing technique, in order to asphyxiate himself. As they were reminded of the bump on Biko's head, however, the inquiry turned from how Biko was injured to why he was given no medical care afterward. By the day after the scuffle Biko was delirious, but his condition was ignored. When it became clear that he was dying, the chief warden chose to have him transported by Land Rover some 700 miles to a prison hospital. He passed his final hours naked on a mat, his legs and arms in chains, his mind rattled, his spirit—who knows of his spirit?

Yet the chief magistrate concluded that "on the available evidence the death cannot be attributed to any act or omission amounting to criminal offense on the part of any person."

In Woods's view, this miscarriage of justice only confirmed the evil of the apartheid regime. He was right, of course. Although his conclusions sprang from his own disposition as a constitutional liberal, in *Biko* he framed them in such a way that they might convince international human rights organizations and people of goodwill generally. "Because the State has not seen fit to indict anyone for the death of Steve Biko, it becomes necessary to indict the state," he wrote, and then went on to do so in the final chapters of his long book.

Why did Steven Biko die? Woods answers the question as a prosecuting attorney would. Biko died because of "the policy of apartheid, the most outrageous affront to all humanity that has ever been devised by collective decision since the dawn of procedural government." *Biko died that apartheid might die.* Like the forty-four other prisoners who died in detention, Biko was a martyr to the cause of justice, but because in life he had been a leader and an example, his death must be seen as exemplary. Characteristically, Woods makes his example rather juridical and abstract. "Because of who he was, because of his special stature—and because of the attendant circumstances," Woods concluded, "the death of Steven Biko symbolizes the ultimate consequence of apartheid with all its implications."

Sir Richard Attenborough based his film *Cry Freedom* on Woods's book, with Woods as a consultant. The film was released a decade after Biko's death, in 1987, at a time when American colleges were being pressured to withdraw their investments in South Africa; owing in part to Woods's efforts, people in the United States and Europe were greatly agitated over the evils of apartheid, and a democratic South Africa seemed a tenable, if remote, prospect. *Cry Freedom* is the story of that growing awareness in the West, and of blacks' strivings toward freedom in South Africa. The film opens with a dramatization of the Sharpeville massacre, in which dozens of black South Africans were killed and their townships destroyed by paramilitary forces. Biko's funeral, the black population's greatest public event of the apartheid era, sits at its center. At the end, the names of those who died in prison roll down the screen, like credits of the ill-termed "peaceful revolution" that was then gaining momentum.

Attenborough is surprisingly unconcerned with the particulars of how Biko died. As Woods (played by Kevin Kline) examines the dead man's corpse in the morgue, a flashback sequence shows Biko being beaten by the guards and writhing in the Land Rover. As played by Denzel Washington, Biko has been a genuine hero—true to the sources, convincing on screen—and the viewer feels the loss acutely.

The film has more than an hour to go, but Attenborough passes over the inquest almost entirely. Instead, he depicts the newly enlightened

Woods defying his banning order so that he might make Biko's life and death known to the rest of the world. Woods is silenced; his family is threatened; finally, he leaves wife and children behind to escape South Africa for London, and there find a publisher for his manuscript.

In *Cry Freedom* Attenborough, drawing on Woods's accounts, reverses the terms of Wood's argument. Woods had made Biko a martyr for all times and places, a witness to universal human rights, and in doing so had established him, in death, as an international figure. With Biko and his story well known—and the cause of a free South Africa gaining momentum—Attenborough was free to depict Biko as a great *national* figure, and his story as that of black South Africans' struggle for justice. *Why did Steven Biko die? So that the people of South Africa might live.*

———

The black Anglican priest Desmond Tutu (now the archbishop of Cape Town) was a leader of church-based opposition to apartheid during Biko's lifetime, and he spoke at Biko's funeral, an open-air ceremony attended by more than 15,000 mourners. In his sermon, he drew equally on liberation theology and the oratory of the U.S. civil rights movement—familiar rhetoric now, but no less powerful for being so—to rejoice in Steven Biko as one who had imitated Christ unto death.

"Oh, God, where are you? Oh, God, do you really care? How could you let this happen to us? . . . God, do you really love us?" With this cry, the anguished cry of the Israelites, Tutu begins his appeal. Like the Israelites, South Africans seek a land of their own; it is their birthright, for all people, white and black, "count because we are human persons, human persons created in your own image." Christian homiletics are harmonized with the appeal to human rights. Prophecy is joined to political pragmatism.

"Let us recall, my dear friends," Tutu goes on, "that nearly two thousand years ago a young man was done to death and hung like a common criminal on a cross . . . Let us recall how his followers were dejected and quite unconsolable in their grief." In a sweeping biblical synopsis, he recalls how "this young man, God's own son, Jesus Christ, had come preaching the good news of God's love for all his children." This young man took the side of the oppressed and the poor and the exploited, and through signs and wonders he showed them the fullness of their humanity and "set them free from all that would make them less than he wanted them to be, fully human persons as free as Jesus Christ showed himself to be." Then he was taken from them, and they grieved, for darkness had overcome them. "But that death was not the end," Tutu declares. "That death was the beginning of a glorious life, the resurrection life. That death was the death of death itself—for Jesus Christ lives for ever and ever. The grave could not hold captive such a gloriously free life."

Tutu proposes that Steven Biko's was such a life. Like Jesus, Biko thirsted for justice and righteousness; like Jesus, Biko showed peace and love to all those who knew him and his work. For Biko—Tutu uses the language of Scripture—had been called by God to be his servant in South Africa, to proclaim God's righteousness by calling blacks to the fullness of their humanity. Biko's great insight was to see that "until blacks asserted their humanity and their personhood, there was not the remotest chance for reconciliation in South Africa." (Tutu fiercely adds, "You don't get reconciled to your dog, do you?")

Biko was a liberator, yes, a champion of the oppressed—but in an instant Tutu turns from celebrating Biko the liberator to appealing to the Christian convictions of South Africans black and white. For Tutu, Christianity is not only God's pact with the oppressed, the black people of South Africa; it is also the only grounds for a claim to human dignity in a country with no other language of common personhood or civil rights. Without reconciliation, Tutu warns, there might come a day of violence, a day when the oppressed will rise up and claim their inheritance by force. "We may, all of us, crash headlong to destruction. Oh God, help us! We cry for our beloved country."

What follows can be read only with the knowledge that the prophecy the Reverend Mr. Tutu ventured that day has come to pass. "Paradoxically, we give thanks to God for Steve's life and his death. Because, you see, Steve started something that is quite unstoppable," Tutu proclaims, then closes with a surge of oratory that frankly recalls the speech Martin Luther King, Jr., gave during the March on Washington in 1963. "We are experiencing the birth pangs of a new South Africa, where all of us, black and white, shall walk tall," Tutu says with confidence. "For all of us, black and white together, shall overcome, nay, indeed have already overcome."

Seldom has the creed of liberation sounded so like the word of God. As eulogized by Tutu, Biko was a martyr as all who die in the name of justice are martyrs: but the measure of justice is not democracy or constitutional law but the law of God, as seen in his solidarity with the oppressed. The blood of the martyrs, if not the seed of the church, is the seed of justice—God's justice. *Why did Steven Biko die?* Tutu's answer is biblical *and* civic, Christian *and* universal. *Biko died because God called him to lead his people into a new South Africa, and only through his death could a new South Africa be born.* Biko led his people into the fullness of their humanity, where, in God's image, they could be free at last.

———∞∞∞———

Aelred Stubbs was no prophet. During the last years of Biko's life, this priest who had known him since he was a boy was divided and confused about his own calling. Eleven months of the year Father Stubbs served as a parish priest in Johannesburg while at the same time supervising the theological education of new ordinands—"training men to be efficient servants of one more facet of 'the system,' the institutional Church." The twelfth month he conducted a ministry to the banned, including Biko, and it was in this work that he found his joy and fulfillment.

Stubbs's ministry was wracked by the tension between Black Theology and traditional ecclesiology. Perhaps this is why Biko was drawn to him, for Biko was also divided about Christianity. He had rejected the historic churches as mere local, temporal institutions whose members had become Christians by accidents of birth or circumstance. He had embraced Black Theology. In 1973 he wrote:

> [Black Theology] seeks to relate God and Christ once more to the black man and his daily problems. It wants to describe Christ as a fighting God, not a passive God who allows a lie to rest unchallenged. It grapples with existential problems and does not claim to be a theology of absolutes . . . It is the duty therefore of all black priests and ministers of religion to save Christianity by adopting Black Theology's approach and thereby once more uniting the black man with his God.

Even so, Biko never renounced the baptismal claims of the Church of South Africa upon him—so as not to offend his mother, Stubbs surmises—and he so valued Stubbs's ministry that he sought out the priest in order to make a confession of sorts (evidently about marital infidelity) before he was jailed for the last time. For his part Stubbs, while a committed churchman, saw Biko as a kind of messiah. "I would have to go back to Jesus himself to find a parallel to the extraordinary pastoral care which Steve had for his own," he recalls in his memoir. "In this particular area I trusted him with the same *kind* of trust I have in Jesus. I know this sounds idolatrous to a Christian believer, but there was nothing idolatrous in my attitude toward him."

Stubbs's memoir, entitled "Martyr of Hope" (it appears in *I Write What I Like*), is a model of Christian self-examination—as much about his own life as about Biko's, but always observing the right relation of the lesser to the greater. Stubbs is determined to understand the nature of his friend's martyrdom. "What did Steve die for? In what sense, if any, can he be called a Christian martyr?" This was no mere case of scruples. As an intimate of Biko's, Stubbs is clearly wary of attributing beliefs to his dead friend or welcoming him back, like a prodigal son, into a church he had stood apart from.

Stubbs begins to answer his questions by presenting a "memorandum" Biko wrote in 1974. It is a virtual catechism of Biko's beliefs, with Biko as both catechist and catechumen. Does God exist? Biko is confident that He does, finding evidence in natural law and conscience. What is God's nature? Biko cannot say. "Suffice it to trace back to him all that happens around us and out of this to begin to understand somewhat his powers."

"But the real stumbling block for Steve was the South African phenomenon of the historic churches," Stubbs writes. In Biko's view the churches are no more divine than soccer clubs. Worship is useless. Truth is not something to be grasped at by this or that church body. Rather, it is to be sought by doing good. Christ did come to earth, and the spirit of the Lord was upon him, but his nature has been obscured by dogma (born of a virgin, true God and true man). The Christ of the Church is abstract and conservative. The true Christ transcends the Church and must triumph over it. So Biko rejected the way of the churches and embraced the way of the "selfless revolutionary" who obeys God's call as he hears it in conscience.

Stubbs considers "selfless revolutionary" an apt description of his friend's calling, but finds it insufficient to his own purposes. His question is whether Biko was a martyr. So he must ask, *Why did Biko die? "Steve died to give an unbreakable substance to the hope he had already implanted in our breasts, the hope of freedom in South Africa,"* Stubbs writes. In that sense he was a martyr—a witness to the hope. But does this entitle the church to claim him as a Christian martyr? Not by any means. If Biko was vague at times about what he believed, he knew what he did not believe. Like Biko, Stubbs is a man of distinctions, and—it must have taken great courage—he does not abandon them in the exceptional case of his friend.

Martyr must be used advisedly. "This Anglican Church," he declares, "does not have the right at present to claim him as its martyr."

"He was too big for the church," Stubbs goes on. The formulation verges on idolatry. Stubbs is after something else, however: "the church of hope," which the churches are meant to announce and point toward. In the church of hope, Stubbs proposes, Biko has already shed his blood; and it is not only the seed of justice, but the seed of the church Christ will encounter at his coming. "In the purified Church that will be reborn out of the destruction of this racist society," Stubbs concludes, "in that Church [Biko] will be venerated everywhere, as he is by some of us now, as a true martyr of Christ, the Christ whom he maybe could not consciously be often in communion with because of the disfiguring guises with which the churches had distorted him." Though no prophet, Father Stubbs recognized prophecy and saw in Biko's strivings for justice the strivings of the universal church toward justice at the end of time.

For years Peter Gabriel always ended his concerts with the same song. A martial drumbeat, a dirgelike guitar riff, and right away almost everyone knew what song it was, but that only made it more powerful. Earlier in the concert Gabriel had sung another dirge, "Lay Your Hands on Me," during which he would enter the crowd from one side of the stage and allow his fans to pass him overhead to the other. With this last song, too, he would work them into somber, brooding, messianic ecstasy.

The song was "Biko," which he recorded in 1980. It closed his third album, as it closes his greatest-hits collection, and it is one of the strongest songs he has ever written. On the albums it opens with a recording of a black South African chorus singing an anthem in Afrikaans; then comes the drumbeat, the dirgelike guitar. The first few lines are spare and evocative: "September 1977—Port Elizabeth weather fine—it was business as usual in police room 609." But the backbone of the song is the chorus. "Oh, Biko," Gabriel cries, over and over, the name sounding like a foreign word for pain, or injustice, or heroism, or all these things. And then: "He a martyr—here a martyr—the man is dead, the man is dead." He slurs the words so that it is unclear whether he is saying "He a martyr" or "Here a martyr" or "Kill a martyr," and the imprecision gives the song its power. It doesn't sound like a song composed on a synthesizer in the 1980s, but like an anthem or a spiritual, a song for the ages.

There are two more verses, and a final refrain—"And the eyes of the world are watching now"—but it is that chorus that lingers as the crowd moves toward the exits. Biko. Biko. Biko. The complications of martyrdom are dispelled, or overwhelmed, through bold assertion. "He a martyr—here a martyr—the man is dead, the man is dead."

The song makes clear that martyrdom is a concept that still has authority in the culture at large. In this cultural sense, the terms of martyrdom are expansive and negotiable. The martyr lives and dies and dies for a just cause, and the martyr is an exemplar whose witness spurs others to thought and action.

In its Christian sense, the terms of martyrdom are more specific. The Christian martyr lives and dies for a just cause and is an exemplar—but in some sense the cause must be Jesus Christ; the example that of the Christian life. The Christian martyr's thought and action must be seen, somehow, as embodying the theological virtues of faith, hope, and love.

Christian or otherwise, the martyr reminds us that it is in individual lives, first of all, that God must be known and justice done. And it is remarkable how the life and death of a martyr like Steven Biko can refract the conflicts of the age.

In any thorough examination of his martyrdom—to choose just one way of approach—the questions of a half-century of Christian ecumenism are thrown up before us, profound and unavoidable.

The views of the churches toward non-Christian religions, for example, and toward social movements that are at most implicitly religious, have changed dramatically in this century. New alignments among the denominations, restatements of doctrine, fresh understandings of the nature of Christian witness, all these are very important—but it is in exemplary lives that they are truly made manifest. Even as the churches undertook more cooperative efforts after World War II, for example, the great ecumenical act of the period was the life of Martin Luther King, Jr., an expression of faith as profound as any declaration of the Second Vatican Council or the World Council of Churches.

In the same way, the life and death of Steven Biko point toward what seem to be the most pressing questions for individual Christians today. Every thoughtful believer has agonized over whether a lived life must be explicitly Christian to announce and enact the gospel message. What to make of those exemplary lives that, although not Christian, point to Christ with such authority? And if one need not be a Christian to bear witness to

Christ, what is the nature of our own Christianity: is it a relative accident of birth and upbringing, a personal choice, or a claim about the way the world was in the beginning and is now and ever shall be?

These questions of the missionaries of old now face all of us, and a martyr is a missionary in reverse. In death the martyr says to others, What I believe is so important that it is worth dying for, whereas in life the missionary says to others, What I believe is so important that it is worth living for. The man is dead: Steven Biko cannot answer our questions, and it is important that we do not try to answer them for him. Christians are enjoined to remember the dead, but to convert the living. Rather than try to convert the dead, we must ask ourselves whether we could urge Christian faith upon the likes of Steven Biko. If so, how? And if not, we've got to ask ourselves whether Christian faith is something we can continue to urge upon ourselves. The question isn't whether we consider Christ worth dying for, but whether we truly consider him worth living for.

In one of her essays Flannery O'Connor pondered the "unbelieving searchers"—Pascal, Kafka, Camus—and their effect on those who do believe. "We begin to examine our own religious notions," she observed, "to sound them for genuineness, to purify them in the heat of our unbelieving neighbor's anguish." Steven Biko was such a searcher. His death forces us to sound our lives for genuineness, and in his anguish we must confront our own.

For Further Reading

Richard Attenborough, *Cry Freedom.* MCA, 1987.

Steven Biko, *I Write What I Like.* Edited by Aelred Stubbs. Harmondsworth, Middlesex: Penguin Books, 1978.

Peter Gabriel, "Biko." On the CD *Shaking the Tree: Sixteen Golden Greats.* New York: Island Records, 1991.

Theodore W. Jennings, "Steve Biko: Liberator and Martyr." *Christian Century*, November 2, 1977, 997–99.

Desmond Tutu, "Oh, God, How Long Can We Go On?" (1977). In *The Rainbow People of God: The Making of a Peaceful Revolution,* 15–21. New York: Doubleday, 1994.

Donald Woods, *Biko.* 3d rev. ed. New York: Henry Holt, 1991.

MARTIN LUTHER KING, JR.

Tennessee, 1968

Martin Luther King and the Reinvention of Christianity in Modern America

by GERALD EARLY

Part One

We will win our freedom because the sacred heritage of our nation and the eternal will of God are embodied in our echoing demands.

    Martin Luther King, Jr., "Letter from a Birmingham City Jail"

"You went to college, right? So what you think white folks want from us?"

"You serious?"

"Yeah, I'm serious."

Reno began slowly, expecting some kind of joke. "They want us to be what they think we are." He paused. "Now what that is depends on the particular white man you are dealing with. You still with me?"

"Yeah. Yeah." The boy was making sense.

"Most of them want to think we're not dangerous. And that means they don't want us to be human. Because if I learned anything at all in college, it's that everybody's just naturally dangerous."

    Discussion between Reno and Ludlow in William Melvin Kelley's novel *A Drop of Patience* (1965)

To talk in terms of Christianity, love, nonviolence is reassuring to the mentality of white America.

    August Meier, "On the Role of Martin Luther King"

Doubtless, the most famous death scene in all of American literature, in a book that has no shortage of them, is the demise of Uncle Tom in Harriet Beecher Stowe's landmark antislavery novel, *Uncle Tom's Cabin*. Although the deaths of Little Eva and Augustine St. Clair have great dramatic impact, their ends are really mere preludes to Tom's gut-wrenching, violent departure. It had to be so if the book was to have any impact on the white American mind of 1852. Little Eva and Augustine St. Clair are white sacrificial lambs; Tom is black, his death the moral and political signification of the one form of resistance to slavery that was sure, in the end, to undo the slave oligarchy. Thus, his death bears the entire political and religious significance of the novel. Indeed, Stowe herself mythified Tom's death, saying that it was the very first scene of the novel she wrote, intimating that its composition, which came upon her as a kind of illumination or spell and came out in one sitting, was inspired by God or was the signal that God was inspiring her to write the book.

Tom dies from the brutal, sadistic treatment of Louisiana planter Simon Legree, a Yankee who runs a savagely efficient plantation and is totally fixated on money. "Legree, like many other planters," writes Stowe, "had but one form of ambition,—to have in the heaviest crop of the season."

Tom resists Legree by refusing to become a black overseer; then he helps a black woman in the field who cannot keep up with the pace of the cotton harvesting. Tom is compelled by Christian duty to act this way. He is willing to participate in an oppressive system. He will work for Legree and never questions Legree's right to ownership over him. But Tom refuses to oppress others. He will not make his load easier at the expense of the other slaves, thus relieving the guilt of Legree and perpetuating the system itself by giving in to its values. Tom will not, in short, individuate his interests, which for Tom would mean giving in to a morality of dog-eat-dog or all-against-all in the killing fields of the plantation. As Tom tells Legree when Legree demands that Tom apologize for his resistance:

> Mas'r Legree . . . I can't do it. I did only what I thought was right. I shall do just so again, if ever the time comes. I never will do a cruel thing, come what may.

Considering the broad and powerfully humane aspect to Tom's essentially nonviolent resistance, this speech sounds almost insipid. Stowe often mistook insipidity for childlike simplicity, which, naturally, is what she was aiming for in her noble African. Stowe does a little better later when Tom is finally beaten to death for not revealing the whereabouts of Cassy and Emmeline, Legree's black concubines who have run away. In Tom's last speech, where he expresses concern for his wife and children, he concludes: "I loves every creatur' everywhar!—it's nothing but love! Oh . . . what a thing 't is to be a Christian!" He forgives Legree and dies.

Nearly everyone knows that "Uncle Tom" is an intraracial epithet of considerable force and disapprobation for a black person (now anyone of an oppressed group) who works against the interests of his or her group and displays servile love for the dominant group. It has been said by some critics, especially those who find *Uncle Tom's Cabin* to be an important, even radical, political novel, that Tom is misunderstood by modern blacks, that most have never read the novel and are led astray by the undying images from the burlesque Tom shows that followed in the wake of this enormously popular book. But it is not likely that Tom would be better appreciated if more blacks today read the novel. (I have never noticed any dramatic changes in black students in my classes when I have taught the novel. They remain generally unmoved and unimpressed by the character.) In Tom's Christian resistance to slavery there is something at the core that is inhumane in what is being asked of him or in what he asks of himself. He is never angry at his oppressors and thus, despite his dignity, he seems debased because he is never dangerous to Legree, at least not in any conventional sense, in asserting his humanity. It isn't that black readers don't understand that Tom's "dangerous" humanity, his resistance, ultimately unhinges Legree. What they refuse to accept is that Tom's resistance never dissuades Legree from destroying him in the first place. Tom's resistance is distasteful to blacks in two ways: he is never able to overcome his helpless posture, and he is too concerned with the soul and fate of his oppressor. This seems too much of a symbolic burden of racial healing for the black to have to bear.

James Baldwin, one of the staunchest and most famous critics of the novel, believed precisely that this symbolic burden was Tom's undoing as both a political and a religious character. In his 1949 essay "Everybody's Protest Novel," he wrote:

> The figure from whom the novel takes its name, Uncle Tom, who is a figure of controversy yet, is jet-black, wooly-haired, illiterate; and he is phenomenally forbearing. He has to be; he is black; only through this forbearance can

he survive or triumph . . . His triumph is metaphysical, unearthly; since he is black, born without the light, it is only through humility, the incessant mortification of the flesh, that he can enter into communion with God or man.

Baldwin here is right, although he thoroughly misreads the novel: in Tom's triumph over his oppressor, he must never threaten the white man as a man but as something "unearthly," a combination of Job, Moses, Christ, the good white Victorian mother, the holy celibate, the Father as nonthreatening, nondangerous, nonaggressive, nonmaterialistic masculinity. To save the African from the theories of scientific racism and theological racism of the nineteenth century, Stowe made him the natural Christian, a transcendent being. What Baldwin fails to understand is that Tom is not merely another black slave in the book or just a religious symbol. He is the archetype of the black leader. He is the most respected slave, by both blacks and whites, on the Shelby plantation before he is sold. He is a role model of how a slave can prosper under the system without losing his dignity. Throughout his travels, he becomes the leader, the slave that all the other slaves look up to, the slave that the masters and traders implicitly trust. He symbolizes the slave's interest and the slave's humanity to the master. After all, even Legree, in his demonic greed, wanted to make Tom a leader on his plantation because he, too, saw this mystical quality. Tom refused to be a leader on Legree's terms. Tom is a martyr. He dies in defense of his people as well as in defense of his humanity, recognition of which will, naturally, transform the twisted psyche of his oppressors.

Moreover, it must be remembered that the title of the book is not simply *Uncle Tom* but rather *Uncle Tom's Cabin,* a location, a domesticity we encounter once in the novel, which, as it turns out, is this idealized beloved southern community—terribly oversentimentalized—where blacks and whites can eat together, black children tumble joyously, and peace reigns through obedience to God. In effect, the novel succeeds at dramatizing with compelling lucidity and considerable magnitude the intersection of American exceptionalism (the salvation history of America as the new Israel) and black exceptionalism (the ironic salvation of the degraded slave in a free land), both serving as the twin, inseparable pillars upon which American theological destiny is built. Black and white abolitionist leaders had said this for years, since the abolitionist movement became a social protest force in the United States, but Stowe dramatized, mythologized what they could only rhetoricize. Stowe showed how American redemption, the meaning of American salvation history, was tied not only to the fate of the African (what would be done with him in American society?) but to his character and his quality of leadership, which would be essential in the redemptive process (what did he have to offer America in its relentless march to messianic empire?). Indeed, what the novel gives us is the black leader, Tom, as the only fully realized, totally idealized, adult male. The black leader will redeem the role of Father in Stowe's feminized domestic sphere, will be the beloved and loving Father around whom will gather the black and white children and adults to hear the Word.[1]

Baldwin wrote this essay at the time that Jackie Robinson was the most publicized black person in America, a virtual black leader, and something of a father figure, especially as at the age of twenty-eight when he broke into the major leagues in 1947, Robinson was old for a baseball rookie. Robinson had been playing with the Brooklyn Dodgers for two years, during which time, under the agreement he made with Dodger executive Branch Rickey (a devout Methodist who may have read *Uncle Tom's Cabin* as a youth, less for its social implications than as an exposition of religious piety), he endured the taunts and insults of both white fans and opposing players. It was nonviolent resistance meant to bring about acceptance of the black ballplayer by white fans and white players through his ability and his noble demeanor. Baldwin was no sports fan but he surely knew about Robinson's exploits and the conditions under which Robinson played ball. (Baldwin did not leave America in his first bout as an expatriate until November 1948. As an inveterate reader of black newspapers and as a resident of New York, he had to know the Robinson saga fairly well.) Surely, a young Martin Luther King, Jr., a second-year student at Crozer Theological Seminary in 1949 and an avid sports fan, knew about Robinson, his example, and his impact. King, by the time Baldwin emerged in the 1950s, was to know about the young black writer, too. He enjoyed Baldwin's writings a great deal. One of his favorite books was Baldwin's second collection of essays, *Nobody Knows My Name,* published in 1962. Baldwin even interviewed King for a profile on the famed Baptist minister in *Harper's.* One wonders what King, who artfully and brilliantly exploited the Uncle Tom archetype to legitimate his own leadership in the eyes of both black and white America, thought of Baldwin's assessment of that character.[2]

Part Two

*I would have to appropriate these white centuries, I would have to make
them mine—I would have to accept my special attitude, my special place
in this scheme—otherwise I would have no place in any scheme.*

James Baldwin, *Notes of a Native Son*

*Martin Luther King has limitations when he functions
politically because he is a churchman.*

Ralph Ellison, 1966

I have always found the term *black leader* to be curious, for while we seem
to have a considerable number of "black leaders" in the United States,
there are and never have been any "white leaders." None of the people
elected to national, state, or local office in the United States, even during
the time when only white men voted and only white men, with few exceptions, were elected, have ever been called "white leaders," even though
many of them believed that they were protecting a white nation. It would
never occur to us to call Abraham Lincoln and Thomas Jefferson "white
leaders," although, of course, they were elected by white men exclusively.
Now, today, Jesse Jackson, we are told by the American press, is a black
leader because he heads an organization that is made up mostly of black
people. Jesse Jackson is a minister who is actively involved in politics. Pat
Robertson is also a minister actively involved in politics. He is not called
a white leader, even though the organization he heads is made up mostly
of whites. Perhaps it will be argued that Robertson has blacks among his
flock, which, I am sure, is true. But then again Jackson has whites among
his. Indeed, when both men ran for president, Jackson had far more white
people vote for him than Robertson had blacks.

Martin Luther King, despite the number of whites who were instrumental in his protest movement, was called a black leader but Billy Graham was never called a white leader. Jerry Falwell and Rush Limbaugh
are not called white leaders, but what appellation would be better? No
one thinks of calling major-league baseball played between 1884 and 1947
white baseball, although that is exactly what it was. The Beatles are never
called "white musicians" or "white recording artists," although they have
sold far fewer records to blacks than, say, Motown artists have sold to
whites. But everyone is always reminded that Motown was a black com-

pany with a roster of black artists. Race is a singular marker in our country. Although we have a group of radical intellectuals and scholars who are determined to "mark" whites, who wish to create a history of the construction of whiteness, blacks remain the stigmatized group, and how they have dealt with their stigma remains a truly vital American tale.

"The terrible thing about being a Negro leader," James Baldwin wrote in his essay "The Harlem Ghetto," "lies in the term itself. I do not mean merely the somewhat condescending differentiation the term implies, but the nicely refined torture a man can experience from having been created and defeated by the same circumstances. That is, Negro leaders have been created by the American scene, which thereafter works against them at every point; and the best that they can hope for is ultimately to work themselves out of their jobs, to nag contemporary American leaders and the members of their own group until a bad situation becomes so complicated and so bad that it cannot be endured any longer. It is like needling a blister until it bursts." Baldwin's last sentence was a metaphor used often by Martin Luther King, Jr. For instance, in his famous "Letter from the Birmingham City Jail," King wrote: "Actually, we who engage in nonviolent direct action are not the creators of tension. We merely bring to the surface the hidden tension that is already alive. We bring it out in the open where it can be seen and dealt with. Like a boil that can never be cured as long as it is covered up but must be opened with all its pus-flowing ugliness to the natural medicines of air and light, injustice must likewise be exposed."

King elaborated on the metaphor when interviewed on *Meet the Press* in the summer of 1966, shortly after the James Meredith March Against Fear. In talking about the hostilities and violence that the civil rights movement had unleashed, King said: "Certainly no one would blame the physician for using his instruments and his skills and his know-how to reveal to a patient that he has cancer. Indeed, one would praise a physician for having the wisdom and the judgment and the power to do that." In one sense, it is not a surprise that Martin Luther King used the language of cure in talking about the aims of the civil rights demonstrations. He was, after all, a reformer within the bourgeois American tradition that dates back at least to Jane Addams and the turn-of-the-century creation of the social-work profession. Indeed, Louis Farrakhan used almost identical language in describing himself and his aims at the recent Million Man March in Washington, disguising himself, despite his fascist trappings, in the lineage of the bourgeois, social-working, education-oriented reformer. In another sense, King was also fired by the millennial righteousness of the abolitionist Christians like Weld, the Tappans, the Grimkes, Frederick Douglass, Henry David Thoreau, Wendell Phillips, Garrison, and Lydia Maria Child of the antebellum era. Declaring racism an illness, saying that whites were in need of a cure, of a demonstration of how their racism could be exposed and treated, was a dramatic shift in how the race problem had been viewed. The Negro may still be a problem, still be sick, but the whites were even sicker and ironically needed the Negro as a physician. Given these two strains, King couldn't help but see himself as a holy healer.

King was not a great or original thinker. Indeed, his ideas were often simplistic, as August Meier, among others, has pointed out, which is what gave them their power and popular appeal. King understood, to use David Riesman's term, the "other-directed" age in which he lived. He knew implicitly that the people of his age were ultimately to judge themselves not on their accomplishments but on their ability to get along with other people. This is why the entire issue of racism became so fantastically, almost luridly, important in the middle of the twentieth century but not the middle of the nineteenth century, which was dominated by the issue of slavery as a political problem, not racism as a psychological and interpersonal problem. But King also understood the inner yearnings of blacks, their need to have a "war," in effect, to show that they were willing to die for their liberation—which was itself, for American Negroes, an explicit act of liberation that would forever change both them and American whites. Thus, Martin Luther King was also a great deal more than simply a successful American reformer in the antinomian Protestant tradition of American social protest. He was the greatest of all Negro leaders in the Western world.

It might seem strange, after all, to call King this—a left-handed compliment. Why not call him the greatest American of the twentieth century, which, I believe, unarguably, he is? Or one of the most important Americans in our history? Who would be as important: Washington, Jefferson, Lincoln, Franklin Roosevelt? King is this, too, without question. But he was important because he was a Negro leader, because, for better and for worse, he operated within this limiting, even degrading framework. As James Baldwin remarked in his lengthy meditation on the black leader (*Harper's,* February 1961):

Now, the problem of Negro leadership in this country has always been extremely delicate, dangerous, and complex. The term itself becomes remarkably difficult to define, the moment one realizes that the real role of the
Negro leader, in the eyes of the American Republic, was not to make the
Negro a first-class citizen but to keep him content as a second-class one . . .
Whatever concession the Negro leader carried away from the bargaining
table was won with the tacit understanding that he, in return, would influence the people he represented in the direction that the people in power
wished them to be influenced.

King had to achieve the impossible of being trusted both by the whites
(as operating in good faith) and by the blacks (as not selling out their interests). Thus, he had to appear nonthreatening to the whites as he, at the
same time, appeared dangerous to them in order to appeal to the blacks.
He did this in two ways: first, through his Christian rhetoric and vision of
millennial America, whose apocalypse was race war, and his insistence, no
matter how much some of his lieutenants thought otherwise, that nonviolent direct action was not merely a tactic but a religious principle
through which the regeneration of America could occur. No matter how
much King and others pointed to Gandhi as the source of his nonviolent
stance—a convenient masking as it gave King the aura of being something of a politically aware black man through his use of another third-
world, "colored" leader as a model—within the American context, it was
simply a reworking of the Uncle Tom archetype as distinct from the Nat
Turner archetype, the two principal archetypes of the millennially religious black leader in both the white and the black American mind. King
needed the rhetoric of Christian forgiveness, love, and commitment not
only to connect to the Christian imagination of the blacks (their inevitable, salvation destiny was freedom) but to appeal to the Christian
imagination of the whites (whose version of apocalypse was not race war[3]
for victory and final supremacy but the voluntary sacrifice of black lives
to more than match their own sacrifice of treasure and privilege). Both
sides had to be convinced that there was a larger concern here than
merely the complaints of mistreated black folk. The soul and future of the
United States were at issue.
Second, King accepted the mantle of the black leader from the white
American press and the white power structure, a mantle they were willing

to confer because King had so successfully transformed himself into a symbol, flexible enough to serve a number of people's interests and ends until, say, 1965. This meant it was in the interest of the white power structure to permit King some success as it was in the interests of the black elite to have King as a major bargaining agent. The whites had to concede something to King from time to time to assure themselves that he was in control, that he could stay in control, of this movement. That King often was not in control was something that for a time worked in his favor, as both important whites and important blacks felt his symbolic value was such that he had to appear at least as if he were in control. In a sense, King never transcended being a Negro leader. He made being a Negro leader a virtually transcendent profession as Uncle Tom did.

I would like to get at what that means in the context of Baldwin's remark in a passage I quoted earlier from "The Harlem Ghetto"; for Baldwin implied something both absurd and tragic about being a Negro leader, someone created by the same forces that are ultimately designed to defeat him. In some measure, the drama of the black leader is the drama of the average black person played out on the level of myth and icon. The black leader lives not merely to gain concessions for his people from the white power structure but through his example to teach his people how to live in the great American paradox of being a black American, which, if not a contradiction in terms, is certainly a disjuncture at times, so large as can float a few large ships of irony and dismay in its watery breach. King was the greatest of all black leaders because his attempt to bridge this disjuncture between black and American absolutely changed the nation—because he made being a Negro not an aberration of the American experience but the very soul and essence of what it means to be an American.

Of all black leaders, King is most often compared to his contemporary Malcolm X, a pastor in his own right and a man of some messianic pretensions, like King, but certainly not a historical figure of the same weight and stature as King. There are obvious differences: King was more connected to the heart of the black community than Malcolm X, that is, the part of the community from which one could not only get money and talent but could also influence how the grassroots think. Despite Malcolm's connections to the ghetto and the hustler's life (which many black people, out of guilt and a bourgeois romanticization of the "low life," continue to think of as the true representation of their community and their culture), King was connected to the largest black mass organization in the country, the National Baptist Convention—through his own Baptist ministry and that of his father and grandfather, both hugely successful black Baptist preachers—and some of the most important black secular institutions: black fraternities and black colleges. By virtue of growing up middle class in Atlanta, he also had access to the heart of the most developed black urban business district in the country. And it was the fraternities, the colleges, the businesses (although some black business thrived on segregation), and the churches that produced the extraordinarily talented leadership cadre that was so important to King, so instrumental to his leadership.

King surrounded himself with often brilliant, always capable people: Lawson, Walker, Young, Shuttlesworth, Abernathy, Carmichael, Jackson, Bevel, Rustin, Levison, and, for a time, Ella Baker. Indeed, as both James Washington and Lewis Baldwin have pointed out, a generation of militant black preachers, from Adam Clayton Powell, Jr., to Kelly Miller Smith, ascended to pulpits in a span from the Depression to the end of World War II, making possible King's Southern Christian Leadership Conference (SCIC), formed in 1957 after the unbelievable success of the Montgomery bus boycott that made King an international hero, because its ranks were mostly made up of black southern ministers. But this access was not mere accident of birth. King took advantage of his birth and did something that seemed unthinkable before he did it: he united a largely apolitical, apathetic black middle class and gave them a political mission and vision. Then, even more amazingly, he was able to link them in direct action protest with the black grassroots. Malcolm X never achieved anything like this. He was unable to effect any sort of meaningful black political coalition, not even a Pan-Africanist one, during his lifetime. He could simply rhetoricize and imagine it. It is therefore no surprise that Malcolm failed so completely when he tried to form his own organizations, the Muslim Mosque, Inc., and the Organization of Afro-American Unity, when he left the Nation of Islam. He was too unconnected with the intellectual and organizational talent pools in the black community to build much of anything (the very pools that Farrakhan wants access to in his bid to reach the black mainstream as the man who can, as it is said, "make the trains run on time" or solve the disorder of the black inner city). Malcolm was a brilliant ideologist and masterful social worker, but he was not a tactician or a good manager of people. King himself was no great administrator, but he was gifted as a visionary and gathered solid administrators around him. But most important, he understood how to plan campaigns and create crises.

Malcolm X's stature among blacks today rests a great deal upon his militant nationalism as truth-telling and unmasking, which mirrors precisely the mood of so-called radical politics both among rappers in the hip-hop nation, as it is called—crude and clever rhetoricizing that is meant to unmask political hypocrisy as it legitimates its own revolutionary, transformational pretensions—and among the postmodernists and radicals in academia, whose crude and clever rhetoric is meant to achieve the same ends. Malcolm's accusation against the civil rights movement was that it was insufficiently international in its scope and insufficiently knowledgeable about Africa, neither of which was, in fact, true. The civil rights establishment understood the international significance of its struggle, and many people involved in it were more knowledgeable about Africa and more involved in African affairs than Malcolm was. But Malcolm's denouncement of the tactics of nonviolent direct action, of King's redemptive love mission, as a naive misunderstanding of both the intractable nature of privilege in American politics and the process of American social change, was a more accurate hit. Malcolm was correct in connecting King with the Uncle Tom archetype, and I think blacks today feel a certain discomfort with King because of that.

Moreover, many blacks are a bit uncomfortable with the revelations about King's character that have surfaced in recent years: the womanizing and the plagiarism.[4] However much one might wish to dismiss these as being, in the one instance, the perquisites of a famous man and, in the other, an irrelevant sin of consequence only in the rather elite world of the intellectual, there is no escaping that they seem to reveal a core of dishonesty in King's makeup. King's womanizing came perilously close to wrecking his leadership. It certainly compromised him as a leader. His inveterate plagiarizing was the sign of a man who did not respect intellectual ownership or the courtesy of intellectual acknowledgment. There was a considerable degree of dissembling in King's posture as moral leader and as intellectual. In this respect, Malcolm as loyal husband and honest intellectual, in this age of beleaguered black male character and the quest for the good black father, all the more strikingly reveals King's limitations.

But there is no getting around the fact that King's achievement far outstrips anything that any other black leader ever dreamed could be accomplished. There are two immediate reasons for this. First, King was the only black leader to speak with a truly prophetic voice and with prophetic authority for at least a significant portion of his public career. Second, King was able to move black people en masse in pursuing their claims as Americans. Indeed, King was able, for a considerable time, to make a significant number of black people demonstrate and sustain a fervent, nearly heartbreaking belief in the American creed, American institutions, and the inevitability of American justice.

The most striking rhetorical metaphor King created as a leader was "the dream," thoroughly unoriginal, even pedestrian but, once again, all the more formidable and memorable because it so conveniently taps into a number of national clichés. With it King so deftly tied black people's aspirations to the nation's; King thoroughly transformed black people from being seen by whites as the sum total of their characterological defects to being ardent, deeply moved believers in the national myth of plenty, self-reliance, and merit. What was this dream of which King spoke? In a speech at Lincoln University in Pennsylvania in 1961, he said: "For in a real sense, America is a dream, a dream as yet unfulfilled. It is a dream of a land where men of all races, of all nationalities and of all creeds can live together as brothers." In the same speech, he spoke of "an inescapable network of mutuality." He said: "Strangely enough, I can never be what I ought to be until you are what you ought to be. You can never be what you ought to be until I am what I ought to be."

How he describes the American Dream here is not quite how the American Dream traditionally is defined. The American Dream may be about diverse people living together but it is also about class-jumping and upward mobility, about which King never speaks. The American Dream is also about material possession, which in sermons like "The Drum Major Instinct" King naturally deplores. The American Dream is about individual fulfillment, but for King this fulfillment can never be achieved through self-reliance but only by community, beloved community. In his most famous speech, "I Have a Dream," given on the steps of the Lincoln Memorial on August 28, 1963, the day of the March on Washington, King said his dream was "deeply rooted in the American Dream," which would, of course, imply that it is not quite the American Dream but something else, possibly the black American Dream or the black Christian's vision of a redeemed America.

King seemed to have to screw up his own belief in his dream when he gave his Christmas sermon at Ebenezer Baptist Church in 1967, a time when King's movement seemed to be unraveling with great and vivid speed. He was denounced from many formerly friendly quarters for coming out earlier that year against the Vietnam War. The Black Power movement had siphoned off virtually all the young people he once had who were committed to nonviolent direct action. The urban riots had unleashed a level of black bitterness and white reaction that made any further talk of redemptive love almost impossible or at least quixotic. King said on that Christmas Eve:

> In 1963, on a sweltering August afternoon, we stood in Washington, D.C., and talked to the nation about many things. Toward the end of the afternoon, I tried to talk to the nation about a dream that I had had, and I must confess to you today that not long after talking about that dream I started seeing it turn into a nightmare. I remember the first time I saw the dream turn into a nightmare, just a few weeks after I had talked about it. It was when four beautiful, unoffending, innocent Negro girls were murdered in a church in Birmingham, Alabama. I watched the dream turn into a nightmare as I moved through the ghettos of the nation and saw my black brothers and sisters perishing on a lonely island of poverty in the midst of a vast ocean of material prosperity . . . I saw that dream turn into a nightmare as I watched the war in Vietnam escalating . . . Yes, I am personally the victim of deferred dreams, of blasted hopes, but in spite of that I close today by saying I still have a dream, because, you know, you can't give up in life.

There is more to King's dream than the usual superficial observation about the need for racial harmony and the quest for a color-blind society. Indeed, I do not believe that King invented the dream as a metaphor about racial harmony or a color-blind society, although in early speeches it is described in those terms. Here King's speech intimates that the American Dream is inescapably tragic. The nightmare and the dream, in Hegelian dialectical union, are forever fused. (Hegel was one of King's favorite philosophers.) That is, King is outlining, in his crisis moment, in his dramatization of his dark moment of the soul as a black leader, the real and very hard costs of achieving the American Dream.

In his novel *Native Son,* Richard Wright suggests that the best that ghetto-dwelling, violent Bigger Thomas can hope for is the welfare-state paternalism of the Daltons, who give money to black colleges and jobs to poor, wayward black boys like himself and who also owe the slum apartment building he lives in. What Bigger learns is that the welfare system created to save him is, through the very mechanism of its creation, the representation of his complete and utter defeat, which reflects nothing more than his own condition of blackness: that the very forces that created him are designed to defeat him.

King created the metaphor of the dream for theological reasons: to give both blacks and whites hope that the race problem in America could be solved. As Lerone Bennett wrote: "It was King's achievement to give men hope." King's dream was to provide a mythical structure to black *status viatoris* and national *status viatoris,* which, as Josef Pieper defined it in his *On Hope,* means "the condition or state of being on the way." Both black people and the United States, according to King's vision, had to understand themselves as being pilgrims in time. The alternatives are fulfillment and nothingness. As *homo viator,* man on the way, King himself as prophet symbolized the way toward fulfillment, toward being. But this could happen only through hope, a theological virtue made up of magnanimity ("aspiration of the spirit to great things," according to Pieper) and humility ("the knowledge and acceptance of the inexpressible distance between Creator and creature,"). Without hope, there is only the paradox of temporal existence without meaning.

It is this black existential realization that King came to on that Christmas Eve. Indeed, in the Christmas Eve sermon, King almost sounds like a blues singer. He makes a specific reference to Langston Hughes and his famous lamentation about black people and their dreams deferred, which dry up like a raisin in the sun—to quote the line that became the title of Lorraine Hansberry's great drama about black people and the American Dream. But King, like the gospel singers who say, "I'm so glad that trouble don't last always," lifts himself up, because, as the singers say, "I got religion in time." He finds the blues singer's victory in his adversity. "The blues," as Ralph Ellison most famously wrote, "is an impulse to keep the painful details and episodes of a brutal experience alive in one's aching consciousness, to finger its jagged grain, and to transcend it, not by consolation of philosophy but by squeezing from it a near-tragic, near-comic lyricism." So, in the end, King, as the great American lyrical prophet, goes from being the awareness of blues to the psyche of the spirituals. He dramatizes finding theological hope and national purpose in the very essence of his people's struggle. This was King's great gift and the meaning of his great sermonic skills. August Meier wrote:

At the heart of King's continuing influence and popularity are two facts. First, better than anyone else, he articulates the aspirations of Negroes who respond to the cadence of his addresses, his religious phraseology and manner of speaking, and the vision of his dream for them and for America. King has intuitively adopted the style of the old-fashioned Negro Baptist preacher and transformed it into a new art form; he has, indeed, restored oratory to its place among the arts. Second, he communicates Negro aspirations to white America more effectively than anyone else. His religious terminology and manipulation of Christian symbols of love and nonresistance are partly responsible for his appeal among whites.

No one was able to do this before he came on the scene. No one has been able to do it since.

Part Three

Mutiny from stern to bow
   Bob Dylan, "My Back Pages"

Tradition! We scarcely know the word anymore. We are afraid to be either proud of our ancestors or ashamed of them. We scorn nobility in name and fact. We cling to a bourgeois mediocrity which would make it appear we are all Americans, made in the image and likeness of George Washington, all of a pattern, all prospering if we are good, and going down in the world if we are bad. These are attitudes the Irish, the Italian, the Lithuanian, the Slovak, and all races begin to acquire in school. So they change their names, forget their birthplace, their language, and no longer listen to their mothers when they say, "When I was a little girl in Russia, or Hungary, or Sicily." They lose their cult and their culture and their skills, and leave their faith and folk songs and costumes and handcrafts, and try to be something which they call "an American."

This is a passage from Dorothy Day's 1952 autobiography, *The Long Loneliness*. Day, one of the founders of the Catholic Worker movement, a frontline battler for social justice issues, was a bourgeois radical from the 1920s who had something like a tradition of radical politics with which to shape her own religious vision of political engagement. This is why she could question Americanism. Martin Luther King had no such tradition upon which to draw. This is why he couldn't. Americans of European descent had a history of radical, anarchist politics in Europe. Americans of African descent had no such history in Africa. It would not matter how much a black American read or knew about African life, tradition, and culture; little of it would be of use in the United States because Africa and the United States are and were such extraordinarily different places. A European memory for a white American was extremely useful, however, because the United States and Europe were and are not so very different. But Day's radical questioning of Americanism and American identity is rooted in an atavistic, even reactionary ideal: the nonmodernist, more holistic, less standardized past of the folk peasant. That a black person must have something like an African memory, even if totally fictive, is something that no one questions much now. King found that concern irrelevant in the shaping of a radical politic. Ironically, King's radicalism grew from his insistent, even provincial belief in the utter sufficiency of Americanism and the utter sufficiency of the social gospel tradition and religious revivals.

In short, King was forced to invent himself as he went along and he grew with his job, remarkably creating a black radical political tradition, not only in what his positions ultimately became but in the criticism that his various positions generated. There would have been no Black Power movement of the vehemence that we had, no possibility for the emergence of a black leftist or socialist movement, and no black nationalist ideology as clearly defined as it became had not King achieved his remarkable stature and so magnetically pushed his own vision.

King was not of age in the 1930s, so the Marxist decade of American history had no direct influence in shaping his mind. Moreover, King's childhood in the 1930s in Atlanta was a far more privileged one than that of most black children and a good many whites, since his father was a successful pastor of a large black church. King felt a degree of guilt about this his entire life. Perhaps this is why he was moved to become a social reformer in the first place: an intense dissatisfaction with the philistine, anti-intellectual nature of black middle-class life. King surely went out of his way in his life to appear neither philistine nor anti-intellectual. The sheer urgency with which he pursued his public career as reformer and the urgency that punctuated his message of freedom now for blacks seemed at least partly driven by a dislike for the apathetic, petty, contrived, and materialistic diversions of the black middle class.[5] Indeed, King would fit almost perfectly the new radical, as defined by Christopher Lasch in *The New Radicalism in America, 1889–1963:* a person who had never been poor who discovered the dispossessed and who also discovered intellectuals.

One of King's heroes was the great black socialist and union leader A. Philip Randolph, so indirectly, of course, King was influenced by the radical politics of the 1920s and 1930s. But King emerged in the post–World War II era, when the United States was engaged in all-out ideological war against radical politics in the form of communism and when liberalism in this country was particularly constrained, disavowing its leftist associations. Liberals such as Trilling, Schlesinger, Mary McCarthy, Reisman, and Bell were all trying to find the center, an absolutely centrist position of liberal anticommunism. Even one of King's liberal Protestant influences, Reinhold Niebuhr, who had Marxist sentiments, tried to do much the same in his tricky balancing of the individual and the community, the citizen and the state, which King copied nearly verbatim. Niebuhr, for instance, wrote in a 1945 article in *Commentary:*

> The consistent socialization of all economic power is no more adequate a solution for our problem than a consistent disavowal of political authority upon economic process. The latter leads to anarchy as the former leads to tyranny. The wisest nations experiment in order to find *a middle way* which will insure a maximum of freedom and security. [Emphasis mine.]

This position of balancing personal freedom and welfare-state security would be King's for his entire public career, the only position possible in a country that was now defining itself almost entirely through the prism of national security. Calling King a "conservative militant," a man who practices compromise and caution, much to the chagrin of more radical civil rights factions, August Meier wrote in 1965: "King occupies a position of strategic importance as the 'vital center' within the civil rights movement." King further emphasized his position as the middle man within the realm of black politics. In his "Letter from a Birmingham City Jail," he said that he stood

> in the middle of two opposing forces in the Negro community. One is the force of complacency made up of Negroes who, as a result of long years of oppression, have been so completely drained of self-respect and a sense of "somebodiness" that they have adjusted to segregation, and, of a few Negroes in the middle class who, because of a degree of academic and economic se-

curity, and because at points they profit by segregation, have unconsciously become insensitive to the problems of the masses. The other force is one of bitterness and hatred, and comes perilously close to advocating violence. It is expressed in the various black nationalist groups that are springing up over the nation.

Another way of seeing King's position as a bargaining agent for blacks was expressed in his *Playboy* interview, where he said: "I mean to say that a strong man must be militant as well as moderate. He must be a realist as well as an idealist." In short, King served as the center between black and white and as the center between black radicalism and black conservatism. It was convenient for King to label black nationalism as "bitter" and "hateful," yet he had to know, in truth, that it was a competing form of black hope that he was bound to disparage. King knew, indeed, that his exploitation of a nationalistic sense of black destiny—he never discouraged references to himself as Moses—was responsible for his success and legitimacy as a leader. What interested King was neither being a conformist nor being a nonconformist—he was both and neither simultaneously—but being able to manipulate the forces of conformity and nonconformity in both white and black politics for the greatest concessions—actual or symbolic—that he could gain.

King's own centrism was expressed in the search for the mainstream of American life into which the black American could integrate. King had been greatly influenced by Gunnar Myrdal's massive 1944 sociological study of race relations, *An American Dilemma*. King was a sociology major at Morehouse, which he attended from 1944 to 1948, and doubtless read at least a portion of this work. The book made clear for King the strategy that other African American leaders played out with less success. If the problem in America was the disjuncture between the American creed of freedom and equality and the existence of blacks as a disenfranchised, pariah group, then the solution was to make the country uncomfortable, embarrassed, downright guilty, explosively tense, about this disjuncture and the hypocrisy it implied until whites were moved or forced to make the country live up to its creed by including blacks as full-fledged citizens.

This was King's version of black Americans' continued quest for absorption, to lose himself in an Americanism he was never permitted to enjoy in order to be himself, to realize himself. The bourgeois homogenization that Dorothy Day deplored in her radicalism was what King sought for blacks in his centrism. For Day and other leftist intellectuals like her, Americanization was the curse of a conformity of consumption. For King and the civil rights leaders, Americanization was the golden door that would open to political and economic power for blacks. Indeed, as Day notes that schools are the centers for this Americanization process, it is worth remembering that her book was written two years before the Brown decision that declared segregated schools illegal. With schools being declared the battleground for the creation of a color-blind society, the process of the complete Americanization of the Negro was now launched with a vengeance. The irony for the civil rights movement was that the Americanization of the Negro rather wound up calling into the question both the process of Americanization and the presumed meaning of the African American presence in American life. In the end, America did not validate black folk as much as black folk wound up validating American democracy.

At first, King may not have realized this implication in the movement, but it became clearer later as his philosophy of redemptive love developed and as his politics became more explicitly leftist or anticapitalist. The irony for Martin Luther King was that the man who started out as a bourgeois centrist became the major force behind the invention of the new popular front in the 1960s and the all-out ideological attack on Americanism as symbolized by—as this new popular front construed things—racism, militarism, and corporate power.

King first tried to create a new popular front with the March on Washington in 1963, an event designed to pull together a coalition of liberal white intelligentsia, Jews, labor unions, liberal Catholics and Protestants, Bohemians and Beats, old social justice radicals of the 1930s, and, of course, blacks to form an antiracism, anti-right-wing political movement. Two hundred and fifty thousand people attended, and 60,000 were white. Here was a version of King's Beloved Community, as he called it, and to many it resembled nothing so much as a kind of leftist utopia.[6] This coalition was to be buttressed on one side by the antiracist assaults of the new wave of sociology, slavery historiography, anthropology. On the second side, it was to be buttressed by the new innovations in popular music with rock and roll, the return of the radical folk music of the 1930s with Dylan, Ochs, Seeger, Odetta, Joan Baez, Buffy Sainte-Marie, and politically self-conscious jazz, all of which extolled the romanticized, even sentimentalized virtues of miscegenation, ethnic consciousness, committed youth, the working-class life, and a bourgeois vision of the liberated artist. By 1965, black popular music, led by Motown Records, had so successfully crossed over that *Billboard* quit running its Rhythm and Blues and Black Music chart. On the third side, the new popular front was to be supported by an activist federal government, particularly activist executive and judicial branches with the Kennedy administration and the Warren court.

It should not seem odd that there was such a huge cultural component for King's new popular front. By the 1950s, black people had become a considerable cultural force in the United States. Indeed, King's fame through his leadership of the Montgomery bus boycott was made possible largely because of the cultural power, the cultural charisma of the Negro. It may be that blacks wielded very little political or economic power in the United States, but they were a significant cultural presence and questions of politics in the United States had relentlessly, since the turn of the century, become more and more questions of culture to be played out in the cultural realm. Norman Mailer's influential 1957 essay "The White Negro" portrayed blacks in a stereotypical light, but it did in fact suggest that blacks were central in the radical transformation of American culture. As Mailer wrote about hipsterism as the transformation of American values: "And in this wedding of the white and the black it was the Negro who brought the *cultural* dowry" (emphasis mine).

The fact that King gave this new popular front a Christian mission was strategically of the utmost importance if the movement was ever to have legitimacy with mainstream liberals and moderates and carry blacks along as well. It was genius of King that he was able to convince so many for so long, as the brilliant black theologian Howard Thurman observed, that racism was not simply un-American in some provincial sense of being against our creed of fair play but was, in fact, a sin against God and that it jeopardized America's special destiny as the new Israel. The major problem that was to dog King until his death in April 1968 was that he could never entirely shake being seen as something of an inadvertent sellout by the younger black radicals, in part because of the very Christian rhetoric that was needed to keep King's coalition alive and keep King vital and distinct on the civil rights scene. The Kennedy assassination, the escalation of the war in Vietnam, the sex revolution, the illegal drug revolution, the emergence of black power, and the nihilistic violence of the black urban riots forced King to reinvent his position and to try to reinvent this new popular front when he gave his 1967 anti–Vietnam War speech at

Riverside Church in New York. By this time, after failed campaigns in Albany, Georgia and Chicago, a moderately successful but costly one in Birmingham, somewhat successful campaigns in Danville, Virginia, and St. Augustine, Florida, and a memorable march from Selma to Montgomery, King had come to the realization that the "vast majority of white Americans are racists." He also saw racism as connected to capitalism and both as the instruments of American neocolonialism. Most of this sort of thinking was stock leftist criticism of American foreign policy of the middle and late 1960s. Despite his continued rhetoric of centrism, that is, of redemptive love and nonviolent direct action (King, after all, was never seen by either the radical left or Black Power advocates as anything other than a bourgeois social reformer till his death), it was clear to everyone that he was now obviously a democratic socialist and a fairly frustrated man.[7]

His last campaign, meant to bring blacks and whites together, the Poor People's march, of which virtually no one at SCLC approved and which he did not live to see, was called by King "a class struggle." He did not have nearly the set of historical circumstances, let alone the moral and political authority to make such a popular-front coalition work in 1967 as it had in 1963. Four years during this extremely accelerated period in American history changed the entire landscape in which King operated, and although, by 1967, he was still enormously useful to the new left, he was virtually useless to bourgeois liberals who opposed his stand against the war, and his position was eroding in the black community, although, of course, because he was clergyman and a man who sacrificed so much for his people, he still was held in high regard. King simply was unable, at this point, to make the rhetorical or symbolic linkage between American exceptionalism and black exceptionalism as he had in the past. Perhaps it was ego, as Carl Rowan suggested in 1967. King was the most influential black person in America at the time. Did he think that whites would really listen to him about the Vietnam War? I doubt if he necessarily thought they would, as they had not really listened to him about anything else. For blacks, by 1967 King no longer was seen as the man with a realistic or compelling solution. Within a period of ten years, from the end of the Montgomery bus boycott in 1956 to the Selma march of 1965, nonviolent direct action and redemptive love had virtually run their course as a political tool for black people in the United States. As Marcus Garvey wrote in October 1919, "No mercy, no respect, no justice will be shown the Negro until he forces all other men to respect him." And for many black people, it seemed impossible to think that any real respect or justice would be gained from nonviolence. Despite the fact that King's actions had produced the Civil Rights Act of 1964 and the Voting Rights Act of 1965, the virtual destruction of the most overt forms of discrimination, and a higher regard for black Americans in the world than they had ever before enjoyed as a result of this extraordinary protest movement, most blacks felt that they had seen few tangible results—drugs, rampant violence, joblessness, utter cultural isolation, single parenthood, and police brutality wracked most northern ghettos—and the white backlash against the gains of the civil rights movement was considerable and vehement. King hardly seemed like a man who was in control of the forces he had set loose. Indeed, King had set loose forces from both the left and the right over which he had no control whatsoever—and which made any seeming centrism for him impossible, if he was to retain any sense of trust from the black community.

"We'll meet on edges soon," folksinger Bob Dylan sang, and that is precisely what King did: he forced various elements of American society to meet on edges, on the very edges of sanity, on the very edges of the new frontier, the urban street. It was in the streets of the cities, north and south, where King through his demonstrations and the energy they set loose had the citizens of the United States committing violence, enacting political repression, venting self-destructive rage on the one hand and praying to God for endurance, mercy, forgiveness, and transcendence on the other. We enacted before the entire world, as both catharsis and salvation, a tragedy and a farce and in doing so completely unraveled Americanism as a legitimate cultural or moral force. It was not Dorothy Day and white radicalism that made homogenization impossible in America. It was King and the civil rights movement. King, magnificently and inadvertently, defeated and discredited the very ideology that he wished to legitimate by having Negroes walk through the sunlit passageway of American bourgeois life. He was the only black in American history who was created and defeated by the very set of forces that he ultimately unhinged.

There are two other brief observations I would like to make about Martin Luther King. First, that King's movement would not have been possible without the rapid increase in the number of professional, educated blacks that came about after World War II. King was able to lead the movement that he did because he so resembled the very black people who made up the movement's organizing cadre. After World War II, there was an intensified sense of militancy in the black communities of the United States, but even more important, with the G.I. bill there was an incredible increase in the number of educated, professional, or potentially professional blacks. Despite the development of the urban black communities of the early Cold War years and the number of black institutions that existed—small businesses, schools, churches—there was simply an insufficient number of such institutions, an insufficient number of career opportunities in the black communities to absorb these restless black folk, especially black G.I.s, who were bursting the halls of Fisk, Morehouse, Howard, Lincoln, and other black, state, and white private schools. The push for integration was simply a social and economic necessity, a safety valve to relieve this pressure. Fortunately, King came up with a creative way to channel this energy by providing a heroic way for the group to press its claims without being wiped out by violence or co-opted by petty concessions. But, simply put, black folk, by the 1950s, wanted integration for very practical reasons: an expansionist middle class wanted more career opportunities. As Samuel D. Proctor, the distinguished pastor of the famed Abyssinian Baptist Church, observed in his memoir, *The Substance of Things Hoped For,* Martin Luther King was a man who knew he was going places and that he was going to be important when Proctor met him when they were both students at Crozer Theological Seminary. King did not lack either confidence or ego when he was a seminary student. He was simply waiting for his opportunity, for his moment. He was fortunate to have been born in the historical circumstance that surrounded him with a large number of black men and women who were just like him in that regard, ambitious for the main chance.

The second observation is that King was deeply influenced by two black athletes, Jackie Robinson and Muhammad Ali. Robinson, as mentioned earlier, signed to play for the Brooklyn Dodgers in 1945, thus becoming the first black ballplayer in the major leagues in the twentieth century. King was then sixteen years old, a sports fan, and still at an age susceptible to hero worship. Robinson, a tough, tense, competitive man who bristled at the slightest hint of offense from whites, endured a barrage of insults from many white fans and from white ballplayers on opposing clubs, which nearly drove him to a nervous breakdown and prematurely grayed his hair. He felt he was a freak for having to endure this treatment without expressing his rage. Robinson, after all, was nearly kicked out of the U.S. Army during the war because he refused to sit in the back of a Jim Crow bus that served his army base. But his endurance was extremely important in helping to pave the way for black acceptance in major-league baseball. What King learned from Robinson is incalculable. King knew about Gandhi's nonviolent protest in India; most black people did, as Gandhi was regularly written about in black newspapers throughout the 1930s and 1940s. But King may have thought that such a method would work only in a country where the whites were in the minority, were essentially a colonizing presence who did not have to look forward to the prospect of actually living with their former subjects as equals. Robinson's endurance taught King that nonviolent protest could be effective in a situation where whites were in the majority. But it was of the utmost importance that in nonviolent protest, black people not look submissive. Robinson was used to being around whites, having grown up in Pasadena and attended UCLA as a star athlete, so he was not intimidated by playing on the same field with them and against them. Robinson looked enraged as a ballplayer, and his controlled rage gave him a nearly transcendent dignity as he was clearly morally superior to those who tried to break him. With the right kind of people, nonviolent protest need not make black people look like they are afraid to fight. After all, Uncle Tom himself, a big, burly, barrel-chested man according to Stowe's description, was not supposed to give the reader the impression that he was afraid or unable to fight. The point of her novel would be lost on white readers if Tom simply didn't fight because he was afraid of whites. He didn't fight in obedience to a higher principle. Everyone knew Robinson could fight back and had the courage to fight back. He *chose* not to and that made all the difference. Moreover, Robinson's integration of baseball graphically demonstrated that it was possible for integration to work, for blacks and whites to be able to work together on a team as equals. It was extremely important, as King well knew, that Americans had this example before King began his movement.

Muhammad Ali was an important influence late in King's career and surely was one of the figures who convinced King to take his stance against the war. Ali's youth, his determination to stand against the draft and take the punishment, his influence among blacks as a popular athlete greatly appealed to King, even though King did not like the Nation of Islam. Partly King's stand against the war was to prevent losing his moral and political influence with young black people who were likely to admire Ali. Partly King's stand was a tribute to Ali and King's subtle attempt at a kind of rapprochement with the Muslims, at least to the extent that they could all be against an unjust war and against American militarism. King gave his famous anti–Vietnam War sermon on April 4, 1967, and Ali refused induction into the U.S. Army on April 28, 1967. So, how did one event influence the other? It must be remembered that Ali's draft problem was headline news across the nation at least a year before King's speech. For instance, it was in February 1966 that Ali was quoted in papers around the country as saying, "Man, I ain't got no quarrel with them Vietcong." It must also be remembered that it was headline news in March 1966 when Ali officially filed for conscientious-objector status. This too was nearly a year before King's speech. Indeed, King secretly met Ali in Louisville in early 1967.

Ali was also the culmination of a politicized black youth movement that started in 1960 with the student sit-in crusade. King did not initiate the student sit-in movement. In fact, the students were not impressed with him when they first met him, derisively calling him "De Lawd." His alliance with them was uneasy. SNCC, the Student Nonviolent Coordinating Committee, formed in 1960, eventually disavowed nonviolent direct action and redemptive love. Yet it was King, more so than any other leader except Ella Baker, who set the entire student movement in motion and, in effect, politicized American youth culture. The civil rights movement was a youth movement—indeed, with so many restless baby boomers that what King did in starting direct-action protests was give many young people, black and white, a sense of identity, purpose, and, finally, adventure. There was an undeniable thrill, even glamour, in the valor and commitment that the street demonstrations and the voter-registration drives demanded.

"In America," James Baldwin wrote, "life seems to move faster than anywhere else on the globe and each generation is promised more than it will get: which creates, in each generation, a furious, bewildered rage, the rage of people who cannot find solid ground beneath their feet." King's failure, like that of the other integrationists, was that he promised more than he could deliver to a new generation of blacks. Like other American prophets, he also promised more than God would deliver in this world— neither complete fulfillment nor utter destruction. King did do something no other black leader had done, no other American leader had really done. He gave a younger generation of blacks a sense of honor, ironically fulfilling an Uncle Tom archetype, for no other African American generation would be so tempered by the chiliastic possibilities inherent in war. No other African American generation would be so shaped by the chiliastic possibilities of its own American fate. No other American generation, bereft of its belief in piety, would be, alas, so disillusioned by the cost of our uneasy racial peace.

Notes

1. It is interesting to note, in this regard, the quotation used by Lerone Bennett in his biography of King, *What Manner of Man,* from an article by Drs. Frederic Solomon and Jacob R. Fishman entitled "Youth and Social Action: Nonviolence in the South," which describes why black youth of the sit-in movement in 1960 were inspired by King's leadership during the Montgomery bus boycott of 1955–56:

> [The Montgomery boycott] occurred when many of these students were about fifteen years old, two years after they heard the Supreme Court tell them that their anger against segregation was justified and sanctioned. Young people all over the South were greatly impressed with the Montgomery boycott. They felt it was a lesson in the practical and emotional "advantages of direct action" in expressing legitimate Negro discontent. Martin Luther King became the image of an assertive male assuming freedom of action with dignity and achieving respectful recognition through successful struggle with the white community (i.e. male community). *In a sense he became the figure that the Negro adolescents wished their fathers might have been and as such became incorporated as part of their ego-ideals.* [Emphasis mine.]

2. Baldwin was never completely sold on the idea of nonviolence or redemptive love, although the latter was certainly a theme in many of his works—that is, the redemptive power of a taboo-breaking carnal love. Part of Baldwin's attraction to King had to do with the fact that King manipulated symbols and used language that Baldwin, as the son of a preacher and a teenaged preacher himself, knew and liked. But it was for this very reason that he felt uneasy about King. As Baldwin's biographer, David Leemings, put it: "Having gone the church route himself and rejected it, Baldwin was naturally uncomfortable with the idea of a clergyman's leading a revolution." When Baldwin first met King he was uneasy about what the minister would think of his latest novel, *Giovanni's Room.*

3. Race war is an old trope in American political and social rhetoric, dating back to both Thomas Jefferson and David Walker. Historian Brenda Gayle Plummer notes that it was particularly prevalent in the overheated rhetoric of the 1960s of both whites and blacks. King was attempting to defuse it with his own vision of a redeemed America. King understood, unlike Malcolm, that blacks in the United States were a minority. They were not a potential nation or a state and could not bargain as such. Malcolm, on the other hand, did question why blacks could not defend themselves against the violent aggression of the whites. Robert Williams, head of the NAACP in Monroe, North Carolina, argued in *Negroes with Guns* (New York: Marzani and Munsell, 1962) that violence against blacks would lessen if blacks had guns. There was also the question of constitutional rights.

Why shouldn't blacks have guns if other Americans lawfully can possess weapons and use them to defend themselves? Or does their race affect the nature of their citizenship in this regard? King's own message must be understood as existing within this context and part of this larger cultural debate concerning blacks and their citizenship rights.

4. King stole forty percent of the first part and twenty-one percent of the second part of his doctoral dissertation, nearly word for word, from another man's work. Why did he do this? He knew academic culture and academic rules: he went to Morehouse at the age of fifteen and graduated from both there and Crozer Theological Seminary before going to Boston University to do his Ph.D. Did he simply not take scholarly work seriously? He took posing as an intellectual and philosopher seriously enough. King's books were largely composed by several trusted lieutenants, although there are enough King thought-clichés and turns-of-phrases in them to convince anyone that he had a substantial input. King wrote books to bolster his pose as an intellectual. He obviously thought it would make him more in the public eye than a mere southern black Baptist preacher. Like Kennedy, Nixon, Jimmy Carter, Theodore Roosevelt, and Booker T. Washington, King thought that writing books would add gravity and authority to his public image. He also thought that his books could get his philosophy to the public exactly as he wanted it.

5. Howard University professor E. Franklin Frazier's classic sociological examination of the black middle class, *Black Bourgeoisie,* published in 1957, discusses these very character traits or flaws. Ironically, King's *Stride Toward Freedom,* about the Montgomery bus boycott, how he became the leader of it, and the political transformation of the very black middle class Frazier condemns, was published in the same year.

6. The March on Washington had its backstage flare-ups and eruptions. The tone had to be politically moderate, because the coalition could not seem, on its face, like a new popular front, but more or less like segments of the Democratic party. There were deep fissures in this coalition because, already, younger blacks resented the presence of white liberals. But King desperately needed this coalition to last at least for this day. John Lewis of the Student Nonviolent Coordinating Committee (SNCC) was forced to censor his inflammatory speech. Bayard Rustin, earlier, had his role reduced because of his homosexuality and Communist affiliations, at the time a deadly combination. Indeed, Adam Clayton Powell had forced King to reduce Rustin's role in the Southern Christian Leadership Conference (SCLC) for the same reasons. King was under pressure from President Kennedy to jettison Stanley Levison because of his Communist past. The march was certainly, to some extent, shaped by Kennedy, who was in on some of the preliminary planning.

7. There are two observations to make about King's democratic socialism: first, King was, like Frederick Douglass before him during the age of abolition, clearly upset with the practice of Christianity in the United States. Douglass, in his 1845 *Narrative,* for instance, adds an appendix explaining that "between the Christianity of this land, and the Christianity of Christ, I recognize the widest possible difference." All Christianity, north and south, that endorsed and supported slaveholding was wrong. This meant, in effect, that Douglass was condemning most white Christianity in America. Martin Luther King's "Letter from a Birmingham City Jail" expresses this same dissatisfaction. In his *Playboy* interview, he is more explicit: "My personal disillusionment with the church began when I was thrust into the leadership of the bus protest in Montgomery. I was confident that the white ministers, priests, and rabbis of the South would prove strong allies in our just cause. But some became open adversaries, some cautiously shrank from the issue, and others hid behind silence. My optimism about help from the white church was shattered." King's move to overt socialism—he always believed in New Deal welfare statism—was part of his vision of fulfilling the Gospels.

On the other hand, this shift would have been seen by someone like nineteenth-century Catholic polemicist Orestes Brownson as the utter corruption of Christianity itself. In his 1849 essay "Socialism and the Church," Brownson wrote: "Socialism is . . . presented in a form admirably adapted to deceive people, and to secure their support. It comes in Christian guise, and seeks to express itself in the language of the Gospel." He went on to argue sarcastically: "The Christian symbol needs a new and a more Catholic interpretation, adapted to our stage in universal progress. Where the old interpretation uses the words God, church, and heaven, you must understand humanity, society, and earth; you will then have the true Christian idea." Brownson's thesis is that fulfilling the natural or earthly good has nothing to do with saving people's souls. Christianity transcends any earthly political system and cannot be served by reforming social ills. Anyone who argues such, he implies, is a heretic.

For Further Reading

Lewis V. Baldwin, *There Is a Balm in Gilead: The Cultural Roots of Martin Luther King, Jr.* Minneapolis: Fortress Press, 1991.

————, *To Make the Wounded Whole: The Cultural Legacy of Martin Luther King, Jr.* Minneapolis: Fortress Press, 1992.

Taylor Branch, *Parting the Waters: America in the King Years, 1954–1963.* New York: Simon & Schuster, 1988.

David J. Garrow, *Bearing the Cross: Martin Luther King, Jr. and the Southern Christian Leadership Conference.* New York: Morrow, 1986.

Martin Lurther King, Jr., *A Testament of Hope: The Essential Writings and Speeches of Martin Luther King, Jr.* Edited by James M. Washington. San Francisco: HarperSanFrancisco, 1991.

The Mirabals

Dominican Republic, 1960

Chasing the Butterflies

by Julia Alvarez

I first heard about the Mirabal sisters when I was ten years old. It was four months after we arrived in this country. My father brought home a *Time* magazine because he had heard from other exiles in New York City of a horrifying piece of news reported there. My sisters and I were not allowed to look at the magazine. My parents still lived as if the SIM, Trujillo's dreaded secret police, might show up at our door any minute and haul us away.

Years later, doing research for the novel I was writing, I dug up that *Time* article. I stared once again at the lovely, sad-eyed woman who stared back from the gloom of the black-and-white photo. As I read the article, I recovered a memory of myself sitting in the dark living room of that New York apartment secretly paging through this magazine I was forbidden to look at.

It was December 1960. My first North American winter. The skies were gray and my skin was turning a chapped, ashy color that made me feel infected by whatever disease was making the trees lose all their leaves. Every evening my sisters and I nagged our parents. We wanted to go home. They answered us with meaningful looks that we couldn't quite decipher. "We're lucky to be here," my mother always replied. "Why?" we kept asking, but she never said.

We had arrived in New York City on August 6, 1960. My father had participated in an underground plot against our dictator, Trujillo. The plot had been uncovered and we had barely escaped capture. We were lucky to be in the United States.

When my father read of the murder of the Mirabal sisters, he must have felt a shocking jolt at what he had so narrowly missed. The sisters were members of that same underground he had bailed out of in order to save his life. Here, just four months after we had escaped, they were murdered on a lonely mountain road. They had been to visit their jailed husbands, who had been transferred to a distant prison so that the women would be forced to make this perilous journey.

And so it was that my family's emigration to the United States started at the very time the Mirabal story ended. These three brave sisters and their husbands stood in stark contrast to the self-saving actions of my own family and of other Dominican exiles. Because of this, the Mirabal sisters haunted me. Indeed, they haunted the whole country. They have become our national heroines, and November 25, the day they were killed, has been declared by the United Nations the International Day Against Violence Against Women.

But I did not become personally involved in their story until a trip I made to the Dominican Republic in 1986. A woman's press was doing a series of postcards and booklets about Latina women, and they asked me if I would contribute a paragraph about a Dominican heroine of my choice. The Mirabal sisters came instantly to mind. Looking for more about them, I visited Dominican bookstores and libraries, but all I found was a historical "comic book." It was disconcerting to read about heroines with balloons coming out of their mouths. On the other hand, any shoeshine boy on the street or campesino tilting his cane chair back on a coconut tree knew the story of the Mirabal sisters. "*Las muchachas,*" everyone called them. The girls.

When I complained to a cousin that I couldn't find enough formal information about them, she offered to introduce me to someone who knew someone who knew one of the Mirabal "children." Six orphans—now grown men and women—had been left behind when the girls were murdered. That's how I met Noris, the slender, black-haired daughter of the oldest sister, Patria. In her early forties, Noris had already outlived her mother by six years.

Noris offered to accompany me on my drive north to visit the rich agricultural valley where the girls had grown up. She would take me through the museum that had been established in their mother's house, where the girls had spent the last few months of their lives.

What happened on that trip was that the past turned into the present in my imagination. As I entered the Mirabal house, as I was shown the little alcove outside where Trujillo's secret police gathered at night to spy on the girls, as I held the books Minerva treasured (Plutarch, Gandhi, Rousseau), I felt my scalp tingle. It was as if the girls were watching me. Here is a page from the journal that I kept on that trip:

> In the bedroom: The little clothes that the girls had made in prison for their children are laid out on the beds. Their jewelry—bracelets, clamp earrings, the cheap costume type—lies on the dresser under a glass bell that looks like a cheese server. In the closet hang their dresses. "This one was Mami's," Noris says, holding up a matronly linen shift with big black buttons. The next one she pulls out she falls silent. It's more stylish, shirtwaist style with wide blue and lavender stripes. When I look down, I notice the pleated skirt has a bloodstain on its lap. This was the dress Patria carried "clean" in her bag the day she was murdered so she could change into something fresh before seeing the men.
>
> María Teresa's long braid lies under a glass cover on her "vanity." There are still twigs and dirt and slivers of glass from her last moments tumbling down the mountain in that rented Jeep. When Noris heads out for the next room, I lift the case and touch the hair. It feels like regular real hair.
>
> We walk in the garden and sit under the laurel tree where "the girls used to sit." Noris says it is too bad that I am going to miss meeting Dedé.
>
> That is the first I hear there is a fourth sister who survived.

Dedé was away in Spain and wouldn't be back until after I had returned to the States. Maybe the next trip, Noris said. "Meanwhile, there are a lot of people you can meet now."

"It's just for a paragraph on a postcard," I reminded her, for I was a little ashamed to be taking so much of her time.

She waved my politeness aside. "It will inspire you," she promised me. Indeed. Maybe she could sense that more than a postcard was already cooking in my head.

One of those people I met was the dynamic and passionate Minou, daughter of Minerva Mirabal. She was four years old on the day her mother was killed. *I remember her sitting in that chair. I remember her leaning down to kiss me, laughing.* Eventually, Minou would share with me a folder of the love letters her parents had written each other during their many separations. Among them, letters they had smuggled back and forth in prison:

> My life, I send you this pencil so you can write me. Tell me everything. Don't keep a sorrow from me.

———⬲———

> Adored one, how many times haven't I thought about our last night together, how full of presentiments we were. I've asked myself a thousand times if I shouldn't have done something to escape capture. What a painful experience this has been. *¡Dios mío!* And then, when I knew you and your *compañeras* had been caught, I wanted to die. I could not bear that large, cruel moral torture of knowing you were suffering what I was suffering. Oh, what long days, what interminable days. All I can do is fill myself with illusions. To be asleep in your arms, my head on your breast, breathing the fresh smell of your skin, our limbs confused in a tender embrace. *¡Vida mía! Tu Manolo.*

I also met Marcelo Bermúdez, another member of the underground who was in the torture prison with the other men. Again, from my journal:

> Marcelo tells the story of the day the girls were captured and brought to the torture prison. The men were already there, naked, packed in cells behind thick walls of stone, silent and afraid. All of a sudden, the girls spoke out in code and the prisoners took heart. "We are the butterflies!" (*Las Mariposas,* their code name.) "We are here with you. If any of you would like to identify yourselves, do so now." Marcelo said that voices started to call out, "I am the Indian of the Mountains." "I am the Hunter of the North Coast." And so on. That's how the group found out that people believed long dead were still alive.

Back in the capital, I recounted the story for my aunt and cousin. "What did the guards do?" my aunt asked.

I had been so caught up in Marcelo's story that I couldn't remember what he had said had actually happened. "Let's see," I told my aunt. And I think that's when I realized that I was bound to write a novel about the Mirabals rather than the biography I had been vaguely contemplating.

———⬲———

But after I wrote my Latina-postcard paragraph, I put the project away. The story seemed to me almost impossible to write. It was too perfect, too tragic, too mythic, too awful. The girls' story didn't need a story. And besides, I couldn't yet imagine how one tells a story like this. *Once upon a holocaust, there were three butterflies.* It sounded maudlin, both reductive and inflated, junky. A paragraph of this stuff was quite enough.

What I was forgetting—and not forgetting—was the fourth sister. It was my curiosity about her that led me back to the Mirabal story. In 1992, during my annual trip "home," I met her—the surviving sister. Dedé, as everyone calls her, invited me out to the house where she and her sisters had grown up and where she still lives.

This meeting opened up the story for me. It was late afternoon, the light falling just so, a deepening of colors in the garden, the rockers clacking on the wooden patio floor. Dedé, very modern in black culottes, a hot-pink shirt, wire-rimmed glasses, recalled this and that in a bright, up-beat voice as if it were the most normal thing to have had three sisters massacred by a bloody dictator and live to drink a lemonade and tell about it. I realized this was her triumph. She had suffered her own mar-tyrdom: the one left behind to tell the story.

It was after this meeting that I decided, once and for all, to write a novel about the Mirabal sisters. I wanted to understand the living, breath-ing women who had faced all the difficult challenges and choices of those terrible years. I believed that only by making them real, alive, could I make them mean anything to the rest of us.

And so I began to chase the butterflies. With my husband, Bill, at the wheel of our rented car, we traversed the island, meeting the people and visiting the places that had been a part of the girls' lives. There were always surprises.

In the National Archives I combed for information about the Trujillo regime. I found many volumes missing and the radio distracting. The "li-brarians" (two young girls doing each other's nails) offered to help. We found a stack of yellowing *El Caribe*s. In the one published the day the girls were killed, November 25, 1960, a warm day was forecast throughout the island with possible rains in the north. A Japanese doctor had regis-tered a machine that proves that human beings snore in thirty different patterns. In *Confidencialmente* it was reported that everyone has the same measurement at the fattest part of the calf as at the neck. María Teresa, the youngest sister, might have read her horoscope for the day: *Libra, Do you* *realize how much effort and materials you've lost? Try to find a way to save your efforts.* Her two sisters had better luck predicted: *Pisces, This is your lucky time. Neptune is now in a benevolent angle for your sign.*

Leaving the capital and driving north, we stopped at Salcedo. I wanted to see the church where the girls had gone to mass, gotten married, baptized their children, mourned their father. From Dedé, as well as from local campesinos, I had heard about Patria's legendary faith. Indeed, in the purse Patria carried the day of her murder I had found her small prayer book. It was held together with a rubber band, the binding falling apart from constant use. Tucked between the pages were scraps of paper with handwritten prayers that Patria had either composed herself or written down as especially efficacious. One to San Marco de León for protection against imminent danger made tears come to my eyes.

Were the other sisters religious? Dedé had raised an eyebrow when I questioned her. "The rest of us were up and down," she admitted. But she confessed that those last few months Minerva began finding her religion again. "When she saw the priests entering the movement, her faith found faith again. It made Patria so glad. Her prayers were answered. Minerva had wanted Patria to join one revolution, the one they would fight with arms. And Patria wanted her sister to join the other revolution, the one you fight with the spirit."

In Salcedo, Bill and I found the church that had housed the girls' passionate or turbulent life of faith. It showed no signs of either commotion: a gray adobe with a red bell tower, quaint and pretty, a place for fairy tales. We wanted to see the inside, but the big wooden doors were locked. We stopped an old man who asked Bill in Spanish if he was a priest. *Cura,* one who cures? Bill deduced. Bill, a doctor, nodded, "*Sí, cura.*" No, I shook my head. "Honey, he's asking you if you're a priest."

"He's not a priest," I said. Then, more bluntly, "He sleeps with me."

"That's okay," the old man said, slapping Bill on the back. Way to go.

We found out why priesthood and pleasure didn't necessarily jar the old man. In order to get inside the locked church, we had to find the priest with the key. He wasn't in the rectory, the old man told us, but over in the discotheque. Bill and I looked at each other, daring each other not to laugh.

A young woman came out on the sidewalk. Her mother owned the pharmacy behind us. Did we want to come in and get out of the sun? Many thanks, but we were headed to the discotheque to find the priest so we could get inside the church. She was too polite to ask what we were up to. But I offered her our story. I was interested in the Mirabals. I wanted to visit the church where they had been married and had gone to mass. The mother came to the door from behind the counter. If you're interested in the Mirabals, why don't you go talk to Doña Leila? She lives right across the street.

Who's Doña Leila? my look said.

"Their aunt. She knew the girls since they were this high." The proprietress of the pharmacy gestured toward her thongs.

"Let's go," Bill said. He had understood enough Spanish to know we were being invited into another story.

So that's how we met the girls' aunt, and how we met many others who had been important to the Mirabal sisters. We even got the priest to come out of the discotheque. ("I get invited to these darn things I have to go to," he explained himself.) He opened the church doors, chatting all the while about his parishioners. "By the way," he asked—and my ears had learned to perk up at the phrase in Pavlovian anticipation of a choice tip or tidbit—"do you know one of Minerva's *compañeras* in prison lives in town? Doña Sina. Shall I give you an introduction?"

Just past the town of Salcedo, we turned off the main road and headed down a dirt road shaded by a canopy of interlacing *amapola* branches. Here and there we stopped to admire one of the lovely *ranchos,* small wooden houses painted bright Island colors with Victoriana bric-a-brac on the gables and shutters of tiny wooden slats for windows. A man and, in a moment, a woman, who had been tying a scarf stylishly around her head, stepped out of one of the *ranchos.* Her makeup matched the extravagant colors of some of the houses: bright lipstick and heavy eyeliner with little tadpole tails at the corners of her eyes. Did we want to come inside the gate?

We sat on their veranda and told them what we were after. We had heard that down this road we'd find Patria's husband's farm. It had been a magnificent, thriving spread, but when the girls were captured, the house was destroyed and the farm confiscated. Did they know where the place was?

Why, of course they knew where the González farm was! "We're all related," the woman explained. "Their mother and my paternal grandmother . . ." They went on to recount how the girls' deaths were reported the very next day in *El Caribe* as a car accident. "We felt those girls' deaths.

Trujillo pretended his hands were clean. Such a tragic accident, he said when he was here. Oh yes, he was here. He made us throw him a big party. And the girls not a month in the ground. Imagine, all of us dressed up like there was something to celebrate, our hearts so heavy, *ay.*"

They directed us to follow the road till it came to a dead end. There we would find what was left of the farmhouse.

You can't miss it: seven concrete pillars stand in the middle of a field. In what would have been the backyard, we could make out the water tank. We climbed over the barbed wire, walked toward the front steps, still visible, past two toppled concrete urns where I imagined Patria grew her sweet-smelling jasmine. She loved flowers.

Bill and I stayed close, stunned at the sight of a great house fallen. Wandering back toward the fence, we found a grapefruit tree with low-hanging branches. We picked one, peeled it, and ate the bittersweet fruit.

At the opposite end of the island in the dry and desertlike northwest, we visited Monte Cristi, the hometown of Manolo Tavárez, Minerva's husband. After they were married, Minerva and Manolo lived there with his parents before moving into their own little "humble house." It was from their own house, one they would never return to live in, that both were taken into custody by the SIM. We walked the hot, dusty streets wondering how we would ever find the house. At the square, we approached an elderly, seated gentleman wearing a Panamá hat and smoking a cigar. Would he happen to know the house where Minerva Mirabal and her husband, Manolo Tavárez, had lived? He looked us over, deciding. Then, he pointed across the street at a tiny pea-green house. "They lived there!" My mouth dropped.

He let that sink in a minute. Then, patting his *guayabera* pocket as if to make sure he was all there, he stood up. "Come on, I'll show you the place. I live there now."

And so it was that we went inside the house in which Minerva spent the last of her married days. Everywhere we went, it seemed we could reach out and touch history. And always there were plenty of living voices around to tell us all their individual versions of that history.

Even the grim trip on the mountain road where the girls were killed brought out the storytellers. Here Trujillo had built one of his many "mansions," kept fully staffed and ready in case El Jefe should decide to drop in without notice. Usually he brought a young lady guest he wanted to try out.

We parked in a shallow ditch off the narrow road and looked up at the crest of the hill and the abandoned house. The gate with the five stars was locked. Two young men appeared out of nowhere: a tall one in a gaudy, disco-fever type shirt and another one with a crippled foot. He walked with a crude crutch, maneuvering easily to show us the way up an incline to a break in the wall. We climbed the mossy, cobbled driveway that had once, I'm sure, been scrubbed by caretakers on hands and knees.

It was here, the boys told us, that the girls were brought after their Jeep had been stopped on the mountain road. El Jefe was waiting for them inside, the boys said. He wanted to have his way with them, especially with the one who had slapped him when he was fresh with her at a dance.

"That would have been Minerva," I said.

"Then, they say, he gave each sister to one of his SIM to terminate."

"Which one went first?" I wanted to know.

"We don't know things like that," the tall, more self-assured one told me.

"Over there." They pointed into the lower garden full of tall grass. "Some stories say they were killed there. Then, they put them in the Jeep with their dead driver. And they drove it up that road there, see." They indicated a steep road that led from the few side-by-side thatched huts they called "the town."

"It was already dark by then," the one with the crutch said. "They pushed the Jeep over the side of the mountain to make it look like an accident."

"Many of the old people heard the crash," the tall one said. "You want to talk to someone who remembers?"

My heart was too full in this grim place. The night was falling. The overgrown garden, the brick buildings, the padlocked doors, the mossy stones that rang with our footsteps were ominous. I said we had to go.

Down below, on the road, the villagers swarmed around our car. Two giggly girls with spreads of missing teeth approached us. Somebody had told them the gringo and his lady were going to make a movie about the Mirabals. "This town needs money," an old grandmother nodded at me. "Let us all be in the movie."

"Okay," I promised them. "If they make the movie, you can be in it." There was general applause, good-bye slaps on the car as Bill and I drove away.

As we descended the mountain, I felt as if we had traveled the whole route of their lives to the place where they had been struck down. And now that I had come to love the girls in my head, I didn't want them to be dead.

"Where to tomorrow?" Bill asked. Maybe a plan would brighten both our spirits.

"Home," I said. I meant Vermont. It was time to hole up and write the novel about the Mirabals that would become *In the Time of the Butterflies.*

¡Que vivan Las Mariposas!

For Further Reading

Julia Alvarez, *In the Time of the Butterflies.* Chapel Hill, NC: Algonquin Books, 1994.

NATE SAINT, JIM ELLIOT, ROGER YOUDERIAN, ED MCCULLY, AND PETER FLEMING

Ecuador, 1956

A Cloud of Witnesses

by STEVE SAINT

As I made my final approach to the short jungle airstrip, I could tell I was coming in a little high. I pushed the flap lever all the way down, but it still wasn't going to be enough to get me down on the tiny mud-and-grass strip. I decided to pick up speed, staying on the approach glide path to get the feel for my next try. I had just spent three weeks building a new airstrip with the Huaorani people of Ecuador, but this was my first landing in Huaorani/Auca territory, and this little strip wasn't exactly what the engineers had in mind when they designed this Cessna 172. Racing down the field just ten feet in the air, I could clearly see the faces of the Huaorani people lining the strip. As I pulled up and banked to the left to start another approach, I could see the river and what is left of the sandbar where my father, Nate Saint, had made his first approach, the very first approach ever in Huaorani territory, just forty years ago. He and fellow missionaries Jim Elliot, Ed McCully, Pete Fleming, and Roger Youderian had set up camp on that little sandbar in hopes of making contact with the primitive Aucas, known for their fierce infighting and hatred of outsiders. The five missionaries had a deep burden to share the gospel message with a people known only for hunting and killing. Their initial friendly contact ended in death by spearing.

On my second try, I was right on the numbers. Crossing the final bushes, I cut the power and the wheels touched down solid, just ten feet from the mark I had chosen. I hopped out to say hello, but I was in a hurry to take off again before the afternoon thunderheads started to drop their torrential rains and trap my little plane in mud, making a takeoff impossible. Dad, I remembered, had flown the Piper Family Cruiser off the beach each afternoon for much the same reason while awaiting the first contact with the "savages," as the Quechua word *auca* means. So much was the same and yet circumstances were so different! The past three weeks I had been carving a new airstrip out of the virgin jungle with "the people" (which is what their own Huaorani word means), some of whom had murdered my father and his friends just before my fifth birthday. Mincaye was one of them. Mincaye, with whom I had just gone hunting, who laughed and joked about everything, who had tried the hula hoop on his first friendly contact with the outside: he had been on the beach that fateful day in 1956. There was no laughing on that visit. Dyuwi, shy, sweet Dyuwi, who hung around our camp each night waiting for a break in the conversation so he could thank *Wangongi* (creator God) for keeping us safe from falling trees, Konga ants, and poisonous snakes: he too had been there. Just a teenager then, and certainly just as shy, he was nevertheless an up-and-coming killer who knew what they had come to do and went about it—no doubt with the same vigor I had seen him demonstrate on a huge stump he'd been working to clear from our landing strip for the last three days. Kimo, who brought his canoe full of provisions so we would have plenty to eat while we worked on the strip, had also been there in 1956. He told me that the last of the five young *cowodi* (foreigners/strangers) had fled across the river, away from the attack, and instead of fleeing into the jungle and safety, had climbed onto a log and called in poor Huao, "We just came to meet you. We aren't going to hurt you. Why are you killing us?" It was this same gentle Kimo who listened to this plea and then ran a nine-foot hardwood spear through the foreigner's chest.

Why did these gentle, kindhearted men I had been eating, sleeping, and working alongside kill my father and his friends? Why did the missionaries not defend themselves with guns against primitive spears? Why leave five young women widowed, nine children fatherless? What had caused the Huaorani to kill the very men who had called to them from the plane that they were friends, who had exchanged gifts with them on a line dropped from the circling plane?

Historically, every encounter with the Huaorani had ended in death, from the sixteenth-century conquistadors to seventeenth-century Jesuits to nineteenth-century gold and rubber hunters. Toward the end of 1955, the oil companies were closing in on Huaorani territory, an area of about 2,500 square miles. This tribe of unknown size and location was seen to be an irritant to development. Not only had they killed oil company employees who ventured into their territory, but they had even laid in ambush outside the big oil camps and killed unsuspecting employees outside their own quarters. Little was said about the raids made by gun-wielding oil company men against the people, but every Huaorani killing was told and retold in the oil camps until "Auca" savagery and killing prowess gained almost mystical power to strike fear into the hearts of even seasoned jungle workers. Soldiers had been dispatched to protect oil camps and there was talk of a military attempt at wiping out this "nuisance." Confrontation was inevitable, and the question was not would the Huaorani be contacted, but who would contact them and with what intentions. Would the contact group take medicines and go in peace to live among the people, or would they go with poison meat and booby traps and guns to see that the nuisance was eliminated or driven deep into the jungle where it would no longer impede the progress of civilization?

Nate Saint, Jim Elliot, and Ed McCully, three college friends working as missionaries in Ecuador, had a burning desire to literally follow Jesus' command to take the gospel message into all the world. They had prayed for years for this primitive group that had never heard the redemption story of peace with God through the death of Christ. Now the men began to feel they should act soon or perhaps lose the opportunity for peaceful contact. The first challenge was to somehow establish that they were friendly and intended no harm, no easy task when you can't speak a common language or safely get close enough to try communicating in any other way. They didn't know for sure where in the jungles the semi-nomadic Huaorani could be found. My father had generally avoided flying over their territory as he delivered goods to various missionaries in the dense jungle, but as the dry season approached (the time most likely to expose a sandbar big enough to land Dad's small plane) he and Ed flew over the area and spotted one small clearing.

The three men rounded out their team with two more: Pete Fleming, a friend of Jim and Ed's, working in Ecuador with the same mission group, and Roger Youderian, who had been working with the Jívaros, known as the "head shrinkers" of the Ecuadorian jungles. A veteran of the World War II paratroopers, Roger possessed a jungle savvy and an ability to live and travel like the Indians.

These five men were not cast from the same mold. Jim was impetuous but focused. Both a college wrestler and a writer, his good looks and physical strength were matched by a deep introspection. Ed McCully, president of his college class, had played football end and won his senior oratory contest. Everyone expected him to go to law school, but something stronger called him to the jungles of the Amazon. Dad was born into an artist's family but picked up a stray gene. He loved the technical and mechanical aspects of life and wanted to use his interest and skills for a purpose that would honor God and outlast the temporal. Flying support for missionaries was a way to fulfill both of his desires. Pete was the youngest of the group, but in some ways the group's sage. Roger was the guy you sent to do the job when it took dogged determination and a complete willingness to get it done. Five common young men whose unifying distinction was less their inherited abilities or acquired skills than their commitment to seek God's will and to carry out his purposes for their lives. They were aware of the risk they were taking but felt it was justified, though they had no idea then of the impact their martyrdom would someday have.

The men studied oil company reports and talked to everyone they could who might give them additional insight into the Huao culture. They began to develop a plan, knowing there was no way to eliminate all danger, but also realizing they each had families and other responsibilities that dictated caution as well as speed. My father and Ed flew back and forth over the jungle and discovered a tiny clearing. They gleaned a short repertoire of Huao phrases from Dayuma, a Huao girl who had fled almost certain death from intratribal spearings and was living on an hacienda outside Huao territory. My father's sister, Rachel, was living with Dayuma and studying the Huao language, sure that God had called her to someday live with this tribe and teach them how to *walk on God's trail*.

The missionaries began making regular overflights to drop friendship gifts from the plane, calling over a loudspeaker, "We like you. We are your friends." Soon they decided to try the bucket drop, a technique Dad had developed to deliver and retrieve items from missionaries who had no airstrip. He circled his plane overhead in tight circles while a long cord with the goods attached was reeled out behind the plane. Air friction on the basket at the end of the line would make the cord cut to the inside of the circle flown by the airplane, while the weight of the basket caused the cord to fall. When enough line was extended behind the plane, the end of the line would actually hang motionless in the air. Letting out more line at that point would make the line drop straight down, where it could be made to hover just above the ground. The Huaorani tell me that when this technique was used, they understood that the gifts were being deliberately offered and signaled their understanding and desire to continue the exchange by tying on gifts of their own. They remember receiving machetes, a metal ax (a prized possession among people who traditionally used stone axes), brightly colored ribbons, and aluminum cooking pots. In exchange, they returned a Huao comb, a feather headdress, smoked monkey, and even a live parrot, which became my childhood pet.

After making thirteen weekly gift drops, Dad located a small sandbar on the Curaray River. By flying over the sandbar and dropping small paper bags of flour at timed intervals, then repeating the process on his own airstrip at Shell Mera, he measured the sandbar to be 650 feet long. It was only about six miles from the Huaorani settlement, although by trail, it would be many, many miles of arduous trekking up and down ridges and across water. (A Huaorani moving at a fast pace could get there in three to five hours.) On January 2, 1956, Dad flew the four other men in one by one and they set up camp on what they called "Palm Beach." They made repeated flights back and forth to the Huaorani settlement so that the people would figure out that the plane was no longer flying off into the distance but landing in their territory.

After three days of waiting on the beach, the men suddenly saw two naked women step out of the jungle onto the opposite bank. Two missionaries waded out into the river to greet them. When it was apparent the women were being well received, a man joined them on the beach. Dad's journal records that the three Huaorani seemed relaxed and acted in a friendly manner. They shared the missionaries' hamburgers and Kool-Aid and carried on an animated conversation as if their every word were understood. The man, whom the missionaries nicknamed "George," made it obvious that he understood the men had arrived in the *ibo* (Huao for wood bee or airplane) and he wanted a ride. Dad took him for a quick spin, which wasn't enough, and then for a second ride over his settlement, where his people saw him in the plane. Dad recorded that George got so excited that he tried to crawl out the open doorway onto the strut, apparently having no concept of how high they were or how fast they were traveling.

Late in the afternoon, Dad and Pete flew out to a friendly jungle station as usual, to avoid getting trapped by a downpour on the frequently flooding river. Shortly afterward, the young girl went into the jungle as abruptly as she had appeared. Soon "George" inconspicuously followed. The older woman stayed on the beach well into the night. (When the missionaries came down from their tree house in the morning, the coals of her fire were still hot.)

The next day there were no visitors, but in an overflight on January 8, Dad spotted a party of ten Huaorani on their way to the beach. (The jungle growth is too thick to be able to see the trail, so this chance spotting probably occurred as the group crossed the Tiwaeno River.) At noon, Dad radioed to my mother, "Looks like they'll be here for the Sunday afternoon service. This is it! Pray for us. Will contact you again at 4:30, over and out." As soon as 4:30 came without word from the always punctual Nate, Mom knew something was wrong and contacted the other missionary pilot. He flew over the beach the next morning, spotting the plane stripped of its canvas covering and one body facedown in the river. Four days later a weary but tense ground party made up of missionaries, Quechua Indians, and military personnel found the other bodies, identifiable only by their watches, rings, and other personal effects. Photos developed from film found in Dad's camera at the bottom of the river, a diary fished out of his pocket, and his watch, stopped at 3:10, seemed to be all there was to tell about the end of his life.

Many times over the years I have wondered what the end was like. When did they realize they were being attacked? Why didn't they attempt to defend themselves? What went through their minds in those last minutes before losing consciousness? They knew that they were dying on a temporary sandbar in an obscure river in unknown territory. Each surely thought about the wife he was leaving behind, who loved him and would miss him like life itself. They must have pictured the nine children among them, one still unborn, who would wonder what happened to Daddy. I imagine they felt they had failed in their objective of taking the gospel to a needy and murderous tribe, as they lay dying, bodies pierced by the wooden spears of Gikita and Nampa and Kimo and Nimonga and Mincaye and Dyuwi.

⸛⸛⸛

After the murders, my aunt Rachel continued learning the Huao language, taking the apostle Paul's words as a personal promise, "Those who were not told will see, and those who have not heard will understand." Dayuma also believed the words Rachel taught her from the Bible and decided to return to her people, to teach them what she had learned about God and the outside world of the *cowodi*. Less than three years after the massacre, Aunt Rachel and Jim Elliot's widow, Elisabeth, had made contact and were living among the tribe. There they practiced basic medicine and began to notate an oral language in hopes of someday translating the scriptures into *Huao-tidido* (the Huao language).

I grew up in Quito, Ecuador, and enjoyed spending school vacations whenever I could with my aunt Rachel among the Huaorani. Being fatherless did not make me unique there: most others had lost family in intratribal killings. Though I knew which men had killed Dad, it was not something I asked about. According to Huaorani tradition, as my father's oldest son I would be primarily responsible for avenging his death in kind, so I never wanted to appear too interested in the particulars. Even Aunt Rachel, who died in 1994 after thirty-seven years with the Huaorani, knew very few of the details.

But finally, in January 1995, during my fifth visit to build a new airstrip and clinic with the Huaorani in just over a year (this time), I asked the evangelist Dyuwi how many times he had killed before he began to walk on God's trail as a young man. We were sitting outside Dayuma's house in the village of Tonnampade, named after one of my childhood friends, Tonna. He became the first Huao martyr, speared while trying to reach his downriver relatives with the gospel. I sat in the shade with Dyuwi and others, some of us swinging in hammocks and some squatting by an open ground-fire. Children played nearby with clipped-winged birds. In a rush of stories, Dyuwi, Kimo, Dawa, Gikita, and Mincaye, all participants that day on the beach, paid me a high compliment by speaking openly of the killing. They knew that all of us have experienced God's forgiveness and that they had nothing to fear from me. As they recalled those days, it occurred to me how incredibly unlikely it was that the Palm Beach killing took place at all; it is an anomaly that I cannot explain.

Though I was familiar with the story as we knew it from the photographs and diaries, I began to hear of a very different drama being played out within the Huao clearing. Nankiwi (the man called "George" by the missionaries) wanted to take another wife. For several reasons, the young girl's mother and brother disapproved. This made Nankiwi furious and he began to threaten to kill the brother. Their disapproval also frustrated the young girl and she, in typical Huao fashion, made a dramatic case out of her thwarted plans, threatening, "If you won't let me marry, then why should I go on living? I'll just go to the foreigners in the *ibo* and let them kill me." Certainly it was no coincidence that of all the small groups of Huaorani scattered throughout their large territory, this group was the one from which Dayuma had fled, and this very girl was her sister. Being of the same stubborn stock as Dayuma, who had escaped to the fearsome "outside," she set off for Palm Beach. Nankiwi apparently saw this as an opportunity to be alone with her and took off after her. One older woman, seeing what was going on and knowing that discovery of their tryst would probably lead to killings within the group, decided to go along as chaperone.

When my father took Nankiwi for a ride and the rest of the tribe saw him in the plane, they decided to go visit the *cowodi,* too. The next morning, they took the trail for Palm Beach. But before reaching the beach, they ran into Nankiwi and the girl, who were unchaperoned. Her brother, Nampa, flew into a rage and was ready to kill Nankiwi. Apparently to divert attention from his own indiscretion, Nankiwi told the group that the *cowodi* had attacked them and they were fleeing. Scoffing as she told me this, Dawa implied that most of the Huaorani found this hard to believe, since Nankiwi had a reputation as a troublemaker. Someone asked about the older woman; "She had to flee another way," Nankiwi lied. As tempers flared, the oldest man, Gikita, took over. He had lived longer than any of the rest and knew better than any how savage and deceptive the outsiders were. While the group made their way back to the village, Gikita began to recount all the killings that had been committed by outsiders. By the time they got home, all fury at Nankiwi had now been refocused on the missionaries. Gikita and Nampa convinced four others to join them to kill the outsiders.

While they were sharpening spears and working up their fury, the older woman returned from the beach. When she saw the men making spears, she knew Nankiwi had lied to them and she tried to convince them that no one had been attacked. She told them the *cowodi* were completely friendly and meant no harm. Listening to her description of events on the beach, Gikita did not understand all that was going on, but he knew enough about the *cowodi* to know that they had never been friendly before, and he was determined that they should be killed.

What I find hard to explain is that killing the *cowodi* only made sense if they had indeed attacked the three Huaorani, since they were otherwise a wonderful resource for the greatly prized and much needed knives, machetes, axes, and cooking pots. Yet, if they had attacked, according to Gikita's logic, they would certainly attack again, and they obviously had the superior technology of guns and an airplane. The Huaorani killed for various reasons: revenge, anger, frustration, fear. Sometimes it took very little provocation. But they always wanted two things: superiority of force and surprise. In contemplating an attack on Palm Beach they knew they would not have a superior force. Six men with spears were hardly a match for five likely armed *cowodi*. If they killed the *cowodi* they knew they would have to burn their houses, leave their gardens, and flee as they always did after attacks, because they knew that other *cowodi* would come in their *ibo*s and find them. Add to this the fact that five of the six attackers were just teenagers, not seasoned killers, and that one witness to the Friday contact insisted the *cowodi* were friendly. Under these circumstances, it seems hard to believe there ever was an attack, yet there was.

On Sunday afternoon, when the killers finally arrived at Palm Beach, they could see there were five *cowodi* and that they had guns. (We know that the guns, which were primarily intended for protection from animals, were usually kept out of sight. The missionaries had vowed to one another before God that they would not defend themselves against human attack, even in the face of death.) Dyuwi tells me that some of the young attackers, seeing they did not easily outnumber the foreigners, got scared and asked Gikita how they could attack. Gikita said that he would first spear each of the five and then the younger men could finish the job. He sent three women over to the far side of the river to distract and separate the missionaries. This seems to have worked as planned. When two of the women showed themselves, two of the men (Jim and Pete, I imagine, since they knew the language best) waded into the river to greet them. Gikita started to rush the three left on the beach but slipped on a wet log under the leaves of the jungle floor and fell. All his spears hit the ground, making a loud noise. The men on the beach turned to see what the noise was, and the element of surprise, the second critical factor, was now also lost. This was too much for the young attackers and they started to flee. Gikita called them back, saying, "We came to kill them. Now let's finish it or die here ourselves." This seems to have at least halfheartedly rallied the troops. Nampa ran across the beach toward the two men in the river, spearing the larger man in the river through the torso. Kimo showed me how the *cowodi* began to claw at his side "like a *gata* monkey that has been shot with a dart." (This was probably the man trying to get his pistol out of his holster, which had a snap-down cover.) As the foreigner began shooting into the air, one of the two women in the shallow river, Nampa's mother, grabbed the foreigner's arms from behind so Nampa could spear him again. Kimo said that when the woman pulled on the *cowodi*'s arms, Nampa was grazed by a gunshot and fell down hard. According to Dawa, Nampa recovered from this wound before dying a year or so later while hunting.

Gikita says he recognized my father from the many overflights and speared him first. A second foreigner ran to help him and Gikita speared him, too (this was most likely Ed). Mincaye said the third man on the beach ran to the airplane, partially climbed inside, and picked up something like he was going to eat it. Mincaye asked why he would do this, and as he mimicked his action, I could see he must have been picking up the microphone to report the attack. Nimonga speared him from the back, and he fell out of the plane onto the ground. When they showed me how he speared him, I knew the man must have been Roger because that is the angle of the spear that is protruding from Roger's body as it is being towed behind the canoe in the rescue-party pictures.

During the attack, the "smaller" of the two *cowodi* who had been crossing to greet the women rushed to a log on the far side of the river and began calling to the attackers in phrases that Kimo and Gikita say they understood to be "We just came to meet you. We aren't going to hurt you. Why are you killing us?" (This was probably Pete, who, though he was tall, was the thinner of the two men in the river when the spearing started. He also knew the language the best.)

"Why didn't he flee into the jungle?" Mincaye emphatically asked me. "If he had fled, surely he would have lived." Instead, he just waited for Kimo to wade out and spear him.

Dawa, one of the three women, told me she had hidden in the brush throughout the attack, hearing but not seeing the killing of the five men. She told me she had been hit by gun pellets in the wrist and just above the knee. (These must have come from random warning shots fired to scare the attackers, because Dawa was hiding on the far side of the narrow river and the men couldn't have known of her presence.) She then told me that after the killing she saw *cowodi* above the trees, singing. She didn't know what this kind of music was until she later heard recordings of Aunt Rachel's and became familiar with the sound of a choir. Mincaye and Kimo confirmed that they heard the singing and saw what Dawa describes as angels along the ridge above Palm Beach. Dyuwi verified hearing the strange music, though he describes what he saw more like lights, moving around and shining, a sky full of jungle beetles similar to fireflies with a light that is brighter and doesn't blink. Apparently all the participants saw this bright multitude in the sky and felt they should be scared because they knew it was something supernatural. Their only familiarity with the spiritual world was one of fear. (Dawa has said that this supernatural experience was what drew her to God when she later heard of him from Dayuma.)

———— ∞ ————

After the killing, the Huaorani showed their customary disdain for their victims by throwing the men's bodies and their belongings in the river and stripping the plane of much of its fabric covering. When they reached their settlement, they burned their houses and fled into the jungle, fearing the retribution from the outside they were sure would come.

As they repeatedly discussed the raid, one inexplicable question haunted the Huaorani: why hadn't the *cowodi* used their guns to defend themselves? If Nampa and Dawa had not been wounded, the answer would have been quite simple: either the men didn't really have guns or the guns didn't work. After the adrenaline rush of any frightening event, it is easy to question what we think we saw or heard. But the Huaorani were certain that the superficial wounds were unintended, since Nampa was hit only after his mother grabbed the *cowodi's* arms and Dawa knew that no one saw where she was hiding. These wounds, actual evidence that the missionaries were capable of defending themselves and chose not to, were a major factor in the Huaorani men agreeing to allow Aunt Rachel and Elisabeth Elliot to come live with them. They had to know the answer: why would the *cowodi* let themselves be killed rather than kill, as any normal Huaorani would have done? This question dogged Gikita until he heard the full story of why the men wanted to make contact and about another man, Jesus, who freely allowed his own death to benefit all people.

Forty years ago, Gikita was an unusually old man in a tribe that killed friends and relatives with the same zeal and greater frequency than they did their enemies. Now he is nearing eighty years of age and has seen his grandchildren and great-grandchildren grow up without the constant fear of spearings. He has repeatedly asserted that all he wants to do is go to heaven and live peacefully with the five men who came to tell him about *Wangongi,* creator God.

My father and his four friends were not given the privilege of watching their children and grandchildren grow up. I've often wished I could have known my dad as an adult, for Mom and Aunt Rachel have often said our thought processes and mannerisms are much alike. (I would like to have known him even if we were very different.) I have trouble distinguishing what I actually "remember" of him and what I have been told. But I do know that he left me a legacy, and the challenge now is for me to pass it on to my children. Dad strove to find out what life really is. He found identity, purpose, and fulfillment in being obedient to God's call. He tried it, tested it, and committed himself to it. I know that the risk he took, which resulted in his death and consequently his separation from his family, he took not to satisfy his own need for adventure or fame, but in obedience to what he believed was God's directive to him. I suppose he is best known because he died for his faith, but the legacy he left his children was his willingness first to live for his faith.

God took five common young men of uncommon commitment and used them for his own glory. They never had the privilege they so enthusiastically pursued to tell the Huaorani of the God they loved and served. But for every Huaorani who today follows God's trail in part because of their efforts, there are a thousand *cowodi* who follow God's trail more resolutely because of their example. The success withheld from them in life God multiplied and continues to multiply as a memorial to their obedience and his faithfulness.

For Further Reading

Cornell Capa, " 'Go Ye and Preach the Gospel': Five Do and Die" and "The Martyrs' Widows Return to Teach in Jungle." *Life,* January 30, 1956, 10–19, and May 20, 1957, 24–33.

Elisabeth Elliot, "Missionaries Live with Aucas" and "Widow's Jungle Life Amid Husband's Killers." *Life,* November 24, 1958, 23–29, and April 6, 1961, 118–30.

————, *The Savage, My Kinsman.* New York: Harper & Row, 1961.

————, *Through Gates of Splendor.* New York: Harper & Row, 1956.

Russell T. Hitt, *Jungle Pilot: The Life and Witness of Nate Saint.* New York: Harper & Row, 1959.

Olive Fleming Liefeld, *Unfolding Destinies.* Grand Rapids, MI: Zondervan, 1991.

Through Gates of Splendor. Video recording, 22 minutes, 1958. Distributed by World Radio Missionary Fellowship, Opa Locka, FL.

Ethel Wallis, *Dayuma's Story.* New York: Harper & Row, 1960.

DIETRICH BONHOEFFER

Germany, 1945

Watching with Christ in Gethsemane

by MARILYNNE ROBINSON

The German Lutheran pastor and theologian Dietrich Bonhoeffer first put himself at risk in 1933 by resisting the so-called Aryan clause, which prohibited Jewish Christians from serving as ministers in Protestant churches. In 1945 he was executed for "antiwar activity." This included involvement in a scheme to help a group of Jews escape to Switzerland in 1941 and a meeting in Sweden in 1942 with the British bishop George Bell at which he tried to secure Allied support for the planned coup against Hitler now known as the Officers' Plot. In the years between, he helped to create and guide the Confessing Church, a movement of Protestant pastors and seminarians who left the official churches rather than accept their accommodation with nazism.

Bonhoeffer was the son of a large, affectionate, wealthy, and influential family. He distinguished himself early, being accepted as a lecturer in theology at Berlin University in 1928, at the age of twenty-three. From the first his lectures attracted students who shared his religious and political views. The divisions in the churches would also have the effect of surrounding him with committed and like-minded people, "the brothers" as he called them, who seem to have answered fairly well to the exalted vision of the church in the world that was always at the center of his theology. To some degree they must have inspired it, having accepted discipleship at such cost. Many of them would be arrested and imprisoned, or be drafted and die in combat.

Bonhoeffer's family were scholars, scientists, artists, and military officers. His own powerful attraction to "the church"—he might be said always to have used the words in a special sense—is apparent in his earliest writing, and also in his decision to be a pastor rather than an academic. He reacted to the introduction of racial doctrine into the polity of the Protestant churches as heresy and led a revolt against it based on the belief that the so-called German Christians had ceased to be the true church. He was active in European ecumenical circles, with the intention of informing the world about the struggle in Germany and of legitimizing and supporting the dissenters.

By "the church" Bonhoeffer means Christ in this world, not as influence or loyalty but as active presence, not as one consideration or motive but as the one source and principle of life for those who constitute the church. This was the resistance position prepared by the formidable work of the Calvinist theologian Karl Barth, Bonhoeffer's teacher and mentor and another early leader of the opposition to nazism. Barth wrote the Barmen Declaration, which rejected the influence in the church of race nationalism together with all other "events and powers, forms and truths" on the grounds that "Jesus Christ, as He is attested to in Holy Scripture, is the one Word of God, whom we have to hear and whom we have to trust and obey in life and in death." [1]

To claim the authority of Christ in this way is the oldest temptation of Christianity, and full of difficulties no matter how sound the rationale behind such a claim or how manifest its rightness in any particular instance. In his theology—that is, in thought and practice—Bonhoeffer corrects against these difficulties with a very strong bias toward grace. His protest, after all, was against exclusivism in the official church, and the church of his contemplation is utterly broad, indefinite in its boundaries. Yet the basis of his ethics is that Christ wills that the weak and persecuted should be rescued, and he must be obeyed; that Christ is present in the weak and the persecuted, and he must be honored. Bonhoeffer's magnanimity and his inclusiveness—which governed his life and cost him his life—are profoundly Christ-centered. Characteristically, he wrote, "An expulsion of the Jews from the West must necessarily bring with it the expulsion of Christ. For Jesus Christ was a Jew." [2]

Bonhoeffer's life and his thought inform each other deeply. To say this is to be reminded of the strangeness of the fact that this is not ordinarily true. Questions are raised about the consistency of his theology, with the implication that his political activity and his death give his writing a prominence it might not have enjoyed on its own merits. But clearly his experience is the subject of his work. His theology is a study of the obedience he himself attempted, together with his students, colleagues, and friends. In 1932 he wrote, "The primary confession of the Christian before the world is the deed that interprets itself." [3] An obedient act owes nothing to the logic or the expectations of the world as it is, but is affirmed in the fact of revealing the redeemed world. Action is revelation.

Bonhoeffer would object on theological grounds to the suggestion that he earned the grace that seems so manifest in both his life and his writing, but the evidence of discipline, of rigorous reflection, is everywhere and most present in his most personal letters, those written nearest his death. Considering the circumstances of his life, so adversarial and then so besieged, and considering what was taking place in Germany and Europe, it is amazing how little notice he gives to sin or evil, how often he expresses gratitude. The church is described, but not its limits. Grace is described, but not its absence. He will not cease to love the world or any part of it: "When the totality of history should stand before God, there Christ stands." [4]

It is obvious from subsequent events that these brave and brilliant spirits did not teach Hitler to fear theology. Nor do they seem to have rescued the honor of the church, which, in popular memory, is at least as roundly blamed as any other institution for the disaster of fascism. The disappearance of religion in Europe, which Bonhoeffer foresaw, is in fact far advanced—despite him and, since he has been sentimentalized as a prophet, in some part because of him. The heresies he and Barth denounced now flourish independently of even the culture and forms of Christianity, beyond any criticism these might have implied. And we have not learned the heroic art of forgiveness, which may have been the one thing needful.

It seems to me that the harshest irony of Bonhoeffer's life and death lies in the use made of him by many who have claimed his influence. Looked at in the great light of his theology, which is an ethics from beginning to end, he is always, and first of all, a man devoted to the church and to religious arts, forms, and occasions, especially those associated with Lutheran tradition. There can be no doubt that his clarity of purpose, his steadfastness, his serenity, were owed to his very devout habits of mind and of life as well. Indeed, it is precisely in these habits that his mind and life are least to be distinguished from each other. He prayed and meditated and read and studied Scripture hours every day, looked forward joyfully to the events of the liturgical year, and, in prison, joyfully remembered them. He preached a sermon on the day he died.

Yet because he posed certain thoughts to his friend Eberhard Bethge about the relationship of sacred and secular, the actual example of his life is lost to an interpretation that devalues "religion" in the sense of religious art, discipline, and tradition, and the very comforts and resources of piety to which Bonhoeffer in his life and writing never ceased to bear witness. In a letter from prison in which he insists that "my suspicion and horror of religiosity are greater than ever," he says also, "I have found great help in Luther's advice that we should start our morning and evening prayers by making the sign of the cross."[5] The contradiction is not at all intractable. Commenting on his aversion to religiosity he remarks, "I often think of how the Israelites never uttered the name of God." Religiosity is a transgression against God's otherness.

"Religion" in the invidious sense common to Barth and Bonhoeffer exists when, in Barth's words, "the divine reality offered and manifested to us in revelation, is replaced by a concept of God arbitrarily and wilfully evolved by man."[6] For Barth, though perhaps not for Bonhoeffer, falseness of some kind is a universal phenomenon of religious consciousness. In any case, the concept is not far from ideas such as hypocrisy or Phariseeism. It is not difficult to understand why this stinging use of the word *religious* would seem appropriate when most of the religious leaders of Germany were eager to embrace National Socialism. But using the word in this sense is a great source of difficulty and confusion, for example in the understanding of Bonhoeffer's famous phrase "religionless Christianity."

The evolution of thinking associated with his name makes Bonhoeffer himself seem an archaic figure, enthralled by that very piety we in his "world come of age" have learned to find strange and suspect. To the extent that his inspired obedience to Christ, that is, his humane devotion to justice in this world, drew from his piety, it is a resource lost to many who might earnestly hope to be like him. And yet, while the abrupt ferocity of the modern world has, for now, been epitomized in Nazi Germany, it certainly was not exhausted in it. If being modern means having the understanding and will to oppose the passions of collective life that can at any time emerge to disgrace us and now even to destroy us, then one great type of modern man is surely Dietrich Bonhoeffer—more particularly, Pastor Bonhoeffer in his pulpit, Pastor Bonhoeffer at his prayers.

⎯⎯ ∞ ⎯⎯

While he never hesitated in his opposition to the National Socialist and anti-Semitic influences in the official churches, at times Bonhoeffer seems to have been uncertain how to respond to them. In April of 1933 he published an article titled "The Church and the Jewish Question," in which he said, "The church has an unconditional obligation to the victims of any ordering of society, even if they do not belong to the Christian community."[7] This might mean "not just to bandage the victims under the wheel, but to jam a spoke in the wheel itself. Such action would be direct political action." In June of 1933 Karl Barth attacked nazism in a stinging public address and sent Hitler a manifesto of protest. Bonhoeffer, with Pastor Martin Niemöller, a martyr in his own right, organized a Pastors' Emergency League to send uncorrupted ministers to serve in parishes whose ministers were influenced by nazism. About 2,000 pastors associated themselves with these initial acts of resistance. If these tempests among the churchmen seem marginal to the events of the time, it should be remembered how alone they were. Bonhoeffer's article was the *first* such defense of the Jewish people.

Then, in October 1933, Bonhoeffer went to England. He had arranged to serve there as pastor to two German congregations. He did not consult with Barth until he had arrived in London, though it had taken him some time to make the arrangements to leave Germany. When he did write to Barth he very respectfully invited a rebuke, and he got one. Barth told him to return on the next ship, or the one after it. But Bonhoeffer stayed in England for two years. While he was there he made arrangements to go to India to be with Gandhi.

Only by the standards of his subsequent life do these choices seem doubtful. During his time in England he worked to establish support for the religious resistance in Germany. It is consistent with the openness of his views that he considered Gandhi's political actions Christ-like and wished to learn from him. He was a pacifist. He was newly ordained into a tradition he loved deeply and could hardly have wished to attack. And the Bethel Confession, which he wrote with Niemöller, and which declared, "It is the task of Christians who come from the Gentile world to expose themselves to persecution rather than to surrender, willingly or unwillingly, even in one single respect, their kinship with Jewish Christians in the Church, founded on Word and Sacrament,"[8] had been watered down before it was circulated and signed by the dissenting pastors. He might reasonably have questioned the prospects of the religious resistance. And in fact, if it were not for Bonhoeffer, his writing, and especially his death, few would remember there had ever been any such resistance.

In 1935 the Confessing Church was founded, the church of the Protestant dissenters. Seminaries were established, and Bonhoeffer returned to head one of them. Later in the same year Heinrich Himmler decreed that the church and its seminaries were both invalid and that those involved with them were liable to punishment. Finkenwalde, Bonhoeffer's seminary, was closed by the Gestapo in September 1937. Twenty-seven former students were arrested. In February of 1938 Bonhoeffer initiated contact with figures in the political resistance to Hitler.

Through all this Bonhoeffer wrote theology—sermons, lectures, circular letters, and books. In a very great degree his writing is characterized by beautiful iterations of doctrine, a sort of visionary orthodoxy: "History lives between promise and fulfillment. It carries the promise within itself, to become full of God, the womb of the birth of God."[9] To understand his method, one must remember his circumstances. He is asserting the claims of Christ in all their radicalism in order to encourage and reassure those drawn to what became the Confessing Church. At the same time he is chastising those who use Christianity as an escape from the evils of the world and from the duties those evils imply, and he is chastising those who have accommodated their religion to the prevailing culture so thoroughly as to have made the prevailing culture their religion. His object is to make core beliefs immediate and compelling, to forbid the evasions of transcendence and of acculturation. He is using the scandal of the cross to discover the remnant church among the multitudes of the religious.

Because of the authority of his example, we look to Bonhoeffer for wisdom and guidance as to the right conduct of life, though he is perhaps more earnest in nothing than in insisting that there is no freestanding code through which goodness can be achieved. In his unfinished late work called *Ethics,* he says:

> The will of God is not a system of rules which is established from the outset; it is something new and different in each situation in life, and for this reason a person must ever anew examine what the will of God may be. The heart, the understanding, observation, and experience must all collaborate in this task. It is no longer a matter of a person's knowledge of good and evil, but solely the living will of God; our knowledge of God's will is not something over which we ourselves dispose, but it depends solely upon the grace of God, and this grace is and requires to be new every morning. [10]

This is an application of the classic Reformation teaching that no one can do the will of God on the strength of his or her own efforts. It is a statement of the faith that God is present and active in the whole of the world—if he were not, he would not have a will to *be* newly expressed in every situation of life. It seems one should be able to extract a secular ethic from the thinking of a man so generous in his views and so positive in his treatment of the secular world as Bonhoeffer, yet to do so is to defeat his clear intention. "Situation ethics" as a form of relativism is obviously not the point, *because* it is what remains of this idea if the active will of God is factored out of it. Later in the same essay he says, "The world, like all created things, is created through Christ and with Christ as its end, and consists in Christ alone."

A scholar coming across such language in an ancient text would quite certainly identify it as a fragment of a hymn. Language of this kind pervades Bonhoeffer's work, which I think may be described as a meditation on it, and a celebration of it. Great theology is always a kind of giant and intricate poetry, like epic or saga. It is written for those who know the tale already, the urgent messages and the dying words, and who attend to its retelling with a special alertness because the story has a claim on them and they on it. Theology is also close to the spoken voice. It evokes sermon, sacrament and liturgy, and, of course, Scripture itself, with all its echoes of song and legend and prayer. It earns its authority by winning assent and recognition, in the manner of poetry but with the difference that the assent seems to be to ultimate truth, however oblique or fragmentary the suggestion of it. Theology is written for the small community of those who would think of reading it. So it need not define freighted words like *faith* or *grace* but may instead reveal what they contain. To the degree that it does them any justice, its community of readers will say yes, enjoying the insight as their own and affirming it in that way.

Theology may proceed in the manner of a philosophical treatise or a piece of textual criticism, but it always begins by assuming major terms. And all of them, being imbedded in Scripture and tradition, behave altogether differently from discursive language. To compound the problem, Christian thinkers since Jesus have valued paradox as if it were resolution. So theology is never finally anything but theology, words about God, proceeding from the assumptions that God exists and that we know about him in a way that allows us to speak about him. Bonhoeffer calls these truths of the church "a word of recognition among friends." He invokes this language of recognition and identification in attempting to make the church real and aware of itself, with all that implied when he wrote. For him, word is act. And, for him, it was.

To a very striking degree, Bonhoeffer's theology returns to formulations that are virtually creedal in their use of imagery taken from the narrative of the sacrifice of Christ. The effect is beautiful, musical. But the language functions not as ornament but as ontology. For him it makes the most essential account that can be made of Being itself. For example, in a late letter famous for the statement that Christianity must be "demythologized" and biblical concepts reinterpreted in a "worldly" sense, he explains, "What is above this world is, in the gospel, intended to exist *for* this world; I mean that, not in the anthropocentric sense of liberal, mystic, pietistic, ethical theology, but in the biblical sense of the creation and of the incarnation, crucifixion, and resurrection of Jesus Christ."[11] Clearly he does not consider such language mythological, and the case could be made that he does not consider it religious either. This fact expresses his belief in the preeminent reality of the cosmic narrative implied in the words *Christ, incarnation, crucifixion,* and *resurrection.* Myth and religion are at the margin. Christ is at the center.

Bonhoeffer invokes such language as the culminating expression of any passionate argument, especially the great Nevertheless, that the world is to be loved and served and that God is present in it. The day after the failure of the attempt to assassinate Hitler, in which he and his brother and two of his brothers-in-law were deeply involved, Bonhoeffer wrote a letter to Bethge about "the profound this-worldliness of Christianity." He said, "By this-worldliness I mean living unreservedly in life's duties, problems, successes and failures, experiences and perplexities. In so doing we throw ourselves completely into the arms of God, taking seriously, not our own sufferings, but those of God in the world—watching with Christ in Gethsemane . . . How can success make us arrogant, or failure lead us astray, when we share in God's suffering through a life of this kind?" These would seem to be words of consolation, from himself as pastor to himself as prisoner. But they are also an argument from the authority of one narrative moment. The painful world must be embraced altogether, because Christ went to Gethsemane.

In 1937 Bonhoeffer published *The Cost of Discipleship.* In it he attacked the "cheap grace" of prevailing Lutheran teaching, which seemed merely to make people comfortable with their sins. "Costly grace" (interestingly, he does not call it "true" grace, though the implications of the distinction would almost justify the use of that word) carried with it the acknowledged obligation of discipleship, that is, obedience: "it is only through actual obedience that a person can become liberated to believe." He says although, as Luther taught, faith is prior to obedience, in effect the two are simultaneous, "for faith is only real when there is obedience, never without it, and faith only becomes faith in the act of obedience."[12] This argument does not cite Paul's Epistle to the Romans or otherwise ground itself in authority, though it means to overturn historical consensus about a crucial Reformation doctrine. The writing comes out of the time at Finkenwalde, from his teaching and his preaching to young men who were making a brave attempt at obedience. Their faith was "worldly," that is, active and costly, not theoretical or doctrinal. He is appealing over the head of conventional theology, to shared experience. This is another form of the "word of recognition among friends," an appeal to the experience of act as witness and as revelation. Bonhoeffer's theology is in its circumstance as much as on the page, and this must surely have been his intention. No other method would have been consistent with his theology.

In 1939 *Life Together* appeared, a book about Finkenwalde as a model of Christian community. Again, the appeal is to experience, an intuition of how life might be, based on the kind of visionary memory that becomes more important in Bonhoeffer's writing as his life becomes more isolated and tenuous. The church, the eternal, present, felt being of Christ in the world, which had always been at the center of his faith and his religious imagination, was or could be seen or apprehended in Finkenwalde or its like: "We have one another only through Christ, but through Christ we really do *have* one another. We have one another completely and for all eternity."[13] The Gestapo, of course, had closed the seminary. His account of it is like mysticism barely concealed or restrained, though all that is being described is a community of the faithful. Visionary memory and anticipation are increasingly the "world" he will cling to until his death. To see divine immanence in the world is an act of faith, not a matter to be interpreted in other than its own terms, if one grants the reasonableness of the perceiver. And Dietrich Bonhoeffer thought and believed his way to a surpassing reasonableness.

In 1939 Bonhoeffer traveled to New York. He had studied for a year at Union Theological Seminary as a young man of twenty-four. He contacted Reinhold Niebuhr, his former teacher, in England, and asked him to arrange an invitation for him to return to the United States. He was at risk of being drafted into Hitler's army. The invitation was made and he was offered a teaching post, but after a month he returned to Germany out of homesickness and a feeling that he would lose the right to influence Germany in the period after the war if he stayed in America. He was no longer allowed to teach in Berlin, and he would soon be prohibited from speaking in public and required to report regularly to the police. But his brother-in-law, Hans von Dohnanyi, was an officer in the Abwehr, the military intelligence, which was a center of covert resistance and which became the nucleus of the Officers' Plot. Dohnanyi took him on as an agent, an arrangement that kept him unmolested and allowed him to travel to Switzerland and Sweden in behalf of the resistance. In Switzerland he spoke with representatives of the Vatican, and in Sweden he described to the English bishop George Bell a plan for simultaneous coups in Berlin and throughout occupied Europe, with support from unions, the military, and the Protestant and Catholic churches. This plan seems to have found no encouragement. During much of this time he lived as a guest in a Benedictine abbey near Munich and worked on the unfinished book titled *Ethics*.

A few months before his arrest in April 1943 Bonhoeffer became engaged to Maria von Wedemeyer, with whom, in keeping with the starchy customs of their class, and then with the conditions of his imprisonment, he was never to spend a single moment alone. He was thirty-seven and she was nineteen. Her family disapproved and only announced the engagement when he was arrested, as a gesture of support. He wrote to her as well as to Eberhard Bethge, imagining a sweetly ordinary domestic life even as bombs crashed into the prison buildings. His letters to her have long theological passages, too, gentler and more lyrical than those written to Bethge.

The fact that he wrote theology in these circumstances, in letters to dearly loved friends that he could not anticipate would ever be published, illuminates all his earlier work. These letters, too, are meant to actualize the sacred, that is, the relationship of love, the ground of shared understanding. Two ideas are essential to Bonhoeffer's thinking: first, that the sacred can be inferred from the world in the experience of goodness, beauty, and love; and second, that these things, and more generally, the immanence of God, are a real presence, not a symbol or a foreshadowing. They are fulfillment as well as promise, like the sacrament, or the church. The mystery of the world for Bonhoeffer comes with the belief that immanence is pervasive, no less so where it cannot be discovered. The achieved rescue of creation brings the whole of it under grace. So moments that are manifestly sacred do not judge or shame the indifference of the world, or its misery or its wickedness. Instead they imply a presence and an embrace sufficient to it all, without distinction. Bonhoeffer is certainly never more orthodox than in seeing the revealed nature of Christ as depending, one might say, on his making precisely this overreaching claim on recalcitrant humankind.

In *The Cost of Discipleship* he wrote:

> Jesus does not promise that when we bless our enemies and do good to them they will not despitefully use and persecute us. They certainly will. But not even that can hurt or overcome us, so long as we pray for them. For if we pray for them, we are taking their distress and poverty, their guilt and perdition, upon ourselves, and pleading to God for them. We are doing vicariously for them what they cannot do for themselves. Every insult they utter only serves to bind us more closely to God and them. Their persecution of us only serves to bring them nearer to reconciliation with God and to further the triumphs of love.

This is the power of Christ that is the weakness of Christ. He is present even where he is forgotten and efficacious even where he is despised.

Such things could not be known about him except in a world like this one. So the secular and the "religionless" are an intrinsic part of divine self-revelation—as, in fact, they were central to the role of Jesus while he lived.

———— ⚬⚭⚬ ————

Watching with Christ in Gethsemane, Bonhoeffer worked at loving the world. In a letter to Bethge he wrote: "It is only when one loves life and the world so much that without them everything would be gone, that one can believe in the resurrection and a new world. It is only when one submits to the law that one can speak of grace, and only when one sees the anger and the wrath of God hanging like grim realities over the head of one's enemies that one can know something of what it means to love them and forgive them."[14] But these exertions of forgiveness did not change his world. Bonhoeffer was in the hands of the SS. This cannot have been irrelevant to the drift of his thoughts about the future of Christendom, nor can the awareness of atrocities he must have had through Hans von Dohnanyi and others. When he says "the time of inwardness and conscience, which is to say the time of religion" is over, and "we are proceeding towards a time of no religion at all: men as they are now simply cannot be religious any more,"[15] it seems to me fatuous to imagine that he is simply postulating a cultural trend that is to be absorbed like others.

He might well have concluded that there is one thing worse than hypocrisy. Yet clearly he is using "religion" in his usual, Barthian sense, albeit with a certain nostalgia. He suggests that the conception of God among the generality of people, the "religious premise," might have been historical and temporary. Insofar as it was, he himself would never have hesitated to call it false. The God of revelation, of Barth and Bonhoeffer, is neither an "a priori" nor a creation of culture. These are the humanist views of God that they both explicitly reject. But "the church" has always lived within religion, usually indistinguishable from it: "If religion is no more than the garment of Christianity—and even that garment has had very different aspects at different times—then what is a religionless Christianity?" In the course of the paragraph Bonhoeffer works his way back to his most characteristic assertion, that Christ is autonomously present, dependent on no human intention or belief or institution. He cannot answer his own question, but he can say, "God is the 'beyond' in the midst of our lives. The Church stands not where human powers give out, on the

borders, but in the center of the village."[16] That "religion" has made inap-
propriate claims, that God and "the church" should stand in opposition to
it, is not a new idea for Bonhoeffer. Surely what is to be noted in all this
is Bonhoeffer's steadfast refusal to condemn the "religionless" world, and
his visionary certainty that it is comprehended in the divine presence.

This is Christ-like only in the manner that the thoughts of a disciple
might have been if one of them had watched with him on the night of his
betrayal. It is striking how Bonhoeffer insists always on the role of disciple,
of one among a company of equals, from which no one must be excluded.
Though he was an aristocrat and aloof in his manner, he seems to have had
no imagination of beatitude which is not a humanly understandable moment with a beloved friend. To Bethge, he wrote of his imprisonment,
"One thing is that I do miss sitting down to table with others. The presents
you send me acquire here a sacramental value; they remind me of the times
we have sat down to table together. Perhaps the reason why we attach so
much importance to sitting down to table together is that table fellowship
is one of the realities of the Kingdom of God."

Neither has he any interest in himself as solitary martyr. He generalizes
from his circumstance to the human condition with a consistency that
leads commentators to forget how extreme his isolation really was, and
how available the idea of martyrdom or abandonment would have been
to him if he had not always transformed his suffering into compassion for
humankind, or for God. It is not hard to imagine what dark night might
have preceded words like these: "The God who is with us is the God who
forsakes us (Mark 15:34). The God who lets us live in the world without
the working hypothesis of God is the God before whom we stand continually. Before God and with God we live without God. God lets the divine self be pushed out of the world onto the cross."[17]

Bonhoeffer's family arranged to help him escape from prison, but he
chose to remain because his brother Klaus was also in prison and might
bear repercussions. He was executed in April of 1945, after nineteen
months of imprisonment. Hans von Dohnanyi died the next day; his
brother Klaus and his brother-in-law Rudiger Schleicher, within the
month. A British prisoner wrote of Bonhoeffer in his last days that he "always seemed to diffuse an atmosphere of happiness, of joy in every smallest event in life, and a deep gratitude for the mere fact that he was alive."[18]

This same prisoner wrote that when he was taken away to his execution, Bonhoeffer said, "This is the end—for me, the beginning of life."

Notes

1. Karl Barth, *Church Dogmatics* (Louisville, KY: Westminster John Knox Press, 1994), 54.
2. Dietrich Bonhoeffer, *The Cost of Discipleship* (London: SCM, 1963), 362.
3. Bonhoeffer, *A Testament to Freedom* (San Francisco: HarperSanFrancisco, 1990), 93.
4. Bonhoeffer, *A Testament to Freedom,* 118.
5. Bonhoeffer, *Letters and Papers from Prison* (London: SCM, 1971), 73.
6. Barth, *Church Dogmatics,* 52.
7. Bonhoeffer, *A Testament to Freedom,* 132.
8. Bonhoeffer, *A Testament to Freedom,* 137.
9. Bonhoeffer, *A Testament to Freedom,* 117.
10. Bonhoeffer, *A Testament to Freedom,* 359.
11. Bonhoeffer, *A Testament to Freedom,* 504.
12. Bonhoeffer, *A Testament to Freedom,* 311.
13. Bonhoeffer, *A Testament to Freedom,* 326.
14. Bonhoeffer, *Letters and Papers from Prison,* 79.
15. Bonhoeffer, *Letters and Papers from Prison,* 122.
16. Bonhoeffer, *Letters and Papers from Prison,* 124.
17. Bonhoeffer, *A Testament to Freedom,* 508.
18. Bonhoeffer, *A Testament to Freedom,* 43.

For Further Reading

Eberhard Bethge, *Bonhoeffer: Exile and Martyr.* Edited by John W. de Gruchy. New York: Seabury Press, 1975.
Dietrich Bonhoeffer, *Christology.* London: Fount Books/Collins, 1966.
———, *The Cost of Discipleship.* London: SCM, 1963.
———, *Ethics.* London: SCM, 1971.
———, *Letters and Papers from Prison.* Edited by Eberhard Bethge. London: SCM, 1971.
———, *A Testament to Freedom: The Essential Writings of Dietrich Bonhoeffer.* Edited by Geffrey B. Kelly and F. Burton Nelson. San Francisco: HarperSanFrancisco, 1990.
Mary Bosanquet, *The Life and Death of Dietrich Bonhoeffer.* London: Hodder & Stoughton, 1968; New York: Harper & Row, 1969.

ETTY HILLESUM

Poland, 1943

Outward from the Camps Themselves

by CALVIN BEDIENT

There are cataclysms that expose the otherwise invisible kernel of the spirit, as when a chestnut clatters on the sidewalk and there it is, the core that, even when hidden, was already new-peeled, that was so by nature: it only needed to be set free. Because the Nazis occupied Holland and persecuted the Dutch Jews, the child Anne Frank went into hiding and, through her now-famous diaries, came out of it a moral example to the world. Exemplary, too, was another Dutch Jew, Etty Hillesum, who, though she intended to become a great writer, never foresaw that it would be her wartime diaries, started in 1942 when she was twenty-seven, that would constitute her legacy to the history of heroic faith and goodness under extreme conditions.

More developed and decided than Anne Frank's, Hillesum's spiritual character, which rapidly deepened and turned crystalline as the situation of the Jews worsened in Amsterdam, was a classic instance of that of the individual who feels responsible for all others and loves them unconditionally; who feels responsible for God, even: "And if we just care enough," she wrote shortly before her deportation from the Westerbork transit camp in Holland to Auschwitz, "God is in safe hands with us despite everything" (Letters, 144).

At the beginning of the occupation, Hillesum had moved from the provinces and occupied a small room in Amsterdam overlooking Museum Square. She quickly formed a fond, if not passionate, liaison with her sixty-year-old landlord, "Papa Han." She had an infectious capacity for enjoyment, was intelligent, and boasted of her "bubbling good humor." She gave private lessons in Russian. She had had several lovers, and on the very first page of her diaries, begun on March 9, 1941, she compares her need to "pour out" as a writer to "the final, liberating scream that always sticks bashfully in your throat when you make love." Outwardly, in short, she gave every appearance of being happily secular, grateful for the life of the mind, the body, and the heart, and unaware of what Emily Dickinson had memorably called "the missing all."

Yet, already on the first page of her diaries, she said that, although love "does indeed suit me to perfection," it was "a mere trifle" compared to what is "truly essential": something "deep inside" her that was "still locked away." She was very soon to give that something a name: the soul. And the soul, for her, exceeded any worldly cause, any evident deserts of the people around her, especially later in Westerbork, where she wrote—in a letter now part of her *Letters from Westerbork*—

> Many feel that their love of mankind languishes at Westerbork because it receives no nourishment—meaning that people here don't give you much occasion to love them. "The mass is a hideous monster; individuals are pitiful," someone said. But I keep discovering that there is no causal connection between people's behavior and the love you feel for them. Love for one's fellow man is like an elemental glow that sustains you.

This was the mystery of Hillesum's faith, this "elemental glow" that seemed to arrive unannounced and unsummoned and to take complete possession of her, to the point of leading her to take steps that put her in the company of those most certain to be sent to Poland and, in all probability, killed. As one of the 100,000 members of the Jewish Council in Amsterdam, even if just a lowly typist, she had the choice of avoiding Westerbork. But what was she doing at the council, which had been mandated by the Nazis, if not helping to send her fellow Jews to a transit camp? "Nothing can ever atone," she wrote, "for the fact . . . that one section of the Jewish population is helping to transport the majority out of the country." Besides, her fellow workers seemed petty, merely self-interested: "God save me from one thing: don't let me be sent to a camp with the people with whom I now work every day. I could write a hundred satires about them." Despite the suggestion that the "elemental glow" is independent of particular objects of love, a self-subsistent reality, Hillesum resisted her own fantasies of becoming a "nun" surrounded by books and golden wheat fields. "God is love," she agreed in a letter from Westerbork, and because of that

> we can extract something positive from life under any circumstances. But we have the right to say that only if we do nothing to escape, even from the worst conditions. I often think we should shoulder our rucksacks, join the others, and go "on transport" with them.

It was Hillesum's calling to the unlimited responsibility of love, of a love at once universal and committed to particular acts of assistance to those in dire conditions (Hillesum was eventually to nurse the sick and dying in the hospital barrack at Westerbork), that made her volunteer to go to Westerbork as a representative of the Jewish Council, after only a few weeks in the Amsterdam office, accompanying the first group of Jews to be randomly swept up from the city streets.

In his rigorous critique of the maxim of neighbor-love in *Civilization and Its Discontents,* Freud argued that "men are not gentle creatures who want to be loved." In fact, he said, "this stranger . . . has more claim on my hostility and even my hatred." Besides, "my love is valued by all my own people as a sign of my preferring them, and it is an injustice to them if I put a stranger on a par with them." Freud meant by "my own people" his friends and family, but the terms *stranger* and *my own people* recall Leviticus 19: first, verse 8, "Thou shalt not avenge, nor bear any grudge against the children of thy people, but thou shalt love thy neighbour as thyself," and then verse 34, "The stranger that dwelleth with you shall be unto you as one born among you, and thou shalt love him as thyself; for ye were strangers in the land of Egypt." The Gospels lift this law of neighbor-love and stranger-love out of the dimming, leveling context of Leviticus (where verse 19, for instance, states, "Thou shalt not let thy cattle gender with a diverse kind," and so on) and universalize it, making it soar beyond the others-in-a-covenant and even the stranger-in-one's-midst and embrace, at its furthest outreach, the commandment to love one's enemies. Freud, of course, found this last the height of unreason. His measuring stick was the heart's reasons, the heart's justness. But the commandment to love one's neighbors *and* one's enemies is not addressed to the heart; its purpose is to instruct, and perhaps even to elicit, the soul. In this context, the soul is the metaphysical organ of the equation "God is love." The heart and the soul are entirely different functions or orders of love. Freud was unable to comprehend the second, to find it reasonable. Of course, it *isn't* reasonable. In its divine unreason it was not only to visit Etty Hillesum but to become the law of her existence. In her, it did not supplant, but it far outshone, the heart.

Heart was what she gave to others selectively. Heart was partiality, affection, erotic love. It was what embraced family and friends. Heart could be an obstacle to the soul's peace, since partiality meant a degree of identification that made a parent's or another loved one's pain more unbearable than one's own. Hillesum might have accepted offers of help to escape Westerbork, for instance, if her parents, so much less rocklike than herself, were not also interned there. Could she not protect them a little by her presence? Speaking of others in the same situation, she wrote, "While each of us would give anything to get away from W., many of us would have to be thrown out before we'd go." Yet, above all, she dreaded being sent to Poland on the same train with her parents; she had a great "fear of seeing them suffer." (As it happened, she was on the same train for the nightmarish three-day journey, but in a different car. And her parents were gassed on their first day at Auschwitz, weeks earlier than she was.) She would much rather go in their stead. It would have been more bearable to see anyone else suffer: they were not "the neighbor," after all; they were her parents. Yet her soul rose up against the partiality of her heart:

> Last night, during yet another hard struggle not to be overwhelmed with pity for my parents, which would paralyze me completely if I succumbed, I told myself it must be wrong to be so overcome with grief and concern for one's own family that one has little thought and love left over for one's neighbor. I see more and more that love for all our neighbors, for everyone made in God's image, must take pride of place over love for one's nearest and dearest.

Hillesum often feared that others would find such sentiments "unnatural," "inhuman"; and they are, in that the soul is not in the domain of the heart. It is disinterested; it is not a part of psychology. It is both in and out of this world.

Soul had an easier struggle against heart, a true victory, in Etty Hillesum's attachment to Julius Spier, a German refugee in Amsterdam whom

Hillesum first consulted to have her palm read. (Carl Gustav Jung had persuaded Spier to turn his astonishing talent for reading hands and palms into a full-time profession; hence the birth of psychochirology.) She later became Spier's part-time secretary and friend—even, according to Jan Gaarlandt (her editor and publisher), his lover. But "lover" may be a somewhat facile label for their relationship, suggesting as it does a passionate abandonment of restraint that was belied by the actual circumstances, not least Spier's continued engagement to a woman in London and Etty's resistance, and growing indifference, to experiencing sensual ecstasy with him. Hillesum idealized Spier, and her love for him fed the question, which her life was soon to answer in the negative, of whether her destiny was to be a woman whose "main interest is the ideal man." But her very ardor for him was infiltrated with the "elemental glow" that placed him, not as the essential object of her love, but as one of the many to be benefited by it as its metaphysical radar swept the world to detect the presence of those in trouble. "I am so glad that he is a Jew and I a Jewess," she said at the height of her feeling for him:

> And I shall do what I can to remain with him so that we get through these times together. And I shall tell him this evening: I am not really frightened of anything, I feel so strong; it matters little whether you have to sleep on a hard floor, or whether you are . . . allowed to walk [only] through certain specified streets, and so on—these are all minor vexations, so insignificant compared with the infinite riches and possibilities we carry within us . . . And I shall help you and stay with you, and yet leave you entirely free. And one day I shall surrender you to the girl you mean to marry.

In fact, from having once envied and even resented Spier's "energy" and "the love he has for everyone," which could make her feel, by comparison, "ineffectual" and which she found insensitive to "times like these" when "we could be ordered at any moment to those barracks [Westerbork] in Drenthe Province," Hillesum, partly by imitating them, came to surpass them. Her own grasp of "the infinite riches and possibilities we carry within us" grew even surer than his. She came to see that "a soul is forged out of fire and rock crystal," is "something rigorous, hard in an Old Testament sense, but also gentle as the gesture with which his tender fingertips sometimes stroke my eyelashes." And because Spier was incapable of such indomitability, she was finally relieved that he was spared the rigors of Westerbork, not to mention Auschwitz. (Spier died in Amsterdam on September 15, 1942, the day the Gestapo came to send him to the transit camp.) "I meet quite a few of Spier's clients and pupils here," Hillesum wrote from Westerbork, "and we always say the same thing: what a mercy it is that he is no longer with us."

Heart and soul, then, were intermingled in her feeling for Spier; but soul was increasingly to predominate, and not least because the man she loved most as a man she also loved most as a moral being, and he was spiritual enough to instruct her in soul's ways. Along this path, eroticism was at once a guide and a distraction. Eroticism, says Georges Bataille, who conceived it as having a religious as well as a sensual dimension, is essentially an experience of unclosed connection, of infinite continuity. Hillesum perhaps begins to search out the larger dimension when she writes, "This afternoon I looked at his expressive mouth and whispered to it, 'Tonight you will be the beaker from which I will sip his breath'" and adds: "Perhaps that is the only real way of kissing a man. Not just out of sensuality but also from a desire to breathe for one moment through a single mouth." But, beyond these confused regions of overlaid sensuality and spirituality, it was Spier's articulation and example of a universal benevolence, his capacity to "understand how women feel" and to give a woman's "'soul' . . . welcome and shelter," together with his Christian posture of prayer, his devoted reading of the New Testament, and his method of healing people "by teaching them how to suffer and accept," that made him, in Hillesum's word, the "mediator" between her and God. After his death, she wrote:

> What energies I possess have been set free inside me. You taught me to speak the name of God without embarrassment. You were the mediator between God and me, and now you, the mediator, have gone and my path leads straight to God. It is right that it should be so. And I shall be the mediator for any other soul I can reach.

More quickly than gradually, Hillesum learned to listen to herself, as she put it; to allow herself "to be led . . . by what wells up within." At the same time, she began reading "the Gospel of St. Matthew morning and night," and Saint Augustine, and soon added Tolstoy; and among her books at Westerbork was a copy of Meister Eckhart. She was astonished by the suddenness and seriousness of her need to pray, and to do so in Spier's Christian fashion, by kneeling—"a posture," she noted, "not handed down from generation to generation with us Jews." Her body even gestured in the direction of genuflection as if born with the pattern already imprinted in it. From having thought of herself in storybook terms as "the girl who could not kneel," she found herself one gray dawn "on the floor, between Han's stripped bed and his typewriter, huddled up, my head on the ground. As if I were trying to seize peace by force. And when Han came in and seemed a bit taken aback by the spectacle, I told him I was looking for a button." Again:

> Last night, shortly before going to bed, I suddenly went down on my knees in the middle of this large room, between the steel chairs and the matting. Almost automatically. Forced to the ground by something stronger than myself.

It was, she thought, "as if my body had been meant and made for the act of kneeling."

"Huddled up," her head deeply bowed, hands before her face—this was not only to "seize peace by force" but to enact a terrible humbleness (stopped, concentrated) before the infinite, still source of all movement. The posture also suggests, without mimicking, a figure that has over the centuries come to occupy the heart of the maxim to love your neighbor: the naked and destitute human being, for instance the man left stripped and wounded by thieves on the way to Jericho in Jesus' story of the good Samaritan (Luke 10:30–31). So it is that Emmanuel Levinas, the greatest modern Jewish philosopher of neighbor-love, writes repeatedly and perhaps tendentiously of the "essential destitution of the Other," that is, "the stranger, the widow, and the orphan, to whom I am obligated."

Of course, the stranger, the neighbor, may not always be in worse circumstances than oneself. It may be the reverse of true humility always to think so. But Etty Hillesum felt so invincible in the profound cheer and tender protectiveness of her faith ("There are moments," she said, "when I feel like a little bird, tucked away in a great protective hand") that she found most of the Jews she encountered relatively destitute, the more so because she was in the privileged minority who were members of the Jewish Council (meaning that, until her identity card was finally taken from her at Westerbork, she had the option of returning to Amsterdam). "They sit here," she said of those who came to the council offices, "and suddenly their need erupts in all its nakedness. Then, there they are, bundles of human misery, desperate and unable to face life." Again: "I no longer shut myself away in my room, God, I try . . . to discover the small, naked human being amidst the monstrous wreckage caused by man's senseless deeds."

Hillesum's diaries (which do not include her days at Westerbork; her last diary disappeared with her at Auschwitz) are filled about equally with notations of her enjoyment of the 10,000 things of this world—the trees outside her window in Amsterdam, roses, good food, poetry, friends—and with prayer, which she couched as a dialogue with the origin and stay and substance of the soul, frequently addressing it as "You" or "God"—dialogue separated off by quotation marks, as if she conceived of it as essentially speech-articulated breath and not mere script, or at least as script being intensely heard as a listening inward to a "voice." Dialogue, or the first-person address, marked an intimacy with the "deepest and richest part" of herself, the "part in which I repose"—the "soul" or, equally, "God."

It was in God that she met others, met them elementally, seeing their suffering as a burden intolerable to the soul's love of peace—yet only the soul could properly take such suffering up and alleviate it. So long as history remained, so long as humanity gave insufficient shelter to God, suffering and love could not be separated. In her days and in her prayers, the path to God was inevitably pulled to the side, like the string of a bow, and the misery of human life notched into it. Humanity was full of evil, but she could not simply withdraw from it; "in every human being," she wrote in her diaries, "I love something of You." The soul is love, and love gravitates to those most in need of it.

She was, she felt, "a floodgate for a never-ending tide of misery." It was not her own misery, except insofar as the image of the soul as "forged of fire and rock crystal" belied the soul's vulnerability, or meant that it was, however hard, transparent to pain. The final words in her last surviving diary are these: "We should be willing to act as a balm for all wounds . . . Never any bitterness about what was done to [others], but always love for those who knew how to bear so much although nothing had prepared them for such burdens"—so she found when she took stock of her feeling at the end of each day. She saw it as foreign to her nature to hate and, or course, unprincipled, too: "every atom of hate we add to this world makes it still more inhospitable." In Westerbork her sympathies were clearly with her fellow internees, disagreeable though she found many of them to be; she could be finely satirical about the camp's commandant, and she was appalled by the brutal, sometimes drunken "green police"— the transport guards who saw more than 100,000 German and Dutch Jews out of Westerbork into extermination camps:

My God, those faces! I looked at them, each in turn, from behind the safety
of a window, and I have never been so frightened of anything in my life . . .
I sank to my knees with the words that preside over human life: And God
made man after His likeness. That passage spent a difficult morning with me.

But her moral indignation and horror remained free of hatred. Was
there not, after all, something "tough and indestructible" in her? And was
there not also suffering on the other side of the enemy lines? "There are
no frontiers between suffering people, and we must pray for them all." In
a letter from Westerbork, she imagines a Marxist friend ("dogged old class
fighter that you have always been") responding to such sentiments in dismay: "But that—that is nothing but Christianity!" To which she retorts,
"Yes, Christianity, and why ever not?"

Hillesum's ambition was to be "*the thinking heart of the barracks.*" The
thinking "soul," to maintain a distinction made earlier: "Unlike the Ori-
entals," she wrote, "we are ashamed of our souls as if they were something
immoral. 'Soul' is quite different from what we call 'heart.' There are
plenty of people who have a lot of 'heart' but very little soul." And what
the soul thinks of—what it thinks—is God, is love. "Once the love of
mankind has germinated in you," she wrote, "it will grow without measure." But love of creation was the greater, the encompassing, love, and
love of the Creator greater still. Hillesum experienced love at all these lev-
els, in all these directions, at Westerbork, as earlier in Amsterdam, with an
intensity that astonished her. The soul, that mystery, existed simultaneously in eternity and time, with God and with humanity—the others, the
neighbors, the "so-called enemies."

Hillesum's youthful capacity to delight in what Michel Serres calls "the
worldwide world" was, as it were, the pagan step up to her eventual love
of the creation as God's. At its deepest, her feeling for material reality,
while it remained erotic, approached what the Greeks called ataraxia, a
peace comparable to soothing the noisy oceanic Venus, the Venus of the
heart, of the bodily cells, she who is repeatedly "impregnated with
Uranus' brush dripping with spermatic and bloody color," as Serres puts
it; it approached the peace of a serenely self-forgetful continuity with immediate reality:

> Last night when I cycled home from S., I poured out all my tenderness, all
> the tenderness one cannot express for a man even when one loves him very,
> very much, I poured it all out into the great, all-embracing spring night. I

stood on the little bridge and looked across the water; I melted into the landscape and offered all my tenderness up to the sky and the stars and the water and to the little bridge.

Again:

From my bed I stared out through the large open window. And it was once more as if life with all its mysteries was close to me . . . I had the feeling that I was resting against the naked breast of life, and could feel her gentle and regular heartbeat. I felt safe and protected.

This is already a peace that passes understanding, even if we view it in Freudian terms as traces of maternally oriented "oceanic feeling." But Hillesum, although "frightened" by the sudden development of her "faith in God," also found and lost and found again a peace that was tinged, as a drop of water may reflect accidental light and shadow, by the sufferings of others. It was a sterner, harder peace than ataraxia, one achieved, again, by vanquishing "our hatred for our fellow human beings of whatever race." Yet it, too, had its vast material world. "We must share our love with the whole of creation":

I am in Poland every day, on the battlefields, if that's what one can call them. I often see visions of poisonous green smoke; I am with the hungry, with the ill-treated and the dying, every day, but I am also with the jasmine and with that piece of sky beyond my window; there is room for everything in a single life.

In this capacious faith, suffering, at the same time that it must continually be confronted as a historical constant, is also a mere part of a life that need never be less than "good and faithful" to the last breath: "living and dying, sorrow and joy, the blisters on my feet and the jasmine behind the house, the persecution, the unspeakable horrors . . . I accept it all as one mighty whole." The "whole" is good, even if certain accidental parts are evil. The whole is just. "In a labor camp I should die within three days. I should lie down and die and still not find life unfair."

What drove Hillesum to the transit camp was, in part, her desire to test her faith that life would appear "meaningful" even in desperate circumstances. To forgo "all personal desires," "offering what little assistance I can wherever it has pleased God to place me," and bear the "labyrinthine and unfathomable network of barbed wire," the mud, mice, overcrowding, and stench, a group of incoming Jews dressed only in slippers and under-clothes ("the whole of Westerbork, in a single horrified and heroic ges-ture, stripped to the skin"), the arrival of carloads of Jews already mutilated elsewhere by the Nazis, the questions of the bewildered old ("there was a little old woman who had left her spectacles and her medi-cine bottle at home on the mantel—could she go and get them now, and where exactly was she, and where would she be going?"), the "animosity between the German and the Dutch Jews," the monstrous punishments (once, fifty inmates were ordered to leave for Poland because one boy panicked and tried to hide to keep from going), orphans and babies ill with pneumonia placed on the trains, indeed "the fear and despair of the thousands and thousands" of inmates, to bear all this and more on an earth that "is gradually turning into one great prison camp" and yet find the beauty of God's earth, of God's creation, which was even harder to bear ("whenever I showed myself ready to bear it, the hard was directly trans-formed into the beautiful. And the beautiful was sometimes much harder to bear, so overpowering did it seem")—this, she said, was "to be placed before Your ultimate mystery, Oh God. I am grateful to You," she added, "for having chosen my heart, in these times, to experience all the things it has experienced." Horrible as "mass murder" was, the soul could with-stand it; it could even be grateful for the discovery of its own strength. "I do not feel that I have been robbed of my freedom," Hillesum wrote; "es-sentially no one can do me any harm at all."

Sitting on the heath in Drenthe "under the great, big starry sky," she could even "feel at home. We are 'at home.' Under the sky. In every place on earth, if only we carry everything with us." Back in Amsterdam for a few months and bedridden with anemia, she remembered the "stretch of heath land surrounded by barbed wire . . . as something almost lovely," and wondered, "How is it that my spirit, far from being op-pressed, seemed to grow lighter and brighter there?" The human beings at the camp were part of "one great, meaningful whole," and not its contradiction. She felt "somehow impelled to return to that spot in the middle of the heath where so many human destinies have been thrown together," and she aspired to "let others see the many inmates, who have to be deciphered like hieroglyphs, stroke by stroke," until they assume their place in one "comprehensible whole." She spent much of her time at Westerbork in "a strange state of mournful contentment." There were moments that approached ecstasy, moments alone on the heath in the evening: "Sometimes when I stand in some corner of the camp, my feet planted on Your earth," she wrote, "my eyes raised towards Your heaven, tears . . . run down my face, tears of deep emotion and gratitude." She quoted from Matthew 5:24, "First be reconciled to the brother, and then come and offer the gift."

Because the soul is infinite with God and stronger than history and evil, "nothing can happen to me," she declared. "My personal fate is not the issue; it doesn't really matter if it is I who perish or another." To want to be "at the center of all human suffering" was part of the soul's "destiny," a reality answering to "a terrible, sacred, inner seriousness." At the least, she wished to be a witness and then a teacher and singer of wisdom. She hoped that there was in her "a little piece of God that might grow into poetry . . . a camp needs a poet, one who experiences life, even there, as a bard and is able to sing about it." She went to Westerbork not in order to die, but to be enabled to live more purely. In a letter from the camp, she wrote:

> If we were to save only our bodies and nothing more than the camps all over the world, that would not be enough. What matters is not whether we preserve our lives at any cost, but how we preserve them . . . If we abandon the hard facts that we are forced to face, if we . . . do not allow them to settle and change into impulses through which we can grow and from which we can draw meaning—then we are not a viable generation . . . New thoughts will have to radiate outward from the camps themselves, . . . spreading lucidity . . . and perhaps, on the common basis of an honest search for some way to understand these dark events, wrecked lives may yet take a tentative step forward.

Hillesum's spiritual greatness was synonymous with her essential humility. She went to Westerbork not so much to exult in her "inner strength," to be its heroine, as to experience the entire humility of it. But this humility should not be confused with weakness or passivity or understood as an apology for one's own existence. One of the most piercing moments in the letters consists of the response that "a stout working-class woman with a kindly snub-nosed face" gave to a mother of a sick child after the mother had sobbed out in the barracks that "they take the sick children away and you never get them back." "There now," the woman almost crooned, "you're just an ordinary Jew, aren't you, so you'll just have to go, won't you?" Kind as may have been this woman's motive, it must be said that to be habituated to being held of no account as a historical and ethnic being and, on the other hand, to be genuinely humble are not the same thing. A fiercely proud Jew who boarded a transport of his own accord, saying that he wanted "the freedom to decide when to go," reminded Hillesum of the answer a martyr gave to the Roman judge who said to him, "Do you know that I have the power to have you killed?": "Yes, but I have the power of letting myself be killed." Hillesum's humbleness was of this latter, formidable kind: an unyielding insistence on the soul's freedom.

Ordered onto a train to Poland, Hillesum was "literally [struck] . . . down" when she learned that her parents and her older brother, Misha, a musical prodigy, were to be transported on the same train. "Within the hour, however," a friend of hers at the camp said in a letter to her friends in Amsterdam, "she had recovered." She stepped onto the platform with "a kind word for everyone she met on the way." She had once announced the terrible goal of going "gracefully into hell" and she lived to fulfill it. Soon after she left the camp in Wagon No. 12, she threw a postcard out of a hole created by one of the car's broken planks. It read: "We have left the camp singing."

For Further Reading

Etty Hillesum, *An Interrupted Life: The Diaries of Etty Hillesum—43*. New York: Washington Square Press, 1985.

———, *Letters from Westerbork*. Introduction and notes by Jan G. Gaarlandt. Translated by Arnold J. Pomerans. New York: Pantheon Books, 1986.

SIMONE WEIL

England, 1943

Love Bade Me Welcome

by ANTHONY WALTON

*Through joy, the beauty of the world penetrates our
soul. Through suffering it penetrates our body. We could
no more become friends of God through joy alone than
one becomes a ship's captain by studying books on navi-
gation . . . In order that our being should one day become
wholly sensitive in every part to this obedience that is the
substance of matter, in order that a new sense should be
formed in us to enable us to hear the universe as the vi-
bration of the word of God, the transforming power of
suffering and of joy are equally indispensable.*

Simone Weil

*The great error of the Marxists and of all the nineteenth
century was to believe that by walking straight ahead one
had mounted into the air. We cannot take a single step toward heaven. It is not in our power to travel in a vertical
direction. If, however, we look heavenward for a long time,
God comes and takes us up.*

Simone Weil

Christian life today seems often to consist of the weary, befuddled attachment to and funding of various faddish left-wing causes in the name of progress and social justice; the use of the church as a sort of community center and support group to comfort, aid, and abet our troubled journeys through the complications of life in Edge City; or the strict doctrinal use of Scripture and tradition as a bulwark from which to fight social change or progress through the guises of antiabortion activism, antihomosexual referendum crusades, a constant harping, without definition, on "family values," and the promised return to the presumed halcyon days of a kinder, gentler America that each day's university study or television talk show makes more clear has never existed.

In light of these circumstances, the most compelling, and perhaps only, issue currently facing Christians in the United States and the other industrialized countries becomes the rationalization in our hearts, minds, and religious lives of the distance between our professed belief in the explicit message of Christ as expressed in the Gospels—faith, hope, and charity—and the demands, exigencies, and limitations placed upon the soul and psyche by the realities of life as it is lived by the Western, industrialized bourgeois in the late twentieth century. And this is not to say that no saintly, committed lives of Christian witness are being lived today; to the contrary, those particular examples of true fidelity to Christ's teachings only expose the emptiness of much general practice all the more harshly.

These folkways of the industrialized church, in fact, seem to be designed, albeit subconsciously, with the goal of obscuring the life and teachings of Christ, all the better to avoid confrontation with the contradictions inherent in modern life. I am reminded of Kierkegaard's befuddlement concerning Danish state church bishop Jacob Mynster, after the late prelate had been eulogized as "a genuine witness for the truth, not only in word and profession but in deed and in truth . . . [in the] whole series of witnesses to the truth which extends through time like a holy chain, from the days of the Apostles to our own day." This panegyric, delivered by the succeeding bishop, Hans Martensen, a former teacher of Kierkegaard's, left Kierkegaard outraged. Bishop Mynster, like all other high churchmen of his day, had lived the life of a pasha, in a church-owned palace with servants and attendants, celebrated by his peers. What, Kierkegaard wondered, did such a life of privilege and acclaim have to do with the life of Christ, the trials of Paul, Stephen, and Peter, the tragic, though hopeful, view of human life as expressed in the Beatitudes, the Epistle to the Romans, and John 3:16? Would the bishop have fought the money changers, or did he not in fact welcome them into the temple and consort with them?

How, exactly, was the late bishop a witness, and to what? In what was to be the last sustained activity of his life, Kierkegaard rigorously attacked—in person, in newspapers and journals, and in books—the Danish state church, the new bishop, Hans Martensen, and, by implication, the complacent status quo of all bourgeois European Christians, saying that which he felt must be said: "Whoever thou art, whatever thy life may be, my friend—by ceasing to take part (if in fact thou dost) in the public performance of divine worship as it now is, thou hast one guilt the less, and a great one, that thou dost not take part in holding God to be a fool, and in calling that the Christianity of the New Testament which is not the Christianity of the New Testament."

Kierkegaard's challenge has stood to this day. Indeed, it is perhaps more acute now, in a time when esteemed evangelist Billy Graham praises Richard Nixon as a paragon of Christian virtue, when a group that calls itself the Christian Coalition seeks temporal power in the most un-Christian of ways, when original media preacher Pat Robertson uses contributions from what is ostensibly worship to build a global entertainment empire—all in the name of Christ. And their opposites on the left are no better, seemingly lost in a labyrinth of New Age hucksterism masquerading as enlightenment, in shallow political causes (almost all overseas—much interest in South Africa, none in the South Bronx), and, in the name of being nonjudgmental, in an unwillingness to choose between or place value on any one thing over anything else—as is seen in doctrinal and denominational ruptures among Quakers, Episcopalians, and Catholics.

Holding God to be a fool. It is significant that Kierkegaard's scathing indictment was directed not at the unchurched but at those claiming to be believers, presumably God's elect. His accusation is echoed and expanded in the life and thought of another great interrogator of the Christian experience who seemed consumed with the conviction that the Christian life must be lived totally, literally, or not at all: the French mystic and martyr Simone Weil. Weil's short life, lived in the shadow of the world wars and Hitler, encompassed a great many activities: academic study, factory work, high-school teaching, philosophical exploration, and political agitation. But it is her lifelong journey to see the spiritual, emotional, and intellectual lives of rich and educated Westerners and their industrial-age societies in the light of the teachings of Jesus, and the Christian life, that constitutes her challenge to the status quo in the late twentieth century.

Simone Weil (pronounced "Vey") was born in Paris on February 3, 1909, the second child of Dr. Bernard and Selma Reinherz Weil. The family was Jewish but was not religious and did not maintain any Jewish identity; when asked, they said they considered themselves "French." Weil's childhood was one of comfort and privilege, in which material wealth was more than matched by parental affection and support. Her beloved older brother, André, was a child prodigy in mathematics (later becoming one of the most important mathematicians of the twentieth century) and is credited with providing her early education, teaching her at home whatever he had learned in school, sharing his books, and in general providing intellectual challenges to Simone at a very young age, all of which developed and fed a hunger for study and mastery that characterized her until her death. At the age of five, Weil had memorized long passages from *Cyrano de Bergerac,* which she loved to walk around the house declaiming. According to her childhood friend and later biographer, Simone Petrement, Weil's favorite lines were the conclusion: "Farewell Roxane, I go to die! / I think it will be this evening, my beloved!"

Weil was sickly as a child and had undergone an appendectomy at age three. Her frequent bouts of illness and bed rest gave her ample opportunity for obsessive reading. She developed a particular passion for the poet Deroulede, memorizing all his work and reciting it to anyone who would listen. She acted out entire scenes from Racine and, with her brother, spontaneously composed and recited poems that had to use preselected words and rhymes. These illnesses probably contributed in some manner to her later empathy and concern for those who were afflicted; but even more, she was marked deeply by the suffering that she saw around her during World War I. Weil's father served as an army doctor, and Simone would have seen much trauma close at hand. As her mother wrote to a friend, "The hospitals are packed to overflowing with sick and wounded . . . We also go almost every day to the hospitals to bring the patients oranges, crackers, and newspapers. And despite all this, one is ashamed to do so little when faced by such boundless misery."

Weil had her own responses to the travail of the war as well, corresponding with a soldier at the front and sending him food and candy, often doing odd jobs like gathering firewood to earn more money to buy treats to send. She also, in a precocious and eerie preview of the last days of her life, refused anything for herself that her soldier did not himself have access to, including honey and sugar. The little girl actually met the soldier in May 1916, but he was killed in action shortly after their meeting, which must have left a searing impression on the child.

When the family returned to Paris after the war, Weil's awareness of and concern with those less fortunate than she continued. One day when she was eleven, Weil disappeared from the family's apartment and was found after some searching standing quietly at a demonstration and rally for the unemployed on boulevard Saint-Michel. About this time she developed her deep and lifelong interest in manual labor, telling Simone Petrement that her interest in workers was fueled by more that a desire for social justice. "I love them naturally, I find them more beautiful than the bourgeois." Later in adolescence, Weil was to say that "the most accomplished and the most human man was the man who was both a manual worker and a thinker."

At age fourteen Weil spent part of a summer working in the fields on a farm in Normandy and in the summer of 1929 surreptitiously worked for several days in potato fields in the farming region of Jura. In 1931 she actually talked a crew of fishermen at Reville into allowing her to go out with them on their runs while her family vacationed in the seaside village; on these trips, she did make-work chores like winding fishing lines. One evening the boat she was working on was caught at sea in a tremendous storm, during which several boats were lost. When Weil's boat returned with all hands, the other crewmen reported with wonder and pride that she had performed as demanded during the storm and had not shown any fear.

At the time Weil was pursuing these interests, she was simultaneously distinguishing herself as a student at the most rigorous schools in Paris, the Lycée Victor-Duruy (where she was the student of René le Senne), the Lycée Henri IV (where she studied with the great philosopher Alain), and the legendary École Normale Supérieure, one of the truly great schools on the planet (its glittering roster of students includes, among others, Jean-Paul Sartre, Simone de Beauvoir, Raymond Aron, and Michel Foucault).

According to Simone Petrement, even at the École Normale, the elite of the elite, Weil's fellow students were awed or intimidated by her. De Beauvoir speaks of being made to feel "inadequate" by Weil, and the other students and some professors followed her lead on social issues. Late in life, in her memoir, de Beauvoir recalled an afternoon when she and Weil had quarreled:

> A great famine had broken out in China, and I was told that when she heard the news she had wept . . . I envied her for having a heart that could beat across the world. I managed to get near her one day. I don't know how the conversation got started; she declared in no uncertain tones that only one thing mattered in the world today: the Revolution that would feed all the starving people on earth. I retorted, no less peremptorily, that the problem was not to make men happy, but to find the reason for their existence. She looked me up and down: "It's easy to see that you've never gone hungry" . . . she had classified me as "a high-minded little bourgeoise."

Even as a student at the École, whenever Weil returned to the Lycée Henri IV to visit and hear lectures, Alain would, as a point of honor, allow whomever he currently considered his best student to sit beside her.

After her undergraduate career, concluded by passing the prestigious *agrégation* examination, Weil began teaching philosophy at a girls' lycée in the remote southeastern French city of Le Puy (thirteen hours from Paris by train), where she proved immensely popular with her students. Some of them later described her to Petrement:

> Her carelessness with dress did not shock us; she was neither affected nor tomboyish; we paid less and less attention to these things, already sensing that Simone Weil's time and thoughts were devoted to occupations of another order. The clumsiness of her gestures, above all of her hands, the special expression on her face when she would concentrate on her thought, her piercing look through her thick glasses, her smile—everything about her emanated a feeling of total frankness and forgetfulness of self, revealing a nobility of soul that was certainly at the root of the emotions she inspired in us, but that at first we were not aware of.

It was rumored that the distant posting was given in punishment for her political views and activities while at the École. During the year, she became heavily involved with the local trade-union movement, both in Le Puy and in the regional industrial center of Saint-Étienne. Weil had obtained introductions to labor leaders from her contacts in Paris and journeyed three hours by train each week to meet with and offer her services to the workers and their leaders. Weil was essentially a syndicalist. This politically agnostic group believed in social transformation through the general strike, through coordinated and societywide action—described by James Forman as the "peaceful but relentless folding of arms that would starve out the capitalists."

Syndicalists strove for worker control in matters of self-management, company policy, production values, and initiatives; thought of all work as intrinsically important and valuable; and viewed the common worker as the most important member of society, the person who created the goods around which economy and society revolved. These views were intimately related to some of the coalescing theories the young Weil was developing and pointed toward her innate deep love of humanity in general and the average, often overlooked, person in particular.

Weil's labor activities were not well received in Le Puy—she had, among other things, led a march of the unemployed on the city council—and she was pressured to transfer to the town of Auxerre. There, the headmistress was so exercised by Weil that she abolished philosophy as a course of study in the school rather than have her return, forcing Weil to move on to Roanne, near Saint-Étienne. In Roanne she finally found a congenial teaching environment and began her serious writing with the essay "Reflections Concerning the Causes of Liberty and Social Oppression." This essay details Weil's concerns with modern society, a society where "Human history is simply the history of the servitude which makes men—oppressors and oppressed alike—the plaything of the instruments of domination they themselves have manufactured, and thus reduces living humanity to being the chattel of inanimate chattels."

In the spring of 1934 Weil took a leave of absence from teaching and in December of that year started a job as an unskilled worker at the Alsthom Company in Paris, taking a room near the factory and intending to live as an ordinary blue-collar person. She had met the progressive managing director of the firm, Auguste Deteouf, through socialist friends, and he agreed to hire her for the shop floor. This was to be a transformative experience for her, even though as a wealthy bourgeoise she was free to leave at any time and reclaim her privilege. She found the factory work to be an education unlike any she had previously experienced, degrading and exhausting. "Each physical annoyance needlessly imposed, each show of lack of respect, each brutality, each humiliation, however trivial, appears as a fresh reminder." It almost broke her spirit. She was tired all the time and found little of the fellow-feeling and fraternity among the workers that she had expected.

In April 1935, Weil left the Alsthom Company for the J. J. Carnaud et Forges de Basse-Indre factory, only lasting a month before being fired for ineptitude. In June she began working at a Renault car factory, surviving for slightly more than two months and suffering several injuries. She summed up her experience: "I could have been shattered. I nearly was . . . I arose each morning with anguish, I went to the factory with dread; I worked like a slave." This appearance of the word *slave* is a crucial development in her thinking; it coincides with her growing spiritual interest in Christianity and the Catholic church and a growing disillusion with politics and revolution. Society was based on obedience, on passively accepting whatever the powers-that-be directed; the entire structure of industrial society was geared toward achieving this result, and no change of any kind would be possible without personal development, psychologically and spiritually. This had been proved in the Soviet Union, in Germany, in Italy, and in France. Great social upheaval had only resulted in "a new boss."

In July 1936 the Spanish Civil War erupted, and this event compelled Weil into action that might seem contradictory to her evolving beliefs but that on closer examination is not. Determined to be of aid to the betrayed republican government of Spain as it fought the forces of Generalissimo Francisco Franco and the fascist nationalists, she obtained journalistic credentials and left for the front. Her feeling was that she did not want to sit comfortably in Paris while a historic verdict was being rendered; she had to participate in the struggle of those who were dying in support of her belief that human beings could live with and among one another in a situation where all had dignity and were valued. Given the rising fascist tide in Europe, she thought that Spain held the last hope for human values on a human scale.

She could not have been more disappointed. She found the peasants illiterate and wretchedly oppressed. And worse, there were deep differences and power discrepancies between those peasants and the army that was purportedly fighting for them: "An abyss separated the armed militiamen from the unarmed population, an abyss exactly like that which separates the rich and the poor." She also contemplated her own death. "If they capture me, they will kill me . . . But it is deserved. Our troops have spilled a lot of blood. I am morally an accomplice." Where was the hope for a free Spain, the last chance for the syndicalist dream? She had learned, to her lifelong chagrin, a lesson we are now, sixty years later, relearning in Bosnia, Burma, central Asia, and Africa: "As soon as men know that they can kill without fear of punishment or blame, they kill; or at least they encourage killers with approving smiles . . . The very purpose of the whole struggle is lost in an atmosphere of this sort. For the purpose can only be defined in terms of the public good, of the welfare of men—and men have become valueless."

On August 20 Weil stepped into a pan of boiling oil and suffered severe burns on her leg and ankle. A cooking fire had been built below ground for camouflage, and she was unaware of the location. Weil had to be evacuated to Barcelona, where her parents took charge of her recovery before taking her back to France. Appalled by both the French national indifference to the fate of the republicans in Spain and France's concurrent military buildup to face the German and Italian threat, Weil drew a chilling and prophetic conclusion about the future of life in Europe: "Capitalism will be destroyed, but not by the working class. It will be destroyed by the development of national defense in each country, and replaced by the totalitarian state. That is the revolution we shall have."

Out of this disillusion a new understanding and maturity began to take shape, hinting at her turn toward religion and martyrdom. "Everything that contributes toward giving those who are at the bottom of the social scale the feeling that they possess a value is to a certain extent subversive . . . all that is highest in human life, every effort of thought, every effort of love, has a corrosive effect on the established order . . . insofar as it is ceaselessly creating a scale of values 'that is not of this world,' it is the enemy of the forces which control society . . . Those who want to think, love, and transpose all purity into political action can only perish murdered, forsaken even by their own people, vilified after their death by history."

In 1937 Weil began to have mystical religious experiences. She describes an experience in a chapel at Assisi, in Italy: "There, alone . . . where Saint Francis often used to pray, something stronger than I was compelled me for the first time in my life to go down on my knees." She was reacting to her suffering in the factory and in Spain, and her life was changing: "What I went through there marked me in so lasting a manner that still today when any human being, whoever he may be and in whatever circumstances, speaks to me without brutality, I cannot help having the impression that there must be a mistake and that unfortunately the mistake will in all probability disappear . . . I received forever the mark of a slave . . . Since then I have always regarded myself as a slave . . . the conviction was suddenly borne in upon me that Christianity is pre-eminently the religion of slaves, that slaves cannot help belonging to it, and I among others." She later described what had happened at Assisi as a mystic transformation, an "insertion of eternity into time," an elaboration of her analogy of the human condition and the deity's role in our lives: "We are abandoned in time. God is not in time."

Simone Weil had two further similarly mystic experiences, the first while listening to Gregorian chant in a Benedictine abbey, which she described as allowing her "to get outside this miserable flesh, to leave it to suffer alone heaped up in a corner, and to find a pure and perfect joy in the extraordinary beauty of the chant and the words." The second epiphany occurred while reading "Love" by metaphysical poet George Herbert:

> Love bade me welcome; yet my soul drew back,
> Guilty of dust and sin.
> But quick-eyed Love, observing me grow slack
> From my first entrance in,
> Drew nearer to me, sweetly questioning
> If I lack'd anything.
>
> "A guest," I answer'd, "worthy to be here:"
> Love said, "You shall be he."
> "I, the unkind, ungrateful? Ah, my dear,
> I cannot look on Thee."
> Love took my hand and smiling did reply,
> "Who made the eyes but I?"
>
> "Truth, Lord; but I have marr'd them: let my shame
> Go where it doth deserve."
> "And know you not," says Love, "Who bore the blame?"
> "My dear, then I will serve."
> "You must sit down," says Love, "and taste my meat."
> So I did sit and eat.

Weil later recounted in a letter her emotions while reading the poem: "It has played a big role in my life, because I was repeating it to myself at the moment when Christ came to take possession of me for the first time. I thought I was only reciting a beautiful poem but, unknown to me, it was a prayer."

Weil's life was on its final course, a counterpoint of regular movement to escape the ever-advancing Nazi threat on the one side, coupled with her constant refusal to officially enter the Catholic church as she experienced an ever-deepening love for Christ. In 1940 she reluctantly left Paris for the city of Nevers, but moved on to Vichy when the Germans occupied Nevers. After the dissolution of the French government and full capitulation to Hitler, Weil and her parents moved to Marseilles, where they spent the winter. It was during this time, while looking for work (as a Jew she lost her teaching privileges), that she met the Catholic priest Joseph-Marie Perrin, who arranged for her to work on the farm of Gustave Thibon. Father Perrin became her confidant and spiritual adviser, talking through with her the various concerns and exceptions she had with Catholic doctrine and striving mightily to get Weil to accept baptism. (He and Thibon are also responsible for the survival of much of her important work.)

In August Weil journeyed to Thibon's farm in the Rhône Valley to work on the grape harvest. Thibon, a deeply serious man who was an aspiring writer and a practicing Catholic, was to become one of Weil's closest friends, though the friendship had a difficult beginning. Thibon found Weil deeply opinionated and argumentative—she refused, among other things, to board in the main house, saying it was "too comfortable"—and the two spent the first weeks of their acquaintance in conflict. But Thibon reports that he slowly noticed the singular kindness and depth of her soul: "She was just then beginning to open with all her soul to Christianity; a limpid mysticism emanated from her; in no other human being have I ever come across such familiarity with religious mysteries; never have I felt the word *supernatural* to be more charged with reality than when in contact with her."

In May 1942, against her will and under extreme pressure from her parents, Simone Weil left France for the last time, sailing from Marseilles to Casablanca, where the family stayed for two and a half weeks before continuing on to New York City. They reached New York in July, joining André Weil, and the senior Weils gratefully settled into an apartment on Riverside Drive, but Simone felt like a deserter from those suffering in

Europe, particularly France, and was already busy plotting her return. In a letter she said:

> It is a very hard thing to leave one's country in distress. Although my parents, who wanted to escape anti-Semitism, put great pressure upon me to make me go with them, I would never have left France without the hope that through coming here I could take a greater part in the struggle, the danger, and the suffering of this war . . . I would welcome *any* degree of danger if only I could do something really useful. My life is of no value to me so long as Paris, my native city, is subject to German domination. Nor do I wish my town to be freed only with the blood of others.

While in New York, Weil campaigned to be allowed to return to France. She wanted to establish a corps of volunteer female nurses who would serve on the front lines of the war, and wrote to French, English, and American officials. While awaiting the replies, she did research at the New York Public Library, attended mass at Corpus Christi parish, and spent time in Harlem, including regularly attending a black Baptist church there. She wrote in a letter, "I am the only white person in the church. After a service of one or two hours, when the atmosphere is established, the religious fervor of the minister and congregation explodes into dances much like the Charleston, exclamations, cries and the singing of spirituals. That's really worth seeing. A true and moving expression of faith, it seems to me." It is not surprising, given her affinities for the downtrodden and outsiders, that Weil gravitated toward blacks while in America. In fact, she told her mother that if forced to remain in the United States she would "go to work in the south with the blacks, and there I am sure I will die because I can't stand this [bourgeois New York City] life."

Finally, through the political manipulations of an old schoolmate, Maurice Schumann, in November 1942 she was allowed to travel to England and begin working for the Free French movement. The nurses corps idea was dismissed, but Weil was given an office job analyzing documents and drawing up plans for the reconstruction of postwar France. Among her voluminous writing from this time is her monumental "Draft for a Statement of Human Obligations." It begins: "There is a reality outside the world, that is to say, outside space and time, outside man's mental universe, outside any sphere whatsoever that is accessible to human faculties. Corresponding to this reality, at the centre of the human heart, is the longing for an absolute good, a longing which is always there and is never

appeased by any object in this world." Among other works, she also wrote
The Need for Roots during this time, as an outline for restoring French culture and community.

In January 1943, she was diagnosed with tuberculosis. In April she was
found lying unconscious on the floor of her apartment, having been missing for two days. She was taken to the hospital, where her decline continued, accentuated by her eating too little food. Legend holds that she
starved herself to death, but apparently it was a combination of a digestive
disorder and the desire to eat only as much as those French citizens living
in Nazi-occupied areas. At this time she also seriously explored the idea
of baptism into the Catholic church, which she had resisted up until that
time because, as she said in her *Spiritual Autobiography*, "I have never once
had, even for a moment, the feeling that God wants me to be in the
church. I have never even once had a feeling of uncertainty. I think at the
present time we can finally conclude that he does not want me in the
church." She also did not want to surrender her intellectual freedom. "So
many things are outside [the church], so many things that I love and do
not want to give up." The year before, she did not see how she could explore the world and various traditions as she desired: "I felt that I could
not honestly give up my opinions concerning the non-Christian religions
and concerning Israel—and as a matter of fact time and medication have
only served to strengthen them." She seemed to be wavering on this at the
end, stating in her "Last Text" that "I have never until now presented a
priest with a formal request for baptism. Nor do I do so now. Nevertheless I feel not the abstract but the practical, real, urgent need to know
whether, if I were to request it, it would be granted or refused me."

After an agonizing summer in the hospital, Simone Weil died of car-
diac arrest late on the evening of August 24, 1943. Her body had almost
literally worn itself out. In the week before her demise, she had experienced several good days and had seemed especially lively and happy the
afternoon preceding her death. Because of the odd nature of her dying,
there was an inquest, at which the coroner described the death as being a
result of "cardial failure due to myocardial degeneration of the heart mus-
cles due to starvation and pulmonary tuberculosis. The deceased did kill
and slay herself by refusing to eat whilst the balance of her mind was dis-
turbed." She was buried in the Catholic section of the cemetery in Ash-
ford, Kent, after a funeral attended by only seven people. A Catholic priest
who had been asked to conduct the service took the wrong train and
never got there.

Jesus said, "If anyone wishes to come after me, let him deny himself and take up his cross and follow me" (Matthew 16:24). Simone Weil met—embraced—the literalness of this challenge, intuitively understanding how one would have to move away from and mistrust "the beast"—the world—in order to see God clearly. Her secular work was in many ways a preparation, an exhaustion of the options that the world offered, until she could see that only one thing, Christ, made sense to her. Weil's desire to follow the teachings of Jesus, and the love and faith they inspired in her, to the end, fiercely, vigorously, and logically, led to her death. Not from suicide, not from a hunger strike, but from a need to witness, to acknowledge and bear the sorrow of the world and act accordingly, regardless of the danger.

In a time when the vast majority of nominal Christians in the Western industrial countries behave like those good citizens in W. H. Auden's poem "Musée de Beaux Arts," contentedly continuing on their various merry ways while ignoring the horror before them, we can begin to see the ways in which Simone Weil, in the spirit of Søren Kierkegaard, is a martyr for our time. She is asking us to look at the world and love it *without consuming it,* literally and figuratively; to take the responsibility for our fellows that true love demands. If we truly look, she says, we will not be able to turn away, to calmly ignore suffering and injustice. We will want to be like Jesus, and we will act upon that wish.

Weil's life and work is a rebuke of the smug illusions that comfort some contemporary Christians and an affirmation of connectedness, of the higher reality that we are all related to one another as human beings and that we cannot avoid or escape one another's fates. She is a challenge to the rich Christians of the West because she forces us to reexamine everything from scratch, to scrape away the years of convention, false or lazy piety, mediocre religious instruction, and self-satisfaction that cloud our vision and keep us from acting on our professed beliefs. We are caught between what we have—what we own—and what we say we believe, between what we profess to value and the cowardice that wealth and comfort place upon us.

When Simone Weil reads a Bible verse, says the "Our Father," she means it; she asks, What does this really mean for those who want to be Christians? This is a radical, unflinching reinterpretation—straight reading—of the Gospels. It is more literal, perhaps, because of her outsider status and her "fresh eyes." *Blessed are the meek . . . Blessed are those who hunger and thirst for righteousness . . . Blessed are the merciful . . . Blessed are the peacemakers . . .* Weil is asking those of us who are Christians to live up to the truths we say we believe, and as a witness to those truths she put her life and health on the line. Close study of her challenge forces us to contemplate the strong possibility that few of us who proclaim to be Christians are what we say we are or actually believe what we claim to believe, especially those of us who profess to be followers of Christ.

How do we live with the images of Zaire, Sudan, Bosnia, Salvador, Mexico, Bangladesh, Brooklyn, Mississippi, Los Angeles—and all the others that float through our homes and imaginations every day—and do nothing? How do we know of these things, do nothing, and call ourselves Christians? Simone Weil protested against this indifference, for that is what it is, our easy acquiescence to the ways of the world. She said very clearly and unapologetically that the way things are is simply not good enough. She could not look away; the world has to be looked at accurately in all its horror to keep us from becoming blind and smug, from thinking that we are masters of that which we are not. The world in its violence and cruelty is what brings us back to God, and God in turn gives us the courage to oppose the cruelties of the human-built world. This is the lesson of the life of Simone Weil, the evidence of her witness, and an interrogation that will stand in rebuke of each and every believer as long as the Christian faith is practiced.

For Further Reading

John Hellman, *Simone Weil: An Introduction to Her Thought*. Minneapolis: Fortress Press, 1982.

David McLellan, *Utopian Pessimist: The Life and Thought of Simone Weil*. New York: Poseidon Press, 1990.

Thomas Nevin, *Simone Weil: Portrait of a Self-Exiled Jew*. Durham: University of North Carolina Press, 1991.

Simone Weil, *The Illiad, or the Poem of Force*. Edited by Ronald Hathaway. Pendle Hill Pamphlet 91. Wallingford, PA: Pendle Hill Publications, 1986.

———, *The Notebooks of Simone Weil*. London: Routledge & Kegan Paul, 1956.

———, *Two Moral Essays: Draft for a Statement of Human Obligations and Human Personality*. Edited by Ronald Hathaway. Pendle Hill Pamphlet 240. Wallingford, PA: Pendle Hill Publications, 1986.

———, *Waiting for God*. New York: HarperPerennial, 1973.

EDITH STEIN

Poland, 1942

A Book Sealed with Seven Seals

by PATRICIA HAMPL

*I have no private life anymore, I told myself. All my
energy must be devoted to this great happening. Only
when the war is over, if I'm still alive then, will I be
permitted to think of my private affairs once more.*

The year is 1914, summer. Edith Stein is twenty-two, a graduate student in Göttingen studying philosophy with the phenomenologist Edmund Husserl. In this passage from her autobiography, *Life in a Jewish Family*, she is instructing herself on her place in the First World War, not the Second, though that is the war that finally claimed her and has fixed her in history as one of "the six million."

Yet it is all there already—the stern high-mindedness barely concealing a raw passion, the longing to plunge into an existence more compelling than a "private life," the urge to be used, even used up, by a consuming reality. There is nothing morbid: the innocent grandiosity—"I have no private life anymore . . . if I'm still alive"—ripples with excitement. This girl, reading Schopenhauer in her rented room on a July afternoon, when a friend runs in with the news that war has been declared, might just as well have been saying, "At last—I can *live.*"

She says that she slapped shut *The World as Will and Idea* ("Oddly enough, I never took up that particular book again") and headed home to Breslau—not so much because it was home but because "Göttingen was in the heart of Germany and there was little likelihood it would get to see any of the enemy except possibly prisoners of war. Breslau, on the contrary, was but a few hours' distance from the Russian border and was the most important fortification in the east. That it might soon be besieged by Russian troops was distinctly possible. My decision was made."

The destination she chose was not home, but history. A flight from the personal into—what? Thrilling danger? But also into a truth more encompassing than "private life." She wished her own life to be absorbed by a vast plot. The first such grandeur she encountered was the Great War. She ran to it. This was only partly a matter of patriotism (though she and her family were fiercely pro-German, then and much later, so assimilated that the anti-Semitism of the prewar National Socialist period struck her mother as implausible, demented, ridiculous). It was clearly Edith Stein's desire to disappear into devotion to a greater good. When a fellow student asked their friend Karl Reinach, a young philosophy professor at the university, if he too must go to war, Reinach replied, "It's not that I *must;* rather, I'm permitted to go."

"His statement pleased me very much," Edith Stein noted. "It expressed so well my own feelings." What appealed to her was the surrender of individual life to a massive reality encompassing everyone. The self was no good if it was merely personal, merely "personality." Rather, as she wrote in her first book, "The self is the individual's way of structuring experience." The self was necessary—but not for itself. It was necessary as the experiencer of "phenomena," of reality as it is absorbed by a life. Self was meant, in a real sense, to be lost. A kind of blessed anonymity attended the most genuine life, the most realized self.

The desire for anonymity is a desire for greatness. True anonymity, of course, is unconscious, unsought. But the instinct, made conscious, to bury the self's small story in the overwhelming text of history—this is a passion for greatness. In her autobiography, Edith Stein emphasized her "conviction that I was destined for something great." Such greatness should not be confused with ambition, for ambition revolves endlessly, and finally hopelessly, around the individual's sense of stardom. Its engine is self-reflexive—whether the ambition looks like arrogance or self-loathing, or sheer willfulness.

The urge toward greatness, on the other hand, is oddly aligned with humility. The purpose is not the "fulfillment" of a self, nor its aggrandizement, but the deft insertion of the self into an overwhelming design. Hence, the sensation of "the loss of self." This quest for greatness always carries as well a charge of relation, of service: at the earliest opportunity, Edith Stein rushed, against her mother's strenuous objection, to work as a Red Cross nurse's aide in a camp hospital for soldiers suffering from infectious diseases. Ultimately, a life seeking greatness is about the loss of the self in the service of a more complete reality. It is a disappearing act. It is, sometimes, a martyrdom. That, finally, is how it came to be in the unlikely life of Edith Stein.

This is the plot: A woman, born into a warm German Jewish family, converts to Catholicism several years after she earns her doctorate in philosophy with a brilliant dissertation published under the title *On the Problem of Empathy*. She teaches and lectures at Catholic colleges in German-speaking Europe for a decade. Soon after her teaching career is ended by the Nazi decree against Jewish teachers in 1933, she enters a Carmelite monastery in Cologne and becomes a contemplative nun. After Kristallnacht, as conditions worsen in Germany, she is moved to a Carmel in Holland on New Year's Eve, 1938. Three years later, two SS officers raid the Dutch monastery and arrest her. A week after that she is sent in a transport to Auschwitz. She perishes in a gas chamber soon after her arrival there.

That is the life. There is a posthumous existence as well, with its own drama. In 1987 Pope John Paul VI beatified Edith Stein as a martyr of the church in a ceremony in a Cologne stadium filled with 70,000 people. There was, not surprisingly, a backlash of protest, mostly from Jewish groups, but also from some chagrined Catholics: what was the church doing appropriating as a martyr a woman who, while she died a committed Christian, was murdered precisely because she was Jewish?

Some of Edith Stein's descendants declined to go to the ceremony. But her niece, Susanne Batzdorff, who lives now in California, did attend. Over the years, she has offered sympathetic help to the Carmelite editors and translators of her aunt's work. But as she sat in the stadium that day, she has since written, "Suddenly it hit me: All these people are gathered here to witness my Aunt Edith Stein declared a blessed martyr of the Catholic church. Yet in August 1942, when a freight train carried her to her death in a gas chamber, no one would help or cry out to stop the horror."

Hers is the inevitable accusation. And interestingly, the question of the propriety of the church's claiming Edith Stein as a martyr of the church rests fundamentally on "the problem of empathy," Edith Stein's defining subject. For if the church cannot see itself as it is reflected by another suffering population, and if it refuses to acknowledge the judgment of that gaze, then it fails in this essential spiritual relation of empathy. For the purpose of empathy is the fullness of reality, of truth. "Empathy," Edith Stein wrote, "offers itself to us as a corrective for self-deception." The point of empathy: I allow myself to be seen through the judgment and clarity of your gaze, acknowledging, as Edith Stein says, that "it is possible for another to judge me more accurately than I judge myself and give me clarity about myself." Empathy seeks truth, and along its difficult way it makes the stunning discovery of compassion as well.

In pursuing Edith Stein's canonization, the church not only displays a troubling insensitivity to Jewish experience, but even more strangely, it denies itself and its people the real benefit of contemplating her death. For if the church relinquished its claim on her martyrdom, Edith Stein could become for Christians the focal point of an act of contrition still desperately needed by the Western world in response to the midcentury horrors committed against Jews and Jewish life in Christian Europe.

As a Catholic saint, she is folded into the canon of church history. But where she is needed is exactly where she placed herself: in between. The Catholic church needs Edith Stein—that's true. Not as a saint of the church, but as a presence who, against all the odds, stands at the midpoint of the evils of midcentury. She should remain a ghost, a figure forever calling Christians toward contrition—the proper Christian response to the Holocaust. What would her niece's response have been at a gathering of Catholics in the Cologne stadium if the occasion had been not a beatification ceremony but a giant open-air act of contrition on the part of the church, extended to Jews living and dead? Catholics must accept the fact that sainthood is not simply a way of honoring a great life; it is inevitably a way of claiming it. The act of contrition must begin with the willingness to relinquish that claim.

Yet this contentious question of Edith Stein's formalization as a martyr of the church, proper to any discussion of the church's habits of cultural appropriation, does not belong to Edith Stein. If there is a problem (and the essays and letters published on the subject make it clear that there is a problem), it is not hers. This ethical question belongs to the church's life, not to Edith Stein's. She remains the riddle containing her seeming contradictions. She, not her "cause" (on either side of the debate), is the fascination. For she is an enigma. That is, she is a life waiting to be read.

Edith Stein bore a crushing burden of paradox with simplicity, certainty, and humility. She went where she had to go—into the Catholic communion when commanded by faith; then, even deeper, into the cloister of Carmel; and finally, crammed into a fetid boxcar, to Auschwitz. For her, the paradox of her life was not a contradiction to be debated but a truth to be lived. She understood quite early that she would be doubly implicated in the crimes of the age as a Christian Jew: "I will always be close to you, to my family, to the Jewish people," she said to her niece Susanne Batzdorff when, as a girl, she asked her aunt why she was entering a Christian monastery *now*, just as attacks on Jews were growing. "And don't think my being in a convent is going to keep me immune from what is happening in the world."

If her life is one of the great conundrums of twentieth-century faith, the mystery does not begin when she converted to Roman Catholicism at the age of thirty. She was one born for mystery, it seems, as genius always is. Jan Nota, a Jesuit priest who knew Edith Stein in her final years in the Carmel in Echt, Holland, has written that the "fascinating thing to me about Edith Stein was that truth did not exist as an abstraction for her, but as something incarnated in persons, and therefore as inconceivable apart from love."

From childhood, when she perceived something to be "true," she had to pursue it, do it, be it—whatever it was. She had been a notoriously riotous, unruly child. "I was mercurially lively, always in motion," she writes, "spilling over with pranks, impertinent and precocious, and at the same time, intractably stubborn and angry if anything went against my will. My eldest sister, whom I loved very much, tested her newly-acquired child-training methods on me in vain."

Then, at about the age of seven, she says the "first great transformation took place in me." It was not the result of an external force, she was sure. She could not explain it, she writes in her autobiography, except to say that "reason assumed command within me." She distinctly remembered that "from that time on, I was convinced that my mother and my sister Frieda had a better knowledge of what was good for me than I had; and because of this confidence, I readily obeyed them." Her "old stubbornness" left her. No one could explain the transformation, but for her it was a natural response to an internal recognition: her behavior changed the instant her perception of "the truth" changed.

Later, the same precise register between perception and action would compel her to behavior far more flagrant than the childhood furies that once caused her mother such pain. But these changes, so inexplicable and even dismaying to those who loved her, were incontrovertible. Once she seized upon the truth, it claimed her and required action. As a result, she wrote, "I was able to sever the seemingly strongest ties with minimal effort and fly away like a bird escaped from a snare."

But if she could so easily "fly away," she flew alone and into skies darker than her protective family could have imagined. In the midst of an unusually close family, she remained inscrutable. "In spite of the great closeness between us," she wrote, "I couldn't confide in my mother more than in anyone else. From early childhood I led a strange double life that produced alternations of behavior which must have seemed incomprehensible and erratic to any outside observer."

The truth was, she wrote, that "within her, another hidden world was emerging, where I would assimilate on my own the things that I saw and heard during the day." As a child she had a naturally heightened sensitivity to suffering, and any observed inequity was writ large in her heart. "Whatever I saw or heard throughout my days was pondered over there"—in her "hidden world." She could not understand how people could laugh at a stumbling, incoherent alcoholic. If anyone spoke of a murder in her presence, she would "lie awake for hours that night, and, in the dark, horror would press in upon me from every corner . . . I never mentioned a word to anyone of these things which caused me so much hidden suffering. It never occurred to me that one could speak about such matters."

No one else had access to this hidden world whence all the "incomprehensible and erratic" behavior came. Her adoring older sisters, already in awe of her grave intelligence and her fierce integrity, despaired of understanding her. So great was her native reserve that they called her, teasingly, "the book sealed with seven seals."

Edith Stein was born in Breslau, Germany (now Wroclaw, Poland), October 12, 1891, on Yom Kippur—a fact, she always thought, that played into her being her mother's favorite. She was the youngest of seven children, some of them nearly adult when she was born. She and her sister Erna, only eighteen months her senior, were the babies, brought up almost as twins.

When Edith was two, her father died suddenly of a heat stroke while he was away on business. Thus began the career of his widow, Auguste Courant Stein, who, against the counsel of her own family, took over the management of her husband's lumber business. The older children helped raise the younger ones, while Auguste kept them all going with her tireless devotion to them and to the business. Against significant odds, she prospered.

A photograph of Auguste, circa 1925 (she was seventy-six and would live another eleven years): The stout body, always dressed in black after her husband's death, suggests solidity rather than anything as frivolous as fat. The face is a stone of certainty, not hard but absolute. The jaw is set, the mouth the most telling feature: lips closed in a firm, almost fierce line, giving away nothing. It is not the tense face of a petty domestic dictator, but all the more resolute: a woman used to command, of necessity.

In a facing photograph in *Life in a Jewish Family,* taken at the same time (when she was thirty-four), Edith sits, hand to deep-clefted chin, gazing at the camera neutrally, not feeling compelled, apparently, to offer any expression. She is an attractive woman, her mouth surprisingly voluptuous in repose. She is waiting to return to her reading: her index finger is inserted in the closed book on her lap, marking her place during this brief intrusion.

By the time these two photographs of mother and daughter were made, much had already been decided. Edith, who was a convinced atheist at fifteen in the liberal idealist way her older brothers and sisters had brought to bear in their mother's orthodox home, had eventually come to belief during her university years, probably influenced by the largely Christian—though not Catholic—circle around Husserl. The Master (as Edith and his other devoted students always called him) was Jewish, though he had become a nominal Lutheran, apparently as a professional protection long before Nazi times.

The decisive moment for Edith occurred, however, when she was visiting philosopher friends in Bergzabern during the summer of 1921. One morning, by chance, she picked up a copy of the autobiography of Saint Teresa of Ávila on a bookshelf. Reading it occasioned one of her galvanizing moments of truth. She was unable to put it down, and sat up all night reading. When she put it down the next morning, she said, "This is the truth." She was baptized in the Catholic church on New Year's Day, 1922.

Auguste was appalled, deeply repelled. "She particularly rejects conversions," Edith wrote to a Catholic friend later. "Everyone ought to live and die in the faith in which they were born. She imagines atrocious things about Catholicism and life in a convent." Going off, against her mother's wishes, to serve in a lazaretto during the war had been one thing, but this was a bizarre infatuation, a monstrous disloyalty.

Worse was to come. On October 15, 1933, three days after her forty-second birthday (on the feast day of Teresa of Ávila), Edith Stein entered the Carmelite monastery of Cologne as a postulant. Her conversion to Catholicism and her conviction of her vocation to Carmel had come virtually together. Before her baptism, she "still cherished," she says, "the dream of a great love and of a happy marriage." Earlier, there had been a fondness (apparently chaste) between Edith and a fellow philosophy student, Hans Lipps. But she was never willing to sacrifice her profession to marriage. Later, after Lipps married and had two small children and his wife suddenly died, he approached Edith Stein again. "Too late," she is reported to have said. This was not the romantic "too late" of disappointed dreams, however, but quite simply the acknowledgment that she was already committed: by then she was baptized, and with her conversion came her vocation to Carmel.

The eleven-year wait between baptism and entrance into the monastery was largely a form of obedience to her spiritual advisers. They cautioned against hasty action on the part of enthusiastic converts. No doubt they also felt Edith's talents as lecturer and teacher had a place in the world. She was willing to be guided in this and was a diligent intellectual worker, turning her philosophical gift now toward Thomas Aquinas, writing and lecturing to Catholic audiences about medieval mysticism and the place of women in the world and in the church. Her writing of the period is lucid, sensible, progressive (she makes a cogent case for sex education in the schools, for example, and argues with un-

canny prophecy about the importance of a wider role for women in religion).

There was another reason to wait. She admitted that at first she had
thought of her baptism as "preparation for entrance into the [Carmelite]
Order." But several months later, seeing her mother for the first time since
her baptism, she realized that Auguste "couldn't handle another blow for
the present. Not that it would have killed her—but I couldn't have held
myself responsible for the embitterment it would have caused."

Before her conversion, she had tried to follow her brilliant *summa* doctorate with a regular university appointment, but the rigidly hierarchical
German academic system was not ready for a woman. No one was willing to sponsor her *habilitation,* the necessary second thesis required for
university appointment. The fervent feminism of her youth met the hard
wall of habit and entrenched power. She spent her professional career at
Catholic colleges and became a much-sought-after lecturer in Germany,
Austria, and Switzerland, in particular.

But clearly, already by 1922, she knew she was a contemplative nun.
She lived in a room adjacent to the nuns' quarters at the college where she
taught, and she attended daily mass, following as well the daily prayers of
the Divine Office. In effect, she managed to mimic a monastic life years
before her entrance to Carmel.

When Edith Stein was asked to reveal the nature of her religious conversion, she refused. There is no essay or memoir, not even a letter to a
trusted friend—nothing—that sheds light on what exactly caused her decisive action. What we know: she read Teresa of Ávila—and recognized
there "the truth." And so she followed it. This had been her pattern since
her "first transformation" when she was a willful seven-year-old and suddenly, inexplicably, felt that "reason assumed command" within her. Now
it was not her mother and her older sister who "had a better knowledge
of what was good" for her. Now it was the Spirit itself.

What she found in Teresa she also kept to herself, though certainly she
is not the first person to have been profoundly affected by that ardent personality. Even today, almost four and a half centuries after she wrote it,
Teresa's autobiography remains the most vivid personal document in the
history of Christian testimony, more spirited and immediate even than
Saint Augustine's *Confessions.* These three—Augustine, Teresa, Edith—

form a fascinating linked-chain of conversions, each in turn liberated from what Teresa calls in her autobiography "the shadow of death," which had left them utterly worn out with interior struggle.

As Waltraud Herbstrith, one of Edith Stein's biographers, notes, the three "shadows" were different for each of them, but the sense of liberation was the same: for Augustine the snare was unbridled sensuality; for Teresa, the surface pleasures of "society" and its tendency to skim over life lightly. For Edith Stein, it was the twentieth-century existential burden: a rationalist, materialist worldview that did not permit the freedom to offer oneself to God. From carnality, to society's distractions, to heady intellectualism: these three figures are cameos of Western civilization's history of spiritual dilemmas.

Edith Stein's reticence about her conversion is striking even in this context of Catholic memoir. It sets her apart from Augustine and from Teresa, for her autobiography does not touch on Christian themes, whereas Augustine and Teresa tremble with the news. Edith Stein's silence bears the particular stamp of her faith—and of her solidarity with her Jewishness. There is nothing "apostolic" about Edith Stein; not a whiff of evangelism pervades her writing. She has no desire to convince anyone of anything—nor to persuade, and absolutely not to convert. What had happened to her, what continued to happen to her thanks to the daily grace of liturgical and contemplative prayer, was a mystery. It was simply to be lived.

That was not only enough, it was hard enough. It is often difficult for Catholics to understand what "contemplative life" is about—or for. But Edith Stein was entering this hidden world (literally, an "enclosure") against a backdrop of incomprehension and even antagonism from her family and professional friends. What on earth was she doing this for? As her mother cried in frustration at her Christianity, "Why did you have to get to know him? He was a good man—I'm not saying anything against him. But why did he have to go and make himself God?"

In fact, it was the full-time nature of the compelling occupation of prayer that sent Edith Stein to Carmel. What is often overlooked, especially in recent times, about the Catholic tradition: in spite of its glaring refusals and inequities regarding women, it remains the only Western tradition that has an unbroken history of providing a respected way of life for women outside the domestic role of wife-and-mother. The work of a nun and of a monk is identical: the *Opus Dei*, the work of God—to pray. Specifically, to pray without ceasing. If this was the call, then Edith Stein must go where that was the business of each day. Such faith had nothing to do either with dogma or with convincing other people of anything. In addition, the choice of Carmel is telling: Edith Stein chose the one Catholic contemplative order whose roots extend past Christianity back into the hermetic tradition of the Old Testament. Carmelites, though they take their rule from Teresa and much of their tradition of contemplative practice from John of the Cross, look back to Elijah as the first "Carmelite."

Perhaps the most striking example of Edith Stein's unwillingness to meddle in the spiritual lives of others (which of course contains the converse: her absolute commitment to following her own conviction, against all inducements otherwise) concerns Edmund Husserl, her revered Master. Though he did not die until 1938, five years after Edith entered the Cologne Carmel, he was already pondering his death and considering religious as well as philosophical questions in 1930 when, in February, Edith wrote an important letter to a mutual friend about him.

Edith was living at the time with the Benedictine nuns at Saint Magdalena college at Speyer where she taught literature and history; Husserl was in Freiburg retired but still writing. They rarely saw each other, and the intimate teacher-student relationship was a thing of the fond Göttingen past. The friend to whom she wrote, a Benedictine nun named Sister Adelgundis Jaegerschmid, was living in Freiburg and so had access to Husserl there. Edith's letter is a response to Sister Adelgundis's mention of a conversation with the Master in which she had managed (she felt) to nudge him along the path of considering "the last things" (in Catholic doctrine: death, judgment, heaven, and hell).

Edith is clearly alarmed by this intrusion into the old man's spiritual process. "I believe one must be on one's guard against illusions," she writes back (immediately) to Sister Adelgundis. "It is good to be able to speak to him so freely about the last things. But doing so heightens his responsibility as well as *our* responsibility for him. Prayer and sacrifice are surely more important than anything we can say to him."

She goes on to make a broader association, distinct from her concern about Husserl:

> There is a real difference between being a chosen instrument and being in a state of grace. It is not up to us to pass judgment, and we may confidently leave all to God's unfathomable mercy. But we may not becloud the importance of

these last things. After every encounter in which I am made aware how powerless we are to exercise direct influence, I have a deeper sense of the urgency
of my own *holocaustum*.

It is eerie, of course, to see that word—holocaust—employed here, almost as if it were a prophetically macabre job description Edith Stein had
written for herself. It would be a mistake to make too much of it. But neither should it be passed over as simply a coincidence, haunting but without significance. For Edith Stein clearly understood—as mystics of all
faiths and "ways" do—that the end point of contemplative life is the oneness that unites the individual with the fullest reality. With God, yes. But
with the suffering world as well. This is why Buddhist monks incinerated
themselves on the streets of Saigon and before the United Nations in
New York during the Vietnam War. They too understood—so literally—
that their own sacrifice would unite evil and its helpless victims in a liberating instant. The collision of radical evil with radical atonement—"my
own *holocaustum*"—is redemption. Edith Stein was irresistibly drawn to it,
as she had been drawn to the earlier conflagration of the First World War
when she declared as a passionate university student, "I have no private
life anymore." She was still trying to "lose her life," now in a frankly religious sense.

This is not to say that she longed for death or imagined foolishly that
she could change anything. The opposite: she saw that even to *speak* to
another, to evangelize harmlessly as her Benedictine friend so naively reported doing, was a misguided action, dangerous even, spiritually and personally for both sides of the equation. She felt that such discussion
jeopardized the root enterprise of active faith: the personal atonement
that every day she saw grow more necessary as the evil took hold of Germany.

As the political situation in Germany worsened for Jews, her focus on
sacrifice grew. "Though she never complained outwardly," one of her students reported later to Waltraud Herbstrith, "nevertheless it was
heartrending to have to see her gentle face contorted in pain . . . I can still
hear her saying, 'One day this will all have to be atoned for.'"

The silence she felt was incumbent on her has made her, strangely
enough, a peculiarly contemporary believer: one whose respect for the
range of beliefs (and disbeliefs) is so strong that "proofs" seem childish.
Only the living, incontrovertible experience itself, mystical and unbidden

and therefore unspeakable, will do. The contemporary believer, even one wrapped in the mantle of the established church, living within a cloister, must give witness in a culture of disbelief, in a secular and, in her case, lawless culture.

This silence did not extend to the repression of her own protest against what was happening, however. Before entering the Cologne Carmel, she wrote—twice, apparently—to Pius XI, requesting an audience to discuss the plight of the Jews, urging him to make a strong statement against this lawlessness. He denied her request for an audience and sent her in reply a papal blessing. Pius XI was very sick at the time, which perhaps mitigates somewhat how history regards this incident. He died soon afterward and was followed by Pius XII, the pope who reigned during the Second World War.

One more thing about Edith Stein's sense of her own sacrifice: it is significant that she used the Latin word—*holocaustum*—and not the vernacular. She was a brilliant Latin scholar and had been drawn to the language from her first study of it. Her use of Latin here and elsewhere is not the flourish of an intellectual fop. In *Life in a Jewish Family,* she says she felt, when she began studying Latin, "it was as though I were learning my mother tongue." This was long before she prayed in Latin or thought of it as the language of the church. Just as the precision of Bach and his elegant resolution of great complexities made him her favorite composer, so it was that of all her languages (and she was a gifted linguist, easily adding Greek and English, French and Dutch, as she went through life), Latin was the tongue that best suited her.

In her autobiography and in the letters, it is clear that when her passion quickens at the edge of the inexpressible, she resorts instinctively to Latin and its crisp, minimalist beauty. It was not for her a brittle, lost language, but the supreme mode of taut expression. Her most intimate revelations revert to Latin, as if there she could be relieved, finally, of the burden of her meaning. And so it is no surprise that when her closest philosopher friend, Hattie Conrad-Martius, asked her the question that every reader now asks—*What caused your conversion?*—Edith Stein replied, *Secretum meum mihi,* my secret is mine (literally, "my secret to me").

Josephine Koeppel, the splendid and meticulous translator of the autobiography and letters, calls this an "amazingly abrupt" response, and yet it is the right one for the new, converted Edith. The great Teresa herself, Koeppel notes, encouraged her nuns "to talk together about spiritual subjects in general, but she frowned on making a display out of one's prayer, or of 'the secrets of the King.' "

Edith Stein, the book her family said was "sealed with seven seals" even when she was a child, remained loyal to mystery and spoke of herself only to the limit of usefulness. The rest, she knew, belonged to her future, her *holocaustum*. It was, in any case, as she said to her closest friend, *secretum meum mihi*.

—∞∞∞—

And what, finally, of that *holocaustum?* Especially the Jewish anguish she saw firing all around her, the anguish that she knew would claim her too. What did this do to her Christian conviction? Where was her solidarity? And did she understand her life as a martyrdom?

Everything suggests that Edith Stein was an unusually integrated person, capable of a high state of contemplative prayer. It seems clear that she adapted naturally to the core of prayer: she understood her vocation as an act of solidarity (or, her old word, empathy) with the suffering of the world. She chose for her name in Carmel, Sister Teresa Benedicta of the Cross. The cross was where she stood. Of all the Christian mysteries—the incarnation, the resurrection, none magnetized her as the cross did. It was *her* mystery, and she made it her name. It was not for her an empty or merely edifying metaphor, but the image of shared, and ultimately redemptive, pain.

Yet in her most telling book, *Life in a Jewish Family,* she does not touch on Christian imagery, on her conversion, or on the story of her struggle. The book covers the years from her birth in 1891 (with backward looks at earlier family history) until 1916. That is, it covers the period before her conversion. But that does not in itself explain the absence of Christian reference, for she was obviously writing it from the standpoint of a Christian life (indeed, she wrote most of it in Carmel and began it at the insistence of a Jesuit friend).

The history of the book's composition is instructive. In January 1933 the Nazis seized power in Germany. Within a few weeks, Edith Stein, like all Jewish teachers, lost her job. She left Münster, where she had recently taken a position, and returned home to Breslau. There, during the next six months, she wrote the first part of the book. She felt "the new dictators" of Germany had so caricatured Jewish life that many Germans, especially younger people, "being reared in racial hatred from earliest childhood," had no idea of the truth. To all who had been thus deprived of the truth, "we who grew up in Judaism have an obligation to give our testimony."

Nowhere in Edith Stein's writing is there the troubling distaste for Judaism and Jewish life that sometimes betrays itself in Simone Weil's work. For Edith Stein, Judaism and, more to the point, Jews are not subject to judgment. They *are*—and are human. Therefore, to be honored in their persons and in their beliefs. And of course, treasured in her own personal life and memory.

In October of 1933, when she entered Carmel, she took up the work of the autobiography again almost immediately and wrote the majority of the text in the next eighteen months in the Cologne novitiate.

A strange project for a postulant to undertake, at her superiors' urging, as her first work in a Carmelite monastery: a detailed memoir of a Jewish upbringing. But her faithfulness to her specifically Jewish identity precluded any diversion from the task she saw as another strict part of her calling: the representation of a real Jewish family to an ignorant (she wished) and hostile (she knew) audience.

She never completed the book, though she tried to return to it. But circumstances intervened. In an effort to find safety for herself and also for her community, she requested to be transferred to a Carmel in Palestine. Too late: the British had already closed that escape route. In the end, she moved to the Carmel in Echt in 1939, aware that she was also transferring to the Dutch monastery the very risk she had brought into the Cologne enclosure. It was impossible for her, carrying Jewish identity papers, to take the manuscript of *Life in a Jewish Family* across the border. But once in Echt, she asked if someone could be found to bring the manuscript from Germany into Holland. A young Marianhill missionary, Father Rhabanus, volunteered. At the border, the police searched his car after all and picked up the bulky manuscript, flipping through the pages idly. "Your doctoral thesis, evidently," the policeman said, and tossed it back in the car, letting him pass through.

Time was running out. Edith Stein wrote only a few pages before the Nazis invaded and occupied Holland. The manuscript had again become a fearful liability. If it was found in a Nazi search (and monasteries were suspicious places), the book would put the entire community at risk. At one point, she buried it on the monastery grounds. Then, fearful of the effects of moisture on her carefully wrapped package, she dug it up again and had a sister hide it elsewhere. It caused her much worry; she was troubled, as well, that her presence jeopardized her community. She also had another pressing project under way: she desperately wished to complete *The Science of the Cross*, her study of John of the Cross, in time for the 400-year anniversary of the father of Carmel in 1942.

She and her superiors began a search for a new sanctuary for her. They were working feverishly on efforts to remove her (and her older sister Rosa, who had also converted to Catholicism and was sheltering at the Echt monastery as a refugee) to a Carmel in Switzerland. Then, on Sunday, July 26, 1942, almost three years after her arrival in Echt, a pastoral letter from the Dutch bishops was read in all Catholic churches, denouncing the Nazi policies toward the Jews.

The next day, "because the Bishops interfered," *Reichskommissar* Seyss-Inquart ordered all Catholic Jews to be deported before the week's end. The official Nazi memorandum listed 722 Jews registered as Catholics throughout the country. A further memorandum, dated July 31, claimed that 4,000 Jews registered as Christians had been gathered in one camp. This information was seen as a threat to induce the bishops to stop their protest of the general deportations.

On August 2, 1942, at 5:00 P.M., after Edith Stein (Sister Benedicta) had, as was the custom, read the point of meditation, the evening hour of mental prayer began. The silence was interrupted several minutes later by a loud pounding on the door that echoed into the nuns' choir. The SS had arrived. Before the nuns realized what was happening, Edith Stein and her sister Rosa were being taken away.

Rosa, terrified, at first became hysterical. Her younger sister turned to go and gently told her to follow. "Come," Edith said to Rosa, "let us go for our people."

Not "to our people," but "for" them. Her *holocaustum* had begun.

They were taken to the transfer camp at Westerbork, from which all Dutch Jews were sent east. They were with other Catholics, some of them also professed religious. On August 6, from Barracks 36 at Westerbork, Edith sent a card to the Echt Carmel, requesting a few necessary items: "woolen stockings, two blankets. For Rosa all the warm underwear and whatever was in the laundry; for us both towels and washcloths. Rosa also has no toothbrush, no Cross and no rosary." Then, strangely radiant, "So far I have been able to pray, gloriously."

It was her last written communication. There was a brief, false, hope of release or "deferments" for these Catholic Jews. Then came news that all such releases were revoked. An Ursuline nun (also a Jewish convert) wrote later of observing Edith Stein when she received this news: "I saw the German Carmelite. Her release had also been cancelled. Pale but composed, she kept on comforting her fellow-sufferers."

A few days later when a group of men sent from the Echt Carmel managed to visit the prisoners in Westerbork, they reported that Edith related everything "in a calm and quiet manner." They had been smoking as she spoke, "and after she finished, in the hope of relieving the tension a little, we jokingly offered her a cigarette. That made her laugh. She told us that back in her days as a university student she had done her share of smoking, and dancing too." They were surprised by her "lighthearted happiness." Later, when the SS patrol signaled the prisoners back into their barracks with a harsh whistle, Edith said, "I am prepared for whatever happens." Apparently, she expected to be sent to a forced labor camp in her native Silesia, to work in the mines.

On August 7, 1942, she and Rosa, along with many of their fellow prisoners, were conveyed by cattle car from Westerbork toward the east.

Final sightings: In 1948 the prioress of the Cologne Carmel wrote that in August 1942 Valentin Fouquet, the stationmaster in the town of Schifferstadt, reported that he heard himself called from the transport that had stopped briefly in the station. A "lady in dark clothes," who said her name was Stein, asked him to tell her friends that she sent greetings and was on her way to Poland.

Then, in 1982, a man named Johannes Wieners published a piece claiming that on August 7, 1942, he had spoken with Edith Stein. There is no proof, only his testimony. He had been working as a postal driver and was assigned to an army post office in Breslau. A freight train came in on the track alongside his and halted. The guard opened the sliding door, and he could see people penned up, "listlessly squatting on the floor. There was a horrible stench coming from the car."

A woman who was dressed in a nun's habit came to the door. "I guess because I looked sympathetic to her, she said to me, 'It's terrible. We don't even have containers to relieve ourselves.' After that, she looked into the distance at Breslau and said, 'This is my home; I'll never see it again.'"

Wieners says he stared at her, and then she said, "We are going to our death."

"That really shook me," Wieners wrote. "I remember that I asked her, 'Do the other prisoners know about this?' She answered very slowly, 'It's better for them not to know.'"

An engine was hooked up to his mail train then, and it pulled out, headed also toward Poland. "But when I got back from internment in 1948," he says, "I read about Edith Stein in a magazine. The minute I saw the picture, I knew it was the sister from August 7, 1942."

That is all there is. Maybe—because the account by Johannes Wieners has no corroboration—it is more than there is. On June 2, 1958, the Bureau of Information of the Netherlands Red Cross sent the nuns in Echt and Cologne a final certification concerning Edith Stein, with information dated February 15, 1950:

FOR REASONS OF RACE, AND SPECIFICALLY BECAUSE OF
JEWISH DESCENT

ON 2 AUGUST, 1942, ARRESTED IN ECHT.

ON 5 AUGUST, 1942, HANDED OVER IN K.L. WESTERBORK AND

ON 7 AUGUST, 1942, DEPORTED FROM K.L. WESTERBORK TO
K.L. AUSCHWITZ.

THE ABOVE NAMED PERSON IS TO BE CONSIDERED AS HAVING
DIED ON 9 AUGUST, 1942 IN AUSCHWITZ.

Nothing more. The mind goes back instinctively to the brief flashes that spark from her memoir as if to live again in her life rather than her death, jots of personal life indelibly inscribed in her account of her "life in a Jewish family." They are the small moments she chose to rescue and reveal as evidence of simple humanity—family parties, mountain hikes with her student friends, as idyllic as scenes out of a German operetta ("No one growing up during or since the [First World] war can possibly imagine the security in which we assumed ourselves to be living before 1914"), dances and jokes, the heated arguments and reconciliations of young intellectuals, the months at the lazaretto, seeing physical suffering and desperation as she never had before, the intensity of her philosophical inquiry, the thrilling proximity to Husserl.

Taking the whole of Edith Stein's life into mind, it is impossible not to see this memoir as part of her sacrifice as well: she is offering up the enormous fact of her family's reality, its appeal, its humanity, to the hostile gaze of a world lit by racial hatred. The Greek root of the word *martyr* is often invoked: it means to witness. But in a deeper recess of the word's etymology there is also a related Sanskrit derivation—from *smar,* to remember. A fierce act of memory then—the will to remember—is the hidden kernel of the martyr's calling. And naturally, the martyr's literary form would be the autobiography.

The strangely instinctive solitude of this woman even as a girl is threaded through this family history. Even when she was quite young, she radiated the dignity of her "hidden world" when she encountered the edge of death by accident one morning when the flame went out in the gas jet of the bedroom she and her sister Erna shared. They lay in their beds, "deathly white, . . . in a heavy stupor." When her sister Frieda discovered them and opened the windows, letting fresh air rush into the room, Edith "returned to consciousness out of a state of sweet, dreamless rest." To her surprise, she says, "what flashed through my mind upon coming to and grasping the situation was the thought: 'What a shame! Why couldn't they leave me in this deep peace forever?' I myself was shocked to discover that I 'clung to life' so little."

She clung, finally, to something firmer than life. But what is the name of that thing? The truth of revelation? Was it the redemptive value of suffering that sustained her? Did she really smile and move through Westerbork "like an angel," as the reports say, playing with the children, helping to knit up the shreds of courage torn from the adults? Did she appear at the cattle-car door, did she know she was heading to her death?

It is gone now with her into the gray midcentury smoke she became. How it all happened, what it meant to her, how she understood it—these are hidden away with the mystery of her conversion, which, as she told Hattie Conrad-Matius, she kept as the *secretum meum mihi,* refusing to divulge, even to her best friend, what she knew each person must find alone.

For Further Reading

Susanne M. Batzdorff, "Catholics and Jews: Can We Bridge the Abyss?" *America,* March 11, 1989.

Waltraud Herbstrith, *Edith Stein: A Biography.* Translated by Father Bernard Bonowitz, O.C.S.O. San Francisco: Harper & Row, 1971.

Edith Stein, *Essays on Woman.* Translated by Freda Mary Oben. Washington, DC: Institute of Carmelite Studies, 1987.

———, *Self Portrait in Letters, 1916–42.* Translated by Josephine Koeppel, O.C.D. Washington, DC: Institute of Carmelite Studies, 1994.

MAXIMILIAN KOLBE

Poland, 1941

16670

by PAUL MARIANI

Though it's not my church, I'm here anyway, kneeling in a pew of this pseudo-Gothic 1920s edifice of Our Lady of Czestochowa in Turners Falls, half a mile from the still-majestic Connecticut, whose waters have flowed through this region for the past hundred millennia. It's the afternoon mass, the 5:30. The pews, varnished too many years ago, creak with every movement of my old knees and sagging hams. The restless eye catches several faded Polish banners with icons of the Madonna sewn onto them by women who long ago turned to dust. The carved-stone stations of the cross along both aisles of the unimposing nave are in Polish, so that I have to guess at the clotted consonants, though I can just make out the names of Jesus, Mary, Simon of Cyrene, Pilate. It's a memory installed in all Catholic churches: Christ's final journey through the crowded market streets of old Jerusalem, one more Jew on his way to be crucified, this one by a contingent of the old Roman XXth, made up of conscript Syrians and Romans.

Why am I here? In part because my oldest son, my namesake, is home for a few days' rest before rejoining his fellow Jesuit Scholastics at Fordham. He lives in a renovated apartment complex called Ciszek House, named for a Jesuit who spent twenty-three years in various gulags for the crime of caring for the spiritual needs of the Russian people. The house stands like a lone beacon in a violent, hardscrabble section of the Bronx made up of a handful of the older Italian families surrounded now by Hispanics and blacks and the crush of new immigrants, mostly Colombians and Vietnamese. Boom-box black vans cruise the streets like sharks nosing for the blood scent.

His first week there, reading philosophy in his room, Paul saw a man beating a woman in the apartment directly across the street. When it dawned on him what was happening before his eyes, he called 911. The scene, he told me, had all the unreality of a piece of street theater, except that it was a real woman being punched in the face. Two days later he watched from that same window as a young cop, out of breath, handed a drug suspect he'd just caught up with the beating of his life. Who did my son call that time? It goes on and on and on, the violence, in the crushing round of things.

Even on vacation Paul quietly, firmly, insists on daily mass, something he says gives order to his day. Praise of God, he explains: a man's or a woman's first order of business. That and the sustenance he will need for the day. Since I already see my son much less than I like, and since soon he will be off again to the ends of the earth—Mexico City, Manila, Xiamen—I don't mind going with him. And if the truth be told, I have come to love the familiar quiet of a church. The year before last, Paul was off with a group of mentally retarded adults in a halfway house in Seattle. Last year it was Guaymas, a port city on Mexico's western border, teaching English, burying the dead, working in a soup kitchen for the hungry. This summer it's the southern coast of China, teaching Chinese teachers English. And though he's fluent in Chinese and would love to be out among the Chinese people, whom he has loved since he was a small boy, he'll wear civilian clothes, his actions will be watched by government agents, and he will be forbidden in any way—except by quiet example—to speak of what is truly on his mind. Still, it's an opening, he says, a way into a country where his fellow priests (Chinese) are still sentenced to long years at hard labor as parasites of the state merely for being priests.

He likes the play of light and shadow here in Our Lady of Czestochowa, he tells me, and he likes the parish priest, a man of Polish-Italian extraction, a former high-school teacher, humble, bright, an archconservative in some ways (no altar girls, thank you, at least not yet). The priest has a self-deprecating sense of humor and shares that intense, Polish vision of the church vigilant that you see in Karol Wojtyla, Pope John Paul II, the first non-Italian pope in half a millennium.

Though the population who attend mass has dropped off in the twenty-five years I've lived in western Massachusetts, there's still a Polish church and a French church and what they call the Irish church here in Turners, though the Irish are mostly gone now. Being an American mongrel—Italian, Swedish, Russian/Polish—with family who were Baptist, Lutheran, Catholic, perhaps even Jewish (or is that merely an old wish I have no way now of ascertaining for certain?), I'm not sure which of these churches I should claim for my own. Besides, I'm all for a stripped, white space with shadows. Call it Benedictine or Shaker: carved stone, polished wood, white walls. Still, Paul has more than half-convinced me that there's much to be said for the clutter of churches like this one with its icons and mass-produced plaster statues and eye-watering incense and wax candles and six altar boys at the midweek mass, their starched white chasubles bedecked with quasi-military medals, as if these kids had fought in Poland's wars for political and religious independence. Over the old high Vermont-quarried marble altar, installed back before the architectural reforms of Vatican II, there's a replica of Our Lady of Czestochowa—the Black Madonna—as much a rallying cry for the Poles as Our Lady of Guadalupe is to the poor and dispossessed of Latin America. Somehow this place is both alien and deeply familiar. Like an old dream.

For several years there was a small painting of a man on the right side-altar here. This, it turned out, was one Father Maximilian Kolbe, prisoner 16670 at the infamous death camp at Auschwitz (or to give it back its Polish name, Oświecim). Kolbe, I'd heard years ago, was a forty-seven-year-old Polish Franciscan (with a German name, ironically) who offered his life in exchange for another prisoner, a man he barely knew. But the Poles had lost so many during the war. What was one more among such a staggering, mind-numbing number?

Here's the story. On the last day of July 1941, in the second year of the war, a prisoner from Father Kolbe's cell block who had been working outside the prison fence to help bring in the harvest managed somehow to make his escape. He had to know from previous attempts at flight that such an escape, even if initially successful, meant the deaths of ten to twenty of his fellow prisoners, who would all be stripped naked, held incommunicado, and deprived of food and water until they died, their corpses "dried up like tulips," as one guard, an eyewitness, poetically phrased it.

At the Auschwitz compound and in the town and fields and railroad yards beyond, the sirens began blaring as soon as the Germans realized that one of the prisoners was missing. Roadblocks were set up for fifteen miles around, and the guards began double-checking to make sure no one else had escaped. Snarling guard dogs were brought out to intimidate the prisoners; the guards themselves—edgy—barked orders. Everyone watched everyone else closely. That evening, after working in the fields, the swamps, the hospitals, the kitchens, the latrines, the prisoners in Kolbe's block—600 in all—were lined up and made to stand at attention. Finally, without being fed their supper, they were ordered to their cells for the night.

The following morning, after the prisoners in the other blocks had had their breakfast of acorn coffee and black cornbread and had been sent off to their work details, the men in Block 14—Kolbe's block—were ordered once again to stand in their assigned rows at attention. All the SS wanted was to know where the escaped prisoner had gone, and surely someone had to know something. As the heat of the day intensified, minute by minute, prisoners began dropping and—since it was strictly forbidden to break ranks—lay crumpled just where they fell. At noon a watery soup was distributed, and those who could still swallow drank it. Then the prisoners went back to standing at attention through the long afternoon. One by one they kept on dropping from exhaustion and heat stroke.

Finally, toward evening, Kommandant Höss's second in command, Deputy Commander Fritsch, attended by his underlings, capos, lieutenants, and the ubiquitous German shepherds, walked out onto the parade ground. He was dressed in a crisply pressed uniform; his black jackboots shone. He had had a good dinner, and now he sauntered up to the prisoners—lined up ten rows deep, sixty to a row. Everyone could see that Fritsch was visibly perturbed; the prisoner, he informed the *Polnisches schweinen,* had not been found. Ten men would therefore be picked at random and sent to Block 11—the pit—where they would be stripped naked and starved to death in reprisal for the one who had yet to be found.

Death, even in the first year of the camp's existence, had long since become a daily fact. One German officer at Auschwitz had already boasted of personally executing 25,000 prisoners, cleanly, each dispatched with a single shot to the back of the head. Monday mornings, as regular as German clockwork, while the rest of the prisoners went about their work, a group of twenty or twenty-five men would be picked at random and executed by firing squad against a massive granite wall. Mass gassings and even mass executions were still months away, and most prisoners still died (as they were meant to) of typhoid, dysentery, infection, slow starvation, exhaustion. Some in despair threw themselves against the high-voltage perimeter surrounding the camp; others were beaten to death with baseball bats or with two-by-fours in front of their fellow prisoners; others were ripped to pieces by the dogs or killed in various insane medical experiments. Others were loaded onto army trucks and taken out of the camp into the surrounding woods to disappear forever.

Like so many others, I have had to live with the bleak reality of the Holocaust all of my conscious life. In the summer of 1945, a child of five, I watched black-and-white grainy images flicker on an early television set in a tenement on New York's East Side. While my parents played cards in the kitchen with friends, I sat transfixed before the tiny screen. Plaintive, otherworldly violin music accompanied images of mannequinlike bodies being bulldozed into hastily made open graves. I saw skeletons in striped prison garb "liberated" by soldiers in khaki uniforms much like the one my father had worn.

None of us here in Europe and America can have escaped the knowledge of the Holocaust, especially the almost total liquidation of the Jews. I have stared and stared, and still my mind cannot get around what happened in the death camps. After the Jews—Polish Jews, German Jews, Russian, Lithuanian, French, Czech, Hungarian, and Italian Jews, Jews from Warsaw and Amsterdam and Paris and Rome, as well as Jews from London and Philadelphia and New York if the Nazis could have had their way—after the Jews it would have been the entire Polish nation the Nazis were bent on liquidating.

Of the six million Poles who perished in the Auschwitz-Birkenau complex, fully half were Jews. By war's end, the Jewish population of Poland, a country that for two centuries had given refuge to this displaced minority, this blessed remnant, when most other European countries had expelled their Jewish populations, had been reduced to 100,000. In 1939—just six years before—there had been 3.1 million Jews living in the country.

But the Poles also lost three million non-Jews, nearly all of them Christians. In that number must be counted one out of every five Polish priests, thousands of brothers and nuns, and virtually the nation's entire professional and intellectual class. Those the Nazis missed the Russian army disposed of, in thousands of incidents, including the infamous executions in Katyn Forest of most of the Polish officer class.

The sad list of those who perished in World War II could go on. Fifty million according to the best estimates, worldwide. The extermination of most of the European Gypsies, anyone suspected of being a homosexual, the physically handicapped, the sick, the retarded. Twenty million Russians died before the war was over. No group escaped, not the Americans, the Canadians, the Australians, the North Africans, not the Free Poles or the English or the Japanese or the Chinese, and certainly not the Germans, many of whom must have known that what Hitler and Goebbels were propounding as a new world order was shit. Each of these victims, if we could get at the truth, was a unique, irreplaceable individual. Even when we die together, it seems, we still die alone, and the world is the poorer for each spark extinguished.

And yet, in spite of these statistics, the Nazi death camps continue to hold a special horror for us. No matter how many times we've heard it before, the bare facts can still plummet one into a depression: half-dead prisoners arriving by train through the yawning gates of Auschwitz, like something out of Dante, only worse. And above the gates the linguistically ambivalent words: *Arbeit Macht Frei. Work Will Free You.*

Kommandant Höss, in his immaculate uniform, standing before the assembled prisoners, bored, addressing each new carload of people as they entered through the gates, commenting airily, pausing as his words were translated into Polish, that the prisoners had not arrived at a health spa. No, this was a German concentration camp, with only one way out: up through the crematorium chimney. If anyone did not like the sound of that, he added, delighted with the music of his own voice, well, he could throw himself at once against any part of the high-voltage fence surrounding the camp. "If any of you are Jews," he added, "you have the right to live no longer than two weeks. Priests one month. The rest of you three months."

"Casimura Szymborski," my father is rasping into the phone, the high metallic nasal pitch of his emphysema noticeably worse. "That was her real name. Your mother's." Then he says, "We used to kid about it"—his voice is plaintive, almost nostalgic. And though he would never admit it, I know he still misses her, though he divorced her twenty years ago and he's been remarried most of that time. "After your grandfather died, Emily"—he means my Swedish-American grandmother, the one from Paterson, the changeling, the alcoholic, perhaps my first love—"she switched your mother's name to make it sound more American. I don't know why. Who knows why that woman did anything she did." It is my father's voice, stranded in the outgoing tide of his life, 400 miles away in his spic-and-span home in Ocean City.

It's the first time I've heard this news, or the first time it's registered, and suddenly the woman who gave birth to me when she was a week shy of her seventeenth birthday and then raised me and my six younger brothers and sisters, the woman I always believed was Harriet, Harriet Green, this woman who has lain still for the past seven years up there in Saint Mary's cemetery, has just been revealed to me in an entirely new light. I've known—or been told, at least—that her father, Harry, was from Poland, or that part of Russia that became Poland once again after World War I: a boy come to the New World with his father. The memory of things is so absolutely fragile, after all. A handful of dust.

Two or three photos have survived. Here's one of him as a young man, perhaps twenty: short, wiry, a sergeant in the U.S. Cavalry, a grin on his face and a repeating rifle slung in its saddle holster along the withers of a magnificent U.S. Army–issue horse named Red. They're somewhere on the Texas border with Mexico. The year is 1916, and Harry is simply one more soldier serving under Black Jack Pershing as he prepares to enter Mexico in pursuit of the elusive Pancho Villa. But this is 1995 and I am fifty-five years old, and the news I have just been handed about my mother strikes me as anything but funny, in spite of my father's laughter. In truth I don't know *what* to do with this belated revelation.

—◆◆◆—

I am talking with a friend of mine who is also the pastor of a large parish church twenty miles south of here in Northampton. Of course he's heard of Kolbe. Saint Maximilian Kolbe, the second person to be canonized by John Paul II, back in 1982. He's heard the story of Kolbe's volunteering his life in place of another man. He thinks there may have been several others who did something similar, including a nun who traded places with a woman who was carrying her screaming child into the gas chambers. He names a Carmelite; he mentions Dietrich Bonhoeffer's witness. There may even be other instances, he adds, instances where the witnesses all perished, leaving no one to tell the story. Still, it must be rare for a person to give up his or her life for another, and that other a virtual stranger.

"It's not the fact that Kolbe traded places," he says, as he shifts his Nissan into fourth gear and we head for the shore. "That may have been something done in a moment and the decision irreversibly locked into place by the machinery of death." What he really wants to know is what led up to Kolbe's decision to act so selflessly, especially when a man has been systematically stripped of his humanity and life has been reduced to trying to survive another twenty-four hours. What discipline, what self-abnegation and steeling of the will had Kolbe already undertaken, he wonders, to be able to step forward when the electric, never-to-be-repeated moment came?

—∞∞∞—

My wife looks up from the newspaper she has been reading. "Did you know that the man whose place that Polish priest took just died?" she tells me. And I stop what I'm doing. That would be Francis Gajowniczek, dead at ninety-four. So the seasoned forty-year-old Polish army sergeant who was ordered that evening into the death cell along with nine other men, and who broke down, knowing he would never again see his wife and his children, a man suddenly granted not just a few extra weeks but a reprieve of fifty-four years when a frail priest in clown's stripes stepped forward to beg permission to take Gajowniczek's place, has only just died. Wine spilling over, laughing, gallons of it, frolic-lavish, as at Cana.

Such an act of self-sacrifice is enough to send anyone into a murderous depression, as Sergeant Gajowniczek said it at first sent him when the impact of what Kolbe had done for him finally dawned on him. Kolbe: a one-lunged, tubercular, frail figure who was known to give his food away to other prisoners, slipping bread into their pockets so that they wouldn't feel embarrassed, a man who just five days earlier had been released from the prison hospital where he'd been confined with his second bout of pneumonia, a man who—Gajowniczek knew—used to hear confessions and say mass in spite of what would have happened to him had he been caught.

Now Gajowniczek and 590 other prisoners watch in disbelief as this man staggers under the weight of another condemned prisoner who cannot get his quaking legs to cooperate and helps him move off toward the death cell. I wonder if Barabbas, wanted for murder and for fomenting riot, and blinking into the sunlight as he was led up from the prison beneath the Roman garrison, felt half as strange when another man, his back raw with the whipping he had just been given, a crown of thorns pressed down on his bleeding scalp, took his place and began shouldering the cross-beam as he was led through the cobbled streets of the city to his death.

"I want to die in place of this prisoner," Kolbe has just said, pointing to Gajowniczek. And then, by way of explanation: "I have no wife or children." And besides, he adds, he is "old and not good for anything." But in truth he is only forty-seven, just seven years older than the man whose life he is exchanging for his own. Besides, Kolbe adds, the man is clearly in better physical condition than he is. It is a brilliant stroke to play to the Nazi mentality, for is it not better that the fit should live and the weak die?

I almost wish Kolbe had not been proclaimed a saint, since sainthood tends in the average imagination to lift a man or a woman to another realm, somehow beyond the human, though the fact is that holiness is a thing faith tells us we ought all to strive for. Kolbe himself was a small man, self-deprecating, modest, his lungs shot through with the tuberculosis he had contracted while a young man studying for the priesthood in Rome. "Marmalade," some of the wittier young Franciscans had called him when he was just starting out as a priest. Slow—one lung will do that to the best of us—and treacly sweet.

Unless you knew him, it would have been difficult to pick Kolbe out of a crowd, either before the war, when he was in charge of Niepokalanow, which by 1939 had become the largest friary in the world, or afterwards, when he was packed off to Auschwitz. For most of his life, Kolbe was just one more black-robed conventual Franciscan living his vow of Franciscan poverty simply, unobtrusively.

So much for appearances. For Father Kolbe was also a Polish intellectual who had earned two doctorates by the time he was twenty-five: his first in philosophy from the Pontifical Gregorian University in Rome when he was just twenty-one, his second in theology from the Franciscans' International College—again in Rome—four years later. In between he was ordained. In the summer of 1919, his studies completed,

Kolbe was assigned to the seminary of Friars Minor Conventual in Kraków to teach church history. Still, his real mission, he believed, was to spread the word of his Lady, the Blessed Mother, to whom he had already dedicated his life.

As a small, rambunctious boy he had had a vision that he shared only with his mother, asking her to keep it a secret (she did, until after his death). It sounds like the stuff of legends, except that the story, as it turned out, is true. The Blessed Mother had appeared to him in church, offering him one of two crowns: a white crown or a red. The white meant a life crowned with chastity, a life of total dedication and singular devotion. The red was reserved for martyrs. The boy asked for the white one, but, not content, asked for the other as well. The beautiful Lady smiled and offered him both.

In 1917, while still in Rome, the twenty-three-year-old Kolbe and six others had formed the Militia Immaculatae (the Knights of the Immaculate), dedicated to conquering the world for God through love and devotion to Mary, the only fully human being, he explained, who had never deviated from soldering her will to God's. Kolbe turned out to be an exceptional Marian theologian and seems to have seen as deeply into the role of Mary in the work of the Trinity as another Franciscan, Duns Scotus, had six centuries earlier. But Kolbe was also a brilliant mathematician and amateur scientist, with a head for complex numbers. As a teenager he used to dream about space travel and of capturing the sounds and images of the distant past and hoped one day to be able to build a machine that would allow him to see what Christ and his mother actually looked like.

The dream turned in time to a dream of founding a city in honor of his Lady. This dream was realized when Kolbe and his fellow Franciscans built Niepokalanow, the City of the Immaculate, still there today and still thriving, in spite of having been dismantled and nearly destroyed during World War II. With no money to his name, the thirty-three-year-old Kolbe went to Prince John Maria Drucki-Lubecki in the fall of 1927 and asked him to donate a large piece of woodland at Teresin, on the outskirts of Warsaw, so that he could build his city for Mary. The prince, disarmed by this persuasive, gentle Franciscan, to his own surprise did just that. From virtually nothing (except God's and his Lady's blessings) Kolbe and his fellow Franciscans—young men with the amazingly right technical skills who flocked to Kolbe's patchwork cabins and tiny chapel—built up the friary and, with the most advanced modern presses, continued to publish and distribute Kolbe's various religious publications.

Kolbe's success as a publisher is by any account nothing short of phenomenal. From an initial run of 1,000 in 1927 the monthly *Knight* had in three years managed a publication run of 350,000. When one considers that this was achieved in a country of 30 million, and that a single copy of the *Knight* often reached not only all members of large families but neighbors and friends as well, the figure swells to over two million, or to one in every fifteen Poles. Somehow the money for such a huge operation, which his superiors insisted be self-sustaining, was found. Once, when he could find no other way to pay the printing bills and was in danger of having his presses shut down by his Franciscan superiors, he went into the church, got down on his knees, and confided his problem to his Lady. Afterwards, he found an envelope on the altar that had not been there earlier in the day. It was an anonymous donation to the Immaculata, and the amount inside was exactly what he needed to pay what he owed. His superiors allowed him to pay with the found money.

As a bookkeeper he was notoriously inept; he would simply open a desk drawer and hand a brother a fistful of bills to purchase whatever was needed, trusting the brother to put back whatever was left over. Kolbe was not one to count costs. For someone like myself who follows the rise and fall of the stock market with the unfailing hope of the invincibly ignorant, slavering in some half-mystical way to strike it rich against the overwhelming odds, such fiscal nonchalance as Kolbe showed leaves me gasping with wonder and admiration. Better that Niepokalanow burn to the ground, he used to say, than that the place should run on a profit. And yet how it flourished! Consider the lilies of the field, his Master and mine reminds us.

Until his initial arrest by the Nazis three weeks after they invaded Poland in September 1939, Kolbe stayed on top of the latest developments in communications, using his knowledge to spread the word of God. Unlike most Franciscans, Kolbe sought out trained friar-technicians—printers, writers, physicians, teamsters, loggers, carpenters, masons, mechanics, cooks—to work in shifts around the clock to get out the Word. There was a war going on out there, Father Kolbe often said, a spiritual war for the souls of the people. Again and again he warned against the worst elements of secularism, modernism, communism, nazism, and freemasonry, stressing in their place the gospel message of social justice. At the outbreak of World War II Kolbe even had two friars in Warsaw training to be aviators to spread the word as quickly and as widely as possible.

Another piece to this amazing story also needs to be mentioned. Sometime in 1929 Father Kolbe met a group of Japanese students traveling in Poland and was struck by their good breeding and manners. He was also struck by the fact that, even after two millennia, the Christian message was particularly hard to come by in vast sections of Asia. And so, in January 1930, he asked his religious superior for permission to travel with four other Franciscans to do his Lady's work in Asia.

Leaving his brother—another capable Franciscan—in charge at Niepokalanow, Kolbe traveled with his companions by steamer through Port Said, and on to Saigon, Hong Kong, Shanghai, and elsewhere. But—in spite of growing a long Confucian beard for his work in Asia—he was repeatedly forbidden by church authorities from opening a friary in the various dioceses he and his fellow Franciscans visited. At last they wound up in Nagasaki, where the bishop, upon hearing that Kolbe had doctorates in philosophy and theology, and needing someone to help train his own diocesan seminarians, allowed Kolbe and his companions to stay if Kolbe promised to teach philosophy in addition to all his other duties. Kolbe agreed.

Incredibly, despite the fact that none of the Franciscans spoke or read Japanese or even knew the customs of the country, and despite hardships that would have crippled most other people ("Heavy snow fell in the night," he wrote in one letter home. "To sleep we had to cover our heads as the snow kept hitting our faces. In the morning our dormitory was absolutely white . . . and the basins full of ice!"), within a month of their arrival the brothers were publishing a Japanese-language version of their magazine.

Twice—in 1933 and again in 1936—Kolbe was called back to Poland on Franciscan business. Often he was dangerously ill with his tubercular lung, feverish, bedridden, sometimes to the point of death. Walking, even breathing, came with great difficulty. In spite of all this, Kolbe insisted on working alongside his brothers, repeatedly refusing special attention or food or clothing. When he returned a second time to Poland, his superiors, fearing for his life, refused to allow Kolbe to return to Japan, insisting instead that he return to Niepokalanow. Without a murmur, as always, when the order was given he obeyed. It was God then who spoke, he believed, and not simply men.

A footnote. When it came time to build a friary in Nagasaki, Father Kolbe chose a site on a hill facing away from the city itself. It was the only land he could afford, and it may well be, as has been suggested, that Kolbe had a premonition to build there. Some greeted the decision to build in that out-of-the-way place with derision. But when the atom bomb leveled the city in August 1945, the friary remained intact. In spite of the harsh treatment shown them during the war, the Franciscans, under the leadership of Brother Zeno, who had been with Kolbe from the beginning, turned the friary and gardens into a hospital and an orphanage, tending to thousands of wounded Japanese and earning the gratitude of a war-ravaged populace.

∞

Facts, told and retold, rubbed clean in the telling. I know I am up against something at once beautiful and terrible here, as I write these words in the comfort of my study, thousands of miles from either Auschwitz or Nagasaki, places that—except in films and stories—I have never seen. I know too that I am removed now from the events of Kolbe's life and death by half a century and more. Gerard Manley Hopkins, the Jesuit poet, wrote in his poetic meditation "The Wreck of the Deutschland" that one could think about tragedy with equanimity when it was others who faced it. So now with me, trying to imagine how I might act if it were I faced with deprivation and loss and death as Father Kolbe was. But how can I? In time, Father Hopkins faced his own slow crucifixion, though it was not in the brinesmart swaggering winter sea as he imagined his heroic German nuns doing out in the Thames estuary on a December night in the winter of 1875, as they called on Christ to save them even as they were pulled under by a freezing, insanely roiling sea.

That was not, as it turned out, what the Lord was calling Hopkins to witness. Instead, Hopkins would show his extraordinary courage by following Christ's will for him in the daily mind-numbing toil of grading thousands of student exams in the shell of a third-rate Catholic university in provincial Dublin, suffering migraines and terrible bouts of depression every day for years among a people who spoke his language but who mostly distrusted him for being an Englishman among an Irish population intent on gaining its independence. It was then, in that seemingly unpropitious time, that Hopkins would be tempered to write his extraordinary poems of desolation followed by consolation, words written in blood, words that have moved and consoled so many thousands of readers—not least myself—in the century since he composed them.

———⟨∞⟩———

It is beyond most of us, I suppose, to imagine Kolbe giving his life for another human being, soldering his will to the will of a loving God. At this level even the most empathic imagination will take us only so far. But there is Kolbe, leading the others in the darkness of that death cell in Auschwitz each day in prayer and singing, hearing their confessions, touching them, comforting them, until even those in the adjoining cells, with similar death sentences, at last stopped their screaming and joined in the prayers and the singing that Kolbe's example had stirred them on to. Kolbe like a paraclete, a comforter, the voices of the others in chorus, hearing the summoning bell of his voice, the voices loud at first, then growing quieter as hunger and exhaustion took their heartbreaking, inevitable toll.

In that hell, deprived of food, of water, of clothing, of light, of air almost, of all vestiges of dignity, the men began dying. When each morning a guard arrived to empty the slop bucket, he always found it empty, so thirst-mad had some of the inmates become. Some curled up into fetal positions and, knowing they would never get out of that hellhole alive, gave up their ghosts as quickly as possible. Some, in adjoining cells—so the reports leaked out years later—went mad and attacked each other like feral dogs, snarling, tearing at each other's flesh. When the strongest managed to crawl toward the guards who came to inspect them, begging for mercy, for a scrap of food, a cup of water, they were clubbed or kicked or simply shot for their trouble.

And each day, when the guards, accompanied by the Polish prisoner who acted as interpreter, entered the cell, Father Kolbe would be standing or kneeling there in prayer. When he gazed at his tormentors, one witness testified, his eyes burned with such liquid intensity that he was ordered to look at the ground. No wonder Kolbe's name quickly made the rounds, even among the SS. Here was a man of courage, an *Übermensch,* a singular priest, more than one guard is reported to have said. Some of the guards, according to the reports of reliable eyewitnesses, suffered psychic trauma. No one, they said, should be able to act as this priest had acted. Somehow, it wasn't right.

o weeks the ten had been reduced to four. Of these, only Fa-
was still fully conscious. By then, too, the cell was needed for
ners, and so a German criminal named Bock, who worked in
the prison hospital, was ordered to inject the surviving prisoners with car-
bolic acid. As Bock approached Kolbe, sitting by the far wall, the priest
stretched out his arm as his Master had before him. It took ten seconds for
the acid to travel up Kolbe's arm before it blew out his heart. Bruno Borgowiec, the German-speaking Polish prisoner who survived Auschwitz
by acting as an interpreter in the death cells, not only lived through
Kolbe's passion but somehow survived the death camp itself. Most potential witnesses were periodically executed by the SS to ensure silence, but
this man survived to give eloquent and vivid witness to what he had seen.

In late 1945, with the war finally over, Borgowiec wrote Kolbe's fellow
Franciscans that, on the day Kolbe was killed, Borgowiec returned to the
cell as soon as the SS had departed. "The other naked, begrimed corpses
were lying on the floor," he wrote, their faces frozen in various contor-
tions of suffering. Only Father Kolbe sat upright, "leaning against the far
wall. His body was not dirty like the others, but clean and bright. The
head was tilted somewhat to one side. His eyes were open. Serene and
pure, his face was radiant." Anyone, he added in case the point had been
missed, "would have noticed and thought this was a saint." It was August
14, the eve of Mary's assumption, body and spirit, into heaven.

<hr>

Shortly before the war, Father Kolbe had told some of those closest to
him that war was inevitable, and that when it came it would be terrible
beyond their wildest imaginings. He also told them that he himself would
not survive it. The Immaculata, his Lady, had other plans for him. Then, he
told them, in the most self-effacing manner he could, that in Nagasaki he
had had a vision of his Lady in which he had been promised heaven. That
was all he could ever bring himself to say about the matter.

As if to underline his unbending conviction that his Lady watched
over him daily, Kolbe and his fellow Franciscans were first released from
prison on December 8, 1939. It was the Feast of his Lady's Immaculate
Conception. When he and his brothers returned to Niepokalanow
shortly afterward, they found that all their presses except for the most
primitive handpresses had been torn from their foundations and shipped

elsewhere by the Nazis. No matter, Kolbe said, and opened the friary to the constant stream of refugees who came begging for food and shelter. He turned no one away and sheltered—among many other displaced persons—some 1,500 Jews. No matter that to do so was to risk great personal danger to oneself and one's community. When a well-meaning Polish woman asked Kolbe if it was a sin to feed Jews when there were so many needy Christians, he told her gently what she should already have known: that Christ would never allow such invidious distinctions, that everyone was her brother and sister.

In the camps in the summer of 1941, the Final Solution—the total extermination of the Jews—had yet to be formulated into formal Nazi policy. At that point Jews made up perhaps 10 percent of the prison population, about equal to their part in the general Polish population, though they were already being segregated by the Nazis from the others. The first specifically Jewish transport, in fact, would not arrive at Auschwitz until March 1942, seven months after Kolbe's death. One man—a Jew—who later became a radio talk-show host in Wilmington, Delaware, and who was a boy of thirteen at Auschwitz in the summer of 1941, remembers how Father Kolbe comforted him like a mother when the boy had lost his family to the Nazis. Doubtless there were others in the camp who might have spoken for Kolbe, but the Nazis left few Jewish witnesses.

Sometime late in 1940, while Kolbe was still at Niepokalanow, the SS in fact had come to see him, secretly, with offers of friendship and impunity from harm. They had papers on him, had been watching him closely, were impressed with his skills as an intellectual and as an administrator. Now they had a proposition for him. After all, Kolbe was a German name, and Kolbe's family had originally emigrated from Germany. They could see to it that he was offered German citizenship and that he was taken to Germany and out of all this hell. Christ in the desert, Kolbe may have thought, facing the tempter. No, he told them in flawless German, he was a Pole, and proud to be counted a Pole. Rebuffed, they did not approach him again until they came a second and final time to arrest him. If there was a way out of this hell, Kolbe knew, it did not lie in making friends with the Nazis.

It is an irony that Saint Maximilian Kolbe's feast day should fall on the vigil of the Assumption. On that day—August 15—permission to bury his emaciated remains having been denied by the camp authorities, Kolbe's body was sent to the crematorium and burned along with the other victims, his ashes mingling with the dust of millions of others. Once, years before, he had told a group of his friends that he would like nothing better than "to be ground to dust for the Immaculate Virgin and have this dust be blown away by the wind all over the world." Now he had his wish.

In that dark, in that hell, then, a small, still, intense light, blossoming against the impossible odds. The memory of prisoner 16670, which should have been obliterated when his ashes were scattered to the winds, instead began spreading like wildfire at Auschwitz among the prisoners and the SS alike: a glory and a sign of contradiction. Some began praying to him, asking his intercession, both those at Auschwitz and others after the war had ended.

There is documented medical testimony, such as the Catholic church requires in cases of sainthood, of miraculous or otherwise unexplainable cures occurring in the name of the proposed saint. Not for the red crown of martyrdom, for martyrdom is itself a sufficient sign, but for the white crown that Kolbe also wished to have: the crown given to those who stand as witnesses to the faith by their teaching and example. One of those cured was Gajowniczek himself, whose advanced tuberculosis of the spine, contracted while at Auschwitz, suddenly and inexplicably disappeared. It was as if Kolbe still watched over this man whose life he had purchased so dearly with his own, brooding and caring like the mother he was. There were others. Those with incurable cancers. A patient in the last stages of acute diabetes. All cured.

——∞——

These are the facts, briefly told, with many omissions. What remains is the consoling, terrible witness of the man himself, a man who, in one of the century's most diabolical moments, spent himself for so many others. He is there as a sign to read as we can, even here in a small Polish church in western Massachusetts, until the mind, the unrecalcitrant, stymied mind of a bottom feeder like myself, grown accustomed over the years to the random flickers of shadowlight at one's feet, looks up trembling into the impossible windswept flame of that love.

For Further Reading

Mary Craig, *Six Modern Martyrs.* New York: Crossroad, 1985. See pages 99–130 and the chapter devoted to Maximilian Kolbe.

Boniface Hanley, *Maximilian Kolbe: No Greater Love.* Notre Dame, IN: Ave Maria Press, 1982.

Ronald Modras, "Pope John Paul II, St. Maximilian Kolbe, and Antisemitism: Some Current Problems and Perceptions Affecting Catholic-Jewish Relations." *Journal of Ecumenical Studies* 20 (Fall 1983):630–39. Addresses the vexing charge of anti-Semitism raised against Father Kolbe at the time of his beatification, a charge that for a time created something of a crisis in Jewish-Catholic relations, though it was subsequently analyzed and successfully rebutted.

Patricia Treece, *A Man for Others: Maximilian Kolbe, Saint of Auschwitz.* Libertyville, IL: Franciscan Marytown Press, 1982. The fullest account to date of the life of Father Kolbe; Treece worked with the nearly 1,000 pages of testimony from the beatification process, supplementing these with other interviews by those who knew Father Kolbe.

OSIP MANDELSTAM

Russia, 1938

M

by MARK RUDMAN

The name Osip keeps moving toward you . . .
　　Paul Celan

"Why is it that when I think of him, I see heads, mounds of heads?" M. said to me once. "What is he doing with all those heads?"
　　Nadezhda Mandelstam, *Hope Against Hope*

Osip Emilievich Mandelstam was born on January 15, 1891, in Warsaw, the son of a leather merchant and a piano teacher. He grew up in St. Petersburg, was sentenced twice to hard labor, and died in 1938 of heart failure in a concentration camp near Vladivostok, as far away as it is possible to be from St. Petersburg while remaining inside Russia. In the last images we have of him he is scrambling to stay alive, rummaging in garbage cans for scraps.

In the manner of Rembrandt, martyr
of chiaroscuro, I've driven deep
into the numbness of time.
My rib—a burning spike in the icy night.
The jailers hover in the indefinite.
The sentry nods out in the darkening storm.

Forgive me, revered
brother, master, prime
mover of the black-green
darkness . . . ; I could be a boy
following the lead of grown-ups as they step
blithely into choppy seas—
and not a man in desperate straits
walking toward a future he
will never see, as
the tribe, shadowed
by furs, under the spell
of twilight, quakes.

265 and 364; Voronezh, February 8, 1937 (my translation)

During his lifetime Osip (Russian for Joseph) Mandelstam published three volumes of poetry, *Stone* (1913), *Tristia* (1922), and *Poems* (1928). He wrote prose of the highest order, prose that is very difficult to categorize, but it consists of essays, ranging from "travel" pieces, like "Journey to Armenia," to discourses on poetry so far-reaching that I am reluctant to call them criticism, like "Conversation About Dante." Few writers are more rewarding to read—line by line, sentence by sentence.

There is no getting to the bottom of Mandelstam. Mandelstam went so far that no one's yet caught up with him.

Born a Jew, Mandelstam later converted to Christianity and was baptized as a Lutheran. It is assumed by some that he did this to escape Russia's rabid anti-Semitism and, more germanely, to avoid the Jewish quota at the school he was to attend; yet for him faith was clearly more than self-protection.

He was never secure in life; never had a proper stipend or job, much less a proper apartment. (I had to restrain myself from referring to him as

"M" in this essay; what stopped me was remembering that Nadezhda referred to him as M. in *Hope Against Hope* and *Hope Abandoned*.) Journals wouldn't publish him because his work espoused humanist values. He survived by the Soviet version of Grub Street, writing children's books and translating novels by Upton Sinclair, Jules Romains, and Sir Walter Scott (though here he played Terence Kilmartin—who updated Scott Moncrieff's translations of Proust—working from an earlier version). During a brief stint as a journalist, he interviewed the young Ho Chi Minh and faulted him on his French. This marginal existence jumped catastrophically to another plane when he began to be pursued by Stalin's henchmen, and he spent the last part of his life, after serving his sentence, in exile, for which he did his best to prepare himself spiritually. But there are limits.

Mandelstam predicted his own exile, that forerunner of more permanent departure, and announced in the title poem of his second book, *Tristia,* that he had made himself an expert in the *"science* of farewells." His exile has precedent externally in his identification with Ovid on the Black Sea, but Pushkin figures just as prominently (although to the non-Russian reader, these latter references are difficult to discern without commentary). The poems are steeped in terror, strewn with black suns, black seas, black sails. "The tree-top laughs and plays / into the day of the axes."

One of the central questions about Mandelstam is why he refused to leave Russia during the period of emigration in the late 1920s, before the doors closed. Nabokov went to Berlin; why didn't Mandelstam? I'm not going to suggest that he stayed in order to be martyred. I don't think that Mandelstam wanted to die. And I offer instead that he became perplexed about where the borderline of fantasy and fact lay between his erotics of exile, as exemplified by his identification with Ovid, Dante, and Villon, and the gruesomeness of being in actual exile.

I had no sooner started writing this piece than Isaac Babel's diaries appeared and two major critics, both Jewish, reviewing them in the same week in the *New York Times Book Review* and the *New York Review of Books,* spoke to this question of being born Jewish in Russia. Harold Bloom writes vehemently: "Russian Jewish . . . appears to be a pure dichotomy." Alfred Kazin is more tempered: "Being a Jew did not bore him [Babel], as it did Pasternak, who could never understand why Jews stuck to their ancient heritage. Unlike Osip and Nadezhda Mandelstam, he never 'felt' Christian."

Pasternak, Jewish on his mother's side, was more overtly Christian than Mandelstam; one would imagine that he endorsed the fictional Yuri Zhivago's assertion that Christianity represents the highest evolution of the consciousness of the Old Testament.

For some Russian writers Christianity was a refuge, an escape: Christ was a human figure that represented a shelter from the anti-Semitic terror. Mandelstam's case is more complex: while he converted to Christianity in his early twenties, the nature of his faith was no less mysterious, ultimately, than everything else we know about him. He wanted to "drink the cold mountain air of Christianity"; to gaze upward where cathedral spires protest against the emptiness of the skies. "The fine arrow of the Gothic belltower is angry," he writes in "The Morning of Acmeism," "for the whole idea of it is to stab the sky, to reproach it for being empty."

Did his obsession with aspiration, flight, heights, and distance have anything to do with his physiognomy? He was frequently described as birdlike, *bazdomnaia ptitsa,* "homeless bird." The constructivist poet Velimir Khlebnikov, punning on the nineteenth-century writer—best known for his "King Lear of the Steppes"—Nikolai Leskov's "steel flea," nicknamed Mandelstam "the marble fly."

———— ✺ ————

In our "wolfhound age," our "tyrant century"—to appropriate two of Mandelstam's more unforgettable epithets—is a man who asserts the divine over the secular in his youth predisposed to the idea of martyrdom? Or is it the explicitly Christian imagery that begins to arouse suspicion of his interest in the sacred? As early as 1912, in a poem about Hagia Sophia ("Holy Wisdom"), the cathedral in Istanbul—and the onetime *sanctum sanctorum* of the Eastern Orthodox church, which had been turned into a mosque by the Turks—he would already assert:

> Hagia Sophia—here the Lord commanded
> That nations and Tsars should halt!
> Your dome, according to an eyewitness,
> Hangs from heaven as though by a chain.
>
> *Translated by James Greene*

The weight of stones is not the matter that matters here: it's the soaring construction of the cathedrals, which have aspiration locked into their stones. "A cobblestone in the hands of an architect is transformed into substance, and the man who does not hear a metaphysical proof in the sound of a chisel splitting rock was not born to build" ("The Morning of Acmeism").

———

The Russian Revolution and its aftermath were a catastrophe for a generation of Russian writers. Absolutely no one escaped unscathed: Yesenin, Mayakovsky, and Tsvetaeva hanged themselves; Nikolai Gumilev, Anna Akhmatova's husband, was shot; Isaac Babel died like Mandelstam, in a camp. And this just begins the roll call. Even the ones who survived, like Akhmatova and Pasternak, lived as displaced persons. They were silenced for long periods as poets. And when they wrote, they devised elaborate codes.

If there ever was a consistent personality, it was Pasternak: he could not even intercede with the authorities on Mandelstam's behalf in a straightforward manner. When, in a now fabled event, Pasternak came to the phone one day having been told that it was

JOSEPH STALIN HIMSELF ON THE OTHER END OF THE LINE

and when he had done with the complaints with which he began every telephone conversation and allowed the dictator to get a word in, Stalin assured Pasternak that Mandelstam's sentence had been commuted and that it was "all right." In the following conversation, though, it was Stalin who reproached *Pasternak,* for not doing more to help his fellow poet and friend. In his own defense, straying from the life-and-death issue at hand, Pasternak chopped logic about the definition of the word *friend* until he was interrupted by Stalin, who asked him:
"But he's a genius; he's a genius, isn't he?"
"But that's not the point."
"What is it, then?"
"We should meet, and talk face to face."
"About what?"
"About life and death."
At this point, the dictator had had enough and hung up; Pasternak could not get him back on the line. The supposed "miracle" of Mandelstam's commuted sentence had already occurred (thanks in part to Pasternak's appeal to Nikolay Bukharin); but Pasternak also succeeded in

preventing Stalin from capitalizing too much on his own noblesse oblige. Pasternak had already prepared the ground for this bizarre interchange by being the only author of note not to append his name to a florid condolence letter signed by thirty-three upstanding members of the Writer's Union after the suicide of the dictator's second wife (official cause of death: peritonitis), and also by brashly writing to Stalin what must have been an unsettling note saying that he, Pasternak, *had been thinking deeply and intensively about Stalin . . . for the first time . . . on the day before Alliluyeva's death.*

I think that Nadezhda Mandelstam is psychologically on target in her analysis of Pasternak's personality. While taking Pasternak's side against those who would have implicated him, she reminds us of his obliviousness to compromise and rapprochement; she (not alone among his acquaintances) found his self-absorption "faintly comic." She uses the word *antipodes* to define just how different Mandelstam and Pasternak were temperamentally, "but since antipodes are by definition located at opposite poles of the same sphere, it is possible to draw a line between them . . . But it is noteworthy that at the end of their lives both of them acted in ways quite at variance with the whole of their previous stands." She means that Pasternak would put himself into conflict with the Soviet literary world by publishing *Dr. Zhivago;* and that Mandelstam would "attempt" an ode to Stalin, when it no longer mattered—the noose was already around his neck.

Pasternak survived by making people scratch their heads about what his "ambiguous givings out" might mean. His art was a matter of not saying what he meant. But indirection came naturally to him just as it did not to Mandelstam. When Pasternak ends the lush, sensual poem—"Summer"—with a reference to a committee on social reform, he still gives the senses and the natural world the last word.

That's how the dust smelled. And the weeds.
And once you got the point
that's how the gentry's decrees smelled:
of brotherhood, equality.

Councils gathered in villages.
Did you, friend, cast your lot with them?
Days glittered in the sorrel
and smelled of wine-cork.

Translated by Rudman with Boychuk

A packed auditorium chanted "sixty-six, sixty-six" when Pasternak prepared to read his translations of Shakespeare's sonnets, and applauded when he reached the line: "And art made tongue-tied by authority." There are ways of defeating censorship without sacrificing your liberty and life for it.

Mandelstam, like Simone Weil, another Jew turned Christian turned martyr, scorned physical comfort. When Pasternak congratulated him on having obtained an apartment by saying "Now you'll be able to write poetry," Mandelstam responded with "The Apartment," lashing out at an attitude he considered precious:

> It won't be the fountain Hippocrene
> that will burst through the hack-work walls,
> but the current of household terror
> in this evil coop in Moscow.

> *Moscow, Furmanov pereulok, November 1933 (translated by Brown/Merwin)*

These are the kinds of issues that stand behind his somewhat perplexing lines about being "no one's contemporary," especially considering what good company, poetically speaking, he was in.

The name Mandelstam has become synonymous with martyr in the same way that the name Kafka is synonymous with persecution. He may be better known in the West for the sufferings he endured than for the works he created. Besides, before he was old enough to have heard of the poets with whom he would later identify, he felt an affinity with his biblical namesake, Joseph.

At the time of this writing, a new edition of Mandelstam's work, with many corrections, is being prepared. Because you sometimes get entirely different images from reading two translations of the same poem, I am slightly squeamish about my own conviction of Mandelstam's stature as a poet, in the density and the velocity of his poems, when I'm essentially dependent upon translations, and in the case of poems memorized by Nadezhda, translations of translations. While I have a certain anxiety in the back of my mind about the truth content of anything I say about his work, I am also convinced that it is his tone that is indelible.

> I never stood under the Egyptian portico of a bank
> With ponderous importance, frowning, in a beaver-fur mitre,

And above the lemon-coloured Neva
No gypsy girl ever danced for me to the crackle of hundred-ruble notes.
Sensing future executions, from the howl of stormy events
I ran to the Black Sea nymphs

> *222 (translated by James Greene)*

He dramatizes what he does not do and leaps into prophecy. It reminds me of the way certain speeches of Shakespeare interrupt history. The tone is always so sure and eerie, your curiosity about the poems is piqued when you encounter them in a form to all accounts so diminished.

This tone comes across in every piece of his prose or poetry, and it is also tied to his martyrdom. Why? Because while he was a fearful person, within this fearfulness lay a terrific, wild, and sometimes savage sense of humor, a levity that leavens his darkest poems and keeps his works purged of self-pity.

The age. In the sick son's blood the deposit of lime
is hardening. Moscow's sleeping like a wooden coffin.
There's no escaping the tyrant century.
After all these years the snow still smells of apples.
I want to run away from my own doorstep,
but where? Out in the street it's dark,
and my conscience glitters ahead of me
like salt strewn on the pavement.

Somehow I've got myself set for a short journey
through the back lanes, past thatched eaves, starling houses,
an everyday passer-by, in a flimsy coat,
forever trying to button the lap-robe.
Street after street flashes past,
the frozen runners crunch like apples;
can't get the button through the button-hole,
it keeps slipping out of my fingers.

> *"1 January 1924" (translated by Brown/Merwin)*

You'd have to leap ahead to Beckett's stylized characters to find a self-description such as this, of the erstwhile lyrical hero as a passenger in a dog-eaten greatcoat, unable to get the button through the buttonhole. Even in desperation he can manage something comic, even histrionic. How absurd I must look, trying to save myself, *moving through the frozen streets in my tattered coat, unable to get the button through the buttonhole* while in the world all is charged with portent, importance, apocalypse.

Mandelstam, like Cézanne, prefers apples to apocalypse. And they come back later, like a musical phrase, in "1 January 1924": "The frost is smelling of apples again." (Mandelstam was captivated by Cézanne's still lifes. "Roses that must have been cut in the morning, solid and rolled tight, unusually young tea roses. Exactly like little scoops of yellow ice cream.")

Mandelstam endears himself to us through the self-deflation of the comic self-portrait: "A passenger like any other," the absolute lack of self-importance of "an internal" (which I had misremembered as "eternal") *raznochinets,* as he characterized Dante (an intellectual, not of noble birth). He is a man who doesn't know how to behave or what to say, much less how to make a bow.

> The inner anxiety and the heavy, troubled awkwardness which attend every step of the unself-confident man, the man whose upbringing is inadequate, who does not know what application to make of his inner experience or how to objectify it in etiquette, the tortured and outcast man—it is these qualities which give the poem all its charm, all its drama, and they create its background, its psychological ground.

This description of Dante is a crucial self-disclosure, a key to what makes the enigma enigmatic. He goes on to insist that Dante's awkwardness, the violent mood changes, the soaring and plummeting of his self-esteem that make it so difficult for him to be him as well as to be around is not something he has imagined; the evidence is strewn everywhere through the *Commedia.*

Another posture Mandelstam likes to assume is that of the failed pedant. "My lack of even the vaguest notion about crystallography—*an ignorance in this field, as in many others, that is customary in my circle*—deprives me of the pleasure of grasping the true structure of the *Divina Commedia*" (my emphasis).

⁓

Mandelstam rarely strays from the problems of time and duration, the intervals in which space curves while the day itself "yawns like a caesura"; orioles sing in the elms; vowel-length is all that counts where classical lines are concerned. Mandelstam is as passionate about the Bergsonian *durée* as he is about cathedrals.

Bergson [the French philosopher], whose profoundly Judaic mind is gripped by an insistent need for practical monotheism, offers us a doctrine concerning the system of phenomena. Bergson regards phenomena not in the order of their subordination to a rule of temporal sequence, but, as it were, in their spatial extent (or perhaps, to keep it closer to Bergson's terminology, in their "duration"). He is interested exclusively in the internal linkage of phenomena. This linkage he liberates from time and considers separately. The phenomena that are thus interlinked form as it were a kind of fan, the panels of which one can unfurl in time, but at the same time it lends itself to a rolling up that the mind can comprehend.

But Mandelstam was not *always* so far away. He liked the Crimea, because it had been spared the ravages of the Revolution; and he reveled in his brief sojourn in Armenia—witness his high spirits in "Journey to Armenia," the last piece of his writing to appear during his lifetime.

The Armenians' fullness with life, their rude tenderness, their noble inclination for hard work, their inexplicable aversion to anything metaphysical, and their splendid intimacy with the world of real things—all of this said to me: you're awake, don't be afraid of your own time, don't be sly . . . Wasn't this because I found myself among a people who, though renowned for their fervent activity, nevertheless lived not by the clock in the railway station nor by that in some institution, but by the sundial such as I saw among the ruins of Zvartnots in the form of an astronomical wheel or rose inscribed in stone?

Everyday life never came easily to Mandelstam. Clarence Brown recounts that after Mandelstam fell in love with a woman doctor in the Crimea, he refused to leave, even when he couldn't pay his rent. The poet who some twenty years later was last seen scrounging around the mounds of garbage not far from Vladivostok was subsequently persecuted by a servant woman with a foul temper who fed him leftovers and scraps. That wasn't the worst of it: "Whenever evil-tempered guests arrived he was evicted from his room and forced to sleep in an unheated storeroom, where he caught cold and an infection that caused his cheek to swell up. With his head bandaged, painted with iodine, he was followed about by a troop of taunting urchins."

Mandelstam was hounded throughout much of his adult life. "Miserable is the man who runs from a dog / in his shadow, whom a wind reaps

at the knees, / and poor the one who holds out his rag of life / to beg
mercy of a shadow." While this situation drove him over the top, it also
helped him arrive at a high tragic pitch, a desperate babble closer to the
outbursts in *King Lear* than anything else I can think of in English. He
wrote one utterly rending poem after another. What we are really talking
about underneath the shifting rubric is intensity—a term that continually
demands to be redefined. He cries out like a man being flayed:

> What shall I do with myself, now it's January?
> The gaping city staggers and clings.
> I think it's the locked doors that have made me drunk.
> I could howl out of every lock and paper-clip.
>
> And after that, there I am, gasping,
> drumming on an icy wooden tub:
> "Somebody read me! Somebody lead me! Somebody heal me!
> Somebody say something on the jagged stairs!"
>
>   *360; Voronezh, January–February 1937 (translated by Brown/Merwin)*

(I thought I had the last stanza memorized, but my "Somebody feed
me!"—for "lead me"—was clearly a projection.)

I am not saying that Mandelstam sought out trouble, but that he early
discerned the poetic use he could make of trouble; trouble as exemplified
by exile. Mandelstam may have undergone an imaginary death via his
identification with Ovid and Villon, just as Keats did with Chatterton.
"Sensing future executions, from the howl of stormy events / I ran to the
Black Sea nymphs." He steeped himself in the literature of exile; he re-
hearsed the unspeakably terrible part he would have to play. He took
steps—Brecht would say measures—to make sure that he could convert
his destitution, his homelessness, into writing; even if he couldn't, both for
lack of a desk and an antipathy to stasis, physically write down what he
was all the time at work composing in his head, he ensured that someone
would.

> I have no manuscripts, no notebooks, no archives. I have no handwriting be-
> cause I never write. I alone in Russia work from the voice while all around
> the bitch pack writes.

This from his scathing and apocalyptic "Fourth Prose," which plays on
the idea that Moscow was the "Third Rome" and—by decree of the

monk Philotheus in the seventeenth century—there would be no "Fourth."

Mandelstam continued to turn to Italy, preferring the wide skies and "the bright, all-human" hills of Tuscany to "the still-young hills of Voronezh"; he praised Dante's Italian for its "infantile phonetics" and the old Italians for their sensual "lust after rhyme." As he writes in "Conversation About Dante":

> The mouth works, the smile moves the verse line, the lips are cleverly and merrily crimson, the tongue presses itself trustfully to the roof of the mouth.
>
> The inner image of the verse is inseparable from the numberless changes of expression which flit across the face of the teller of tales as he talks excitedly.
>
> For that is exactly what the act of speech does; it distorts our face, explodes its calm, destroys its mask.

Mandelstam was so disoriented he wrote almost no poetry for about five years in the mid-1920s. But when his silence ended he became the only productive Russian poet during the 1930s. His tragedy was that he could not, if he was to speak, censor himself internally. Mandelstam, intrigued with martyrdom as early as "The Lutheran" ("Our candles make a twilight at noon"), was propelled on a trajectory toward the dwindling future long before he wrote "The Stalin Epigram," the poem that sealed his fate as a martyr.

Mandelstam divined in the condition of the exiled poets an ingredient he wanted in his poetry: a tone; a sense of addressing someone intimately yet from a distance. Distance is never far from him. It's significant that he would fasten on *Tristia,* one of Ovid's least-read texts, as a source. The poems in *Tristia* are one-to-one, written to specific people—whom Ovid did not name for fear of implicating them.

> My heart is with you. Only my husk is here.
> The skies above me are frosty. Even the stars here
> 　　shrivel with cold. Beyond, there's the Bosporus,
> the Don, the Scythian marshes, and then nothing but ice,

empty uninhabited wastes, the world's
dizzying edges, vacant as death itself.

Translated by David Slavitt

While complaining that he hasn't got the peace of mind he needs to
compose poetry, Ovid casts his net wide over turbulent skies, agitated waters, and domestic squalor. He could range without straining from the
perturbations of the Black Sea raging in its chains to a litany of complaints
about the quality of life in the grubby backwater of Tomis to which he
had been dispatched. Uprooted, in desperate straits, Ovid continued to
experiment with poetic genres, to practice and perfect the one thing no
one could take away from him: his art.

Ovid's lesson went straight to Mandelstam's unconscious. Certain lines
imply that Mandelstam imagined himself exiled, like Ovid, from *Rome*.
"Rome is far. And he never loved it." As early as in his first book, *Stone,* he
reveals Italy as his spiritual home: "I was born in Rome and Rome has
come back to me."

Here, amid the quiet fading of nature
Far from the Forum and the Capitol
I hear Augustus, and on the earth's rim I hear
The years rolling, like the sovereign apple.

Translated by Robert Tracey

Mandelstam, like Robert Graves, is convinced of the importance of
what he called "the addressee." It is typical of bad poetry—such as the
type Hopkins referred to as "parnassian"—that it is addressed to too general an audience, everyone and no one. (Whitman is one of the few who
could address "a great audience"—perhaps because it existed solely in his
head.) "I and one other" is how Mandelstam characterized his attitude toward his audience. In his essay "On the Interlocutor," Mandelstam goes
after the early Russian symbolist Konstantin Balmont, his case in point,
for lacking "the precious consciousness of poetic rightness . . . because he
does not have a constant interlocutor." According to Mandelstam this
leads him toward obsequiousness and insolence, a tone deafness that un-
dermines imagination in favor of rhetoric or empty eloquence.

Readers can relax only when they sense a certain ease or comfort between the poet and the "addressee" or "interlocutor"—what Mandelstam

termed a "concrete listener." The tension between the poet and the concrete listener breeds attention. As Simone Weil has written unforgettably in *Gravity and Grace,* "Absolutely unmixed attention is prayer."

Addressing poems to an intimate other also broaches the problem of information—both its presence and its absence—that can, if not baffle the reader, prevent anything like a complete understanding. But a complete understanding is probably a misnomer where every true poem is concerned, because of the dimension of time, which prevents everything from happening at once. And poetry and quickness—as Mandelstam argues in "Conversation About Dante"—are allied.

> The quality of poetry is determined by the speed and decisiveness with which it embodies its plan of action, its commands, in diction, the instrumentless, lexical, purely quantitative nature of word formation. One must run across the full width of a river, crammed with Chinese junks moving simultaneously in various directions—this is how the meaning of poetic discourse is created. The meaning, its route, cannot be reconstructed by interrogating the boatmen: they will not tell how and why we were leaping from junk to junk.   *(my translation)*

Mandelstam was tattered but free until 1934, when someone who had heard him recite "The Stalin Epigram" informed. The poetic trope of exile, which he embraced so early in his career (through his three main poetic alter egos, Villon, Ovid, and Dante), predicted his martyrdom.

History alters Mandelstam's fate, turning him into both a Dantesque poet and a character in Hell.

> Our lives no longer feel ground under them.
> At ten paces you can't hear our words.
>
> But whenever there's a snatch of talk,
> it turns to the Kremlin mountaineer,
>
> the ten thick worms his fingers,
> his words like measures of weight,
>
> the huge laughing cockroaches on his top lip,
> the glitter of his boot-tops.
>
> Ringed with a scum of chicken-necked bosses
> he toys with the tributes of half-men.

One whistles, another meouws, a third snivels.
One for the groin, one the forehead, temple, eye.

He rolls the executions on his tongue like berries.
He wishes he could hug them like big friends from home.

286 [November 1933] (translated by Brown/Merwin)

This poem, "The Stalin Epigram," may have sealed his fate, but Osip Mandelstam had been a man on the run for a long time and, even under the best of circumstances, he didn't have the constitution for it. Mandelstam was a ruined man already: frail, penniless, homeless, and slightly mad, when Stalin, in what he wanted to be regarded as an act of charity, sentenced him to five years of hard labor instead of executing him. Russia loves its poets to death.

Stalin missed that Mandelstam had understood him, in that "The Stalin Epigram" wasn't an *entirely* negative portrait of a world-class butcher; it showed a cognizance of his power, and how successful he was in exercising his will. He found death delectable where other mortals would quail. Lowell put a stress on this with "After each death, he is like a Georgian tribesman, / putting a raspberry in his mouth." Stalin may have been a tyrant, but he wasn't a cipher. And he cared—too much and in the wrong way—about what poets thought of him.

The human-animal metaphors in the poems, which became more rending and brutal as time went on, were already predominant in an early essay about François Villon, who "lived in Paris like a squirrel in a wheel, without knowing a moment's rest. He loved in himself the predatory lean little beast and cherished his own shabby little hide." (Mandelstam must have invited such comparisons too. One of his neighbors in the years following the Revolution, Mikhail Leonodovich Lozionsky, saw Mandelstam as a cross between a rabbit and a snow leopard.)

In Lowell's version of "The Stalin Epigram," his half-men "make touching and funny animal sounds." Merwin goes with "One whistles, another meouws, a third snivels." Bernard Meares risks—preceded by the padded *"servile* half-human hordes"—"Some mewl, some grizzle, some moan." Mandelstam never tires of reminding our hubristic species just what we really are made of.

My animal, my age, who will ever be able
to look into your eyes?

Who will ever glue back together the vertebrae
of two centuries with his blood.

The buds will go on swelling,
the rush of green will explode,
but your spine has been shattered,
my splendid derelict, my age.
Cruel and feeble, you'll look back
with the smile of a half-wit:
an animal that could run once,
staring at his own tracks.

  135, "The Age," 1923 (translated by Brown/Merwin)

I have been enchanted by Mandelstam's poem "On the Sledge" ever since
I first encountered it in Robert Lowell's lively, vivid version in the anthology *Poets on Street Corners*. (Why have Lowell's "imitations," which
make up in energy what they lose in accuracy, been so vilified? You learn
something else about the original poems after you have read one of Lowell's tense, heightened "versions.") As for "translations," this is one of the
instances where I prefer "scholar" Clarence Brown's translation to the one
he later collaborated on with W. S. Merwin.

On a sledge overlaid with straw,
Ourselves but partly covered by the fateful bast,
We rode through immense Moscow
From the Sparrow Hills as far as the familiar little church.

But in Uglich children play at knucklebones
And there's a smell of bread left in the oven.
I am conveyed about the streets bareheaded
And in the chapel three candles glimmer.

Not three candles burning, but three meetings—
And one of them had God's own blessing on it;
There is to be no fourth, and Rome is far away—
And Rome He never loved.

The sledge dove into the black ruts
And people were returning from the open place for strolling.

Thin mouzhiks and cross old women
Shifted at the gate from foot to foot.

Raw distance seemed to blacken with the flight of birds
And bound hands went numb.
They're bringing the Tsarevich, the body numbs with terror,
And now the amber straw's been set on fire.

In the title poem of Mandelstam's *Tristia,* the collection in which "On the Sledge" appears, Mandelstam reminds us that everything has happened before and will happen again and that only the flash of recognition brings delight. This poem, as resistant as it is to paraphrase, still has a kind of inevitability, the inevitability of doom. Mandelstam's life too was heading toward its inevitable end, which took the form of martyrdom.

There is no one consummate translation of "On a country sleigh, laid out with straw" and yet all of them allow me access to the poem, or something in the poem that shines through—that fascinates me, like an unsolved mystery; which the poem probably is in its original Russian. But the litany of place-names—"Sparrow Hills," "Moscow," "Uglich" (the latter goes so well with "Tsarevich")—sets up its own tension of opposites. Lowell puts a weight on this in his version. He foregrounds the issue of place, with the implicit opposition (lurking behind every stone in Russian literature) between Moscow and St. Petersburg. "Somehow we got through the miles of Moscow, / left the Sparrow Hills, and found the small, familiar church / Then in Uglitch the children play knucklebones."

Around the time he composed "On the Sledge," Mandelstam wrote enthusiastically about Pasternak's *My Sister—Life,* and he would have encountered and marked a poem called "Sparrow Hills" where the litany of nouns denotes the natural world: "in the heights, thoughts simmer in the white foam / of woodpeckers, fir cones, clouds, pine needles, and heat" (my translation).

In Uglich the children play knucklebones.

There is a splendid consonantal clatter, harsh *ch* sounds that are full of foreboding—a prelude to terror. Different renderings of the line, with different syntax and arrangements, also succeed—although one would assume there to be only one way to utter such a natural sentence. In the Merwin/Brown version, the line ("Children in Uglich play at knuckle-

bones") sounds like something in an early imagist poem, when the movement's formal concerns were still pristine and close to those of the
Acmeists, whose manifesto Mandelstam authored. You can see why the
poem clearly would have engaged Lowell, whose opening line to his own
"A Quaker Graveyard in Nantucket"—"A brackish reach of shoal off
Madaket"—also prefigures a death as a kind of sacrifice. The splendid play
of consonants in the English of "In Uglich the children play knucklebones" falls right into a loose, decasyllabic anapestic trimeter, and the
fourth stanza is another you have to work hard to ruin in English: the
sledge moving down into the black ruts while vaguely menacing "Thin
mouzhiks and cross old women" kill time, absently converging around it.
It is like the image of van Gogh's crows flying over the wheat field *into* his
face.

Translation is a form of criticism; when Clarence Brown writes, "And
the people were returning from the open place for strolling," it is his way
of signaling what the reader needs to know. The literal, prosaic quality of
the line interacts almost jarringly with the rest of the stanza and the
poem; it would have been easy to intensify here, but he abjures the lure of
the smooth, "cool" solution. Lowell misses the swift, fluid beauty of Mandelstam's construction when he, against the grain of the original poem,
stops time with "The men were all bones, the women were crows."

Mandelstam's work is saturated in Russian history; he writes intimately
about great events. Because of the mysterious death of Tsarevich Dmitry,
"Uglich" is as familiar a name in Russia and as encrusted with associations
as the "Alamo" is to Americans. The multiplicity of tones and layering of
allusions make even his short poems resemble Elizabethan plays in minia-
ture. The line ("In Uglich the children play knucklebones") also brings to
mind the opening shot of Sam Peckinpah's Eisensteinian Western, *The
Wild Bunch,* where children play ants-devour-the-scorpion before they
set the whole makeshift nest of twigs on fire. (Mandelstam dissed the cin-
ematograph with its "celluloid tapeworm" but was drawn to a painting of
Degas in which he "elongates the bodies of the horses approaching the
finish line at the race track.")

The non-Russian reader can identify the tone, and divine the aura of
mystery in "On the Sledge," without knowing that the poem takes off
from what Pushkin called "the smells of ancient Russia" or that the reference to Rome ("There is to be no fourth, and Rome is far away") echoes

the line from the closing stanza of *Eugene Onegin* ("Some are gone already, and those [who remain alive] are far away")—as well as the entire theme of *Tristia*. Even the reader who knows that the poem was addressed to Marina Tsvetaeva may not know that even this is layered—that while the "three meetings" may refer to her, "Marina" makes an implicit reference to the Polish princess Marina Mniszek, who was seduced by Czar Boris Godunov's usurper, the selfsame Tsarevich Dmitry who will soon be burned on the amber straw and whose very name carries with it the period of Russian history known as the Time of Troubles.

Why "bound hands"? It's said that the Tsarevich was an epileptic. But who is conveyed bareheaded through the streets like a captive? Mandelstam? The Tsarevich? Marina Tsvetaeva's biographer, Victoria Schweitzer, detects this strain of fatalism in Mandelstam: "as he took Russia into himself, as he began to see himself as a part of Russian history, he also foresaw his own doom. 'On a country sleigh, laid out with straw' is Mandelstam's answer to Tsvetaeva's various prophecies; it is his first premonition—and acceptance—of his own fate." And yet this is an aesthetic victory, his happening upon what would give his poetry its frame."

In one of his first poems, Mandelstam claimed to be so tired of life he could accept nothing from it, but he loved his "poor earth" because it was the only one he had seen. Then in a feverish haze he remembered rocking, on a plain wooden swing in the distant garden, under the tall dark firs. And toward the end of his life, he "could be a boy / following the lead of grown-ups as they step / blithely into choppy seas." In order to extinguish melancholy, Mandelstam contemplated reading only children's books, having only childish thoughts, and abandoning everything adults deemed valuable. He echoes Christ's teaching—you must become as little children—in this poem to the children of the future: one of his last utterances.

> Mounds of human heads recede in mist.
> Unseen in their midst, I grow small. But in books
> we were raised on and games children play
> I will rise from the dead to say—: the sun.
>
> [1936–37] (my translation)

For Further Reading

Clarence Brown, *Mandelstam*. New York: Cambridge University Press, 1974.

Nadezhda Mandelstam, *Hope Against Hope*. New York: Macmillan, 1976.

————, *Hope Abandoned*. New York: Macmillan, 1974.

Osip Mandelstam, *The Complete Prose and Letters*. Translated and edited by Jane Gary Harris. Ann Arbor, MI: Ardis Press, 1979.

————, *The Noise of Time: The Prose of Osip Mandelstam*. Translated by Clarence Brown. New York: Penguin, 1993.

————, *Selected Poems*. Translated by James Greene. New York: Penguin, 1992.

————, *Selected Poems*. Translated by Clarence Brown and W. S. Merwin. New York: Simon & Schuster, 1973.

————, *Stone*. Translated by Robert Tracey. New York: HarperCollins, 1993.

Boris Pasternak, *My Sister—Life*. Translated by Mark Rudman with Bohdan Boychuk. Evanston, IL: Northwestern University Press, 1993.

PATRICK PEARSE

Ireland, 1916

Poetry, the Body, and Violence

by PEGGY O'BRIEN

[I]t would take sensible, level-headed experienced men to guide a great agitation; none such were associated with the Sinn Féin agitation. It was guided by feather heads and dreamers, hence only mischief and worse than mischief could attend it . . . the Crazy Rebellion was the work chiefly of a lot of Crazy Poets. This has surprised people as far away as Chicago.

Jasper Tully, writing for the *Wicklow People,*
May 6 and June 10, 1916[1]

Poets have their own religion or profane equivalent, and one of its tenets, more a mystical inclination, is that rhyme can be synecdoche, the part standing for the whole. Rhymes as tightly packed as walnut shells appear to offer themselves up to the poet as much as to the reader as little, meaty truths. Rhyme appears designed to package paradox compactly, the metaphysical and physical in tight symmetry. I cannot even say the name Pearse to myself without completing the equation with "I write it out in a verse" and then continuing to recite the rest of Yeats's puzzling conclusion to "Easter 1916," all the more provocative for being superficially resounding:

I write it out in a verse—
MacDonagh and MacBride
And Connolly and Pearse
Now and in time to be,
Wherever green is worn,
Are changed, changed utterly:
A terrible beauty is born.

The rhyme between "Pearse" and "verse" seems as much an organic given as the lobes of the brain, suggesting that, if as readers we make an incision down the line where the two words join, an insight will unfold rewarding faith about the mysteries of both martyrdom and poetry. That is the religious approach that the poem unfortunately, through its seeping ironies, none more than in the conclusion, asks us to resist. The poem interrogates the equation between patriotism and martyrdom, not unconnected to the further equation made by some between Catholicism and Irish nationalism. This insidious link is not made explicit by Yeats in his elegy but it is the second cultural given, that to be truly Irish is to be Catholic, for which Pearse bears considerable responsibility. "Easter 1916" asks us to resist with skepticism these fusions, transcendence generally.

Bewildered, Yeats asks what could be worth both the loss of life and the loss of poetry. These two terms, life and poetry, form the alternative equation made by the poem. His private interest in the patriots (apart from MacBride, Maud Gonne's husband, who never fails to prick Yeats's rage, jealousy, and scorn) is that two of the executed insurgents invoked, Patrick Pearse and Thomas MacDonagh, were poets. Yeats, unconcerned about concealing his own vanity and guilt, ponders the special poignancy of their sacrifice as young poets:

This man had kept a school
And rode our wingèd horse;
This other his helper and friend
Was coming into his force;
He might have won fame in the end,

So sensitive his nature seemed,
So daring and sweet his thought.

Pearse was executed at the age of thirty-six by the English for his part in the Rising, an armed insurrection for independence from British rule carried out by a handful of Irish in Dublin starting on Easter Monday April 24, 1916, and lasting for less than a week. Besides his martyrdom Pearse left behind a modest literary legacy, plays and stories and most importantly for Yeats a handful of poems. The contemporary reader, anticipating the rhyme between Pearse and verse and knowing the accepted status of Pearse now as a minor poet, can't help latching on to the derogatory connotations of verse today: "staves," non-poems, earnest efforts lacking in the first intensity. But Yeats, I believe, is using verse to mean the rudiments of poetry, its metrical grid, its stanzaic structure, and wondering how Pearse could live without poetry any more than Yeats's poetry could exist without these basic supports. Yeats is acknowledging Pearse's potential, not just the few true poems but the flashes of the real thing in much of his work: the lyrical exquisiteness, barely contained passions, a natural gravitation to extremes tempered by a "cold eye," intuitive, mesmerizing rhythms, and most of all an urgency of address that necessitated even in his brief career experiments with form.

In his conclusion, Yeats seems, at one level—in the touch of rhyming-chiming jingoism—to be reprehending Pearse particularly for his declension from poet to demagogue. That Yeats can even suggest such criticism in the midst of eulogy indicates the value he places on poetry as a receptacle for complexity, emotional and intellectual, a use to which Pearse was never fully able to put the form and may explain his willingness to lose its consolations. Yeats is able to present conflict with a formal clarity and proportion that in the moment of the poem contain its tensions. Contradictions don't evaporate in the poem's ether; rather they are suspended in it in a seemingly ideal arrangement like sun and moon.

"Easter 1916" is a troubled poem, and the deliberately forced, upbeat conclusion doesn't convince tonally. Read as parody it becomes a cautionary tale. This puts Yeats in the position of both commemorating the dead and subverting their legacy, a posture that extends his meditation throughout on actual nonparticipation and imaginative involvement. Even hinting at the cant of patriotism, not least its predictable rhythms, warns the reader of its dangers. This conclusion comes at the weary end of a process that has been driven by self-examination. The poet earns closure on his own terms.

The poem, after all, pivots on self-interrogation, and the basic question asked, no doubt prompted by the internalized voice of Maud Gonne, is why Yeats also didn't physically participate, risk his life and poetry for Ireland. His answer must include a justification of poetry, as profound in its own domain as the fight for national independence in the political. The poem charts the process of discovering and defining a poetic that eschews completely ephemeral effects for essential aims and consequences, finding even a limited social role. In the first stanza Yeats, flaying himself for past superciliousness, presents himself then as an Ascendancy snob, engaging with fervid Nationalists only to the degree of snagging a story to deliver at "the club." By the end of the poem, when he ritualistically names the dead, who deliberately are not named in the second stanza where their accomplishments in life are mourned without myth getting in the way, Yeats provides an answer to how poetry may also serve. He can use the names at this concluding moment because by then the poem has restored individuality, corporeality to the participants by returning them to an imagined, real context. Each in turn has been rescued from inert hagiography. Memory is rendered visceral by the poem's emotional honesty. Irony and sincerity mingle to guarantee a comprehensive response, much harder to digest than the pabulum of patriotism.

This paradoxical stance, however, would not be possible without a further degree of discovery about the poetic process. The third stanza succeeds both in stamping Yeats's genius on the meditation and justifying his decision to remain on the margins of action and thereby live. Here he shows how the retention of a living perspective is necessary for an understanding of tragedy. He demonstrates the power of such immediacy by radically breaking with the temporal flow of the poem, which up to this point has been retrospective, symptomizing the grasp the event has on imagination. Even though the form is meditative and allows for digression, the leap into immediacy in the third stanza feels sudden, a deliberate snapping to attention, a focusing on the here and now, "minute by minute" time. Here he re-creates with mimetic fidelity the temporal and spatial fluency he witnesses from the window of his tower where "minute by minute" things change, changes that may not appear as important as the transformation of many individuals into the monolith of history, the "stone in the midst of all"; but the poem, bent on preserving dichotomy, makes it clear that there are changes and changes, hence the repetition "changed, changed utterly." Two temporal orders are jostling for priority and the poem negotiates between them, mitigating both extremes. Yeats can only restore individual identities to the martyrs by looking at them through the scrim and frame of his own ever distracting identity immersed in the living, plural moment: "The horse that comes from the road, / The rider, the birds that range / From cloud to tumbling cloud." The poet must remain in the living stream if only to reproduce the infrangible presence of loss and disorientation represented by the stone.

The spectacle of Pearse's martyrdom raised and still raises the question of the relationship between poetry and action. It asks as an example whether poetry has a certain sufficiency to itself, whether it has the power to be transformative or whether its function and in fact virtue lie in adhering to obstinate circumstance. Pearse's witness asks whether the complex man seeking simplicity and transcendence must relinquish poetry, which ontologically opposes these states. William Irwin Thompson, whose book *The Imagination of an Insurrection* was published originally in the 1960s and recently republished, still contributes to an understanding of these questions. While Thompson is less strong in his grasp of the nuances of Irish history (especially in light of the spate of recent historical reassessment, much of it revisionist, prompted by over two decades of Troubles in the North), still he has much to say on a theoretical level about the relationship between the political and poetic acts. While never doubting that Yeats is a major poet and that the poets of 1916 are not, Thompson makes two observations that assist in an overall reevaluation of Pearse. The first is that the poem's prerogative, as distinct from that of political action, is to give vent to, indeed lay out for inspection, complexities that both history and personality find difficult to accommodate.[2] Political action rooted in external conflict requires an eradication of internal conflict to occur, that in order to make history an individual must cease making himself. On the other hand, quite paradoxically, the gesture of political action, supremely the sacrifice of a life, can be a self-defining moment commensurate with art. The entire body becomes the artist's medium, the unbroken shape of the gesture it makes the equivalent of formal coherence in a poem.

To look at the sweep of Pearse's short, intense career is broadly speaking to notice a movement away from art to politics. While Pearse never stopped writing and in fact wrote some of his most spontaneous and bold work shortly before, even just before, his death, his image of himself increasingly became that of a rhetorician and finally a martyr. Here is a sketch of his biography.[3] First, Pearse's parentage is not homogeneously Irish. His father was from England, a stone carver of monumental sculpture, an artisan of the first rank who created many of the noteworthy altars and pulpits in Dublin and the surrounding area. James Pearse, who had intellectual and artistic ambitions, was of Unitarian, freethinking stock and emigrated on his own to Ireland for work. He converted to Catholicism during the course of his first marriage to an Irishwoman who soon left him a widower. His second wife, Margaret, Patrick's mother, was a devout, unintellectual Irish Catholic. The firm that James Pearse established, Pearse and Sons of Richmond Street off what is now Pearse Street, became a very successful business under the father's chisel. Under the sons alone, when the father died in 1900, the firm went into gradual decline. Really only one son, Willie, who had artistic talent and studied painting, tried to keep it going. Willie, however, was increasingly drawn into his older brother's orbit, serving simultaneously as confidant, companion, colleague, acolyte, comrade, and surrogate wife. The two brothers were almost inseparable, and one of Pearse's best poems, "On the Strand of Howth" ("On the strand of Howth / Breaks a sounding wave; / A lone sea-gull screams / Above the bay.")[4] reads less like a poem of fraternal love than romantic love and separation. (Willie in a short-lived stab at separateness was in Paris studying art.) The gradual erosion of the business as the entire family became recruited to pursue Pearse's star signaled the onset of serious financial problems for them all. Pearse's mission from the beginning required relinquishing the world.

Pearse had from the start a separate, ill-defined, all-consuming, and ineffable destiny, some unique trajectory that only found the name of martyrdom posthumously. His search, beginning with words, can look like a struggle to find the word. He began his professional life with a halfhearted attempt at being conventional. He studied for the bar, succeeded, but never really practiced. His extracurricular involvement with the Gaelic League held far more magnetism for him and would soon claim all his time. Pearse had fallen under the charismatic sway of John O'Leary, the old Fenian celebrated in the refrain of "September 1913" ("Romantic Ireland's dead and gone, / It's with O'Leary in the grave"). Soon Pearse took on with a wholeheartedness far exceeding Yeats's the romance of the west of Ireland. Pearse learned Irish even though not being a native speaker brought suspicion on him from purists within the League and nearly blocked his advancement in the organization. Typically this impediment served only to redouble his devotion to the movement. Even at this stage, however, his messianism is utterly intelligent. While echoing the thoughts and sentiments of many contributors to cultural nationalism around him, Pearse's own writings about the depredations subsequent to the death of a language suggest a poet's involvement with words. For example, in a rebuttal to an argument that political autonomy should take precedence over linguistic, Pearse makes the claim for language as the very source of identity: "In truth, the language movement is not merely more important than the political movement, but it is on a different and altogether higher plane . . . [P]olitical autonomy . . . may . . . be necessary to the continued existence of the Nation—in the case of Ireland it probably is—but it is not, in itself, an essential of nationality."[5]

Already, however, the "higher plane" holds Pearse in thrall and, when he does eventually switch to embracing political autonomy as a goal, politics will enjoy that unearthly address. Even in these early formulations of a purpose, language exists in a context that includes the political, however much it exists to be transcended. Elevation at any cost above everything sordid, finally the world itself, will propel Pearse to the end. It will claim his mere body and determine a risky politics of no compromise. The rarefied for Pearse always triumphs because he is addicted to refinement. In this early phase, spirituality and art are automatically linked, implying a deeper connection between egoism and religion: "literature is the revelation of the author's soul . . . his interpretation of a fragment of life."[6] This early articulation demonstrates Pearse's innate immunity to contradictions lurking beneath the surfaces of his willed syntheses, like the dissonance of "soul" and "fragment," the unitary and the fragmentary vibrating side by side.

Any investigation of Pearse and martyrdom has to take account of his various, imperfectly analogous models for self-sacrifice, from the pre-Christian, Celtic hero Cuchulain, to Irish patriots of the past, Wolf Tone and Robert Emmet, to the timeless image of Christ on the cross. Each of these metaphors for martyrdom nests comfortably inside his mind within the others, interchangeable and equal, for the task that's being served is self-definition, finding a consummate metaphor for a complicated man. Each of these models reflects an aspect of Pearse's personality, different

variations on the theme of idealism and self-sacrifice. To watch their inter-
play in Pearse's rhetoric is also to witness an attempt at integration in their
author. Pearse can collapse Cuchulain, Tone, and Christ into one consummate martyr just as he tries to compass his discordant selves. One of the
greatest ironies of a life bent on purity is that it could so readily eradicate
important differences—historical, political, doctrinal—both within and
outside the self in the service of, for want of any better word, a "dream."

Pearse's biographers and critics perennially face the choice of taking
the high or low road to explain him. Generally speaking, the later into the
century commentary occurs the more it is couched in terms of the psychological, political, and economic rather than the spiritual, the more in-
clined toward detached criticism than hagiography. This is partly because
establishment Ireland, especially the academy, has felt the need to distance
itself from the imago of Pearse, which so easily defies reason in the popular imagination. Whenever the life is confronted closely, however, three
crucial developments must be interpreted. The first transition is from immersion in language and the language question climaxing in Pearse's
editorship, from 1903 to 1909, of An *Claidheamh,* the Gaelic League's
newspaper, to his equal immersion in the cause of Irish education. Pearse
not only founded in 1908 a school for boys, Saint Enda's, but wrote about
his theories of education, grounding them in a respect for the sacred individuality of each boy. His religious instincts, therefore, migrated from a
mystical attachment to language to an idealization of boys.

While he never officially gave up his position as headmaster, Pearse became diverted. In 1914 he sailed to America, ostensibly on a fund-raising
mission for Saint Enda's, which rapidly became an initiation into the efficient, determined Fenianism epitomized in America by John Devoy. It
was on this tour that Pearse discovered his considerable power as an orator, the cornerstone of his vocation as a martyr. The second transition,
therefore, was from education to politics. The parabola is from thought to
action, from defining the self first by inner and later by outside forces. His
final leap at the very end was from talk of violence to violence itself. This
move mirrors in microcosm his entire career. Pearse never loses the urgency to communicate announced by his editorship; it is just that his language changes, eventually becoming the hieroglyph of that final climactic
sacrifice, a gesture freighted with a lifetime's significance, an apocalyptic
moment distilling an obscure search. The sacred individuality of language

had translated itself into every boy's nobility and finally seemed the destiny of God's chosen people, the Irish. That the people are clearly a projection of one individual, Patrick Pearse, male, Catholic, celibate, is the reason that his legacy is fraught in contemporary Ireland.

The man himself refers his choices to a higher power, casting his entire life in a numinous glow: "We do not know what God has intended for us, but we can be sure of this: that He has appointed for us no trifling work."[7] Whether to take such claims as self-aggrandizement or self-abnegation is a problem. Pearse's most recent biographer and harshest critic, Ruth Dudley Edwards, limns him as a man jumping from one hastily conceived and neglected project to another, leaving a mess of bad debts and unexecuted good ideas in his wake. Pearse defends the variousness, extravagance, and sheer impracticality of his ways in a late poem, "The Fool," which was written in English, the expeditious language he chose the closer he came to martyrdom. The poem betrays the need the son of James Pearse had to carve his own epitaph, taste the Yeatsian pleasure of instructing posterity:

> Since the wise men have not spoken, I speak that am only a fool;
> A fool that hath loved his folly,
> Yea, more than the wise men their books or their counting houses,
>   or their quiet homes,
> Or their fame in men's mouths.

In yet another poem, "I Have Not Garnered Gold," however, he vows the opposite about his intentions and his bequest. Hardly indifferent to immortality, here he makes it the only compensation for not garnering gold:

> Of riches or of store
> I shall not leave behind me
> (Yet I deem it, O God, sufficient)
> But my name in the heart of a child.

In a poem frequently memorized in Ireland, one particularly memorable phrase stands out, "the heart of a child," because it contains much of the Pearse enigma. Not only do children figure prominently in his poetry but there are recurring images of the pietà, mother and child, even the child at the breast, for example in "Lullaby of the Woman of the Mountain": "Little soft mouth that my breast has known, / Mary will kiss you as she passes." In "To a Beloved Child" the child's mouth is also fetishized:

"Laughing mouth, what tortures me is / That thou shalt be weeping." Pearse was placing all his hopes for immortality in the mouths of children, the boys he taught at Saint Enda's. His poetry, his own mouth's efforts at recognition, would remain by this decision dilatory and occasional. In abandoning language and placing all his hope in the ephemeral rewards of teaching and administration, he was taking a large risk, given his desires. His final sacrifice more truly guaranteed "his name in the heart of a child" and yet demanded the price of his own body, the mouth his own mother once gazed at. The cost incurred when a man's name is wrenched from his living body is suggested in "Easter 1916" in lines that nearly do break up to weep, lines evoking mother love, the affirmation of another it be- stows: "our part / To murmur name upon name, / As a mother names her child / When sleep at last has come / On limbs that had run wild." So preoccupied is Pearse with the introjected image of himself as a child in relation to the mother that one of his final acts on earth is to place words in his own mother's mouth, scripting her response to his and his brother's deaths, the ultimate, paradoxical projection into the future and rewriting of the imperfect past:

I do not grudge them: Lord, I do not grudge
My two strong sons that I have seen go out
To break their strength and die . . .
But I will speak their names to my own heart
In the long nights;
The little names that were familiar once.

In founding Saint Enda's Pearse was building a structure in which safely to explore this powerful, internal drama between parent and child, the cir- cular dynamic in which he plays both parts. His virtual abandonment of this project in education is perhaps the most mysterious nub in his career. There has been a tendency in recent years to focus on the homoerotic in Pearse and see it, specifically its repression, as a major source of momentum in his life, a determining agent. The potency of this source is not in doubt, but there are others less visible, less amenable to analysis, less hospitable to a modern sensibility. Pearse's moral, spiritual, and psychological in- scrutability is his most compelling trait, and the concatenation of various often contradictory impulses in him determines his choices, often lurches into decision. Reading Pearse, like reading anyone, includes but is not ex- hausted by a reading of the self; both acts of interpretation demand as a

starting point some predicating of the place assigned to the sexual and spiritual as causes. The spectacle of Pearse, however, demands an especially rigorous examination of one's own premises about the formation of that
elusive entity we once called character.

Pearse's declaration regarding the founding of Saint Enda's can be read
as pathological or noble depending on these premises. It certainly lends
itself with ease to reading his life as a sexual allegory:

> I am conscious of one motive only, namely, a great love of boys, of their
> ways, of their society; with a desire, born of that love, to help as many boys as
> possible to become good men. To me a boy is the most interesting of all liv-
> ing things, and I have for years found myself coveting the privilege of being
> in a position to mould, or help to mould, the lives of boys to noble ends.[8]

The statement, however, innocently exposes the bare bones of the
most recalcitrant contradiction in Pearse through that juxtaposition of the
word *coveting,* with its suggestion of insatiability, and the phrase *noble ends,*
a denial of base humanity. Dudley Edwards, who does much to stress the
roles of money and sex and raw ambition, even petty politicking in the
drama, is perfectly and consistently direct, however, in her estimation that
Pearse's homosexuality remained latent. I believe, further, that Pearse's obsession with young boys hinged utterly on his introjected image of himself as a young boy and that the maintenance of this radical innocence was
the single most powerful psychological drive in him. The center would
not hold without this pristine, shining axis. It is also true that this second
phase of his career represented a courageous deepening of consciousness,
an exploration of preconscious, even preverbal identity: powerful, frightening, exciting springs of energy. In the intense light of these even half-
made discoveries, poetry, as he was for the most part decorously practicing
it, paled.

Pearse at this time published what is by now a famous pamphlet, *The
Murder Machine,* an unflinching exposé of the worst abuses of the English
examination system in Ireland based on what Pearse regarded as a blood-
less, dull, standard curriculum. *The Murder Machine* is an impassioned plea,
backed up by a commonsense pedagogy, for the individuality of the child.
It refashions in educational theory Pearse's thoughts on art, that the individual soul is the only worthy object of attention. Pearse's byword now is
freedom. The Edenic myth of Fionn and his following of young boys, the
Fenians, wandering in total freedom in Ireland's primeval forests, is the

presiding conceit. Given this cherishing of the identity of each boy, a conviction lodged with transparent sincerity, any transgression of personal, corporeal boundaries on Pearse's part becomes unlikely. Nonetheless this exemplary piece of advocacy for liberal reform contains the seed of another, subtler form of oppression: the cult of personality. The essay foreshadows the troubling blurring of religion and personal ambition, the fusion of Christ image with self-image, the confusion of self-apotheosis with mystical transport, that remain Pearse's fatal signature. Already the paradigm of the teacher-student relationship is that of master and disciple. Pearse characteristically jumps from one metaphor of ideal education to another, from pre-Christian Fionn and his boy warriors, to the medieval Irish practice of fosterage, to Christ and his disciples. Whatever the ruling example, however, the constant is the spectacle of power. A large part of Pearse's worry about the status quo is that it has brought about a loss of reverence for teachers, the demise of the teacher as an irresistible force.

As evidence of the angelic innocence of the man, however, *The Murder Machine* contains a conceit for the thwarting system that naively exposes much more an author caught in phantasmal tentacles. Pearse's choice of figure seems the cryptic record of an unidentified, very likely unconscious, personal trauma cast as a collective, colonial experience. His fervor of description sounds uncannily like repressed anxiety:

> I have often thought that the type of English education in Ireland was the Laocoon: that agonizing father and his sons seem to me like the teacher and the pupils of an Irish school, the strong limbs of the man and the slender limbs of the boys caught together and crushed in the grip of an awful fate.[9]

Again psychological splitting in Pearse allows him to identify simultaneously and circularly with the crushed boys entangled with this exaggerated phallus and the powerful father. Pearse's father, not coincidentally a sculptor, died when Pearse was twenty, just as he was entering manhood. Yet as so often happens in Irish cultural history, a personal struggle genuinely mirrors and fuses with a national one. Pearse seems poised on a knife edge, both coming into consciousness of the erotics of abuse and determined to locate its source exclusively elsewhere, someplace other than the self, in England, his father's birthplace. There is, it goes without saying, no direct correlation between the content of art and the psyche, but the act of metaphor, like the act of projecting the personal onto the national, must imply a distancing from threatening material. This distancing cooperates with Pearse's conscious volition to act for good. The cost he pays is being distanced from a complex personal and cultural truth, preferring to inhabit in consciousness an oversimplification of his own and Irish identity. For example, by anglicizing the enemy he makes Irishness the vehicle for un-real, unhealthy, finally untenable purity, a displacement that reverberates still in Ireland. Saint Enda's would be a sanctuary for Irish boys, the adjec-tive and noun holding equal weight in Pearse's mind, another equation. And yet the repressed returns with deadly accuracy and in mufti, the usual disarming combination. Pearse nearly destroyed Saint Enda's, pushing it to the edge of bankruptcy, by insisting on the purchase of an old Anglo-Irish estate, once occupied by his hero Robert Emmet in the foothills of the Dublin Mountains. He was driven to reclaim for Fionn and his boys the lost domain of the Father.

Within the proscenium arch of Saint Enda's, Pearse began to explore his inner drama. Given his first love affair with language, it's not surpris-ing that he became intrigued with the possibilities of words combined with spectacle. Theater became his new passion and Saint Enda's became known for its dramatic productions. On one famous occasion Yeats, for whom Pearse gained increasing respect the more Pearse's conception of freedom soared beyond localities of language, came to a production at the school but couldn't find a seat and stood through the whole play. The school's repertoire included the predictable adaptations of myth and folk-lore, but its crowning achievement was a Passion play performed on the Abbey stage. The final tableau, significantly exchanging language for pure spectacle, was of the crucifixion. The performance outraged some and moved others, a division prophetic of the subsequent reception of Pearse's final sacrifice. The crucifixion on the Abbey stage enacted by Pearse's boys eerily predicts the execution of their master, mentally crucified even as he entered early middle age.

This shift from poetry to performance, predicting an imminent transi-tion from education to politics, may indicate a need to compensate for a felt lack in his poetry, precisely of corporeality. There are many echoes in Pearse's poems of the early self-absorbed, disembodied Yeats. For example, the opening lines from Pearse's "To a Beloved Child"—"Laughing mouth, what tortures me is / That thou shalt be weeping; / Lovely face, it is my pity / That thy brightness shall go gray"—recall the melancholy about aging in the young Yeats's "The Pity of Love"—"A pity beyond all telling / Is hid in the heart of love." Yeats will use this fear of ephemeral-ity to wage war with time through poetry, a battle partly fought through making poetry bend to complex, human imagination. Pearse will bring literal muscle into his art by resorting to the body. A clue to why his practical abandonment of poetry becomes a certainty leaks through the poems, through phrases like "what tortures me." To the degree that the poems are real poems, touching a nerve, they produce anxiety, tap into excruciating experience. Maturation seems so painful that much of the time it is conducted in the poems behind a veil of sentimentality, idealized youth, diaphanous beauty, Ireland, and maternal love.

The most audacious and intriguing, even shocking poem in Pearse's limited oeuvre is the "Little Lad of the Tricks." I am assured by native speakers that the poem in Irish carries with it a much greater insouciance than in English. Irish, I am also told, allows for a different, more humorous and accepting version of the body. Nonetheless the poem's betrayals, even in the Irish, of Pearse's unconventional inner life were sufficient for MacDonagh to warn him off the poem. Translation seems incapable of disguising the unprecedented degree of Pearse's candor here, an unusual playfulness with tone and, most daring of all, a dramatic airing of his own proclivities. To read it, however, is to understand MacDonagh's concerns for one entrusted with the development of boys. The creepy feel, the sadistic sheen of the voice is that of a headmaster:

LITTLE LAD OF THE TRICKS

Little lad of the tricks,
Full well I know
That you have been in mischief:
Confess your fault truly.

I forgive you, child
Of the soft, red mouth:
I will not condemn anyone
For a sin not understood.

Raise your comely head
Till I kiss your mouth:
If either of us is the better of that
I am the better of it.

There is a fragrance in your kiss
That I have not found yet
In the kisses of women
Or in the honey of their bodies.

Lad of the grey eyes,
That flush in thy cheek
Would be white with dread of me
Could you read my secrets.

He who has my secrets
Is not fit to touch you:
Is not that a pitiful thing,
Little lad of the tricks?

Two pressure points alert us to the tension Pearse was under. Their cu-
mulative pathos is immense: "I will not condemn anyone / For a sin not
understood" and "He who has my secrets is not fit to touch you." In the
same way that Pearse in his prevailing psychodrama is both child and master, here he is both errant "Lad of the Tricks" and corrupt authority. He
exposes himself as both instinctively in touch with illicit yearnings and
innocent of illicit acts. This notorious poem, sitting just on the cusp of
self-knowledge, ironically exonerates Pearse in my eyes from all possible
charges of actual pedophilia. This poem, which goes such a salutary distance in pursuit of a dialogue between opposed but connected selves, em-
ploying the antiphonal voices and ambiguities that poetry can offer, marks
sadly the beginning of a campaign of self-censorship in Pearse. The lava of
this eruptive personal material was bound to find another outlet.

Through hearing the ghost of Walt Whitman in Pearse's poetry we become sadly conscious of possibilities missed—not just for self-exploration
through poetry, but poetry and culture revolutionized by self-realization,
not physical force. It is Whitman's voice, offering Pearse culturally unprecedented opportunities for formal and emotional latitude, that rings,
vigorous and proud, through one of Pearse's final poems, "The Rebel," an
appropriate vehicle in which to emulate the infamous American icono-
clast. Whitman is written all over "The Rebel": the uneven, often extraordinarily long lines, its incantatory rhythm, its hypnotic repetitions, the
sustained mode of direct address, the assumed intimacy with the reader,
and finally a conclusion that posits the fusion of reader and author, a favorite Whitman strategy drawn from a poetics of seduction, not that far
from demagoguery. This is the voice of America from which Pearse had
recently returned, the free swing and lope of the rhythm, one long exha-
lation of freedom on the eve of the Irish nation's bid for it:

I am the flesh of the flesh of these lowly, I am the bone of their bone,
I that have never submitted;

I that have a soul greater than the soul of my people's masters,
I that have vision and̃ prophecy and the gift of fiery speech,
I that have spoken with God on the top of His holy hill

. . .

And now I speak, being full of vision;
I speak to my people, and I speak in my people's name
    to the masters of my people.
I say to my people that they are holy, that they are august, despite their chains.

An American cannot read this, read the word *holy* in relation to human beings, and not think of *Howl* and the entire tradition of Whitman's scions, both the consolidation and the weakening of that strand of American poetry that converts the Puritan idea of a personal covenant between the individual soul and God into a new covenant between the individual body and romantic imagination, hence Allen Ginsberg's "The asshole is holy." It is obvious that Pearse read Whitman and was seduced by him, by the exuberance of his stride and the breadth of his vision of personal freedom. Pearse must have also registered Whitman's sexual frankness; but, crucially, Pearse swerves away from this corporeal content, does not choose to imitate it, rather separates it from a spiritual thrust. In effect he appropriates only half of Whitman's poetic. It is a choice both culturally determined and determining.

Compared to Yeats, Whitman sets both a dangerous and a useful example in relation to form, pushing the balance between static and kinetic, ordered and chaotic qualities in a poem to near breaking point. And Whitman's predilection seems equally indigenous, a product of America. The deep inhalations and exhalations that are not only simulated by his rhythms but determine them seem required by America, the vast imaginative strides it takes to cross the continent, which Whitman does often in one line, from Long Island to the Rockies. He plays daringly with scale, too, inspecting a scab of lichen and then turning to consider the Atlantic. He regards time as a medium in which to step manfully over centuries. Above all, like Pearse, his eye is always on posterity, the inheritance his vision will represent after his death. But the great sustaining paradox of Whitman that keeps him a poet is that, although we are to look for his decomposed and infinitely recyclable body under our footsoles, he lodges this instruction not just in a poem but in a poetic form that mimics the integrity of the body itself, its natural lineaments, its breath. Whitman teases himself and the reader with the potential for stepping out of the

body and off the page but in fact stays contained in both. This preservation of circumstantial, corporeal reality seems mysteriously bound to the
preservation of poetry. You might say that the retention of the skin of the
poem implies a correlative acceptance of the skin of the body, that the
two are dependent, in some mystical, mimetic relationship, and that when
one is abandoned, despaired of, not valued, the other is, too.

There is one particular poem by Pearse that indirectly discloses the
reason that he had to abandon poetry, abandon it with the same unconscious necessity that others pursue it. This poem, "Why Do Ye Torture
Me?" has a reflexive irony at its center that is like the irony of Yeats's "The
Circus Animals' Desertion," only in reverse. The Yeats poem is about not
being able to write a poem. Pearse's is a poem about why the forsaking of
poems is the only sane and prudent choice, given the emotional pressure
behind creation. Like "The Little Lad of the Tricks" it reveals a quite dras-
tic split in personality plus a perversion, not sexual, of natural instinct into
demonic energy that requires absolute quashing. The poem assigns to sexual energy a split-off, emblematic status, utterly separate from a notion of
integration:

> Why are ye torturing me, O desires of my heart?
> Torturing me and paining me by day and by night?
> Hunting me as a poor deer would be hunted on a hill,
> A poor long-wearied deer with the hound-pack after him?

It ends forebodingly:

> No satisfying can come to my desires while I live,
> For the satisfaction I desired yesterday is no satisfaction,
> And the hound-pack is the greedier of the satisfaction it has got—
> And forever I shall not sleep till I sleep in the grave.

The hound pack of disowned and demonized desires inevitably pur-
sues tirelessly. It must. It seeks recognition; unaccepted, it will chase Pearse
off the written page where conscious acknowledgment might occur. It
will eventually push him even off the template of identity perceived as the
body, propel the mortal man in the direction of immortality, pure idea,
where the pack of hounds can find no remnant of human flesh to con-
sume.

When an integrated identity, distinct and shaped, is not introjected
there can be a compensatory flooding into the world beyond the self, a

survival tactic, literally trying to find oneself. The whole of existence can be allegorized out of a failure to read the self with modest accuracy. The irony of Yeats as an example in relation to Pearse is that Yeats can commit this hegemony and keep it poetry, in tension with its own implosion, a mind doubting its constructs. In Pearse we see a collapsing of boundaries necessitated by an intolerance of illicit desires and the isolation of living with this torture: the failure of the dreamed ideal to inhere in the real. Division itself becomes painful, not least the separateness of the poem from the poet. The poem fails in self-sufficiency, receding infinitely into doubleness. Wallace Stevens, in contrast, an example of a poet thriving on doubleness, not only makes this fugacity of the first idea his cohering, tragic theme but builds a poetic on the epistemology of partial knowledge, perpetual loss. The mystic in rapture doesn't speak, since words always mean atomic fission, splitting absolutes. Yeats, like Pearse, may regard the entire cosmos as entropy waiting for systematic, adequate imagining in order to release its full, teleological potential, but always, at some level, Yeats is self-ironically aware of how much he is using the positing of absolutes as a way dialectically of guaranteeing their subversion, a poet's strategy, a way to barter for the next poem, a sort of intellectual wickedness.

Pearse, unassailably sincere, could never indulge in such games, however sublime. Finally the inbred playfulness of the poet isn't his. Even Dudley Edwards grants Pearse this probity, placing it in a constellation with other less attractive attributes: priggishness, captiousness, impetuousness, arrogance, impracticality, inflexibility, obtuseness about others. Desmond Ryan, an earlier biographer and Pearse's student, colleague, comrade, and lifelong friend but nonetheless a detached witness, grants Pearse a megalomaniac streak but confines it to the intellect. Ryan never personally observed Pearse's zeal spilling over into a bullying of other people, let alone violating their bodily integrity, a subject Ryan doesn't even broach in the 1930s. Still Ryan's judgment squares with Pearse's writing, where chronic transgressions, conflations prompted by a terror of mental fission, appear to be only between categories in the mind: body and soul, self and the people, self and God, the people and God.

This final conflation worries most. In "The Rebel" the line "I that have spoken with God on the top of His holy hill" strikes an ominous note, as the opening phrase of a piece of music that will climax in the crescendo of this man's martyrdom. It will fall on the ears like a note of heresy or mystical imagination, depending on the listener. To many Irish, from historians and politicians to the plain people, the most troubling aspect of the Pearse legacy is that it has sanctioned in the name of God so many immoral acts. The arrogance behind declaring one man as a voice for the people and the people as the voice of God many regard as a great part of the present problem in Ireland. Time and again in attempts to create dialogue in the North, stress is laid on the importance of recognizing differences, preserving distinctions, and realizing that the achievement of true pluralism depends on this rigor. The degree to which Pearse impeded the development of secular thinking in Ireland is a fair question.

Pearse's gradual entrancement with the demagogic potential in words is part of this need to collapse boundaries, finally between speaker and audience. The seduction began dramatically with Pearse's trip to America, where he was put on the speaking circuit. In this role he discovered his rhetorical talents. Dudley Edwards presents a man who insidiously abandons his specific project of raising funds for Saint Enda's and begins to deliver Fenian diatribes, preaching to the converted. Suddenly the primary exchange is not between one's inner, conflicting selves, but between self and the audience, locked in collusive, mutually congratulatory agreement. Manipulation rather than truth becomes the goal. A perversion of Whitman's sacred breathing occurs: energy passes, like artificial respiration, from speaker to audience and back again, and the unbrokenness of that circle is the measure of success. Whitman, of course, ultimately asserts this oneness with his listener but only after establishing the inimitability of the self, especially the sexual self, with uncompromising honesty. Pearse doesn't do this in his poems, let alone in front of his early-twentieth-century, Catholic, Irish American audience. This unholy commingling of self with others is utterly remote from the sacrosanct doctrine of individuality that was Saint Enda's credo. This is evidence of a master so addicted to the acquisition of disciples that favor not truth becomes the purpose of expression.

Pearse's loneliness is incalculable. In America he began to enjoy the power that the arabesque of the spoken word could have to meld differences and merge the speaker with the listener. The capacity for gesturing inherent in language seems to lure Pearse more and more as the Rising comes closer. In his graveside panegyric to O'Donovan Rossa, the pinnacle of his rhetorical career, Pearse ends his famous speech, constantly quoted by Republicans now, with "Ireland unfree shall never be at peace,"[10] words that echo still off gable ends in Catholic Belfast and Newry. There is also a section in the speech that makes clear the degree to which belief in the transformational power of sacrament provides a solution to personal conflict, the redemption of all merely personal shortcomings. O'Donovan Rossa, most historians agree, was not an especially distinguished man or even inspired patriot. Pearse's praise is so overblown that the rhetoric of his hyperbole almost becomes autonomous from its much less spectacular subject. Pearse is willing this transubstantiation by invoking the overarching metaphor of the Eucharist. Pearse claims to be "In a closer spiritual communion with him now than ever before or perhaps ever again, in a spiritual communion with those of his day, living and dead . . . speaking on their behalf as well as our own, we pledge to Ireland our love, and we pledge to English rule in Ireland our hate." Nothing could be simpler, which it is why this is rhetoric, not poetry. Having held the hundreds of thousands who attended that funeral hostage to his words, Pearse walked home from Glasnevan Cemetery alone.

In the final moments of Pearse's life his allegorizing reached manic lengths. The inversions and perversions, the wild departures from truth, even from the distinct but crucial responsibility metaphor entails, are legion. Perhaps the most outrageous example occurs in the pamphlet *The Sovereign People,* published in March 1916, a month before the Rising. There, desperate to construct a single historical imperative in a climate of ideological and interpersonal division in the run-up to the event, Pearse gives everything that has happened in the name of Irish independence thus far biblical authority and inevitability. Finding in history the balance between the part and whole, incident and divine intention, which Whitman saw in the idea of the United States, a paradox mirrored in his poems by the plethora of detail contained by the single imagination, Pearse began to read history through himself. He is the apogee, like Christ, toward which all prior history prophetically advances. His martyrdom will be his self-apotheosis. His four evangelists are the patriots Tone, Davis, Lalor, and Mitchel.[11] If the ordinary reader, even one familiar with Ireland, doesn't recognize all of these names immediately, or senses that some are not as illustrious as others, that is a sign of Pearse's then hermetic gnosticism.

This is also the time when the doctrines of the Incarnation, the Eucharist, and the Resurrection, the vivid image of Christ on the cross, so dominate Pearse's public language that any leftover, predatory, personal desires are consumed in the euphoria of an idea of transcendent, national destiny:

The great, splendid, faithful, common people—that dumb multitudinous throng . . . which starved in the Famine . . . who wept in Gethsemane, who trod the sorrowful way, who died naked on a cross, who went down into hell, will rise again.[12]

The "dumb throng" finds a single, eloquent voice in Pearse. And this is the time when Pearse begins talking of bloodshed being a "cleansing and a sanctifying thing."[13] In "Peace and the Gael" (December 1915), he asserts that "the old heart of the earth needed to be warmed with the red wine of the battlefields" and finds most restorative of all the blood of young men. Most depressing of all, in Pearse's perverse but sadly prophetic figure, it is the personified land itself, turning on the natives, that requires this sacrifice.

The unorthodoxy of Pearse's religious motifs shocked one Father Francis Shaw. In an essay on this subject published in 1970 after Shaw's death, the priest takes serious issue with Pearse's blasphemous rhetorical flourishes. He accuses Pearse of being "aggressively unorthodox," adding as a qualification and an indictment: "I accept without question the sincerity and reverence of Pearse . . . but one has to say that objectively this equation of the patriot with Christ is in conflict with the whole Christian tradition and explicitly with the teaching of Christ."[14] This attack on Pearse by a cleric, however, by no means seals Pearse's spiritual fate.

The hermeneutic routes to assessing any martyr are probably standard. And modern-day analysis is a form of inquisition. Finally, after all the questions are asked, I defer to mystery in relation to Pearse. There is sufficient evidence of an inexplicable spiritual energy to baffle all reductive attempts to make him a victim of either circumstance or his own psychology, or both. The steadily burning necessity for what Yeats calls unity of being in the man, in addition to his limpid sincerity, makes even the most cynical observer balk at merely natural explanations for his life. Seeing the push toward religious ecstasy as a displacement of a frustrated search for sexual ecstasy doesn't do justice to the sheer unworldliness of his ambition. Pearse's persistent goal is the achievement of an unsullied spiritual truth. Even a quite early description of poetry indicates this bias; he describes a real poem as "The clear detection of and statement of some naked truth, the touching of some bedrock foundation." However slight the physical yearning in this definition, its speaker places himself in a noncorporeal domain, seeing the things of this earth from above: "for a moment one sees with the awful clearness with which God sees."[15] The intense desire to enact a gesture of pure noncorporeality becomes Pearse's purpose for living and dying. As such he is the father figure of the morally and politically disturbing practice of self-immolation in Armed Republicanism. According to this Republican tradition, Bobby Sands is Pearse's son, hence the caution with which the more constitutionally minded approach Pearse. Distancing through debunking also goes on. The gentler tactic might be to grant Pearse his piety, thus teasing further individual conscience in Ireland out of the web of cultural mandate. Acknowledging the genuineness of Pearse's spiritual hunger is not equivalent to accepting the morality of the hunger strikes or physical force as a solution to the political hunger that persists. Pearse's composite, highly personal metaphors needn't be ours. We can parse his syntheses and still allow the validity of some of their parts, disallowing that of others, according to the lights of the individual, the sacred object after all of Pearse the educator. Pearse's unorthodoxies, we must always remember, are the canon law of a completely personal religion.

At the end of his life, however, Pearse had gathered such momentum in his quest to transform his own carnal being that individuality too was bound to be a casualty. He was bound by the same token to abandon language for a much less plural, less representational form of expression. His death was intended to epitomize the fusion Yeats expresses in not being able to divide the dancer from the dance in "Among School Children." Pearse intended his death to be an indivisible, eloquent gesture resisting deconstruction, even literal translation. From his first words on language Pearse betrays the beginnings of an obsession to make words transcend themselves, become silent, motionless, the body's dream of itself. Poetry is meant to "make us better, happier, holier."[16] The value of a poem is not merely innate, not limited to aesthetic effects or even to stark truth telling, or a compromising combination of these two ends; rather there is a moral and metaphysical imperative too. Pearse here is applying to poetry an injunction derived from his own experience, that the truth as one finds it, circumstantial truth, is not pure enough for poetry. To assert this higher truth, imagination must exert a will over circumstance and matter. In relation to the national question he put it this way: "No nation is snuffed out except by its own will. If the glory of a nation is extinguished by its own cowardice or its own despair, a second age is there if it strives properly for it. God never abandoned the nation that did not abandon itself." Later:

"God promised intellect and will to everyone of us . . . If we do not work to fulfill the counsels of God, He cannot fulfill these counsels for us."[17]

Every account of Pearse's short life recounts the swiftness of his conversion to the strategy of violence. His slide from cultural nationalism to armed resistance was precipitate, occurring between 1914 and 1916, and was more an epiphany than a strategic decision. The impending revolution provided the perfect vehicle for total transformation and redemption of the man and the nation as one. The poignant final irony of Pearse's life proves his spirituality better than any other detail. After all his talk of carnage, when Pearse actually saw blood in the General Post Office, much of it shed by his own students, he fell into an instant depression, a classic "dark night of the soul." Those days under siege were days under spiritual siege; he became a prisoner of his own self-doubt. His conversations with his brother and Thomas MacDonagh were incessant and incessantly centered on precisely the moral and spiritual and political questions many ask of him now. Clearly the daimon or God who led him to this destination didn't speak through the usual channels of language or rational thought or even received values. The most persuasive argument for the validity of Pearse's spiritual experience is that transport wasn't his final conscious experience, a morphology in keeping with all we know of mysticism. Pearse faced in the end a stark, harsh reckoning with his own limitations. Baffling even future skeptics, Pearse did come to resemble Christ: Christ in Gethsemane.

On a political level, one particularly salient conundrum of the Rising is how effective this botched job was and not just as a result of the executions, which, as they continued through most of May 1916, hardened Irish opinion against the British. These deaths would have been less shocking were it not for the caliber of the men who died, the tragic, central fact of Yeats's poem. It is precisely because the course of Pearse's short life includes so much resonant experience, making it truly a pilgrimage, that he remains a compelling mystery. The thrust of his campaign, chiefly against the flesh, still exerts a dubious influence in Ireland; but Pearse didn't invent this strain in Irish culture. Rather he gave it a powerful voice and an even more powerful witness in this century. This denial of the body is a recurring theme in Irish cultural and religious history. In the twelfth century, for example, Ireland possessed one of the most famous pilgrimage sites in Europe, Lough Derg, where a penitential ritual pivoted on the beneficial spiritual effects of self-mortification. Dante wrote about it, as did Ariosto and Seamus Heaney. The pilgrimage to "Station Island" in a small bog lake in northwest Ireland still goes on.

So, in a sense, does the cultural tradition of spiritual transcendence. It is impossible to conclude a meditation on Pearse without considering briefly the status of his legacy now, and there is no better lens to look through than Heaney. Recently, an arresting emphasis on edification has surfaced in Heaney. There is no doubt that Heaney has risked his Christian soul throughout his career by remaining the muse's faithful acolyte, standing as he received the Nobel Prize, therefore, shoulder to shoulder with his Irish antecedent, Yeats. But Heaney's recent declarations distance themselves considerably from the ostentatious hedonism in Yeats's "words alone are certain good." Heaney, while professing to have left self-punishment behind, has adopted a new position, which still cleaves to the somewhat less recent contours of a primarily abstract purpose for poetry. Emphasis on a strict, in fact thanatologically driven, metaphysics of rarefaction may have given way to the promotion of spiritual and moral uplift, but both postures have in common a resistance to circumstance.

Locating Heaney in a cultural tradition that includes the poets of the Rising, that Crazy Poets' Revolution, is also apt because Heaney's whole career has been spent developing in tandem with the Troubles in the North. Like Yeats he has often had to assert the salutary claim of independence for poetry from direct political responsibility, salvaging his craft from polemics. Heaney, in fact, being a Northern Catholic, has had to muster moral and artistic courage continuously for the last twenty-five years over this matter. But he has also had to live with the example of the 1916 poets, not for what they could mean to him as exemplars of the discipline but for the cultural precedent they laid down about poetry and politics. Pearse especially, elevating spirit unquestioningly over the body, makes self-sacrifice appear inexorable and obligatory. If this seems a far-fetched claim with regard to Heaney, one only has to consider Yeats's disbelief and shame in recognizing the gravity of MacDonagh's choice, that he gave up poetry for death when "He might have won fame in the end." Yeats's self-flagellation in "Easter 1916" is child's play compared to what Heaney has inflicted on himself for remaining marginal to communal suffering in the North.

When the Nobel committee awarded the prize, in their citation they made the explicit connection between Heaney's poetry and the politics of his place and historical moment. Heaney for his part is open in the Nobel acceptance speech, "Crediting Poetry," about having had to maintain the contorted position as a poet of considering almost exclusively the responsibilities of poetry to the suffering around him rather than to other claims, like pleasure or joy. He recalls with affecting frankness the self-punitive asceticism that has been too much and for too long a part of the creative process for him:

> Which is why for years I was bowed to the desk like some monk bowed over his prie-dieu, some dutiful contemplative pivoting his understanding in an attempt to bear his portion of the weight of the world, knowing himself incapable of heroic virtue or redemptive effect, but constrained by his obedience to his rule to repeat the effort and the posture. Blowing on sparks for a meager heat. Forgetting faith, straining towards good works. Attending insufficiently to the diamond absolutes, among which must be counted the sufficiency of that which is absolutely imagined.[18]

But "diamond absolutes"? What are they? And is there such a thing on earth or in poetry, both distinct alas from the realm of mystical experience, as "that which is absolutely imagined"? In the opening paragraph of the title essay, "The Redress of Poetry," in his new prose collection, Heaney quotes the words with which Stevens ends his essay "The Noble Rider and the Sound of Words," where concluding a long and tangled meditation Stevens says of imagination: "It is a violence from within that protects us from a violence without." The attraction of this statement for a poet from Northern Ireland is obvious. Stevens, however, begins the essay with a long, meandering, in fact vacillating discussion of Plato's dialogue, *The Phaedrus,* particularly Plato's conceit for human nature, a charioteer with two horses galloping across the heavens, one animate being or the soul, the other inanimate being, presumably the body. Stevens's response to the trope is complex and cumulatively not supportive of Heaney's current position. In snatches Stevens records the following thoughts:

> The statement is a moving statement and is intended to be so. It is insistent and its insistence moves us. Its insistence is the insistence of a speaker, in this case Socrates, who, for the moment, feels delight, even if casual delight in the nobility and the noble breed . . . Yet we do not quite yield. We cannot. We do not feel free . . . . The imagination loses vitality as it ceases to adhere to what is real . . . What happened as we were traversing the whole heaven, is that the imagination lost its power to sustain us. It has the strength of reality or none at all.[19]

Although Stevens says the question of whether Plato believed in the soul or not is immaterial, clearly whether the reader does or not is crucial. Stevens is seriously challenging the power of imagination, in particular metaphor, the stock-in-trade of poetry, to be transformative, to convert. Yeats and Stevens are mirror images of each other: Yeats setting up absolutes with ringing confidence only to erode them in time; Stevens refusing to yield but constantly registering the paradoxical pressure of incipient belief. There is always something prior to and beyond the poem.

It is Yeats's example that appears to be uppermost in Heaney's mind as he stands at the podium in Stockholm. Perhaps these consummately oracular lines from Yeats's "The Tower" illustrate for Heaney the "sufficiency of that which has been imagined":

> Death and life were not
> Till man made up the whole,
> Made lock, stock and barrel
> Out of his bitter soul,
> Aye, sun and moon and star, all
> And further add to that
> That, being dead, we rise,
> Dream and so create
> Translunar Paradise.

Is there any more dramatic example of "insistence" in the canon, of sheer will trying to determine poetic truth? The tone of authority cows the reader, at least in the moment; but for how many contemporary readers does this moment carry over from the page into ordinary living? Personally, like Stevens, I "cannot yield." As readers, however, most of us are lazier then Stevens, more indulgent of poetic license; we learn early on to suspend disbelief, allow the theater of the poem to occur but preserve our own doubts simultaneously, knowing that truth is multiple and that Yeats here, for instance, is accurate about not just a mood of desperation but a metaphysical possibility, one of many the agnostic reader adds. Surely Stevens's point about adhering to reality, allowing for a relativism, is that a poem's tone also discloses the degree of this adherence by its rigor, its willingness to take the shape of inconvenient facts. Even Pearse, intent on poetry making us "better, happier, holier," in describing poetic truth inserts a suggestion of its often unwelcome mien: "There is sometimes a harshness in the relentlessness of this truth-telling, a pain in the pleasure of this revelation."[20] With that mention of pain, of course, the reader can practically hear the hoofbeats of Pearse's speedy escape into masochism, one of many small rehearsals of martyrdom. Where genuine accommodation of unwelcome truths occurs, however, we can hear reluctant resignation in a voice.

In the Nobel speech Heaney's tone has less resignation than ebullient authority in it, the note of "insistence" Stevens identifies as forceful but not always convincing, though perhaps a tone required of Heaney by the occasion in Stockholm. Nonetheless Heaney comes as close to prescribing for poetry as ever I can remember him doing:

> . . . we want the poem to be not only pleasurably right but compellingly wise, not only a surprising variation played upon the world, but a retuning of the world itself. We want the surprise to be transitive, like the impatient thump which unexpectedly restores the picture to the television set, or the electric shock which sets the fibrillating heart back to its proper rhythm.[21]

On one level this sincerely lodged wish accommodates Stevens's stern reservations. I take it that when Heaney asks that the poem be not just "pleasurable" but "wise" this is like Stevens demanding that the imagination draw its energy from reality or fail. Heaney is demanding quite simply and romantically that beauty be truth. In the way, however, that he goes on to define truth, through metaphors that escalate quickly from the trivial to the profound, he leaves this reader at least unable to assent, again to yield. He tries to win the reader over with the sentiment of his remarks rather than their veracity. Who cannot be moved by the completely human wish that poetry have the power of restoring life? Who does not want, for that matter, like Yeats, to live forever? But the triumph of this passage is a rhetorical one only. I see a mood, a very human one, true to the moment, but not a mature, durable, ultimately wise outlook, one that combines the certainty of death with intimations of transcendence. I do not hear the paradoxical resignation and elation of "Enough / To know they dreamed and are dead." Heaney's life-affirming words may seem at the antipodes from Pearse's suicidal rant; but both avoid the middle ground of compromised reality. The "diamond absolutes" dazzle both.

When Yeats asks "Did that play of mine send out / Certain men the English shot?" ("The Man and the Echo") the question is sincere, the worry precisely that his words have been transitive. The poet's guilt is that the rhetorical momentum of his words may have been mistaken for a final achievement, ripped out of the containing form of art and loosed on the world, that the precisely intransitive necessity of art has been over-looked or underestimated. Is Heaney by stressing the transitive in art pos-sibly trying to compensate for an imagined failure of action on his part or even a cultural heresy, putting his faith absolutely in poetry?

As an American whose entire adult life has been intimately and profes-sionally connected both with Ireland and with poetry, I can only be apprehensive about Heaney's recent pronouncements. While I can appre-ciate and applaud Heaney's bravery in resisting the entrenched secularism of modernism and the nihilism of postmodernism by sticking up for an indigenous, unforced spirituality in his own culture, it does not seem a service to poetry or Ireland for him to appear doctrinaire. I can also admit that my own thinly veiled biases, particularly toward a poetics of agnosti-cism, stem from my American background, undiluted by many years of living in Ireland. (Actually my biases may as easily be construed as a re-sponse to this direct experience of Irish conformism.) It is, however, that word *transitive* that instills fear in me most, because when words are hauled off the page, their implications can run riot. They don't always obligingly jolt a machine or an organ into animation; they can just as likely feed ma-niacal obsessions, lead to appalling acts. The web of interwoven, mutually qualifying meanings made by a poem rarely survives intact transported into another language or even paraphrased in its own. Even less does it survive action.

When Patrick Pearse was executed for treason at 3:00 A.M. on a cold spring morning, his brother Willie, with whom Pearse habitually con-versed in baby talk, was summoned for a final interview with his brother. Somehow the timing went awry. Willie heard the fatal shot ringing as he crossed the cobbled yard of Kilmainham. All the unfathomable humanity of Pearse, from that baby talk to his passion and piety, was lost to the liv-ing world in that quintessentially flawed, quotidian moment.

Human interpretation finally seems hobbled by human limitation, the possibility of seeing many truths, the impossibility of seeing one. We can-not solve the mystery of Pearse. The secular skeptic in me sees a man who reached the rim of a self-knowledge he didn't want, couldn't absorb with-out violating an idea of purity that was central to his being; but where, I then ask, as Stevens would put it, did that "first idea" come from? That is where mystery begins. The answer keeps sourcing itself in a place beyond the pale of ordinary knowledge, calling for an extraordinary explanation.

In the end I refer back to Yeats, who at his best doesn't explain but points in the direction of truth. It is consoling that Yeats too could be puzzled, unable to read finally the meaning behind Pearse's last, formally coherent but inscrutable gesture:

> When Pearse summoned Cuchulain to his side,
> What stalked through the Post Office? What intellect,
> What calculation, number, measurement, replied?

Yeats crystallizes the mystery of Pearse for us in a rhetorical strategy, asking a question of a question. He further humanizes Pearse, adding an unbearable pathos to the sacrifice, by depicting Pearse at the very end as not simply acting on faith but asking himself the final question. In doing this, taking this risk of interpreting the man's last imaginings, Yeats is doing the human work of poetry. We see Pearse, in a single, economic line in Yeats's poem "The Statues," summoning Cuchulain to his side in a final attempt at fusing myth and reality: a transcendent idea of himself and the fact of himself. It is as though Yeats, summoning Pearse's double and allowing us to see these two selves, like the ultimate rhyme, allows us also to receive a glimpse of Pearse's soul. The line registers on the reader's imagination like a snapshot of extraterrestrial life or of the spirit visibly leaving the body at the moment of death. The line hovers between the achievement of a unity and maintenance of a dualism, and the temporal order of things is also ambiguous. Is a splitting occurring or a synthesis imminent? These dualities just extend the endlessly receding dichotomous truth of Pearse's end. William Carleton, the nineteenth-century Irish writer who converted to Protestantism, went to Lough Derg as a young, impressionable, pious Catholic youth and vehemently recorded later his conviction that the trouble with self-mortification is that it has the ironic consequence of only heightening a sense of the flesh. Similarly, our final image of Pearse is supremely carnal, a slumped body bleeding.

The final moral image is a compromised one. Can we strictly define Pearse's end as martyrdom when all along he displayed a savor for suicide? Surely real martyrdom is thrust upon one; but then again, to bow to my own skepticism in another direction, surely such demands for purity, especially in the mortal eyes of the survivors, are unrealistic, absolutist. Yeats, anticipating all this ratiocination, makes it implicit that all we are viewing in the poem and the spectacle of Pearse's end is figure, trope, just as Cuchulain was a conceit for Pearse the man. Human beings are incapable of glimpsing unclothed absolutes. The questions only proliferate, fugacity increasing the more an absolute is even entertained: "What intellect / What calculation, number, measurement replied?" The human mind, even poised on the edge of a belief in what Heaney speaks of in "Joy or Night" in *The Redress of Poetry* as "an overall purpose to life," can't conceive of such far-reaching meaning, except in the formal guise of the measured monuments to human imagination we've witnessed on the earth—the statues, the poems, the idea of the Incarnation. And yet irony reverberates even here. There is the intimation in "The Statues," ever so slight, the merest brush of connotation, of the dire possibility that measurement may not provide adequate containment for the coming, certain flood of revelation. Total knowledge beckons us with menace; in the moment of the poem we thank God we do not know.

Notes

1. J. J. Lee, *Ireland, 1912–1985: Politics and Society* (Cambridge: Cambridge University Press, 1989), 35.

2. William Irwin Thompson, *The Imagination of an Insurrrection: Dublin, Easter 1916* (West Stockbridge, MA: Lindisfarne Press, 1982), 114–15.

3. Ruth Dudley Edwards, *Patrick Pearse: The Triumph of Failure* (Dublin: Poolbeg Press, 1990). For the facts of Pearse's biography, but not always the interpretation of them, I have relied on Dudley Edwards.

4. All quotations of Pearse's poems were taken from Desmond Ryan, ed., *The 1916 Poets* (Westport, CT: Greenwood Press, 1979).

5. Dudley Edwards, *Patrick Pearse*, 71.

6. Dudley Edwards, *Patrick Pearse*, 92.

7. Dudley Edwards, *Patrick Pearse*, 99.

8. Dudley Edwards, *Patrick Pearse*, quoting from *An Macaomh* (*The Youth*), the Saint Enda's school magazine, 124.

9. Seamus Deane, ed., *The Field Day Anthology of Irish Writing* (New York: Norton, 1991), 2:291.

10. Deane, *Irish Writing*, 2:293–94.

11. Deane, *Irish Writing*, 2:294.

12. Dudley Edwards, *Patrick Pearse*, 258.

13. Dudley Edwards, *Patrick Pearse*, 179.

14. Deane, *Irish Writing*, 3:592.

15. Dudley Edwards, *Patrick Pearse*, 169.

16. Dudley Edwards, *Patrick Pearse*, 18.

17. Dudley Edwards, *Patrick Pearse*, 98.

18. Seamus Heaney, *Crediting Poetry* (Loughcrew, County Meath, Ireland: Gallery Press, 1995), 19–20.

19. Wallace Stevens, *The Necessary Angel* (New York: Vintage, 1951), 4–5.

20. Dudley Edwards, *Patrick Pearse,* 169.

21. Heaney, *Crediting Poetry,* 16.

For Further Reading

Seamus Deane, ed., *The Field Day Anthology of Irish Writing* (3 vols.), vol. 2. Derry, Northern Ireland: Field Day Publications, 1991.

Ruth Dudley Edwards, *Patrick Pearse: The Triumph of Failure.* Dublin: Poolbeg Press, 1990.

J. J. Lee, *Ireland, 1912–1985: Politics and Society.* Cambridge: Cambridge University Press, 1989.

Desmond Ryan, *The Man Called Pearse.* Dublin: Maunsel, 1919.

———, ed., *The 1916 Poets.* Westport, CT: Greenwood Press, 1979.

William Irwin Thompson, *The Imagination of an Insurrection: Dublin, Easter 1916.* West Stockbridge, MA: Lindisfarne Press, 1982.

Charles de Foucauld

Algeria, 1916

Little Brother of Jesus

by Robert Ellsberg

When I was twenty-four I decided to become a Roman Catholic. Like many prospective converts I was inhibited for some time about announcing my intentions—as much out of the fear of sounding dramatic as I was fearful of being talked out of it. For five years I had lived as a member of the New York community of the Catholic Worker, the radical movement founded by Dorothy Day. Many people supposed I already *was* a Catholic. Dorothy knew otherwise, though she never raised the subject. As a convert herself, she had a good deal of respect for the workings of grace. Meanwhile, silently, she included me in her prayers.

The first priest to whom I expressed my interest, a Dominican, responded, "Why on earth would you want to do that?" (He was shortly to leave the priesthood.) I turned instead to a French priest who lived in a small apartment in my neighborhood on the Lower East Side. He was, I knew, a member of the Little Brothers of the Gospel, a community inspired by the French desert father, Charles de Foucauld. Not that I knew anything about Foucauld. But I knew that the Little Brothers, who lived a contemplative life in the midst of the poor while supporting themselves through menial labor, represented the kind of holiness that had attracted me, so mysteriously, to the Catholic church.

Brother Peter, as he was called, worked as a janitor in the Municipal Men's Shelter. Though quiet and almost painfully shy, he radiated a type of solid authenticity. He had spent a number of years in America but still struggled with his English. And yet he once delivered the best sermon I ever heard—at least the best sermon that consisted of only one line: "There are two kinds of people in the Gospels: there are the good people, and there are the sinners, whom Jesus loved."

In a simple ceremony on Holy Thursday I was received into the church in the chapel of the Little Brothers. The chapel consisted of a room set aside in one of their tenement apartments. Afterward I went to see Dorothy Day in her room at Maryhouse, a shelter for homeless women. At the time she was eighty-two and only a few months away from her death in November. It was she, more than anyone, who had brought me to the Catholic church. But as I was shortly to leave New York and the Catholic Worker, her embrace that evening combined an element of farewell as well as welcome. We began to talk about the Little Brothers and Dorothy mentioned her devotion to Charles de Foucauld.

"I used to have a book about him somewhere," she said. And as was often the case with Dorothy, the recollection of some book or object had the power to make it appear at her fingertips. "Why, here it is," she said, reaching for an aged volume on the crowded shelf beside her. It was an English translation of a book by René Bazin, the first biography of Charles de Foucauld. It was this book, I later learned, that had inspired the foundation of the Little Brothers many years after Foucauld's death. "Would you like it if I gave it to you?" she asked. Of course I said I would like that very much. She dutifully inscribed the book and handed it over.

Dorothy's copy was heavily underlined and annotated with her distinctive script. It included a photograph of Charles taken toward the end of his life: a weather-beaten figure in a white robe who, but for his piercing eyes and astonishing smile, looked much like many men I had met on the Bowery. On the back of the photograph Dorothy had written, "Charles de Foucauld, pray for us and all who pass through the doors of the Catholic Worker."

So I passed through her door for the last time. When Dorothy died that fall I finally took down and read the life of Charles de Foucauld that she had commended to me. There at last I learned the story of the man in the photograph, the man to whose prayers she had commended me and who in mysterious ways had come to play a part in my own story.

On the evening of December 1, 1916, Charles de Foucauld was roused from his prayers by an urgent knock on the door of his hermitage in Tamanrasset, a remote outpost in the Saharan desert of Algeria. Foucauld, the only Catholic priest within many hundreds of miles, was known as the *Marabout,* or holy man. It was a mark of respect on the part of his Tuareg neighbors. Devout Muslims, they respected the Frenchman's piety and good works, though they were not tempted to share his faith.

Despite the isolation of his hermitage, Brother Charles was accustomed to receiving visitors at all hours. Part of his mission as a "little brother of Jesus" was to remain available to the needs of his neighbors. But lately he had taken unusual precautions. The reverberations of the Great War in Europe were felt even in this isolated corner of the desert. He had been warned that Tuareg rebels, inspired by a brotherhood of Muslim fanatics, might be looking for an opportunity to strike a blow against the French infidels. Thus he had lately fortified his hermitage, and he did not answer a knock at the door without determining the identity of his caller.

The desert sand had muffled the sound of camels and the dismounting of the forty armed men who now surrounded his little fort. The caller identified himself as the mailman. In fact he was a local tribesman, known to Charles, who had accepted a bribe to transact this betrayal. Trustingly, Charles unbolted the door and reached out his hand, only to be roughly seized. The rebels poured in and bound his arms. While some subjected him to interrogation, others searched the hermitage for valuables. Charles did not answer their questions, but only seemed to pray silently while a fifteen-year-old boy pressed a rifle against his temple. When twenty minutes had elapsed a noise was heard, the sound of two approaching camels. Charles started to move, whereupon his frightened guard shot the priest through the head.

Foucauld's lonely death was in character with the solitude and obscurity of his life. He had spent years in the desert preparing the way for followers who never arrived, and his efforts had ended this way, with a shot in the dark, a sound quickly absorbed in the cold sand of the surrounding dunes. Compared to the rivers of blood then flowing through Europe, it was a relatively unremarkable event. No one could have anticipated the extent of his later influence, the fact that several congregations would trace their foundation to his inspiration, that indeed Charles de Foucauld would come to be regarded as one of the most significant religious figures of the twentieth century. But in fact the path between his death and his later influence is far less remarkable than the path that led to his final appointment in Tamanrasset.

Viscount Charles Eugène de Foucauld was born in Strasbourg on September 15, 1858, to a proudly aristocratic family. Throughout his childhood he was regaled with stories of his ancestors' honor and of their history of service to cross and crown. The Foucaulds, he learned, had fought in the Crusades and stood beside Joan of Arc at Orléans, thus earning the family a title and a coat of arms emblazoned with a heroic motto: *Never Retreat*. Of the varieties of valor, however, his pious mother paid special tribute to the example of Armand de Foucauld, archbishop of Arles, who had died a martyr during the revolutionary terror of 1792. But Charles's mother was given little time to impart her faith and ideals. She died in childbirth when Charles was six, a loss compounded only six months later by his father's death from tuberculosis.

Charles and his younger sister were entrusted to their maternal grandfather, a retired colonel already in his seventies. The colonel excelled in discipline, and he had great hopes as his grandson matured that the boy would carry on the family tradition. But for Charles such hopes were not sufficient to fill the yawning void he felt within. Lacking any wider purpose or ambition, he turned increasingly to frivolous diversions and the indulgence of his considerable appetite. He had little interest in studies. Any religious faith he might once have known had been casually discarded along the way. Nevertheless, to oblige his grandfather he agreed to apply to the military academy of Saint-Cyr. With special tutoring he managed just to squeeze through the entrance examinations—allowance being made for his family name. No special connections, however, could help him squeeze his overfed body into a regulation uniform. For this a private tailor was commissioned. As a result, in years to come, even when he had become a scrawny hermit, he would be affectionately known by his comrades in the elite officer corps as "Piggy."

Charles looked resplendent in his uniform. But the uniform did not make the cadet. His years in the academy were distinguished only by the frequency of his official reprimands. It might be supposed that such a figure would earn the disdain of the more disciplined cadets. In fact, he carried off his escapades with such *joie d'esprit* that he seems instead to have endeared himself to his classmates, many of whom would remain his life-long friends. As one of them later recalled, "If you have not seen Foucauld in his room, clad in his white flannel pajamas buttoned with frogs, sprawled leisurely on his divan or in a commodious armchair, enjoying a tasty snack of *pâté de foie gras,* washing it down with a choice champagne, then you have never seen a man really enjoying himself."

By this time, following his grandfather's death, Charles had come into a considerable fortune—the better to underwrite his epicurean tastes. His room became the site of extravagant entertainments. He was generous in sharing the contents of his wine cellar and the services of his personal barber. But occasionally he went too far. One time he slipped off base in disguise, defying a confinement to quarters, in order to keep a dinner engagement with his mistress, a certain Mimi. When the ruse was discovered and he faced his superiors, he explained that he could hardly do otherwise—a commitment to a young woman was a matter of honor. This was not the military definition of honor, but for sheer audacity it apparently won passing marks. He managed to escape with a severe reprimand.

From Saint-Cyr Charles was passed on to cavalry school. There he graduated in 1879, eighty-sixth in a class of eighty-seven. The Inspector General described him as "a remarkable person . . . with no thought for anything except entertainment." His first posting was to North Africa, where he quickly got into trouble for sending Mimi on ahead, passing her off as the Viscountess de Foucauld. In light of the ensuing scandal, Charles was informed that he must make a choice—either Mimi or the army. Without hesitation he made his choice: he resigned his commission and returned to France and to his scandalized family. They retaliated by putting his finances into the hands of a trustee.

He had scarcely arrived in Paris, however, when he applied to rejoin his old unit. News had reached him that his comrades were about to go into battle against Arab rebels and he could not bear the thought of sitting on the sidelines. And so he bade farewell to Mimi—this time forever—and returned to Algeria.

This was to be the turning point for Foucauld, the moment when a different side of his personality began to emerge. To everyone's surprise, he fought valiantly in battle and demonstrated considerable skill as an officer. The more lasting effect of this experience, however, was a new fascination with the North African desert and its people. After only six months in active service, long enough to rehabilitate his honor, Charles again resigned his commission to pursue an ambitious and dangerous mission. He had decided to undertake a one-man geographical expedition to Morocco, a vast territory as yet unexplored by Western outsiders. Because of the risks facing any lone Christian in this Muslim country, Charles disguised himself as a wandering Jewish rabbi. For eleven months he traveled the country, armed only with a sextant and compass, finally emerging with the material for a book. When it was published in 1885 he was awarded the gold medal of the French Geographical Society.

Back in Paris Charles's family was delighted by his new evidence of discipline and purpose. But already his restless heart was stirring in a new direction. The experience of Muslim piety had made a lasting impression on Charles, and he found himself increasingly drawn to the religion of his youth. As he wrote, "My exposure to this faith [Islam] and to the soul living always in God's presence, helped me understand that there is something greater and more real than the pleasures of this world."

An irresistible force was drawing him, where he could not say. But over and over, as he restlessly roamed the streets of Paris, he repeated a prayer: "My God, if you exist, make your existence known to me." In the fall of 1886, after finally overcoming his inhibitions, he made his way to the church of Saint Augustine where he sought out Abbé Huvelin, a famous confessor and spiritual director. Finding Huvelin in his confessional he described his predicament and asked the priest to recommend some Christian reading. Huvelin, with inspired insight into the character of this seeker, told Charles that what he needed was not to be found in books. All that he needed to do was make his confession, receive communion, and he would believe. Charles complied, and at once he felt his life transformed. He left the church that day determined to give himself entirely to God. As he wrote later, "As soon as I believed there was a God, I understood that I could not do anything other than live for him. My religious vocation dates from the same moment as my faith."

The question for Charles now was what form this vocation should take. At the suggestion of Huvelin—into whose hands he fully entrusted himself—Charles undertook a pilgrimage to the Holy Land. There he spent several months visiting the holy shrines and following the footsteps of Jesus in the actual towns and countryside where he had walked. This experience would ultimately have a decisive impact on his life. But all that was clear at this point was his determination to embrace a life of prayer and poverty. The austere Trappist order seemed to offer the best means of fulfilling this calling. And so Charles renounced his fortune, applied to the Trappists, and eventually settled in a monastery in Syria, the most remote and impoverished community he could find.

Charles dutifully applied himself to the discipline of monastic life. He stuck it out for over seven years. But it did not satisfy his yearning. For one thing it fell short of his imagined ideal of poverty. Despite the famous rigors of the Trappist life, Charles found it altogether too comfortable. "We are poor in the eyes of the rich," he wrote, "but not so poor as our Lord was." When a papal order slightly mitigated the Trappists' dietary rules to allow a bit of oil or butter on their vegetables, Charles was indignant: "A little less mortification means so much less offered to the Good Lord; a little more spent on feeding us means so much less to give the poor . . . Where will it all stop?" When he was once sent on a pastoral errand to the hovel of an Arab Christian who was dying of cholera, Charles was appalled to acknowledge the contrast between the dignified simplicity of the monastery and the actual poverty of a common peasant.

At the same time, Charles had begun to question whether it was really to any traditional monastic life that he was called. He had been increasingly haunted by an insight from his sojourn in the Holy Land. What impressed him then was the realization that Jesus, though the Son of God, had lived the majority of his life as a poor man and a worker. As a carpenter in Nazareth Jesus had, in these lowly circumstances, embodied the gospel message in its entirety, before ever announcing it in words. From this insight it occurred to Charles that the "hidden life" of Nazareth, and not the monastery, should be the model for his own spirituality.

It took a while for Charles to obtain a dispensation from the Trappists; he was at this point within months of making his final vows. Huvelin, too, was reluctant to endorse Charles's impetuous plan. But eventually Charles was free to return to the Holy Land, to Nazareth itself, where he found a position as a servant at a convent of Poor Clares. Calling himself simply Brother Charles he spent three happy years in this occupation, dividing his waking hours between his minimal chores and a far more rigorous schedule of prayer. He exulted in the thought that he was living in the same place where Jesus had spent thirty years of his life and where "I have now the unutterable, the inexpressibly profound happiness of raking manure."

But though Charles aspired to emulate the "hidden life" of Jesus, his evident holiness eventually attracted the attention of the mother superior of the Poor Clares. She convinced Charles that he had a more important mission to perform in the world and urged him to become a priest. Though Charles felt unworthy of ordination, he found himself exhilarated by the dream of founding a community of like-minded brothers.

Once again Charles turned to the counsel of Huvelin, who expressed his opinion in blunt terms:"You are not made, *not at all made,* to lead others." Nevertheless he acquiesced in Charles's enthusiasm to set forth again on the next stage in his spiritual journey. In particular, he helped arrange for him to return to France to undergo a year of training for the priesthood. Shortly after his ordination in 1901 Charles returned once more to North Africa. To enact his new mission, he had concluded, it was no longer necessary to live in the actual town of Nazareth."Nazareth" might be any place. And so he returned to Algeria, to the oasis of Béni-Abbès on the border of Morocco. His goal was to develop a new model of contemplative religious life, a community of "Little Brothers" who would live among the poor in a spirit of service and solidarity. In the constitutions he devised for his planned order he wrote,"The whole of our existence, the whole of our lives should cry the Gospel from the rooftops . . . not by our words but by our lives." He was now forty-two, ready at last to begin his true mission.

Béni-Abbès was a predominately Arab settlement, though also the site of a French garrison. As a French colony, Algeria was administered under military authority. Since it was the policy of the French government to avoid any provocation of the Muslim population, Charles could hardly have established his hermitage without approval from the military authorities. But here, and not for the last time, his old connections proved invaluable. Many of his classmates from the academy had risen to positions of authority in the colonies, and they were only too willing to assist a former comrade—even one whose career had taken such an unlikely turn.

Ostensibly, Charles's mission was to divide his time between service to the Arabs and pastoral duties among the garrisoned troops. He was the only priest within 250 miles. Thus, a good deal of his time was spent saying mass and hearing confessions from the soldiers. But his heart was with the mass of his Arab neighbors to whom Christ was as yet unknown. He dressed like one of them in a coarse, white robe, with a leather belt around his waist. His only distinguishing marks were the rosary tucked in his belt and an emblem of his own design—a red heart with a cross—sewn over his breast. His aim was not to convert the Arabs but rather to offer a Christian presence in their midst.

Ultimately, Charles regarded himself as simply the advance agent for a community of Little Brothers. But no followers ever came. There were not many at the time who could even comprehend his novel approach to mission; fewer still who could endure the extreme, nearly impossible, standards of asceticism that Charles embraced. He had traveled far from the days when he had lounged on a sofa, feasting on oysters and pâté. Now he worked hard by day, spent half the night in prayer, slept on the bare ground, and subsisted on a diet of dates and boiled barley. His former abbot, one of those to whom he frequently appealed for helpers, was realistic to observe, "I fear he would drive a disciple mad by excessive mental concentration before killing him by excessive austerities."

After several years in Béni-Abbès, Charles began to find the isolated outpost too congested for his taste. In 1905, on the lookout for a more remote setting, he accepted an invitation from Colonel Henri Laperrine, an old classmate and now the commander of the Saharan Oases, to tag along on an expedition to the Saharan interior. Thus Charles discovered the rugged Hoggar region—a barren plateau surrounded by dramatic volcanic mountains, deep in the heart of the desert. Charles was enchanted by the complete isolation of the region and by its mysterious inhabitants, the Tuaregs. They were a seminomadic people, famous for their ardor in battle, easily recognized by their peculiar complexion, their skin dyed blue from the color of their distinctive veils. If he were to live here he would be the only priest within sixty days of desert travel. The attraction was irresistible. He decided at once to move his hermitage here to the village of Tamanrasset. Laperrine, for his part, had hoped for such an outcome; it pleased him to imagine that through this priest a bridge might be formed to the remote tribal peoples of the Saharan interior. Who was better equipped for such a mission than Piggy?

His new home, Tamanrasset, was hardly a village at all. Twenty families lived in this settlement, halfway up a mountain at an elevation of 4,600 feet. A small oasis nourished a few tufts of grass and sustained the meager gardens and small herds of goats on which the people subsisted. By day the sun was mercilessly bright, with temperatures reaching 120 degrees Fahrenheit. At sunset the mountaintops caught fire in a crimson blaze. By night the temperature could drop seventy degrees, while the sky was illuminated by a sea of stars. With time Charles came to know that sky so well that he could better navigate in the dark than he could by daylight.

Choosing a spot just out of sight of his neighbors, he built himself a house of stones and reeds. It consisted of two rooms, each about six by nine feet and a little over six feet high. Ever hopeful regarding the arrival of fresh recruits, Charles eventually constructed a "refectory" and "parlor" and a series of additional cells, each of the same claustrophobic dimensions. At the center of it all, when he was finished, was a burning lamp, indicating the presence of the Eucharist—to the eyes of faith, the very presence of Christ himself, here among the most abandoned and neglected. Charles spent hours each day prostrate before that lamp and the box beside it. Meanwhile his letters, filled with chatty details of his daily life and spiritual reflections, were punctuated by the plaintive appeal: "My only regret is that I am still alone . . . Try to send me some brothers . . . I would so love to have a companion who would be my successor." But this was not to be.

The years passed. Foucauld grew older. The plump young cadet had given way to a gaunt figure of middle age, bearded, almost bald, his skin darkened by the sun. His smile revealed missing teeth, while his eyes burned with a passionate intensity. From the time of his arrival in the Hoggar he had struggled hard to master the Tuareg language. The fruit of his study was recorded in a massive Tuareg dictionary, a manuscript completed shortly before his death and later found among his papers. Otherwise it was a life spent with little sign of outward accomplishment.

Nevertheless, as he wrote to a friend, "Living alone in the country is a good thing; one can act, even without doing much, because one becomes one of them. One is approachable, because one is so small." It was thus a fruitful loneliness, a way of being available to his neighbors. He had little to offer them but his friendship, his care, and occasional medicines. They had no use for his religion. But having overcome their initial suspicions of this strange foreigner who had traveled so far to share their poverty, Charles was accepted by the people of Tamanrasset. From there, by the ancient channels of bedouin communication, his reputation extended throughout the Hoggar.

In 1908, after two years in Tamanrasset, Foucauld obtained a dispensation from the Vatican to say mass by himself, without a server, as well as permission to construct a tabernacle for the reserved Eucharist. And so he was not entirely alone. "To receive the grace of God," he wrote to a Trappist, "you must go to a desert place and stay awhile. There you can be emptied and unburdened of everything that does not pertain to God.

There the house of our soul is swept clean to make room for God alone to dwell . . . We need this silence, this absence of every creature, so that God can build his hermitage within us."

The spiritual path of Charles de Foucauld was modeled on the hidden life of Jesus in Nazareth, a way of constant abandonment to the love of God, whether in the silence of desert spaces or in the midst of others. There is no doubt that in embarking on this path Foucauld prepared himself to give everything and that he carefully calculated the cost. Already in 1897, while living in Nazareth, he had written in his journal:

> Think that you are going to die a martyr, stripped of everything, stretched out on the ground, naked, hardly recognizable, covered with blood and wounds, violently and painfully killed . . . and wish it to be today . . . Think of this death often, prepare yourself for it and judge things at their true value.

It was a remarkably prophetic meditation. Was it also evidence of a morbid imagination? If so, it was a natural feature of a spirituality centered so closely on the imitation of Christ. "We cannot possibly love Him without imitating Him," he wrote. "Since He suffered and died in agony, we cannot love Him and yet want to be crowned with roses while He was crowned with thorns . . . We must love Him just as He loved us, in the very same way."

All the same, it seems that for Foucauld the consciousness of impending sacrifice grew over time to a steady conviction. Scattered throughout his journals one finds such statements as these: "To prepare oneself constantly for martyrdom, and accept it without a shadow of reluctance, like the divine Lamb, in Jesus, through Jesus, for Jesus." "I must try and live as if I were to die a martyr today. Every minute I must imagine I am going to be martyred this very evening." And in a booklet found on his body on the day he died: "My wish is to live as if I were to die a martyr today."

Foucauld was granted this wish; so he lived, and so he died. And yet is it entirely accurate to describe Foucauld as a martyr? Among the motivations of those who killed him it is possible to discern a variety of factors beyond simple "hatred for the faith." But this is undoubtedly true with most martyrs, whose witness to Christ is inevitably complicated by cultural, ethnic, or political interests. As for Charles de Foucauld, it must be acknowledged that, despite his desire to live a hidden life as a brother to the Tuaregs, he was finally unable to obliterate his identity as a son of France, and a former officer.

Foucauld deplored certain features of colonial rule, especially the failure of French authorities to check the ongoing commerce of slavery. But he continued to affirm an idealistic notion of France's role in bringing civilization and Christian morality to the benighted peoples of the Sahara. His criticism of colonial policy was that it failed to reflect its exalted purpose. As he wrote to a friend:

> I suffer as a Frenchman to see the natives not being ruled as they ought. On the contrary, the moral and spiritually inadequate condition of these peoples is made all the worse by treating them as no more than a means of material acquisition. What the natives learn from the infidel Frenchmen who proclaim the doctrine of 'fraternity' is neglect, or ambition, or greed, and from almost everyone, unfortunately, indifference, aversion and harsh behavior.

In another place he wrote, "If we act according to our lights, if we civilize instead of exploiting, in fifty years Algeria, Tunis and Morocco will be an extension of France. If we do not live up to our duty, if we exploit rather than civilize, we will lose everything and the union we have created from these diverse peoples will turn against us."

Throughout his years in North Africa Foucauld maintained friendly relations with the army. In a sense he had no other choice if he was to pursue his mission. But at the same time many of the officers were truly old friends from his earlier life. They consulted him about conditions in the interior and he readily provided intelligence about the terrain, about the best location for encampments, and about the dangers of bandits and rebels. The army in turn regarded him as a kind of French agent in the Hoggar. It was a role Charles did not positively decline.

The outbreak of World War I, which intensified conflicts between the army and rebel tribesmen, enhanced Charles's value to the colonial enterprise. Many of his army friends were recalled to the trenches in Europe, and Charles himself inquired about the chances of serving as a stretcher bearer. It was his old friend—now General Laperrine—who instructed him otherwise: "Stay in the Hoggar. We need you there." And so in his own corner of the world Charles was prepared to do his part.

In April 1916 a French stronghold at Djanet on the Libyan frontier fell to an army of Senoussi rebels. The Senoussi were a brotherhood of Muslim nationalists, drawn from a number of ethnic groups, united in their determination to drive the foreign infidels from the land of Islam. Warned that the Senoussi were drawing near to Tamanrasset, Charles decided to build a small fortress. Using local materials, over a period of months he managed to raise a formidable structure with walls a solid meter thick. He finished the fortification on November 15. Visiting officers were impressed and asked his permission to store supplies and weapons inside. Foucauld raised no objection.

It is difficult today to reconcile the image of Foucauld the French patriot with the image of Charles, the Little Brother of Jesus. By the same token one can imagine with what ease the Senoussi warriors who broke into his fort on December 1, who bound his arms, shot him, and left him bleeding in the sand, might confuse the holy *Marabout* for a representative of France. For their careless violence they were rewarded with the contents of his fort. Aside from supplies of food, they recovered six cases of ammunition and thirty carbines. They left his Tuareg dictionary scattered in the courtyard, along with the apparently worthless tabernacle, not to mention his body, all discovered later by French troops. Such are the complexities of Charles de Foucauld and the ambiguities of his death. By the end he had managed to combine the heroic ideals of both his grandfather the colonel and his pious mother, all reflected in the family motto: Never Retreat.

Foucauld himself was aware of the ironies of his existence. Daily he confronted the weakness of his faith and the ambiguities of his witness. In the end those ambiguities ran deeper than he could acknowledge. But he prayed that if he made his small offering in love, then God would purify his intentions and bring forth the harvest from his small seeds. Ultimately, the meaning of his life, distilled with the passage of time, had nothing to do with carbines, forts, the honor of France, or even the matter of his death, but with the spiritual vision he summarized toward the end of his life:

> Jesus came to Nazareth, the place of the hidden life, of ordinary life, of family life, of prayer, work, obscurity, silent virtues, practiced with no witnesses other than God, his friends and neighbors. Nazareth, the place where most people lead their lives. We must infinitely respect the least of our brothers . . . let us mingle with them. Let us be one of them to the extent that God wishes . . . and treat them fraternally in order to have the honor and joy of being accepted as one of them.

Failing the joy of being accepted as one of them, there was another joy. On the last day of his life he wrote a letter to his cousin Marie, which was left sealed and ready for the mailman:

Our annihilation is the most powerful means that we have of uniting ourselves to Jesus. One finds one doesn't love enough, that is true, but Almighty
God, who knows with what He has molded us, and who loves us much
more than a mother can love her child, has said that He will not cast out
those who come to Him.

At that point he heard the knock on the door, the sound for which he
had trained his ear: "Illness, danger, the prospect of death, it is the call.
'Here is the Spouse: go forth to meet Him.'"

For Further Reading

René Bazin, *Charles de Foucauld: Hermit and African Explorer.* London: Burns Oates & Wash-
    bourne, 1923.
Charles Lepetit, *Two Dancers in the Desert: The Life of Charles de Foucauld.* Maryknoll, NY: Orbis
    Books, 1983.
Marion Mill-Preminger, *The Sands of Tamanrasset.* New York: Hawthorn Books, 1961.
Silent Pilgrimage to God: The Spirituality of Charles de Foucauld. Maryknoll, NY: Orbis Books, 1977.
Jean-François Six, *Witness in the Desert: The Life of Charles de Foucauld.* New York: Macmillan,
    1965.

MARIA GORETTI

Italy, 1902

Maria Goretti — Cipher or Saint?

by KATHLEEN NORRIS

And you will know the truth,
and the truth will set you free.
　　John 8:32

Exploitation is at the heart of Maria Goretti's story, so much so that I wonder if it is possible to write about her in the late twentieth century without exploiting her further. In an odd way she reminds me of Marilyn Monroe. A virginal peasant girl canonized as a "martyr of purity" by the Roman Catholic church and a Hollywood sex goddess martyred on the altar of celebrity would seem to have little in common. Yet both make a witness to the perils of being female in life *and* in death. Their lives, their deaths, have been appropriated, squeezed for every drop of meaning by those who have not necessarily had their best interests at heart. Very little is known about Maria Goretti, and all too much about Marilyn Monroe, but each in her own way has become a cipher, a blank page on which others write to suit their own purposes. Both have been so consistently ill-used that they make us cry out, "Enough, already; let her rest in peace."

The bare facts of Goretti's story sound familiar to anyone who reads a newspaper. In 1902, at nearly twelve years of age, she was knifed to death in an attempted rape. Her murderer, who had threatened her in the past, was Alessandro Serenelli, the son of her father's partner in tenant farming, a boy she'd known for much of her life. When Maria was younger her destitute parents had moved, with their seven children, to a farm in the Pontine marshes of Italy in a desperate but futile attempt to better their circumstances. It was there that the father died of a fever, leaving his wife and children vulnerable to increased economic (and sexual) exploitation. It was there that Maria Goretti received her first communion and also took on considerable domestic labor while her mother and older siblings worked in the fields. She was murdered in the kitchen of the rented house that her family shared with Alessandro and his father Giovanni.

The apparatus of hagiography so quickly entered into the telling of Goretti's story that one must proceed with caution in interpreting even the simplest facts concerning her life and death. In an article entitled "Maria Goretti: Rape and the Politics of Sainthood," Eileen J. Stenzel has written, "To read the lives of the saints literally is to misunderstand the polemics and politics of sainthood." Stenzel discovered, in teaching an undergraduate course on Catholicism, that the story of Saint Maria Goretti inevitably polarized her students. "Some," she writes, "would claim that the rationale for [her] canonization was understandable given the social climate of the 1950's. Others were outraged that the Roman Catholic church would ever have said that a woman is better dead than raped."

But the literalism that would hear that as the church's message obscures the complexities of Goretti's story and ignores the economic and social realities of her time and place, a rural Italian village of the early twentieth century. As Stenzel points out, it was "the world in which Maria struggled to survive [that] promoted the belief that a woman was better dead than raped." And by canonizing her, the church has seemed to many to agree. Ironically, it is the church's own eagerness to promote Goretti as a model of chastity that has fostered such cynicism and obscured the most profoundly religious elements of her story.

Hagiography is one of humankind's stranger endeavors. That a child, an illiterate peasant at that, should become of such importance to the Roman Catholic church in the mid-twentieth century that it expanded its official definition of martyrdom in order to canonize her seems ironic to skeptics but to the faithful is evidence of grace. Thomas Aquinas had opened the door back in the thirteenth century, writing that "Human good can become divine good if it is referred to God: therefore, any human good can be a cause for martyrdom, in so far as it refers to God," but until Maria Goretti's canonization in 1950, martyrs were considered by the church to be those who had clearly died for their faith. As Kenneth Woodward explains in *Making Saints,* the church decided that "technically, [Goretti] did not die for her faith. Rather, she died in defense of Christian virtue—a significant though by now routine expansion of the grounds on which a candidate can be declared a martyr."

Goretti thus earned herself a place in the history of hagiography, paving the way for other twentieth-century martyrs such as Maximilian Kolbe. She also exposed a fault line in the church's historical treatment of the virgin martyrs, young girls who were executed during the persecutions of Christians in the second to sixth centuries. That they had died because they were Christians was never in dispute, but in accounts of their martyrdoms from the fifth century on, it is their commitment to preserving their virginity that is emphasized. Many of the stories relate the miraculous interventions that occurred when Roman officials sentenced the girls to be sent to brothels. Butler's *Lives of the Saints* (1880) typically praises Saint Agnes for her "voluntary chastity," for "purity," and for "joyfully preferring death to the violation of her integrity."

That "joyfully" rankles these days, and maybe always did. But in terming Goretti "the Saint Agnes of the twentieth century," and in expanding the definition of martyrdom to include Goretti as a "martyr of purity," Pope Pius XII laid to rest the old ambiguity surrounding the virgin martyrs. His use of Goretti proved not ambiguous at all; as Woodward relates, the church immediately set about to make her "the heroic embodiment of the church's sexual ethics." And, as Scott Hoffman notes in an essay on Goretti, the church intended this concept of purity to embrace "not only chastity, but [many] other virtues in opposition to the modern world."

Maria Goretti's canonization process was remarkably swift. Her canonization was, in the words of one hagiographer, "unique in the history of the church" because her mother, brothers, and sisters were able to be present. To the modern mind, Goretti as saint seems suspiciously convenient. The Catholic church needed a saint who could promote traditional values to teenagers and their parents in the wake of postwar modernism, and as Kenneth Woodward relates, Goretti soon became, in Italy at least, "the church's most popular icon of holy virginity after the Virgin herself . . . a saint whose story had become symbiotic with the church's teachings on sexual purity." The purposes to which the Catholic church wished to put Goretti are made abundantly clear in the address given by Pius XII at her beatification in 1947, when he termed her "a ripe fruit of the domestic hearth where one prays, where children are educated in the fear of the Lord, in obedience of parents, in the love of truth, and in purity and chastity."

Maria Goretti, cipher, was well on her way toward becoming a media event. The sermon preached in Union City, New Jersey, on the day after she was canonized, and covered by the New York Times, sounds eerily familiar in mid-1990s America. The priest called Goretti "a saint of the Christian home" who stood for divinely ordained family values and against "parental absenteeism and juvenile delinquency." He blasted Hollywood movies and the popular press in general for "lurid descriptions of sex crimes and of the lives of notorious murderers," and even took a stab at comic books, which he termed "the marijuana of the nursery." In his paper on Goretti, Scott Hoffman notes, dryly, "St. Maria Goretti had arrived on the Jersey shore."

Maria Goretti comics were apparently okay; they were a staple of the small industry that Goretti became in America during the 1950s. She was promoted with such fervor by the American church, held up so insistently as a model for the families of postwar baby boomers that Hoffman wonders, "Did [Goretti] die for Christ or the middle class?"

Reading the devotional literature about Goretti that was aimed at American Catholics, one is tempted to say that she died for whatever purpose one wanted her to. In Helen Walker Homan's smarmy Letters to the Martyrs, for example, Goretti becomes a beacon of anticommunism. As the martyred Saint Agnes stood against the Roman Empire, Homan finds that Maria Goretti represents the "Christian principles not compatible with those of a totalitarian State." Another of Goretti's hagiographers, Monsignor James Morelli, makes Goretti an American patriot. In his book about Goretti, entitled Teen-Ager's Saint, he writes that now that the world is "drawing itself into two enemy camps, Communism and Christianity, . . . Our church and our country have no use for weak, lukewarm souls who are always ready to give in to evil . . . The hour has come for hardy, tough fighters who loyally and openly live a fully Christian life under the banner of the Church."

Several writers stop just short of praising Goretti for her illiteracy. "Heaven forbid that anyone think . . . that the key to sanctity is illiteracy," Mary Reed Newland writes in *The Saints and Our Children*. "What God is showing us . . . with the life of this saint is that He alone *can* be quite enough." While this has interesting theological implications, particularly for liberation theology, such subtleties are lost on the hagiographers of the 1950s. Devotional pamphlets such as *The Cinderella Saint* tended to romanticize Goretti's poverty. And Monsignor Morelli, in a chapter entitled "The Little Madonna," takes the opportunity, over Goretti's dead body, to complain about educated women. "Look at all the 'career girls,'" he writes, "who can't even mend a torn dress, or cook a simple meal, let alone manage a household." (Goretti's selfless dedication to domestic responsibilities, especially after her father died, is much praised in all the accounts of her life.) The career girls, the monsignor finds, "don't compare to the little unlettered Italian girl who had a better way of writing."

Taking a quick turn into the darker corners of 1950s Catholic spirituality, Morelli continues: "With her way of writing, Saint Maria Goretti wrote in letters of blood a page of history which is her undying glory. Perhaps some of our modern educated girls, who seem to have spent all their wisdom attending to trifles and serving self, could reflect on the great lesson of Maria Goretti." One must ask: *what* lesson? Better unread, *and* dead?

Several of Goretti's hagiographers have found the saint useful for teaching children about chastity in an age in which, as Mary Reed Newland writes, "the devil [has so] successfully convinced the world that God made [sex] for pleasure alone." Writing of Goretti as a "model of chastity," Newland finds her murderer to "stand for all the boys and girls whose minds and souls have been ravished by dirty literature, pornographic pictures, suggestive movies," and the like. "Like so many young people," she writes, "he became preoccupied more and more with passion and lust because no one had turned his mind in a different direction." This, of course, is the role of the Catholic parent, and Newland challenges them all to do as Goretti's parents did, "parents *who knew they were supposed to raise saints but had no way of knowing they would*. They knew little else but that to do God's will in all things is the secret of sanctity. How well they taught this child!" (Newland's emphasis).

The passage that follows, a dizzy mixture of sanctimonious prudery and sound practical advice on sex education, culminates, predictably, in a passage reminding girls that they must be careful to dress modestly and explaining that the pain of menstruation is "part of the great privilege that goes with being a girl, whom God has given the gift of life-bearing." The grain of truth in all this—that the ability to bear a child is a wondrous and mysterious thing and not to be taken lightly—is overshadowed by the sheer bizarreness of Newland's prose. Her essay typifies what is wrong with the standard hagiography of Saint Maria Goretti; its excesses of masochistic piety cloud whatever genuine religious value the work might have for the reader.

Newland speaks, for instance, of the considerable insults that Maria and her mother, Assunta, suffered at the hands of the more well-to-do Serenellis, father and son, as "the means by which [the women] died their daily death to self . . . the purification . . . that God permitted in order that these two souls be prepared for the gift of martyrdom." To the modern reader this suggests nothing more than the woman-as-doormat school of theology, which is still used in the most conservative Christian churches to keep women from leaving abusive marriages. Appallingly, Newland continues: "The mother must willingly surrender the child who would wear the crown."

Newland even projects onto Goretti a sophisticated awareness of her upcoming death. Given that her assailant had threatened her in the past, the terror of his presence in that household should not be minimized. But what Newland does with it is obscene, an unappealing blend of Jansenism and gnosticism. She suggests that what Maria Goretti knew of the sacraments—a priest preparing himself to "give his body to God to do His holy will," or a married couple planning "to beget with God's help the souls He has known forever"—helped her prepare for her own martyrdom, being "willing to die rather than sin, [even] willing to die rather than permit her neighbor to sin." This is a lot of weight to put on an innocent eleven-year-old, but where Maria Goretti is concerned, the hagiographers have shown no shame.

The nastiest use of Maria Goretti is found in Monsignor Morelli's *Teen-Ager's Saint,* in which he gives a clinical description of the cause of her death, telling his young readers that Serenelli's knife had "penetrated the thorax and penetrated the pericardium, the left auricle of the heart and the left lung . . . the abdomen, the small intestine and the iliac." He follows this with a strangely enthusiastic description of each of the eighteen stab wounds and their locations on Goretti's body, adding that "victory was hers. Doctors testified in their statement that her virginity emerged from the fight absolutely unsullied."

Presumably, Morelli's visceral overkill was designed to take a teenager's mind off sex. Unless, of course, that teenager were a budding sexual psychopath; then the passage would have the opposite effect, appealing to the worst prurient interests. The appalling mix of sexual repression and fascination with Goretti's wounded body makes her not only a cipher but a version of the *Story of O*, a perfect model of pornographic surrender. A Catholic friend recalls that a statue of Goretti was placed at the foot of the stairs at his boys' school. "I guess on our way out the door every day," he says, "she was supposed to remind us where sex could lead."

Girls often got a milder version of Goretti's significance. One friend recalls, "If you had an impious thought, you were supposed to pray to her, but I never understood why. Somehow she was supposed to help you to be good." She comments that a picture of Goretti, "looking demure, crouched in a corner while a man in the foreground held a knife," was merely confusing to her. "I never understood just *why* he was attacking her. It was never explained to us." Even more confusing were devotional books such as *My Nameday—Come for Dessert,* which praised Maria Goretti for her courageous defense of chastity and included a recipe for a "virgin martyr dessert soufflé."

The real girl, of course, was as lost in all this as any rape victim caught in the system between a politically ambitious D.A. and a media-savvy defense attorney determined to make a saint of the assailant by castigating his victim. It comes as no surprise that Giordano Guerri, the Italian journalist who in 1985 published a book accusing the church of having invented Goretti's martyrdom, suggested that Goretti was not so innocent, that she had intended to give in to Serenelli all along.

What possible relevance does Maria Goretti have today? I was pleased to find Eileen Stenzel's article about her in a book on violence against women, less pleased by its densely ideological prose, its air of preaching to the converted. At first glance, Stenzel seemed to be just one more person using Goretti to promote her own political agenda, identifying Goretti as "a challenge to the current position of Rome that women cannot be ordained because women cannot represent Christ on earth." But the delicious irony in Stenzel's calling Goretti a "pastoral testimony to the priesthood of women" is that she is concentrating, far more than Goretti's conventional hagiographers, on the truly religious elements of her sanctity, which is centered on forgiveness.

Witnesses have testified that as Maria Goretti lay dying, she forgave her assailant and expressed the desire to see him in paradise. Several years later, when he was in prison, she appeared to him in a dream and caused him, finally, to repent. He spent the last years of his life as a caretaker in a monastery. That a mere girl could have the power to so change a man is a challenge to the patriarchal status quo. And as Stenzel points out, there is considerable theological significance to this aspect of Goretti's story. "Maria did not urge [Serenelli] to seek out a priest for forgiveness," Stenzel writes. "She forgave him. God did not send angels to a sleeping prisoner; Maria appeared to him and forgave him." Goretti, then, may be seen to represent Christ, much like Saint Barbara, a virgin martyr of the second century, the saint one prays to when in danger of sudden death. Barbara's intercessions are believed by many to be an adequate substitute for the presence of a priest and the administration of last rites, and she is sometimes depicted holding the chalice and the host.

Much of our difficulty with Maria Goretti comes from the fact that her hagiography is of the nineteenth century, but she is a twentieth-century martyr, one with great significance in an age when violence against women is increasingly rejected as a norm and properly named as criminal violence. Ironically, it is the overload of devotional material and sappy titles such as "Lily of the Marshes" and "Lily of Corinaldo," designed to prove Goretti's sanctity, that makes it so difficult for people to take her seriously today. The real child, whoever she was, was quickly and thoroughly encased in the straitjacket of conventional hagiography. Like almost all young saints, she is said to have been "without whims, a saint, an angel," whose "unusual piety had an almost adult quality," and who, despite her destitute circumstances, had "a natural grace and a certain inborn refinement" and practiced "the everyday virtues with perfection."

Unfortunately, it is precisely this kind of language that obscures for modern people what is most believable about Maria Goretti: that as a pious child of a peasant culture she may well have resisted rape in religious terms ("No, it's a sin! God does not want it!" is what her would-be rapist reported that she had said to him). It is also conceivable that she would have forgiven him on her deathbed, again for religious reasons.

Something about Maria Goretti must have struck a spark with the women of the village who tried in vain to stop her bleeding, the ambulance drivers who carried her by horse-drawn cart to the nearest hospital, the doctors, nurses, and priests who attended her on her deathbed. In the traditional manner of saint-making, it was local acclamation that brought Goretti's case to the attention of the Vatican. I like to think that somehow she touched hard people in a hard time and place: her innocence; the radical fact that a young girl had dared to resist a man; the appalling consequences she faced as a result. Apparently there was something in the child's recounting of the attack, and in her mother's grief, that compelled her neighbors, the police, the nurses, to keep retelling the story.

Maybe it was no more than the need to believe that a brutal, needless death might be somehow useful and have religious meaning. Who can blame them if they exaggerated? Or if Maria Goretti's mother, Assunta, in her grief declared that her daughter "in all her short life had never been disobedient" and suddenly recalled that Maria had responded to her first communion by promising, "I shall always be better." Maybe those around Maria Goretti as she died were struck by the courage of someone deemed by her culture to have no significance at all. Peasant cultures are notorious for not valuing girls, except as cheap labor with a potential for motherhood.

In his book *On the Theology of Death,* Karl Rahner speaks of martyrdom in terms of Jesus' declaration in John 10:18: "I have the power to lay down my life and to take it up again." Rahner remarks, "This is particularly true at that moment when we seem most fully under the domination of external forces: 'nobody takes my life; I myself lay it down.' And this is exactly what happens in the martyr's death; it is a free death." Rahner emphasizes that he is speaking of an extreme situation and a liberty that cannot be obtained by any other means: "In that death which is violent," he writes, "which could have been avoided, and which is, nevertheless, accepted in freedom, the whole of life is gathered in one moment of ultimate freedom."

I don't find it hard to believe that Maria Goretti is a martyr in the classic sense, that she died for her faith, after all. To say anything less is, I believe, to continue to relegate her to the status of a cipher. In our age virginity seems little enough to make a fuss over; many girls see it as a burden to be shed as soon as possible. It is difficult for us to conceive of a girl refusing to allow a violation of what she surely saw as her God-given bodily integrity, even though it cost her life.

Why should Maria Goretti be so hard for us to understand and accept? A recent *Newsweek* contains a grim account of a married couple in Canada who habitually kidnapped, tortured, raped, and sometimes murdered teenaged girls. Because they videotaped their victims, the defiance of one fifteen-year-old, Kirsten French, is on record. "Ordered to perform a particular sex act," the article notes, "she refused, insisting, 'some things are worth dying for.'" The girl never gave in, even when her tormentors showed her the videotaped death of another of their victims.

I am not suggesting that this young girl is better off "pure" and dead than raped and alive. I am stating emphatically that in this extreme situation, no doubt having realized that her death was inevitable, she had every right to act as she did. To choose a free death. Of course it's sad to think of this as freedom, to imagine an adolescent having to make such a choice. But surely we recognize—Maria Goretti and Kirsten French force us to recognize—that girls are targets in this world. In Thailand, female infants are sold to brothels. In America, girls as young as ten years of age are made to walk the streets by their families or pimps taking advantage of runaways. We take it as a matter of course that girls will be stalked, raped, murdered—if not on the streets, in our popular entertainment. If one dares say to her attacker, "Some things are worth dying for," there is nothing joyful about it, except possibly deep within, some inner defiance, purity, and strength that defies the sadist and the power of his weapons.

The mystery of hope, of holiness, infuses such defiance. I am haunted by the idea that Kirsten French's killers may have responded to this spark of holiness in her. They had dismembered the corpse of a fourteen-year-old girl they'd killed the year before. It was a videotape of her torture and death that they showed to Kirsten French in an attempt to intimidate her into submission. This may signify nothing at all, but it is the stuff of hagiography, that the body of Kirsten French they buried intact.

I am haunted also by the countless women whose names we'll never know who have faced their rapists with a holy resistance, and possibly even forgiveness, known only to themselves and God. Many societies, including our own, paint themselves as respectable by denying the commonplace, daily reality of reported and unreported rapes. Maria Goretti as cipher allows us to cling to our lies. But Maria Goretti as saint can free us, as a powerful symbol of the grace of healing for those wounded by rape and sexual abuse, both rapist and victim. Resistance to evil and forgiveness are the heart of that grace.

But comfortable untruths die hard. In a world in which some cultures still believe that a woman is better off dead than raped, we are wary of accepting the resistance of Maria Goretti and Kirsten French. As we read of them, sitting in our comfortable chairs, we think, surely, they had another way. Maybe not. It is not a cipher, but a real girl, who says the "no," who becomes a warrior in the face of death, insisting that "some things are worth dying for" or "God does not want it." Maybe only those who have faced that moment of terrible freedom have the right to agree. Maybe only a saint's example can bring us to forgive.

For Further Reading

Berchmans Bittle, O.F.M. Cap., *A Saint a Day.* Milwaukee: Bruce Publishing Co., 1958.

Pietro DiDonato, *The Penitent.* New York: Hawthorn Books, 1962.

Scott Hoffman, "How Do You Solve a Problem Like Maria: St. Maria Goretti in the Post–Counter-Cultural World." *The Critic,* Fall, 1995, pp. 86–98.

Helen Walker Homan, *Letters to the Martyrs.* New York: David McKay Co., 1951.

Helen McLoughlin, *My Nameday—Come for Dessert.* Collegeville, MN: Liturgical Press, 1962.

Monsignor James Morelli, *Teen-Ager's Saint, Saint Maria Goretti.* St. Meinrad, IN: Grail Publications, 1954.

Mary Reed Newland, *The Saint Book.* San Francisco: Harper & Row, 1979.

———, *The Saints and Our Children.* New York: P. J. Kenedy & Sons, 1958.

Kathleen Norris, "The Virgin Martyrs: Between 'Point Vierge' and the 'Usual Spring.'" In *A Tremor of Bliss,* edited by Paul Elie. New York: Harcourt Brace, 1994.

Karl Rahner, "Dimensions of Martyrdom." In *Martyrdom Today,* edited by Johannes-Baptist Metz and Edward Schillebeeckx. Concilium Series. New York: Seabury Press, 1983.

———, *On the Theology of Death.* New York: Herder & Herder, 1961.

"Sex, Death and Videotape." *Newsweek,* May 29, 1995, 53.

Eileen J. Stenzel, "Maria Goretti: Rape and the Politics of Sainthood." In *Violence Against Women,* edited by Elisabeth Schüssler Fiorenza and M. Shawn Copeland. Concilium Series. Maryknoll, NY: Orbis Books, 1994.

E. B. Strauss, "St. Maria Goretti." In *Saints and Ourselves,* edited by Philip Caraman, S.J. Garden City, NY: Image Books, 1958.

THE BOXER REBELLION

China, 1900

Martyrs Among Us

by BARBARA LAZEAR ASCHER

In the optimistic fashion of many nineteenth-century midwestern
Americans of faith, Eva Price believed in the good of others. She believed that the Golden Rule had within it a rule of reciprocity and
that whatever befell her was part of God's grand design.

The life to which she was called would not necessarily bend to these
beliefs.

Born Eva Jane Keasey in Constantine, Michigan, on August 18, 1855,
she grew up to marry Charles Price, eight years her senior and a native of
Richland, Indiana. After ten years of marriage and a quiet life on a tree-
shaded street in Des Moines, Iowa, the two made a decision perplexing to
family and friends. At the age of thirty-six, Charles determined to move
to rural Oberlin, Ohio, and enroll in Oberlin College's Theological Seminary. Eva, who was interested in evangelical Christianity, was also to enroll but would soon drop out in order to care for two young children.

These cannot have been easy times. Eva and Charles were by far the
oldest freshmen at the college, tuition depleted their savings, and Eva's
family disapproved. The reasons for this life change can only be surmised.
Charles's brother Francis, an 1883 graduate of Oberlin, was a highly regarded missionary in China. Perhaps he inspired Charles or perhaps his
example pressured the younger brother. But given the hardship incurred

by their decision, it is most likely that Eva and Charles, sharing a deep faith, felt "called" to leave life as they knew it and to surrender to what they believed was God's will.

At the time, Oberlin attracted many such students. Between 1877 and 1886, one out of every four graduates became ministers. It was not unusual for graduates of the Theological Seminary to become missionaries for the American Board of Commissioners for Foreign Missions. Charles was inspired by the Christian missionary movement that had gained steady momentum in China since the Great Famine of the late 1870s. This disaster, which had claimed 5.5 million lives, was viewed by evangelical Christians from America and England as an opportunity to aid the Chinese and at the same time create a sympathetic response to missionary efforts. The Industrial Revolution had also sparked the call to convert. It was a widely held missionary belief that great scientific and technological advances could only be realized in Christian societies. Thus motivated, Charles applied to the board for a missionary assignment, fearing that he would be considered too old for the rigors of conversion.

Had he known of the board's fervor for Christianizing the world before the approaching millennium, he would have had less apprehension. There was little time for thoughtful evaluation of applicants, considering the job to be done and the short time in which to do it. The board was determined to bring the gospel "to every creature" in "heathen" Asia and to settle for "no less than the moral renovation of a world."[1] To that end, they tossed missionaries over borders like so many Ping-Pong balls over a net. There was no time for language training or background briefing. The millennium was coming. Just get the balls over the net.

Oberlin's Shansi mission in China's remote interior was on the verge of collapse. A missionary wife had been sent home in the wake of a "scandal," and another missionary was dismissed for his doubts about the divinity of Christ. The board reasoned that a mature, older couple like the Prices might be able to salvage and stabilize the situation. They dispatched them immediately with one piece of information about their destination. The climate, the board assured them, was "healthy."

On the eve of departure Eva received a letter from her sister Mary Eltha. "So you and Charlie have decided to go to China. Well, I wish for our sakes and your children's that you would stay in the United States . . . Well, you know your calling and if you are determined to go so far all we can do is pray." Eva responded, "I know we had very little encouragement when we came here to Oberlin, but Charlie has done nobly . . . and will be able to work more for the good of the world than he could have done had we not come here. It is an honor to be permitted to be in the active work of spreading the gospel, especially in heathen lands."[2]

The family dynamics ring forth in these brief epistles. Hurt, fear, and rejection met by guilt and justification. It may explain the tone of forced cheerfulness in Eva's letters written home during the time the Prices served in China. Mary Eltha's sense of abandonment was not unfounded. Her sister was moving 15,000 miles away to one of the most remote Chinese provinces, a journey requiring three arduous months. The mail would take equally long to reach home, and there would be no visits back and forth. There would be none of what constituted midwestern family life in the late 1880s—cousins growing up in close proximity, shared picnics, church suppers, Christmas gatherings. Following God doesn't necessarily sit well with families.

In July of 1889, Eva, age thirty-three, and Charles, age forty-one, departed for San Francisco with their two young children, the infant Donnie and four-year-old Stewart. They sailed first for Yokohama, Japan, then boarded a coastal vessel heading for China. Two weeks after leaving Japan, as they clung to the deck in heavy rain and squalls, they sighted their destination rising from the dark sea, gloomy, forbidding, and shrouded in gray.

As their excitement grew, they held the children up for a look. From this distance they could not guess that their arrival would be greeted with suspicion. They had not been informed that a result of China's defeats in recent wars was a growing hatred of foreigners. How could they anticipate, as they approached with hope and goodwill, that they would be perceived as an arm of Western expansionism?

Nor were they aware that brother Frank who awaited them was despairing that so little had been accomplished by the mission. In ten years of evangelizing, there had been only one genuine convert. The rest had been "rice Christians," those who professed Christianity in order to get salaried jobs with the mission. He was losing hope that missionaries could surmount the language barrier, widespread opium habit, determined worship of idols, and "the deceitfulness and vileness of the heathen heart," which "closes the ear to the Gospel message."[3]

Had they known any of this, Eva and Charles might have had second thoughts, but thus unencumbered they continued on. God and the Industrial Revolution were on their side.

Once ashore they traveled by train to the end of the tracks, then made the remaining 500 miles of the journey into the interior by boat and mule litter—six days on the Clear River until the river became too shallow to navigate, then across mountains by mule. Occasionally, the animals toppled off the precarious paths to their deaths hundreds of feet below. Eva watched with terror and clung more tightly to her young children. Each river navigated, each mountain crossed seemed a door closing on the Prices' former life. Closed and locked shut. When at last they descended onto the Shansi plateau, the view that awaited them was of bare, rocky ground covered with lead-colored loess.

For the next ten years this was to be Eva's home, where she would battle relentless dust that worked its way through windowsills and doorjambs, into her teeth and the folds of all her belongings. Here she would survive brutally hot summers and the cold, dry winds of unforgiving winters for which her one small, inefficient stove was no match. Here she would struggle to sustain herself with her belief in God, the redemption of the world through Jesus Christ, and her calling to save the heathens.

The missionaries were children of a time that told them they were blessed and that it was their Christian duty to share these blessings with those less fortunate. They believed that they were following God's will. But the stubbornness of this conviction prevented questioning the interpretation of that will. They arrived in China with their Bibles, antimacassars, and unwavering faith that they could save people not asking to be saved.

Eva shared the common belief that prosperity was dependent on Christianity. She wrote home comparing herself with one of the Chinese women on whom she regularly called. "What if my lines were set in such hard places? What if, instead of an earnest christian, my husband were an opium user with a lot of other bad characteristics? What if, instead of my pleasant home, with all the comforts and advantages that come through christianity, knowledge, hope, faith, books, pictures, good food, comfortable clothes, beds, and cleanliness, I had to live in such a comfortless, poor, mean, barren home as hers?"[4]

Like most nineteenth-century Americans, she and her colleagues were unschooled in Far Eastern history. They were unaware that China's scientific advancements, among them the magnetic compass, gunpowder, and mechanical clockwork, had preceded the Industrial Revolution by hundreds of years. This now-barren plateau that was their home had once been so rich in resources that Marco Polo described it as a "great centre of trade and industry, which supplies great quantities of the equipment needed for the Great Khan's armies."[5]

Before settling in, the Prices got rid of the "hideous" dragon heads adorning each corner of their compound and removed two "horrid" dogs at the entranceway.[6] All Chinese traces were removed from their home and replaced with rocking chairs, potted plants, and side tables covered with lace doilies. To enter was to come home to Iowa. From inside the high walls of their compound you would hardly know where you were.

Some of this isolation was based on a legitimate fear of disease. The missionaries were frequently without a doctor, and when there was one, the distances were so great that death rather than disease often awaited him. Open sewers, dead bodies, garbage, and contaminated wells aided the spread of typhus and typhoid. Smallpox was rampant.

Donnie, Eva's beloved baby, could not be protected by walls or caution; he died in 1892 at the age of three. In a letter to her family she wrote, "You can still remember when God called for little Harris and how he brought a great blessing to your souls through the affliction. And now when I am called to write to you that He wanted our little Donnie too and we gave him back to Him with joy even, you must not grieve for us nor think of us as stricken and suffering but as looking up into the Heavenly Father's face with trust, peace, and gladness that He has enabled us to so willingly give back this precious, precious little one we had for three and a half years . . . Don't think either that it was because we are in China that caused his sickness . . . No! It was God's time and He called him home."[7]

Let us bear in mind that she was writing to the people who would think that this happened precisely because Eva had taken her children to China. She was defending a decision that perhaps even she was shaken to question. But, even given these considerations, this is where I lost Eva. When does faith become fantasy? When do faith and stubbornness merge and become something else? When does faith require closing one's heart to the very real effects of grief—depression, despair, anger, remorse? Can one truly love a God who "wants" a child and therefore gets him? What kind of God is that? Did God "want" the children recently killed by a bomb explosion in Oklahoma City? Is God "taking back" the children of Bosnia and Rwanda? Did Eva's God "want" the Chinese children who died with such regularity that burial was dispensed with and the small corpses simply flung over the village walls? Does martyrdom require this brand of belief?

Who was Eva's God? One who sent affliction but who also helped "us to bear this affliction he had to send to us for His own wise purpose."[8]

Four years later, elder son Stewart became gravely ill and the Prices determined to return to the States to seek treatment. He was thirteen years old when he died in Oberlin on February 7, 1897. Soon thereafter, his bereft parents set sail once again for China. Before departing, Eva wrote home about the effects of the suffering caused by her children's deaths. "My heart aches at leaving you all . . . more than it did eight years ago. My capacity for loving has enlarged in all the discipline of sorrow we have had and I love you all more perfectly than ever before."[9]

It was here in her heartbreak that I could join her. It was here that I began to understand that what binds us to one another is suffering. We think that it is love, but without suffering, love remains exclusive. Suffering is the mother of compassion. This is where I could see Eva as the martyr Oberlin College was later to proclaim her to be. But, unlike Oberlin, I was to see this not in the physical death she would suffer at the hands of the Boxers, nor in her putting herself in danger to follow what she perceived to be God's will. Eva's martyrdom occurred when her heart, in breaking, broke open.

Having lost two children, the support of family, the proximity of friends, thus stripped to her soul by the fires of suffering, she began to sense that she was supported by a mysterious love that emerges from ashes. In turn, she was able to love expansively. Suffering breaks us open to grace.

—⁂—

Here is where I began to know Eva, for I too had suffered loss and been surprised by the love that moved into what I perceived to be a void. The death of my thirty-one-year-old brother, Bobby, to AIDS connected me in some mysterious way to all who suffer.

Through this connection I was brought to the bedside of Brother Adam, an Episcopal monk. Adam had been increasingly weakened by AIDS and was now close to death. His serene acceptance of his circumstances prompted me to ask if he would speak to me about suffering. "The Christian belief that suffering is somehow 'good' continues to perplex me," I admitted. "Martyrdom has some nasty post-Freudian connotations. Especially for women."

He smiled from his bed, "Suffering is a reduction of life to what it is. There are no longer distractions. Suffering serves to focus you. It focuses and deepens. It makes you aware of what really matters."

And what is that?

"Love. The love we share. Love has been made trite. Look at television. Whatever they could get wrong about love, they do. Suffering relieves us of the superficiality of 'looking for love.' You know, looking for someone who's 'fun to be with' or 'lovely to look at, lovely to hold.' That's not what's important. It is the love that comes from suffering that is deep and abiding."

He assured me that he was not speaking of self-inflicted suffering, of those who wear hair shirts or beat themselves in the name of God. No, he spoke of the inevitable suffering that comes of being alive.

"Everything has within it love and hate, joy and suffering. You find what you seek, and I seek love. And I choose to joyfully embrace my suffering."

To embrace, he asserted, was not to seek pain but to accept it. The simplicity surprised him.

"By focusing, you realize, 'Wait, that's all I have to do?' Yes, that's all we have to do. It's not a program of what you have to be, how you're supposed to act, you just accept this which is given. It's right there for the taking."

And like Eva's suffering, Adam's "gave God the opportunity to break through and tell me that he loves me." Suffering made him "more vulnerable than before I was sick. Before I was busy seeking the love of God, but I didn't know it as I know it now."

Saint John of the Cross believed that anguish was God's act of purification. He compared us to logs that must be burned away to porous ash before God can enter. It seemed to me that Adam, wasting away in his bed, glowed with purity. "Out of intense suffering comes great joy," he said.

And what of God's will? What of Eva's "grand design"?

"I don't believe that it is the will of God that I suffer, but that I embrace it because it is my life. I didn't choose AIDS, but I can choose to use it to help others and myself."

I was reminded of Phillipe Malouf, a monk paralyzed in a fall, who admonished, "Don't waste your suffering."[10] Following the despair of his accident, and out of constant physical pain, he became part of Mother

Teresa's "rosary of compassion around the world." Believing that suffering is a school for holiness, Mother Teresa organized the "rosary" so that those who work with the poor can gain strength from those who are ill and incurable. Today the rosary consists of more than 4,500 ill and incurable people who daily offer up their suffering for the work of 3,000 Missionaries of Charity in eighty countries. According to Mother Teresa, the Missionaries depend on the strength gained from these offerings of the afflicted, who, in turn, are healed if not cured.

Adam reiterated, "I think it is God's will that we find our place in the universe. And that we buy the whole thing, that we embrace all of life. We have to be willing to buy it all, and our mortality is part of it. Jesus couldn't avoid death and neither can we."

Eva was buying it all when seven months after Stewart's death she boarded a ship to return to China. Suffering had focused her. All that mattered was love, and although she could not understand the Chinese, although she was lonely in her isolation and inability to communicate with them, her love would serve as an example of God's grace.

One of the great mysteries of Christianity is that suffering lifts the veil that separates us from one another. I don't know any other path to understanding Jesus' prayer in John 17:20–22. "I do not pray for these alone, but also for those who will believe in Me through their word; that they all may be one, as You, Father, are in Me and I in You; that they also may be one in Us, that the world may believe that You sent Me. And the glory which You gave Me I have given them, that they may be one just as We are one."

I have struggled with this concept my entire life as a practicing Christian, and I now understand that comprehension would never have come by way of my mind. It is only when the heart has been split open that the truths of Christianity can flow in. I was astonished, upon reading John at a time of great pain, to suddenly think, "This might actually be true." At the same time, the sensed separation between myself and others began to blur. Only suffering could have brought me to this place, could burn away my defensive intellectualizing and allow me to receive another kind of knowledge, could allow me to know of our interconnectedness and to accept the strange paradoxes of Christianity; through suffering we are healed, and in our brokenness we heal others.

Eva had a fleeting, almost prophetic sense of this at the time of Donnie's death. She wrote home, "It may be this 'little child will lead them' to the heavenly land, and that we can do more for China by giving this precious baby back to the Savior than in any other way."[11] But it was not until her suffering increased that the mystery of God's work was revealed. Suffering would open her to something beyond Christian duty; it would open her to love that would extend to the family that failed to support and the Chinese who failed to understand her. Eva had been awakened into life just in time to meet her death.

Not long after the Prices' return, in the summer of 1899, a great drought served to solidify the Chinese determination to purge the country of "foreign devils." As the days grew hotter and parched soil cracked open to surrender withered crops, the peasants blamed the "barbarians" (missionaries) for lack of rain. Another Great Famine was feared.

A sense of helplessness in the face of approaching disaster caused the peasants to swell the membership of the loosely united I Ho Chuan, referred to by Westerners as the Boxers. In the beginning the Boxers limited their practice to rituals enhancing spirit possession; however, each day without rain shifted the focus from ritual to murder. As fear of famine bred rumor, the missionaries who kept away the rain were also said to sell Chinese babies into slavery and to cut human forms from paper, give them life, and set them free to harm the Chinese. It was claimed that they conspired with the gentry to keep the peasants in poverty and that a missionary ship had been discovered carrying a cargo of human organs and female nipples.

On the cusp of the twentieth century, the fury swelled, erupted, and spilled blood throughout China. By the time the Boxer Rebellion was quelled by equally violent foreign forces in late 1900, more than 185 Protestant missionaries and their families, 47 Roman Catholic clerics and nuns, and at least 32,000 Chinese Christians had been slain.

Most were caught unaware. Their isolation and lack of political savvy had kept them ignorant of how close and violent the danger was. When they finally realized it, many tried to leave, but it was too late. Their houses were set on fire. They were shot as they rode their mules between villages.

Charles and Eva Price, along with five other missionaries and their children, were told that they were to be escorted to safety. They climbed into a mule wagon. The women spoke of their delight in leaving the growing tensions in the area. Soon all would be well.

Within half an hour of departure, at a preassigned landmark on the trail, the "escorts" left the entourage. Boxers emerged from behind the trees, raised their guns, and killed them all.

Martyrs? Eva expanded my understanding of martyrdom beyond the bloody sacrifice of ancient Christians. It was through her simple declaration of increased love for her family, not her heroism in returning to China, that I understood martyrdom as a gift given rather than a goal sought; as something requiring availability rather than spiritual pyrotechnics. Martyrdom, it turns out, is strangely intimate. Rather than being the sole province of heroes past or of those far nobler than ourselves, martyrdom belongs to all who, in opening to life's suffering, open to the flow of grace. Martyrs aren't relegated to history. They move among us.

Notes

1. Nat Brandt, *Massacre in Shansi* (Syracuse, NY: Syracuse University Press, 1994), 23.
2. Eva Jane Price, *China Journal, 1890–1900* (New York: Scribner, 1989), xxii.
3. Brandt, *Massacre in Shansi*, 37.
4. Brandt, *Massacre in Shansi*, 70.
5. Brandt, *Massacre in Shansi*, 16.
6. Brandt, *Massacre in Shansi*, 40.
7. Price, *China Journal*, 72.
8. Price, *China Journal*, 73.
9. Price, *China Journal*, 151.
10. Dominique La Pierre, *Beyond Love* (New York: Warner Books, 1990), 147.
11. Price, *China Journal*, 73.

For Further Reading

Nat Brandt, *Massacre in Shansi*. Syracuse, NY: Syracuse University Press, 1994.
J. Gernet, *China and the Christian Impact: A Conflict of Cultures*. Translated by Janey Lloyd. New York: Cambridge University Press, 1985.
Stephen Neill, *A History of Christian Missions*, 2d ed., rev. New York: Penguin, 1986.

AFTERWORD

To Witness Truth Uncompromised

by DANA GIOIA

The twentieth century has reminded Christians that the history of their faith is inextricably bound with the sacrifices of its martyrs. Their example is not incidental to the Church's identity; it offers vital proof of the faith's continuing authenticity. Martyrs are not historical relics of Christianity's initial development, early believers risking death to convert others to the faith. They represent the eternal challenge of believers to witness their faith in a fallen world. Their lives and deaths also stand as testimony to the almost incomprehensibly vast violence that has marked the present age.

To most late-nineteenth-century Western Christians, martyrdom had become an unusual and slightly exotic concept—a tragic event located either in the past or on the fringes of colonial empires. The missionary or native killed in a foreign persecution represented a real but remote risk faced by a relatively small number of believers. Martyrdom was something that occurred *elsewhere*. In that geographical entity once called Christendom, such heroic witnessing of the faith seemed an increasingly marginal concept. The nineteenth-century Western mind believed deeply in moral progress, and supporting evidence seemed everywhere—the abolition of slavery, the emergence of trade unions, universal education, rising literacy, national self-determination, expanded civil liberties, increased religious tolerance, as well as myriad scientific and medical advances. Enlightened

Christians could not help becoming swept up in this positivistic fervor. The emergence of a just and tolerant Christian civilization, at least in Europe and North America, seemed to many not merely possible but historically inevitable.

The twentieth century, however, tragically demonstrated that moral progress is neither linear nor inevitable. The dialectic of history pushes forward slowly and painfully. No sooner has some form of tyranny been banished than it reemerges in a new and equally pernicious form. The price of justice is unending struggle. Perhaps the most frightening lesson of the century has been how easily good impulses turn to evil ends. The nationalistic hunger for self-determination among nineteenth-century Germans and Italians became the militaristic fascism of the 1930s. The utopian egalitarianism of Russian progressives eventually justified the Great Famine and the gulags. Cambodia's desire to transcend colonialism created Pol Pot. These are lessons no one wanted to learn, but they are forgotten only at great moral risk. And yet these bitter lessons are being forgotten. The century is not yet over, but to most Americans the idea of martyrdom has once again begun to seem remote and abstract.

Western Christians often seem resigned to religious intolerance in other places. They show little surprise that persecution and martyrdom follow Christians in non-Christian societies. Recent religious persecution in China, Myanmar, Sri Lanka, Uganda, and Pakistan appear almost inevitable because Christians are minorities in those nations. Cultural and political animosities sometimes motivate these attacks more than do essentially religious issues. To established local power, Christianity often seems a threatening, Western importation (just as two millennia ago Roman civil authorities considered it a threatening, Eastern importation). The rights and safety of religious minorities always remain uncertain in times of political and social upheaval. But the modern persecution of Christians in Western nations—Germany, Russia, Mexico, El Salvador, Colombia—and the murderous struggle between Christian factions in Ireland and Rwanda suggest something more unsettling. Perhaps true professing Christians are always a minority *everywhere,* even in ostensibly Christian societies. The example of professing Christians always runs the risk of disturbing political authorities. Contemporary Christians need to understand this troubling issue, and the best place to begin is the example of modern martyrs—the believers of our own age who were forced to choose death rather than spiritual betrayal.

Courage and sanctity are no safeguards against oblivion. Contemporary culture lives so completely in the present tense, especially in America, that it has little time for the past. One of the central tasks of intellectuals has become to hold on to the past and study its lessons. The early church recognized the importance of martyrs by painstakingly collecting and preserving their names and stories. But how can one memorialize the myriad Christians who have died for their faith in the present century? Their numbers run into the tens of millions. How many modern martyrs went bravely to their deaths unrecorded—in gulags, concentration camps, "reeducation" centers, prison yards, or isolated country roads? Their testimony will never be told. It is important, therefore, that Christian intellectuals do not allow the memory of martyrs whose persecution was chronicled to disappear into history's abyss. Their examples constitute an essential part of the modern Christian heritage. Their struggles demonstrate the enduring moral strength generated by even a few individuals resisting a vast evil. Would it be too much to hope that by this century's conclusion the names of Maximilian Kolbe, Dietrich Bonhoeffer, and Edith Stein might become as well known as the names of Hitler's generals?

Who were these Christian martyrs? What were the crimes that earned them death? The examples of Dietrich Bonhoeffer, Maximilian Kolbe, Archbishop Romero, and Edith Stein are vividly presented in this book, but it is a worthwhile exercise to list a few of their contemporaries. Bernhard Lichtenberg, the provost of the Berlin cathedral, protested the execution of the insane and died in transit to Dachau. Inspired by Pius XI's 1937 anti-Nazi encyclical, which condemned Hitler's racism and religious intolerance, Franz Jägerstäter, an Austrian peasant and father of three small children, refused military service to fight in Hitler's war and was beheaded. Father Franz Reinisch refused to swear an oath of allegiance to Hitler and was executed. Heinz Bello, a medical student, expressed his dissatisfaction with German militarism during a fire watch and pointed to a cross that had been left in a barracks, saying, "So long as there is a God in Heaven, there is a limit to what can happen on earth." He was machine-gunned at Tegel prison in Berlin. His last words were *Omnia ad maiorem Dei gloriam!* ("All for the greater glory of God!").

The crime of these people was not active political resistance (though other Christians chose that path); their offense was moral resistance, the refusal to accept evil into their lives. They did not voluntarily seek death, but they faced it heroically. During his trial Bello refused offers to escape to Switzerland. Immediately before his verdict was read, Bello refused the opportunity to escape during an air raid, although his own solicitor urged him to. He accepted death as the cost of witnessing.

These four men are only a few martyrs from one nation. What of the multitudes who died elsewhere? Some we know by name. In 1927 Miguel Pro, a young Mexican Jesuit, was executed under false charges of political conspiracy by the viciously anticlerical government of Mexico. Chinese missionary Lizzie Atwater died in the Boxer Rebellion. Most modern martyrs, however, remain both nameless and numberless. No one knows how many Armenian Christians were murdered by the Turks in the genocidal attacks from 1894 to 1915, an event still officially denied by Turkey. Was it one million? One and a half million? When every member of a family or every inhabitant of a village is slaughtered, who will keep count? How many hundreds of thousands died in Uganda, Cambodia, Ethiopia, China, and Zaire? Modern martyrology consists of imponderables. The only response is not to capitulate before what went unrecorded but to begin with what is known. There will be no shortage of verifiable candidates. Examining the martyrs of the present age, however, is more difficult than it would first appear because the political storms to which they fell prey are sometimes still raging.

Discussions of modern martyrs often tumble uncontrollably into political debates. Critics on both ends of the political spectrum habitually dismiss martyrs of opposing ideological persuasions. A leftist, for example, might characterize a turn-of-the-century missionary killed in China as a hapless victim of imperialism, just as a rightist might claim that an activist Latin American priest died for mostly political reasons. Such narrowly secular interpretations not only trivialize the Christian idea of martyrdom; they also misunderstand how martyrdom inevitably brings religious and political worldviews into conflict.

Virtually all martyrdoms contain a political element. The paradigm of Christian martyrdom is the individual who refuses to bend his or her faith to the demands of political authority. The martyr represents the heroic integrity of the conscientious individual resisting the expedient moral compromises of the collective society. Although the martyr's resistance is fundamentally spiritual, the state will inevitably view it in political terms. To secular authority, all dissent is political. To suggest that anyone but Caesar decides what must be rendered to the state is sedition.

Martyrdom as a clash between secular and sacred duty dates from the beginnings of Christianity. As Kenneth Woodward states in his irreplaceable study, *Making Saints,* "Jesus himself was persecuted for attacking the Temple authorities," and early Christian persecution originated in refusals to worship the emperor as divine or participate in state-mandated religious festivals. The Roman ruling class put little spiritual credence in their crowded pantheon or imperial divinity; religious observance was a civic requirement, an individual's acknowledgment of the state's authority. The political elements of ancient persecution now tend to be overlooked. One rightly remembers the early martyrs as spiritual figures. Modern martyrs also deserve to be commemorated for the religious beliefs they died for—not the often fraudulent political charges by which the state prosecuted them.

If martyrs resist secular authority, the form of their dissent remains quintessentially Christian. They do not fight power by political means but steadfastly insist on the moral and spiritual nature of their dissent. Their resistance echoes Christ's answer to Pilate at His arraignment, "My kingdom is not of this world: if my kingdom were of this world, then would my servants fight." Christ's passion and death remain the inescapable model. As Woodward observes, the martyr repeats the pattern of Christ's sacrifice:

> The classic Christian martyr is an innocent victim who dies for the faith at the hand of a tyrant who is opposed to the faith. Like Jesus, the classical martyr does not seek death but freely accepts it when challenged to renounce his faith or otherwise act contrary to Christian values. Also like Jesus, the classical martyr forgives his or her enemies.

The martyr's task is not armed resistance; nor is it even passive suffering. Persecution and death are only the by-products of the martyr's true role—to witness the truth uncompromised. It is no coincidence that the etymological root of *martyr* contains no hint of death or suffering; *martyr* simply means "witness." The martyr lives by Christ's words to Pilate, "For this cause came I into the world, that I should bear witness to the truth." As W. H. Auden wrote, "In the special case of Christ, the God-Man dies to redeem sinful mankind; the ordinary human martyr dies to bear witness to what he believes to be a saving truth, to be shared by all men."

Imitatio Christi, the imitation of Christ, has been the guiding principle of believers since apostolic times. Each time and place requires Christians to emulate Jesus in different ways. The propagation of early Christianity demanded martyrdom. All the apostles but John died violently for their faith. The first Christians understood what Bonhoeffer called "the cost of discipleship." There is often a sense of joyous acceptance of the mortal danger of the faith. "For me to live is Christ," wrote Paul in Philippians, "and to die is gain." The early martyrs understood, as Martin Luther observed in the Augsburg Confession, that the Church itself was the community of those "who are persecuted and martyred for the Gospel's sake." "The blood of the martyrs is seed," wrote Tertullian. The seasons of history determine when that seed needs to be resown.

The twentieth century has reminded all conscientious Christians of the full cost of discipleship. Many thousands, perhaps even millions of believers followed Christ's example even unto death. "When Christ calls a man," wrote Bonhoeffer, "he bid him come and die." He continues:

> It may be a death like that of the first disciples who had to leave home and work to follow him, or it may be a death like Luther's, who had to leave the monastery and go out into the world. But it is the same death every time— death in Jesus Christ, the death of the old man at his call.

The strength of the martyr is the knowledge that the death of the old individual allows a new life to emerge. Roman commentators often puzzled at the odd joy with which the early martyrs met their deaths in the arena. When the governor of Pergamum condemned Carpus and Papylus to death by agonizing torture, the two condemned men ran to the amphitheater to meet their fate more quickly. The joy of martyrs is the exhilaration of victory—not secular, but spiritual triumph. It is the conviction that their deaths will not only gain them personal salvation but also eventually undermine the system that oppresses them. The sheer absurdity of this second conviction in political terms needs no elaboration, and yet history repeatedly vindicates their wild idealism. Nazi Germany and the Soviet Union now belong to the past no less than ancient Rome. A tyrant can kill bodies but not ideas; especially not ideas the just consider worth dying for. The moral example of martyrs not only outlives the empires that persecute them; it gradually transforms them.

Modern martyrs have understood the communal significance of their deaths. The examples of Christ and the early martyrs have shown them the efficacy of sacrifice. Two weeks before he was gunned down at the altar, Bishop Oscar Romero described his probable fate to a Mexican journalist in words that recall Paul and Tertullian as much as liberation theology:

I have often been threatened with death. Nevertheless, as a Christian, I do not believe in death without resurrection. If they kill me, I shall arise in the Salvadoran people . . . Martyrdom is a grace of God that I do not believe I deserve. But if God accepts the sacrifice of my life, let my blood be a seed of freedom . . . A bishop will die, but the church of God, which is the people, will never perish.

Likewise, in Tegel prison a few months before his death, Bonhoeffer jotted down, "Death is the supreme festival on the road to freedom." The martyr suffers joyfully because, as Bonhoeffer noted elsewhere, "suffering is the badge of true discipleship."

The martyr dies not only to preserve his or her own integrity but also to demonstrate the imperishable integrity of the entire Church. Each martyrdom, therefore, implicitly strengthens the Communion of Saints, the spiritual interdependence of all Christians living and dead. If the role of martyrs is to face persecution and death, the duty of the living is to re-member them. Remembrance of their sacrifice is the Church's con-sciousness of its own identity in a secular world. Their commemoration also has moral and political significance. "The struggle against power," wrote Milan Kundera, "is the struggle of memory against forgetting." To forget their persecution makes its easier for such atrocities to be repeated. Planning the dismemberment of Poland, Hitler dismissed—in one chill-ing remark—suggestions that the world community would object to Germany's aggression. The Führer merely retorted, "Who remembers the Armenians?"

No century has mounted so vast or sustained an attack on Christianity as the present one. International communism alone assaulted the church on a hitherto impossible scale. And yet at the end of the century com-munism has all but passed away while the church survives. In fact, the combined persecutions of modern totalitarian states had at least one un-intended but wholly beneficial effect—Christian ecumenism. The savage materialism and lethal intolerance of modern totalitarian governments have helped Christians of all persuasions to understand the essential unity of their beliefs. (Their persecution has also enlarged Christian sympathy for Judaism, just as the Nazi Holocaust demonstrated the intrinsic evil of anti-Semitism.) The wounds of the twentieth century have miraculously helped heal the lingering ones of the Reformation. Today, unlike in 1900, Catholic, Orthodox, and Protestant are now more likely to recognize and celebrate the many things that unite them rather than the few that keep them apart. Catholic bishops have requested an ecumenical martyrology. The Lutherans have added Pope John XXIII to their calendar of saints. Leaders of the Catholic, Orthodox, and Anglican branches of Christianity pray together publicly and concelebrate the sacraments. Even the book you now hold in your hands—written by members of diverse creeds—represents the fruit of modern persecution: the conviction that the church Christ instituted through his apostles should be one.

The totalitarian state will never comprehend the real power of the church. "The Pope!" scoffed Stalin. "How many divisions has *he* got?" Peter and Paul commanded no legions, and yet they defeated an empire. For all their political expertise, Caesars ancient and modern have never understood what they sought to abolish. "The power of the Church," writes Pope John Paul II in *Crossing the Threshold of Hope,* "has lain in the witness of the saints, of those who made Christ's truth their own truth . . . in the Eastern and Western Churches these saints have never been lacking." John Paul continues:

> The saints of our century have been in large part martyrs. The totalitarian regimes which dominated Europe in the middle of the twentieth century added to their numbers. Concentration camps, death camps—which produced, among other things, the monstrous Holocaust of the Jews—revealed authentic saints among Catholics and Orthodox, and among Protestants as well . . . In eastern Europe the army of holy martyrs, especially among the Orthodox, is enormous . . . This is the great multitude of those who, as is said in the Book of Revelation, "follow the Lamb" (cf. Rev. 14:4). They have completed in their death as martyrs the redemptive sufferings of Christ (cf. Col. 1:24) and, at the same time, they have become *the foundation of a new world, a new Europe, and a new civilization.*

As Christianity enters its third millennium, the link between contemporary faith and its apostolic origins must once again be deepened and renewed. Like Christianity's initial century, our age has been invigorated by "a cloud of witnesses." The suffering of these modern martyrs has been inconceivable, their loss in human terms immense. It is the challenge of today's Christians to let their example animate the church. "The blood of martyrs is the seed," but only the living can cultivate the fruit of their sacrifice. They gained the grace to lose their lives for an ideal. We must pray for the grace to lead our lives in the same pursuit. Without facing a firing squad, we also can hope to meet death with the prayer, *Omnia ad maiorem Dei gloriam.*

Death, where is your sting?

About the Contributors

Julia Alvarez was ten years old when her parents were forced to emigrate to the United States from the Dominican Republic, shortly before Trujillo was assassinated. Her first novel, *How the Garcia Girls Lost Their Accents*, was named a Notable Book by the *New York Times Book Review* and by the ALA and was awarded the Pen Oakland/Josephine Miles Award for excellence in literature. Her collections of poetry include *Homecoming* and *The Housekeeping Book*. A professor of English at Middlebury College, Alvarez lives with her husband in Vermont.

Barbara Lazear Ascher is the author of two collections of essays, *Playing After Dark* and *The Habit of Loving*, as well as a recent memoir, *Landscape Without Gravity: A Memoir of Grief.* She is a frequent contributor to the *New York Times.*

Calvin Bedient teaches in the English department at UCLA. He has published a number of books, including *He Do the Police in Different Voices: "The Waste Land" and Its Protagonist.*

Susan Bergman's essays and poetry have appeared in *Antaeus, Ploughshares,* and *North American Review,* where she is a contributing editor. Her first book, *Anonymity,* was published by Farrar, Straus & Giroux in 1994. Her forthcoming work of fiction is called *The Buried Life.* She lives outside Chicago with her husband and children.

Gerald Early is the Merle Kling Professor of Modern Letters at Washington University in St. Louis, where he is also the director of the African and Afro-American Studies Program. He won the 1994 National Book Critics Circle Award for *The Culture of Bruising: Essays on Prizefighting, Literature, and Modern American Culture.*

Paul Elie is an editor with Farrar, Straus & Giroux and the editor of *A Tremor of Bliss: Contemporary Writers on the Saints.* A Roman Catholic, he has written about religion and other subjects for *Commonweal, The New Republic, Lingua Franca,* the *New York Times,* and *New York Newsday.* He is currently writing a group portrait of Flannery O'Connor, Thomas Merton, Walker Percy, and Dorothy Day.

Robert Ellsberg is editor-in-chief of Orbis Books. A former managing editor of the *Catholic Worker,* he has edited a number of books including *Dorothy Day: Selected Writings, Gandhi on Christianity, Carlo Carretto: Selected Writings,* and *Fritz Eichenberg: Works of Mercy.* He is currently writing a book of daily reflections on saints for our time.

Carolyn Forché is the author of *Gathering the Tribes,* which won the Yale Series of Younger Poets Award in 1976, and *The Country Between Us,* for which she received the Lamont Award of the Academy of American Poets. Her most recent books include *The Angel of History* and an anthology entitled *Against Forgetting: Twentieth-Century Poetry of Witness.* She teaches writing at George Mason University and lives in Maryland with her husband and son.

Dana Gioia is the author of two collections of poetry, *Daily Horoscope* and *The Gods of Winter;* two critical collections, *Can Poetry Matter: Essays on Poetry and American Culture* and *The Barrier of a Common Language: Essays on British and American Poetry;* and *The Madness of Hercules,* translated from Seneca.

Patricia Hampl is the author of two books of poetry and several prose works, including *Virgin Time, Spillville,* and the now classic memoir *A Romantic Education.* A 1990 MacArthur fellow, she is professor of English at the University of Minnesota. She lives in St. Paul, Minnesota.

Ron Hansen's most recent books include the anthology *You've Got to Read This* and the novels *Mariette in Ecstasy* and *Atticus.* He is the Gerard Manley Hopkins Professor of the Arts and Humanities at Santa Clara University.

Nancy Mairs's books include a volume of poetry, *In All the Rooms of the Yellow House,* which won a 1984 Western States Book Award; three collections of essays, *Plaintext, Carnal Acts,* and *Voice Lessons: On Becoming a (Woman) Writer;* a memoir, *Remembering the Bone House: An Erotics of Place and Space;* and a spiritual autobiography, *Ordinary Time: Cycles in Marriage, Faith, and Renewal.* Her current project is entitled *Waist-High in the World: (Re)Constructing (Dis)Ability.* She and her husband live in Tucson, Arizona, where they are active in the peace and justice community.

Paul Mariani is the author of three books of criticism, five books of poetry, and biographies of three poets—William Carlos Williams, John Berryman, and Robert Lowell. His most recent books are *Lost Puritan: A Life of Robert Lowell* and *The Great Wheel: Poems.* He is completing a biography of Hart Crane. Mariani is Distinguished University Professor at the University of Massachusetts at Amherst, where he has taught since 1968.

Kathleen Norris is the author of *Dakota: A Spiritual Geography* and several books of poems, including *Little Girls in Church.* She is currently at work on nonfiction, a book of essays entitled *The Cloister Walk,* and a reminiscence of Elizabeth Kray, a woman Stanley Kunitz once described as "one of the best friends American poets ever had." She lives in South Dakota.

Peggy O'Brien is a poet, teacher, and critic. She is director of the Irish Studies Program at the University of Massachusetts, Amherst, where she is also attached to the English department. A native of Massachusetts and a graduate of Mount Holyoke College, she lived for nearly twenty years in Ireland, for most of that time taking a graduate degree and then teaching at Trinity College, Dublin. She now divides her time between Amherst and Dublin.

Marilynne Robinson is the author of the prize-winning novel *Housekeeping* and of a nonfiction work about Great Britain, *Mother Country*, which was nominated for the National Book Award. Her short work has appeared in *Harper's, Granta, Esquire, The Paris Review,* and the *New York Times Book Review.*

Mark Rudman's recent books include *The Nowhere Steps; Diverse Voices: Essays on Poets and Poetry;* a long poem, *Rider,* which received the 1995 National Book Critics Circle Award in Poetry; and *Realm of Unknowing: Meditations on Art, Suicide, and Other Transformations.* His new book of poems is entitled *The Millennium Hotel.* He teaches at New York University and Columbia's School of the Arts.

Steve Saint, a pilot and the son of Nate Saint, moved in 1995 to Ecuador with his wife and children to work with the Huaorani people to build an airport and a hospital.

Anthony Walton is the author of *Mississippi: An American Journey* and a chapbook of poems, *Cricket Weather.*

Larry Woiwode has published a number of novels, including *Beyond the Bedroom Wall* and *Indian Affairs.* His most recent books are *Silent Passengers,* a collection of short stories, and *Acts,* a personal commentary on the books of the Bible. In 1995 he received the Award of Merit from the American Academy of Arts and Letters "for distinction in the art of the short story."